Critical Media Studies
INSTITUTIONS, POLITICS, AND CULTURE

Series Editor
Andrew Calabrese, University of Colorado

Advisory Board

Recent Titles in the Series

Culture Conglomerates

Consolidation in the Motion Picture and Television Industries

William M. Kunz

ROWMAN & LITTLEFIELD PUBLISHERS, INC.
Lanham • Boulder • New York • Toronto • Oxford

ROWMAN & LITTLEFIELD PUBLISHERS, INC.

Published in the United States of America
by Rowman & Littlefield Publishers, Inc.
A wholly owned subsidary of The Rowman & Littlefield Publishing Group, Inc.
4501 Forbes Boulevard, Suite 200, Lanham, Maryland 20706
www.rowmanlittlefield.com

P.O. Box 317, Oxford OX2 9RU, UK

British Library Cataloguing in Publication Information Available

Library of Congress Cataloging-in-Publication Data

Kunz, William M., 1961–
    Culture conglomerates : consolidation in the motion picture and
television industries / William M. Kunz.
        p.   cm. — (Critical media studies)
    Includes bibliographical references and index.
    ISBN-13: 978-0-7425-4065-1 (cloth : alk. paper)
    ISBN-10: 0-7425-4065-0 (cloth : alk. paper)
    ISBN-13: 978-0-7425-4066-8 (pbk. : alk. paper)
    ISBN-10: 0-7425-4066-9 (pbk. : alk. paper)
    1. Motion picture industry—Ownership—United States.   2. Television
broadcasting—Ownership—United States.   3. Consolidation and merger
of corporations—United States.   I. Title.   II. Series.
PN1993.5.U6K86 2007
384.55′10973—dc22

                                                                                2006002901

Printed in the United States of America

♾™ The paper used in this publication meets the minimum requirements of
American National Standard for Information Sciences—Permanence of Paper for
Printed Library Materials, ANSI/NISO Z39.48–1992.

Contents

Preface and Acknowledgments

Sumner Redstone is a lifelong Democrat and a consistent contributor to the standard-bearers of the party, from Edward Kennedy to Tom Daschle to Al Gore. He is also the chairman of both CBS, which conservative commentators targeted for an alleged "liberal" bias in its news division under Dan Rather, and Viacom, parent corporation of MTV, which the Parents Television Council accused of "targeting kids with sex, drugs and alcohol" in a 2005 report. With such a dossier, one might predict that Redstone supported John Kerry in the presidential election in 2004, and he did make financial contributions to Kerry's campaign. Less than two months before the general election, however, Redstone endorsed George W. Bush. His reason was simple: a Republican administration is a "better deal" for Viacom.

That "deal" is the deregulation that allowed Viacom to benefit from vertical integration through the ownership of a broadcast network, CBS, and major motion picture studio, Paramount Pictures. That "deal" also permitted horizontal integration in the Viacom Television Stations Group to a point where it reached close to 45 percent of television households nationwide at the start of 2005, with multiple stations in six of the top ten markets. The Federal Communications Commission (FCC) sanctioned further consolidation and concentration in 2003 with clear support from George W. Bush, although the U.S. Court of Appeals for the Third Circuit remanded most of those rules to the Commission for further consideration while Congress altered one as well. The role of the executive, legislative, and executive branches of the federal government in the process, in addition to the FCC, raises serious questions.

When students examine ownership and regulation of media industries for the first time, it is natural for them to focus on corporations such as Viacom and Time Warner or individuals such as Michael Eisner and Rupert Murdoch.

Some conclude that these corporations and individuals are "evil" given their apparent quest to dominate the production and distribution of our culture. It is important for them to understand that these corporations are doing what is natural, that conglomeration enables businesses to control more of the market, take advantage of economies of scale, and reduce their exposure to fluctuations in the supply of essential materials and services. Too much concentration, however, undermines democratic societies, which is where the role of the government in setting reasonable limits is so critical. Ted Turner put it in rather basic terms: "As a business proposition, consolidation makes sense. The moguls behind the mergers are acting in their corporate interests and playing by the rules. We just shouldn't have those rules."[1] This part of the equation is more difficult to grasp.

Culture Conglomerates progresses from a supposition that the rules of the game are indeed flawed and that too much consolidation has occurred. One of the cornerstones of this position is a basic belief that it does matter who owns the media. This is true whether the focus is on the dissemination of news and information or in the promotion of dominant values and ideologies and construction of models of thought and behavior for imitation in entertainment programming. This means that it is significant that ownership of all the prominent cable news channels—CNN, CNN Headline News, MSNBC, CNBC, and Fox News Channel—reside within three major multinational conglomerates: Time Warner, General Electric, and News Corp. It is just as important, however, that these same corporations own major motion picture studios, Warner Bros., Universal Pictures, and Twentieth Century Fox, respectively.

In the fall of 2001, Robert McChesney and Benjamine Compaine engaged in an online debate about media ownership via the openDemocracy website, in which Compaine asked, "Where is the evidence?" Less than twelve months later, the FCC released a collection of reports from its Media Ownership Working Group that supported deregulation, but nothing was resolved, not even the outcome of the analysis. Mara Einstein, the author of one of the few studies to originate outside the Commission, took issue with the FCC argument that her findings on the relationship between the diversity of program genres and the Financial Interest and Syndication Rules supported deregulation. She went so far as to write an editorial in *Broadcasting & Cable* in the spring of 2003 entitled "Dereg? We should Talk Re-Reg" in which she begged that her research be used as intended: to "stimulate wider discussion on media ownership, media diversity and the underlying economics that guide media content."[2] The debate is intense because the stakes are high, and the research that is central to this book hopefully will add some depth to this discussion.

The examination of ownership and regulation is a perilous process since the next big deal is just around the corner, and it is impossible to predict when the federal government will change the rules of the game. The protracted battle in the courts and Congress both before and after the FCC released new ownership rules in 2003 slowed that wave of consolidation in broad-cast television. This provides a moment to analyze and reflect on what has transpired over the last two decades. So does the creation of NBC Universal, which matched the last of the nonaligned broadcast networks with a major motion picture studio. The end of the NBC mating dance might freeze the corporate links between networks and studios, at least for a short time. And once changes in ownership and regulation do take place, and it is inevitable that both will, the historical dimension of this project will provide insight into how we got to this point in time and, perhaps, even insight to predict what will happen next.

Some of the changes in ownership and control that follow will no doubt be significant. The announcement in December 2005 of the intended Viacom ac-quisition of the live action unit of DreamWorks SKG, following unsuccessful negotiations between the studio and NBC Universal, aligned the most promi-nent independent motion picture production and distribution company with a major studio. The significance of such a change in the control of DreamWorks is clear. Other potential changes are far less significant. Viacom completed a breakup in January 2006 with the "old media" assets, including CBS and In-finity radio, under the control of Les Moonves and the "new media" assets, including Paramount and MTV and other cable networks under the control of Tom Freston. This is not a true breakup, however, and ownership of both corporations, CBS Corp. and Viacom Inc., will remain in the hands of Sumner Redstone. The motivation for the split was the Viacom stock price, with ex-ecutives arguing that the old media sector was holding back the new media segment.

This tale of domination begins with the stories of the major motion picture studios and broadcast networks, the hearts of the media conglomerates that dominate the creation and dissemination of film and video culture in the United States and around the world. The names will become quite familiar: Disney, NBC Universal, News Corp., Sony, Time Warner, and Viacom. With this as a foundation, the next step will be to examine the impact this ownership and control has on two areas of cultural production and distribution, motion pictures in theaters and prime time programming on the broadcast networks. The final step will be to connect the ownership and control of this content to the cable and satellite programming services that have become such a part of American culture. This might be the most important part of the puzzle, since the abundance of outlets that cable and satellite services promise has justified so much. Such outlets take on different colors, however, when ownership resides in the hands of a select few.

This book progresses from a fundamental position that ownership in media industries does matter. I followed two distinct paths to reach this conclusion. The first is more traditional and evolved through studies in the political econ-omy of communication as well as research on ownership and regulation. The second is more unusual, as I reached the same conclusions over the course of two decades working in sports television at the network level. As a producer with ABC Sports on a full-time and freelance basis before and after the Disney acquisition of Capital Cities/ABC, I witnessed how the influence of ownership trickles down through a corporation. The circumstances were different but the patterns similar during five years as a vice president and senior producer at Turner Sports, a period that bridged the creation of AOL Time Warner.

Those who claim that ownership does not matter want to see the smoking gun, the directive from senior management to cover a particular story or promote certain values. Such edicts often do not exist, but ownership still influences decision-making. There was far more interest in interactive endeavors within Turner Broadcasting after AOL joined Time Warner on the letterhead than before. The reasons are obvious. Ambitious individuals who want to advance must first understand a corporate culture and ownership is a critical component of that ethos. There are reminders of this undeniable fact even for those who want to hide their heads in the sand. There were constant reminders of the Disney ownership of ABC after 1996, from free tickets to the theme parks to advertisements for Disney films on the envelopes that contained paychecks. One can discount the importance of such connections, but even the most ardent journalist is aware of such ownership ties when a story moves close to home. In a 1998 interview on National Public Radio, Michael Eisner sent out a warning when he stated that the ABC brass knew that his preference was for the news division not to cover Disney.

This book is built upon research conducted over the last decade, but it would not be what it is today without the backing of two prominent political economists. Janet Wasko introduced me to the political economy of communication at the University of Oregon and helped me develop the analytical tools I needed to make sense of what I had experienced in the television business. She remains a mentor and friend, and I would not have completed this book without her support. The same is true of Eileen Meehan at Louisiana State University. She helped me hone in on what this book was all about and became a strong advocate for its publication. I am grateful to both of them for their guidance and encouragement. I am also indebted to Brenda Hadenfeldt and Bess Vanrenen for their support of *Culture Conglomerates* within Rowman & Littlefield Publishing Group.

This book does not address the state of sports television, but friends at ABC Sports, NBC Sports, and Turner Sports in the United States and Nine Network in Australia long provided insight and support, even when some did not understand the desire to teach and conduct research of this type. I am also grateful to the remarkable group of announcers at ABC Sports who showed me the ropes and taught me the importance of research when I began in sports television, from Jim Lampley and Al Trautwig to Jim McKay and Frank Gifford. At the opposite end of the trail, my colleagues at the University of Washington, Tacoma have been a source of encouragement over the last three years, while my students in the Political Economy of the Media and Communication Regulation & Policy provide inspiration to dig deeper and explain this material better.

I am most indebted to my family. Moving back-and-forth between television and academia has not always been easy, and many have questioned my judgment. My family, however, has been steadfast in its support. This begins with my parents, Tom and Anne Kunz, and extends to a remarkable group of sibling, in-laws, nieces, and nephews. First on the list is my partner through this strange journey, my wife Miyuki Taguchi. She supported the decision to pursue a PhD, endured the years at Turner when I was on the road so often, and backed the return to the academic world in 2003. She also assumed an unequal share in the care of our toddler twins, Maya and Tomo, so that I could finish this manuscript. The publication of this book is a testament to her love and support.

NOTES

1. Ted Turner, "Break Up This Band!" *Washington Monthly* 36, no. 7/8 (2004), 32.
2. Mara Epstein, "Dereg? We Should Talk Re-reg," *Broadcasting & Cable*, 28 April 2003, 50.

1

❖

Why Ownership Matters

At News Corporation we value the relationships inside our company, and the creativity that they continuously inspire. We are building an unrivaled platform but it is the performance that counts. Distribution for us is merely a means to an end—to ensure we can market our real product—and that product is content.[1]

The News Corporation Limited

The preamble of the 1998 annual report for The News Corporation Limited reveals a great deal about the conglomerates that dominate the media industries in the new millennium. In the corporate culture of News Corp., the Fox Television Network and Fox-owned and operated stations are not there to serve the public interest, convenience, and necessity as Congress mandated in the Communications Act of 1934. Instead, these properties are part of an "unrivaled platform" that gives News Corp. a pipeline into television households in the largest of cities and the smallest of hamlets around the world. This access comes through broadcast networks such as Fox and Network Ten in Australia, cable channels such as Fox News Channel and National Geographic Channel, and satellite systems such as DirecTV in North America, BSkyB in Europe, FOXTEL in Australia, and StarTV across the full expanse of Asia. In the corporate culture of News Corp., Twentieth Century Fox is not just a major motion picture production and distribution company, one that is also quite prominent in the production of television programs. Rather, it manufactures the "real product" of News Corp., and "that product is content."

The creation and dissemination of cultural content has elicited concerns for generations. There was a time when structural barriers existed between the

1

film and television industries in the United States, a time when cable television was a mechanism for the retransmission of signals rather than a fierce competitor for the broadcast networks to reckon with. The fundamental changes in the structure of these industries demands a new approach to the examination of old issues. To understand the implications of consolidation, one must explore two distinct but related questions: how did the current organization of the motion picture and television industries evolve, in other words, how did we get here; and how does this structure impact the production and distribution of cultural products, in other words, what does it mean? Each of these questions is critical to a deeper understanding of these industries and the impact of two decades of deregulation and conglomeration at the local, national, and international levels.

The first question, how did we get here, addresses historical changes in the structure of these industries and the scope of federal regulation of media industries. Some within the Federal Communications Commission (FCC) contend that technological determinants mandate that the rules of the game must change, to "reflect the media environment our children see, not the ones that our grandparents saw."[2] While it would be ludicrous to deny that the media landscape is quite different than it was even two decades ago, the technological deterministic argument, the notion that technology is autonomous and determines social progress, conceals the imprint of those who fight for such changes as well as those who benefit. The second question, what does it mean, requires one to examine these industries in an integrated manner, looking across traditional barriers to understand how these media monoliths function in the real world. The true impact of a prime time television program in a modern media conglomerate extends beyond the ratings it can command for a network and includes its value in syndication to owned and operated stations and cable outlets and in foreign markets, just as the domestic box office is just one revenue stream for a motion picture.

The phenomenal success of *The Simpsons* touches on most of these topics. The animated series has anchored the Fox prime time schedule on Sunday nights for the better part of two decades, but this just breaks the surface of its contributions to News Corp. Reruns of *The Simpsons* debuted on Fox-owned and operated affiliates in 1994 and helped oftentimes marginal stations rise to prominence in their local markets. On the other side of the world, *The Simpsons* contributed to the success of the News Corp.-owned Network Ten and StarTV, although one can only wonder how Apu Nahasapeemapetilon, owner of the local Kwik-E-Mart on *The Simpsons*, translates to the Indian audience on Star World. All that was missing was a full-length feature film, and Twentieth Century Fox Animation confirmed in 2004 that one was in the initial stages of development.

It is important to understand the degree to which decisions made within Congress and the FCC enabled News Corp. to wring the most out of *The Simpsons*. How the Commission defined a network allowed News Corp. to elude the Financial Interest and Syndication Rules and produce the series within Twentieth Century Fox Television, broadcast it on the Fox network, and sell the syndication rights for millions of dollars. Congress, meanwhile, eased ownership limits with the Telecommunications Act of 1996 and allowed News Corp. to control even more of its local affiliates, which gave the corporation additional in-house outlets for *The Simpsons*. The FCC even assumed a critical role in the creation of the Fox network, with the Commission accepting the dubious assertion that $2 billion paid to Metromedia for six local stations in 1985 came from Rupert Murdoch rather than News Corp. This allowed Murdoch, who became a naturalized U.S. citizen after he announced the deal, to avoid FCC rules that limited foreign ownership to 25 percent of a local station. An FCC investigation in the 1990s revealed that 99 percent of the capital used in the acquisition came from News Corp.

The attitude toward the production and distribution of cultural products evident in the News Corp. annual report points to the need to take a more integrated approach to the examination of media industries, since it is clear that such connections are made within the conglomerates themselves. There is little question that these sentiments have existed for generations. Film in the United States developed as a commercial pursuit in which profit maximization was a fundamental objective. The Supreme Court, after all, argued in 1915 that "The exhibition of moving pictures is a business, pure and simple, originated and conducted for a profit like other spectacles."[3] In the 1920s, the production, distribution, and exhibition of motion pictures assumed the characteristics of an industry, and there has been little deviation from that basic structure since then.

Broadcast radio and television were supposed to be different, mandated to serve the public interest in exchange for the use of the public airwaves. The Radio Act of 1927 introduced the public interest, convenience, and necessity as a discretionary licensing standard, while *The Great Lakes Statement* declared that "Broadcasting stations are licensed to serve the public and not for furthering the private or selfish interest of individuals or groups of individuals."[4] Such sentiments were noble, but in the midst of this debate, the government made a series of decisions that contributed to the development of a network-dominated, advertiser-supported, private sector–owned broadcast structure. Powerful commercial interests, including NBC and CBS and the National Association of Broadcasters, were able to frame the public debate and promote the notion that the commercial structure was the lone configuration suitable for democratic societies. CBS founder William Paley put it in simple terms: "He who attacks the fundamentals of the American system of broadcasting . . . attacks democracy itself."[5]

This structure advanced countless private interests long before Rupert Murdoch acquired the Metromedia station group and launched the Fox network. At that point, however, even the hope that Congress and the FCC would hold the corporate parents of these broadcast outlets to a higher standard was disappearing. Mark Fowler, Commission chair under Ronald Reagan, promoted a particular interpretation of the public interest: "The perception of broadcasters as community trustees should be replaced by a view of broad-casters as market participants . . . the public's interest, then, defines the public interest."[6] While one can argue that this sentiment is consistent with the com-mercial orientation of the motion picture and television industries in the United States and the commodification of cultural products, and with the establishment of the marketplace as the ultimate arbitrator of good and bad, the News Corp. annual report suggests the elevation of this process to new levels. Cultural products, from films to recorded music to magazines, have become little more than the software that is needed to feed vast empires.

News Corp. is not alone in the production of "content" that can be packaged, and repackaged, and generate revenue in different corporate sectors. Disney, NBC Universal, Time Warner, and Viacom have all elevated such cross-pollination to a science. The models differ from conglomerate to conglom-erate, and some attempts are more successful than others are. The NBC Uni-versal integration of Bravo and USA Network into the Olympic family in 2004 was a success, while the Viacom two-step at the Super Bowl earlier that year, the MTV production of the Janet Jackson-headlined halftime show on CBS, was a sensation but for all the wrong reasons. Disney is the most aggressive in the pursuit of such synergies, and the ultimate creation is one that can create revenue for each of the four divisions within The Walt Disney Co.: Media Networks, Studio Entertainment, Parks & Resorts, and Consumer Products.

The Lion King grossed over $300 million at the domestic box office alone in 1994, but in the decade that followed it generated total revenues in the billions. There are few areas of Disney that Simba and the gang did not touch. In 1996, for example, *The Lion King* made its broadcast television debut on ABC on the first weekend of the November sweeps, a critical period for broadcast networks and the first prime time season for ABC under Disney control. A special edition DVD of *The Lion King* released in 2003 generated over $150 million in revenue, not including sales from a new line of consumer products that accompanied its release. The Broadway production of *The Lion King*, meanwhile, continued to gross over $1 million a week at the New Amsterdam Theater in 2005. *The Lion King* experience points to the need to take a more integrated approach to the examination of ownership.

GROWTH OF THE MARKETPLACE: FROM LOCAL TO GLOBAL

There was a time, albeit brief, when the marketplace for motion pictures and television programming was local, rather than national or international. That was the case when the first Kinetoscope parlor opened its doors on Broadway in New York in 1894 and when W2XBS telecast Franklin Roosevelt's opening address from the World's Fair in New York in 1939.[7] In both industries, it was not long before production and distribution became national, and then international, and the local origination of content became rare. This is most evident in the film business, where revenue generated in foreign markets has long been critical to the bottom line. In 2004, the Hollywood majors and mini-majors such as Miramax Films and New Line Cinema generated $9.2 billion at the foreign box office alone.[8] Two marquee films, *Harry Potter and the Prisoner of Azkaban* and *Shrek 2*, combined to surpass $1 billion at the foreign box office, 30 percent more than they generated in North America. And this was just the beginning.

The market for film and television products has expanded to a dramatic degree over the last quarter-century, thanks in large part to the evolution of commercial television outlets around the world. There was a time when the foreign market for American films and television programs was limited to theatrical distribution and broadcast television, and even broadcast options were somewhat limited since public service-oriented networks that favored noncommercial programming were most common in other nations. The evolution of communication satellites, development of cable television, and proliferation of commercial broadcast networks, not to mention home video, transformed the global marketplace. While motion pictures remain prominent, these changes have made television the central piece in the puzzle. Edward Herman and Robert McChesney argue that "TV is the defining medium of the age, and it provides the basis for an integrated global commercial media market."[9]

There are countless examples of this phenomenon. The most prominent letters in cable television in the United States—CNN, MTV, and ESPN—brand cable and satellite services that span six continents and extend the reach of Time Warner, Viacom, and Disney. In 2005, CNN International reached over two hundred countries and territories two decades after its launch. MTV joined CNN in the international arena with the debut of MTV Europe in 1987, and the Viacom network completed its circumnavigation of the globe with the launch of pan-African MTV Base in the spring of 2005. ESPN took two approaches to world domination, owning or licensing twenty-nine different international networks in mid-2005, including ESPN Latin American and ESPN Africa, in addition to a 50 percent equity interest in ESPN Star Sports in Asia, a joint venture with News Corp. The penetration of these conglomerates is perhaps most evident with The Disney Channel, which launched new services in Cambodia, Palau, Thailand, and Vietnam over the first six months of 2005.

The U.S.-based motion picture studios and broadcast networks have a tremendous advantage in the international marketplace. Laissez-faire economists would argue that American producers respond to the demands of sovereign consumers, that the invisible hand of the free market dictates what films and television products are produced, and how they are distributed. The simplistic power of this position was evident in the Warner Communications annual report from 1982, which proclaimed that there was a "natural demand for entertainment the world over."[10] The success of American-made cultural products in foreign markets is far more complicated, however.

The nature of film and television products makes them conducive to mass exportation. Since almost the entire cost of a film or television program is incurred in the production of the first print, economies of scale dictate that producers should distribute a film to as many markets and outlets as possible.[11] The United States is home to the largest media market in the world, which provides substantial capital for the production of films and television programs; revenue generated in foreign markets is oftentimes an added bonus. It is difficult for indigenous producers in smaller markets to overcome this advantage. Hamid Mowlana argues that there are two central causes of the widespread importation of popular culture: the inability of domestic producers to meet the demand that new technologies create and the inferiority of domestic products when compared to foreign imports.[12]

The role of the state is also quite significant. What is absent from the Warner Communications document is any mention of the United States government, or the Motion Pictures Association (MPA), which represents the major U.S.-based motion picture production and distribution companies in their international operations.[13] These omissions are significant, since the Department of State, Office of the United States Trade Representative and the MPA, often called the "Little State Department," are critical to the success of American films and television programs in international markets. The American troika demands that foreign markets are open for Hollywood to exploit, while the oligopolistic nature of the American market makes it all but impenetrable to foreign products.[14] The exportation of cultural products improves the trade deficit, but the U.S. government also argues that "trade follows films," that motion pictures and television programs provide a mechanism through which to advertise American products and disseminate ideologies.[15]

The importance of these organizations and the prominence of these ideas were evident in a series of trade disputes in the 1990s. Among the most contentious issues in negotiations between the United States and Canada over the North American Free Trade Agreement were Canadian quotas and protections for its culture industries. Similar issues arose in the Uruguay round of the General Agreement on Tariffs and Trade (GATT), with Jack Valenti leading a crusade against national quotas and subsidies. This included a European Union directive that mandated that at least 51 percent of all programs on broadcast television networks be of European origin. The French and Canadian positions in these disputes are important to consider.

The foundation of their arguments is the basic idea that the cultural nature of film and television products makes them different from other goods and services. French Prime Minister François Mitterand advanced the official French position in a speech in the fall of 1993:

> Creations of the spirit are not just commodities; the elements of culture are not pure business. Defending the pluralism of works of art and the freedom of the public to choose is a duty. What is at stake is the cultural identity of all our nations. It is the right of all peoples to their own culture. It is the freedom to create and choose our own images. A society which abandons to others the way of showing itself . . . is a society enslaved.[16]

Similar themes are evident in the words of Pierre Juneau, head of the Canadian Broadcasting Corporation (CBC) through much of the 1980s: "There can be no political sovereignty, therefore no authority over their own lives, their own future, without cultural autonomy and vitality."[17] Such a position stands in stark contrast to that of Fowler, the head of the FCC at the same time Juneau ran the CBC, who once equated a television to a "toaster with pictures" and argued that the television industry needed no more regulation than that of any other household appliance.

TELEVISION IN AMERICAN CULTURE

There is little question that the transnational expansion of the U.S.-based motion picture studios and television networks has had a profound impact on media markets around the world, but what is often not discussed is the impact of such expansion on American households. The FCC and other federal agencies have authorized numerous mergers and acquisitions based on the argument that modern media conglomerates must be massive to compete in the global marketplace, and such combinations have created countless new revenue streams. Herbert Schiller argued that while American industrial preeminence has declined at the international level, the domestic production and international distribution of "packaged consciousness" is "booming."[18] What is the impact of this drive to dominate international markets on the production and distribution of cultural products at home?

The importance of the conglomeration and concentration of broadcast and cable television, and other media industries in general, are dependent in large part upon the importance one ascribes to television content. Politicians, educators, and communication scholars have long debated the significance of broadcast and cable television in American households. The dominance of the broadcast networks has deteriorated to a dramatic degree with the proliferation of cable channels, but it would be difficult to overstate the prominence of television at the turn of the century. One study measured television usage in the United States at an average of seven hours and twenty-four minutes per household per day, including two hours and forty-eight minutes per day for children under the age of twelve.[19] Another study concluded that by the time American children graduate from high school, they have spent more hours watching television than they have in school.[20] Congressional mandates and FCC policies to increase educational programming, and decrease indecent and violent programming, are reactions to the conspicuous consumption of television in American households.

The influence of television, in the opinion of others, extends far beyond the dearth of educational material and abundance of violence, however. Television has assumed a prominent position in the dissemination of images and ideas, reinforcement of dominant ideologies, and in the social, political, and cultural discourse in the latter half of the twentieth century. Douglas Kellner argues that television takes on a critical role in the "structuring of contemporary identity and shaping thought and behavior."[21] Television has undertaken functions once ascribed to "myth and ritual," including "integrating individuals into the social order, celebrating dominant values," and "offering models of thought, behavior, and gender for imitation."[22] Fundamental to this argument is the belief that television is a force for enculturation and not just a medium that serves entertainment and information functions.

These are critical differences, most evident in debates within the halls of Congress and the FCC. While legislation was passed and policies enacted to mandate the inclusion of a V-chip in new television sets, and the Janet Jackson incident at the Super Bowl in 2004 ignited new debates over indecent material on television and radio, regulations that limit the ownership of media outlets have all but disappeared. The decade between 1994 and 2004 witnessed the unsurpassed consolidation of media properties, with a series of mergers and acquisitions that are the hallmarks of this period: the merger of Disney and Capital Cities/ABC, the Viacom acquisitions of first Paramount Pictures and then CBS, the creation of NBC Universal, and the combination of Time Warner and Turner Broadcasting. Four of these deals involved broadcast networks, four involved major motion picture studios, and all of them involved enormous collections of cable channels. Viewed from within the framework Kellner presents, such a concentration of channels of communication is quite significant, and quite perilous.

ABUNDANCE OF OUTLETS VERSUS DIVERSIFICATION OF SOURCES

The fragmentation of the television audience, and the media marketplace as a whole, fuels claims that the prominence of television has diminished, and, in turn, rendered questions related to ownership unimportant. This argument has justified the deregulation of media industries over the last two decades. Michael Powell advanced the main elements of that position in a speech to the Media Institute in April 1998:

> With scarcity and the uniqueness of broadcasting such demonstrably faulty premises for broadcast regulation, one is left with the undeniable conclusion that the government has been engaged for too long in willful denial in order to subvert the Constitution so that it can impose its speech preferences on the public . . . the time has come to move toward a single standard of First Amendment analysis that recognizes the reality of the media marketplace and respects the intelligence of American consumers.[23]

Powell delivered this speech before he became chair of the FCC, but such themes remained prominent throughout his tenure.

Broadcast television advocates could not have drafted a more favorable speech. The denunciation of the scarcity doctrine reached to the foundation of broadcast regulation, since the paucity of broadcast frequencies was one of the cornerstones for the public service mandate. What is most significant is that an individual empowered to regulate broadcast television in the public interest voiced such sentiments. While one can argue whether broadcast outlets remain scarce, one cannot refute the fact that broadcasters use public airwaves under federal licenses that are allocated free of charge, although the control of those same frequencies make broadcast stations worth millions. The basic position that Powell endorsed was consistent with the marketplace approach that the FCC advanced for two decades, one that stressed abundance in the television marketplace. Increases in the number of television households nationwide that subscribe to cable and satellite services, and the multitude of programming services available, are central to this argument.

What is not even a consideration in such arguments is the concentration of ownership in the motion picture and television industries, and the degree to which a small cadre of corporations dominate both of them, utilizing their market position to extend their influence into more and more endeavors. When one traces the ownership of motion picture studios, broadcast networks, and cable programming services, the same corporations appear time and time again. While it is impossible to refute the claim that the sheer number of outlets has increased, it is far simpler to question whether such abundance has resulted in a true diversification of cultural products. Graham Murdock argues that, "diversity is not multiplicity. It is possible to greatly increase the number of channels and the number of goods in circulation without significantly extending diversity. More does not necessarily mean different."[24]

This is where the concentration of ownership becomes critical. The potential for 500-channel cable and satellite services fueled the argument that diversification will be a by-product of multiplication, but one must question such assertions. There is an important difference between an abundance of outlets—what is often called numerical diversity—and the presence of a full range of voices in the marketplace of ideas—what is often called viewpoint or source diversity. There is no question that the penetration of cable and direct-broadcast-satellite television services has increased the number of television channels available in most American households, oftentimes to a dramatic degree. In the 1990s, for example, the average number of channels available in television households almost doubled, from 33.2 in 1990 to 62.0 in 1999, and that was before digital cable and satellite services penetration became significant.[25] Mere numerical abundance, however, does not guarantee a diversification of voices.

The faith that Powell and other Republican members of the FCC placed in the marketplace was evident when he declared the scarcity doctrine obsolete in 1998 and again after the Commission released its relaxed ownership rules in 2003. In an editorial in the *New York Times* that summer, Powell wrote of the "shrill" rhetoric and argued, "If the problem is lack of diversity among the media, then the fact is that the United States has the most diverse media marketplace in the world. There are more media outlets, owners, variety and diversity now than at any point in our nation's history."[26] There is no question that the penetration of cable and satellite systems increased the number of available services, but far less convincing is the contention that this resulted in more owners, more variety, and more diversity.

WHY OWNERSHIP MATTERS

The issue of ownership in media industries reaches to the core of societies and cultures. The American conception of the media evolved from the founding notions of a representative democracy, within which the media, in theory, make self-government possible through the creation of a "marketplace of ideas" that challenges citizens to grapple between truth and falsehood in a "free and open encounter."[27] Within the liberal-pluralist paradigm, the concentration of ownership of media organizations, newspapers in particular, is a central concern since the dispersal of power and a plurality of elite individuals and groups is essential so no one can dominate the "marketplace of ideas." The reaction within the halls of Congress and of the public at large to the FCC decision to eliminate the Newspaper/Broadcast Cross-Ownership Prohibition in most markets in the summer of 2003 reflects this concern.

The same apprehension persists within the critical paradigm, although the reasons for it are more complicated. Within this framework, power extends beyond the overt use of power to influence the decision-making process, and the covert use of power to control the political agenda and determine what remains outside of the political debate. Power involves the molding of perceptions, cognitions, and preferences, a process that does not reveal the imprint of power. Steven Lukes argues that this allows the dominant class to control discourse so that individuals accept the existing order of things because they cannot imagine an alternative, or because it appears natural or unchangeable, divinely ordained or beneficial. Such a framework introduces the ideological role of the media.

The questions raised in this study are central to the critical political economy of communication, which is most concerned with the production of culture, and how changes in the array of forces influence the production and distribution of cultural products, and, in turn, limit or liberate the public sphere. This approach is at the other end of the critical spectrum from cultural studies, which is most concerned with the construction of meaning in cultural texts. Within the political economy of communication, power is understood at the point of production. Peter Golding and Graham Murdock argue that among the four historical processes that are central to critical political economy, the most important is the extension of corporate reach.[28] The issues of ownership and control grow more prominent with the increased dominance of conglomerates, which provides them with "an unprecedented degree of potential control over the range and direction of cultural production."[29]

A basic question in the political economy of communication addresses the allocation of resources and actions taken to influence this allocation. Dallas Smythe argues that the political economy of communication is concerned with the "structure and policies of these communication agencies in their social settings," and "how mankind arranges to allocate scarce resources with a view toward satisfying some needs (and leaving certain other needs unsatisfied)."[30] These basic questions are quite significant, establishing a point of departure between political economic analysis and economic theories that embrace notions of the invisible hand of the market. Smythe provides a rather precise definition of political economic analysis in the form of two questions: "(1) Who gets what scarce goods and services, when, how and where? . . . (2) Who takes what actions in order to provide what scarce goods and services, when, how and where?"[31] These core principles inform two focal points of this study: the examination of ownership and control in the motion picture and television industries and structural elements, including federal regulation, that encourage or curb consolidation and concentration.

This examination of ownership and regulation of the motion picture and television industries takes the road less traveled. Horizontal and vertical integration and diversification have transformed these industries since the mid-1980s. Given this change, the measurement of concentration in one of these industrial sectors would present a piece of the puzzle, but the larger riddle would remain unsolved. To understand the full implications of federal deregulation and the consolidation and concentration that has occurred, one must now examine ownership vertically within industrial sectors and horizontally across traditional barriers. Within this framework, the vertical connection between the Fox Television Network and its owned and operated affiliates is just as significant as the links to Twentieth Century Fox on one side of the production and distribution equation and FX and Fox Movie Channel on the other. In the end, one must understand concentration in terms of the production and distribution of a type of visual culture, in this case film and video products that are distributed via broadcast, cable, and satellite services as well as in theaters and on home video. This framework speaks to the second question posed at the outset, what does it mean?

It is also important to explore the first of these questions, how did we get here? This requires the examination of two related but distinct issues: how did ownership and control change over the last quarter-century, and how did the executive, legislative, and judicial branches of government and FCC contribute to this change, in either a green light or red light fashion. At the start of 1984, FCC rules limited group ownership to just seven local television stations; at the start of 2005, Sinclair Broadcast Group owned 62 stations. It is critical to address how this growth has changed the nature of ownership at the national and local levels, but it is also essential to examine who has taken what actions to contribute to such changes. Each of the branches of government impacted on the station ownership rules, which was most evident in the first half of the decade. In 2001, the U.S. Court of Appeals for the D.C. Circuit remanded the existing 35 percent ownership limit to the FCC for further consideration. In the spring of 2003, the FCC voted to raise that cap to 45 percent as part of a mandated biennial review of ownership rules. That fall, a Senate-House conference committee added an amendment to an omnibus spending bill that rolled the ceiling back to 35 percent, but the White House stepped into the battle and worked out a compromise with Republican leaders that established a 39 percent limit.

In the end, one must reconsider the argument that Michael Powell advanced in the summer of 2003: "the United States has the most diverse media marketplace in the world." There is little question that there are more media outlets, but has such multiplicity resulted in diversity? One must reassess the claim that Graham Murdock made, that it is possible to "increase the number of channels and the number of goods in circulation without significantly extending diversity."[32] One must consider these questions, moreover, looking across the motion picture, broadcast television, and cable television industries rather than isolated within one media sector. That task lies ahead.

NOTES

1. The News Corporation Limited, "Annual Report," 1998.

2. Michael Powell, ABC's World News Tonight with Peter Jennings, 15 May 2003.

3. *Mutual Film Corporation v. Industrial Commission of Ohio*, 35 S. Ct. 387 (1915).

4. The Radio Act of 1927, Public Law 632, 69th Congress (1927); Federal Radio Commission, *In the Matter of the Application of Great Lakes Broadcasting Co.* 3 FRC Ann. Rep. 32 (1929).

5. Quoted in Robert W. McChesney, *Telecommunications, Mass Media, & Democracy: The Battle for the Control of U.S. Broadcasting, 1928–1935* (New York: Oxford University Press, 1993), 251.

6. Mark S. Fowler and Daniel L. Brenner, "A Marketplace Approach to Broadcast Regulation," *Texas Law Review* 60, no. 2 (1981–1982), 209–10.

7. Tino Balio, ed., *The American Film Industry*, revised ed. (Madison: The University of Wisconsin Press, 1985); Erik Barnouw, *The Golden Web: A History of Broadcasting in the United States, Volume II – 1933 to 1953* (New York: Oxford University Press, 1968).

8. Don Groves, "Indie Spirit Takes Hold of O'seas Auds," *Daily Variety*, 7 January 2005, 4.

9. Edward S. Herman and Robert W. McChesney, *The Global Media: The New York Missionaries of Corporate Capitalism* (London: Cassell, 1997).

10. Quoted in Balio, *American Film Industry*, 588.

11. The first print is a term used in the production of motion pictures. It represents the up-front costs associated with the production of a film, including preproduction costs such as script development and postproduction costs such as editing and scoring.

Costs associated with production are often broken into two groups: above-the-line expenses for actors and creative crew and below-the-line costs for technical crew, facilities, equipment, etc. The term is also applicable to television programs, although all such programs are not shot or edited on film.

12. Hamid Mowlana, *Global Information and World Communication* (New York: Longman, 1986).

13. The Motion Picture Association was formed in 1945 as the Motion Picture Export Association of America and renamed in 1994.

14. This was most evident long before World War II, as in 1925 the United States exported some 235 million feet of motion pictures and imported seven million feet. Thomas H. Guback, "Hollywood's International Market," in *The American Film Industry*, 465–467.

15. Mark Wheeler, "'Trade Follows Film': Hollywood and U.S. Trade Policy" (paper presented at the Political Science Association Conference, 5–7 April 2005).

16. Quoted in Jean-Pierre Jeancolas, "From the Blum-Byrnes Agreement to the GATT Affair," in *Hollywood and Europe: Economics, Culture, National Identity: 1945–95*, ed. Geoffrey Nowell-Smith and Steven Ricci, 57–58 (London: British Film Institute, 1998).

17. Quoted in Marci McDonald, "A Futile Struggle to Withstand U.S. Culture," *Toronto Star*, 9 October 1993, C4.

18. Herbert Schiller, "On That Chart," *Nation*, 3 June 1996, 16.

19. Nielsen Media Research, *2000 Report on Television* (New York: Nielsen Media Research, 2000).

20. P. J. Long and Gerette Buglion, "Summary of Research on the Effects of Television Viewing," in *"un-TV" guide* (10 October 1996).

21. Douglas Kellner, *Media Culture* (London: Routledge, 1995), 235.

22. Kellner, *Media Culture*, 235.

23. Michael K. Powell, "Willful Denial and First Amendment Jurisprudence" (speech to the Media Institute, 22 April 1998).

24. Graham Murdock, "Large Corporations and the Control of the Communications Industries," in *Culture, Society and the Media*, ed. Michael Gurevitch, Tony Bennett, James Curran, and Janet Woollacott, 120 (London: Methuen, 1982).

25. Nielsen Media Research, *2000 Report on Television*.

26. Michael Powell, "New Rules, Old Rhetoric." *New York Times*, 28 July 2003, A17.

27. John Milton is credited with originating the notion of a "marketplace of ideas" in 1644, although the phrase was not mentioned in his speech, "For the Liberty of Unlicensed Printing," to the Parliament of England known as *Areopagitica*. John Milton, *Areopagitica* (Folcroft, PA: The Folcroft Press, Inc., 1969), 58–59.

28. Peter Golding and Graham Murdock, "Culture, Communications, and Political Economy," in *Mass Media and Society*, 2nd ed., ed. James Curran and Michael Gurevitch (London: Edward Arnold, 1991).

29. Murdock, "Large Corporations," 120.

30. Dallas Smythe, "On the Political Economy of Communications," *Journalism Quarterly* (1960).

31. Smythe, "Political Economy of Communications," 564.

32. Murdock, "Large Corporations," 120.

2

❖

Conglomeration in the Motion Picture Industry

When the Academy of Motion Picture Arts and Sciences announced the nominations for the Academy Awards in 1993, *Daily Variety* heralded it as "Independents Day for Oscar."[1] Two of the five nominations for best picture went to "independent" films, *The Crying Game* and *Howard's End*, while four other films distributed outside the major studios fared well in prominent categories. *Howard's End* producer Ismail Merchant viewed the Oscar recognition as a "great endorsement of the independent spirit."[2] Flash forward four years, and the *Washington Post* used an almost identical headline, "Independents Day for Oscar Nominations," when the contenders were announced in 1997.[3] This time, four out of five best picture nominations landed outside the majors, with *The English Patient, Shine, Fargo,* and *Secrets & Lies* so honored. Once again, the "independents" ruled the day. The headlines were similar, but beneath the surface, the stories were quite different.

Miramax Film Corp. was a principal in both these Oscar campaigns. In 1993, it earned acclaim for bringing low-budget wonder *The Crying Game* to theater screens while also releasing two other films that received multiple nominations, *Enchanted April* and *Passion Fish*. Four years later, Miramax claimed the best picture prize for *The English Patient*, which collected nine Oscars. Much changed between 1993 and 1997, however, and Miramax and *The English Patient* failed the first test of independence, the financing of the film. Within weeks of the 1993 Academy Awards, The Walt Disney Co. acquired Miramax for between $60 million and $65 million.[4] Miramax cofounder Harvey Weinstein stated at the time that, "We are autonomous so we green-light the movies, we make the financial decisions, the creative decisions."[5] A central pillar of the deal, however, was that Disney would finance all future Miramax films.[6] *The English Patient* reflected the traditional model of studio financing, as Miramax contributed $27 million to the production of the film after Fox Searchlight walked away from the project. Those millions came from the deep pockets of Disney.

The conglomerate that purchased Miramax was also quite different from the studio that Walt Disney created. When *The English Patient* captured the Best Picture Oscar in 1997, Miramax was just one of four production units Disney owned—alongside Walt Disney Pictures, Touchstone Pictures, and Hollywood Pictures—and the studio had production deals with various producers, directors, and actors. In addition to the horizontal integration that these companies represented, Disney had also become a diversified media conglomerate through its acquisition of Capital Cities/ABC, which was finalized in 1996. This changed the face of the corporation, as the deal included the ABC Television Network and its owned and operated stations and a financial interest in a collection of cable channels, including ESPN, Lifetime, and A&E. The addition of ABC created vertical integration between the network and Disney's television production units, including Walt Disney Television and Touchstone Television.

The transformation of Disney from a corporation that derived 70.4 percent of its revenues from theme parks in 1980 into a diversified media conglomerate that generated 66.6 percent of its revenues from its media networks and studio entertainment divisions in 2004 is neither isolated nor unique. This makeover, in fact, featured the three interlinked but distinct processes that move industries from differentiation to concentration: integration, diversification, and internationalization. Integration is the most significant to this discussion. Horizontal integration occurs when companies consolidate and extend their control within a particular sector and maximize economies of scale and shared resources through the addition of more units at one level of production, distribution, or exhibition. Vertical integration occurs when companies with interests at one level of the production, distribution, or exhibition sequence extend their operations into other stages in order to better rationalize this process. In both cases, greater control over the market is the main objective.

All of the major media conglomerates followed the basic pattern evident in the evolution of Disney in one form or fashion over this period. Rupert Murdoch and News Corp., for example, took a different approach to integration and diversification, but the results were quite similar. While Disney spent $19 billion to obtain Capital Cities/ABC Inc., News Corp. launched the Fox Television Network from scratch. While Disney spent millions to acquire Miramax, News Corp. created Fox Searchlight, Fox 2000, and Twentieth Century Fox Animation in-house. The strategies were different, but the outcomes were the same. At the heart of both these conglomerates lies the same basic pursuit: the production and distribution of content. These cases point to the need to take a more integrated approach to the examination of ownership and bridge boundaries that often separate media industries. And the logical place to start is with the major studios and production companies that create film and television content.

THE FOUNDATION FOR THE AMERICAN SYSTEM

There was a time in the 1920s when the motion picture studios that remain prominent today could still be linked to the individuals who created them: Harry Cohn and Columbia Pictures, Adolph Zukor and Paramount Pictures, William Fox and Fox Film Corp., Carl Laemmle and Universal Pictures, Walt Disney and Walt Disney Pictures, and Jack, Abe, Harry, and Sam Warner with Warner Bros. William Fox was the first of this group to lose his empire when the stock market crash forced him to sell his interest in the Fox Film Corp. in 1930. Walt Disney was the last, as he remained in control of the studio that bears his name until his death in 1966. The movie moguls who created Hollywood might have passed away long ago, but the basic commercial orientation and studio dominance of the business remain true to its roots and the impact of this on the industry is profound to the present day.

The commercial nature of the production and distribution of motion pictures in the United States was evident in the name of one of its earliest and most significant manifestations, the "nickelodeon." It is important to consider that this machine was not named after the images or ideas that it could project or the art form that it could become. Rather, it was named after the "nickel" that it could command from customers. When the nickelodeon dwindled and feature-length films became the norm, the economic potential of films remained central to discussions. When D. W. Griffith's *The Birth of a Nation* opened at the Liberty Theater in New York on March 3, 1915, it began a forty-four consecutive week run with an admission price of $2.00, the equivalent of over $36 in 2005 when adjusted for inflation. The birth of the star system in the same period drove the salaries for such actors as Mary Pickford and Charlie Chaplin to as high as $10,000 a week.[7] Stars reduced the risks associated with production, which made capital more available, fostered the creation of more sophisticated marketing campaigns, and mandated higher ticket prices at the box office. All of these developments support the argument that film in the United States developed as a commercial, profit-oriented activity.

It is quite valuable to compare the evolution of film in the United States with that of other media. The ideals of American newspapers, for example, are an outgrowth of the liberal political tradition reflected in the writings of John Milton, credited with the origination of the notion of a "marketplace of ideas" in 1644. Milton defended the faith of intellectual liberalism, arguing, "truth will prevail over error when both may be freely tested by investigation and discussion."[8] A fundamental assumption of American society is that democracy thrives in the United States, in part, because of the information made available to the public through the media. Thomas Jefferson wrote in 1787 that "were it left to me to decide whether we should have a government without newspapers, or newspapers without government, I should not hesitate a moment to prefer the latter."[9]

Such discussions stand in stark contrast with those associated with motion pictures in the United States at the outset of the twentieth century. The

Supreme Court ruled in 1915 "the exhibition of motion pictures is a business pure and simple, originated and conducted for profit."[10] That business orientation was one reason used to deny motion pictures protection as speech under the First Amendment in this period. Radio received such protection, and broadcast regulations and policies that emerged in the 1920s reveal the difference, once again, between how film and some other media were treated. The Radio Act of 1927 established serving the public interest, convenience and necessity as a licensing standard for local broadcast stations, which carried over to television. This and other documents reveal how the roots of film and television, now often equated as entertainment media, arose from very different philosophical roots.

(Film in the United States did not evolve as a medium for public communication, nor as an art form. It was a profit-oriented, commercial activity. The prime motivation for many involved came not from the images and ideas that they could present but from the profits that they could derive from the machines that projected those images and ideas.) This demands a different approach to the examination of motion pictures, since it is impossible to consider films as "autonomous creations, independent of economic institutions."[11] (Rather, one must consider the industrial mechanism that "produces and disseminates our culture,"|since this system controls, influences, and impacts the selection and development of content, the relationship between the different players within the industry, and the ownership and control of the production apparatus.[12]

POLICY AND REGULATORY FRAMEWORK

The philosophical distinction between a medium treated as a business, "pure and simple," and ones expected to serve the public interest has clear implications when the focus turns to policies and regulations. The Supreme Court decision that included the "pure and simple" argument involved a state statute that allowed for the censorship of films that were "to be publicly exhibited and displayed in the state of Ohio."[13] There is little question that censorship is a clear form of regulation, be it at the federal, state, or local level. The regulation of motion pictures takes different forms, since one could include self-regulation and self-censorship within the regime. In the case of motion pictures, this began in the 1920s when public cries for censorship led to the creation of the Motion Picture Producers and Distributors of America and the implementation of the Motion Picture Production Code in 1930. This pattern continues into the present day, with distributors and exhibitors still working collectively within the Motion Picture Association of America (MPAA) rating system. Sidebar 2.1 discusses self-regulation in more detail.

There are few specific federal regulations that limit the activities of motion picture production and distribution companies. The federal government has even weakened the antitrust limitations codified in the Paramount consent

Sidebar 2.1
Self-Regulation in the "American System"

When the ABC Television Network broadcast *Saving Private Ryan* in November 2004, almost two dozen affiliates preempted the award-winning film. The reason was simple: fear that the Federal Communications Commission would deem the violence and language included in the battle scenes in *Private Ryan* to be profane or indecent.[1] The ABC broadcast of the World War II epic was not the first time controversy arose from the graphic content of the film. In 1998, the Rating Board of the Motion Picture Association of America (MPAA) gave *Saving Private Ryan* an R rating for "intense, prolonged realistically graphic sequences of war violence and for language." At the time, the *Hollywood Reporter* speculated that the film would have received a NC-17 rating if Steven Spielberg had not produced it. The one difference between the 1998 debate over *Saving Private Ryan* and the 2004 storm was that the federal government had no hand in the former.

The role of the MPAA in the rating of motion pictures in the United States challenges one to rethink traditional notions of regulation. The common definition of regulation relates to government rules or laws that control the activities of businesses or consumers, restrictions that prevent the occurrence of undesirable activities. In most nations around the world, the classification of motion pictures would fit within this definition. In Malaysia, for example, the state-run Malaysian Film Censorship Board requested ten minutes worth of cuts from *Saving Private Ryan* and banned the film when Spielberg refused to do so. In Canada, film classification occurs at the provincial level under provisions of The Motion Picture Act, and while the ratings might differ, the role of the state remains constant. In the case of *Saving Private Ryan*, the film received an 18A rating from the Film Classification Office in British Columbia, but a 13+ rating from the Regie du Cinema in Quebec.[2]

The censorship and classification of motion pictures in the United States began much as the Canadian system operates, with control located at the state and local level. Chicago passed an ordinance in 1907 that required exhibitors to receive a permit from the police before showing a film, and Pennsylvania, Kansas, and Ohio established state review boards between 1911 and 1913. The landmark Supreme Court case of *Mutual Film Corporation v. Industrial Commission of Ohio* in 1915 upheld the Ohio statute that established a state board of film censors. In an oft-repeated pattern, the studios were quick to react. Prominent producers and distributors created the National Association of the Motion Picture Industry in 1916 and later adopted a code of standards that specified subjects and situations whose depiction was unacceptable in motion pictures in an attempt to beat back censorship programs. That group became the precursor to the Motion Picture Producers and Distributors of America (MPPDA).

The creation of the MPPDA in 1922 and the self-regulation it promoted was consistent with the historical period in which it emerged. In the 1920s, Secretary of Commerce Herbert Hoover promoted the notion of an "associative state" in which institutions could facilitate cooperation between government and business. Trade associations such as the MPDDA and National Association of Broadcasters (NAB), also formed in 1922, became the main mechanisms for achieving coordination and what Hoover called an "assured transition to an American utopia." Such organizations

(Continued)

assumed a prominent role in the creation of an "American system" that was different from the framework for regulation evolving around the world at that time. In the case of broadcast radio, the NAB assumed a prominent role in the promotion of an advertiser-supported, privately owned system and then worked hand-in-hand with the Federal Radio Commission and Federal Communications Commission in the writing of rules and regulations that assured the outcome it desired. In the case of motion pictures, the government ceded most such roles to the industry and allowed regulation to occur outside the halls of government.

The major studios created the MPDDA at a time when sensational headlines coming out of Hollywood, including the manslaughter trial of Roscoe "Fatty" Arbuckle, fueled calls for government control of the film business. It came in the aftermath of Federal Trade Commission charges that Famous Players-Lasky Corporation was monopolizing first run exhibition. Much as it did in the 1960s with the selection of Jack Valenti to head the MPAA at a critical point in its history, the association reached into government and named Will Hays, former chair of the Republican National Committee (1918–1921) and then Postmaster General (1921–22), as its first president. Hays promised to impose a set of moral standards on the movies, but Hollywood largely ignored his initial forays. This included a list of "Don'ts and Be Carefuls" issued in 1927 that included "Pointed profanity," "licentious or suggestive nudity," "The illegal traffic in drugs," and "Any inference of sexual perversion."[3]

The more formal articulation of such ideas was set forth in The Motion Picture Production Code of 1930, better known as the "Hays Code." The MPPDA strengthened the production code in 1934 with the creation of a Production Code Administration and subsequent mandate for a certificate of approval. The code is an interesting document that says a great deal about self-regulation. The preamble to the code stated that, "though regarding motion pictures primarily as entertainment without any explicit purpose of teaching or propaganda, they know that the motion picture within its own field of entertainment may be directly responsible for spiritual or moral progress, for higher types of social life, and for much correct thinking." Such "correct thinking" related to a range of behavior, including crimes against the law, sex, vulgarity, obscenity, and profanity. The code prohibited nudity and stated, "Excessive and lustful kissing, lustful embraces, suggestive postures and gestures, are not to be shown" so as not to "stimulate the lower and baser element." An amendment in 1939 detailed words that were prohibited in motion pictures, including alley cat, broad, bat, hot, and slut when applied to a woman.

The code is all the more remarkable when viewed in the current context, an age when "lustful kissing, lustful embraces" are a staple of motion pictures. This is most evident with the limits placed on violence:

I. Crimes Against the Law

These shall never be presented in such a way as to throw sympathy with the crime as against law and justice or to inspire others with a desire for imitation.

1. Murder

a. The technique of murder must be presented in a way that will not inspire imitation.

b. Brutal killings are not to be presented in detail.

c. Revenge in modern times shall not be justified.

2. Methods of Crime should not be explicitly presented.
   a. Theft, robbery, safe-cracking, and dynamiting of trains, mines, buildings, etc., should not be detailed in method.
   b. Arson must be subject to the same safeguards.
   c. The use of firearms should be restricted to the essentials.
   d. Methods of smuggling should not be presented.
3. Illegal drug traffic must never be presented.
4. The use of liquor in American life, when not required by the plot or for proper characterization, will not be shown.

It is interesting to contemplate how many of these prohibitions films such as *Kill Bill, Vol. 1* and *Kill Bill, Vol. 2* might have violated in addition to the notion that "revenge in modern times shall not be justified."

What was most significant about the production code is that the system was voluntary and had no basis in law. That, in time, contributed to its demise. In the 1950s, Otto Preminger directed a series of films that violated the code and released them without the certificate of approval. *The Moon in Blue* (1953) was the first film to use the words "virgin," "seduce," and "mistress," while *The Man with the Golden Arm* (1955) and *Anatomy of a Murder* (1959) dealt with drug abuse and rape, respectively. Alfred Hitchcock released *Psycho* (1960) without the seal because of its themes. All of these films were successful at the box office, which was a death knell to the code. In the same period, the Supreme Court ruled in *Burstyn v. Wilson* that the banning of a film in New York because it was "sacrilegious" was unconstitutional, extending First Amendment speech rights to films for the first time.

The formal death of the Hays Code came in 1966 when Jack Valenti moved from the White House to the MPAA and the release of *Who's Afraid of Virginia Woolf* prompted a debate over appropriate language when "screw" and "hump the hostess" were allowed, but the code administration mandated that "screw you" was replaced with "god damn you." The MPAA established the now familiar rating system, including the G, PG, and R ratings, in 1968. The new system was altogether different from the old, but the one constant was that the federal, state, and local governments were not involved and the system had no legal authority. The "voluntary rating system" was the creation of the MPAA, National Association of Theatre Owners (NATO), and International Film Importers & Distributors of America (IFIDA).

What is perhaps most significant about the MPAA system is that it became a model for other media industries. In 1985, in the aftermath of a Congressional hearing that Tipper Gore and the Parents Music Resource Center headlined, the Recording Industry Association of American (RIAA) agreed to provide a Parent Advisory Label for releases that contain explicit lyrics. The administration of this labeling system remains within the purview of the RIAA. A decade later, similar pressure led to the creation of TV Parental Guidelines under the control of the MPAA and NAB. Around the same time, the Entertainment Software Association created the Entertainment Ratings Rating Board to provide information about video and computer game content. At face value, there is little that these systems have in common. While most motion pictures fall within the PG, PG-13, and R classifications, comparable television shows carry TVPG, TV14, and TVMA labels, and video games are identified as E10+ (Everyone

(Continued)

10 and older), T (Teen), and M (Mature). At their root, however, these systems are all an outgrowth of notions of an "associative state" that Hoover advanced in the 1920s and self-regulation that has been prominent ever since.

NOTES

1. ABC aired the film on Veterans Day in 2001 and 2002, and the FCC ruled that the unedited version of *Saving Private Ryan* was not indecent. In 2005, the FCC once again ruled that the film was "filled with expletives and material arguably unsuitable for some audiences, but it was not indecent in the unanimous view of the Commission."

2. The "18A" in British Columbia required persons under eighteen years of age to be "accompanied" by an adult, while the "13+" in Quebec extended the same restrictions only for those under thirteen years of age.

3. Geoffrey Nowell-Smith, ed., *The Oxford History of World Cinema* (New York: Oxford University Press, 1996), 239.

decrees, discussed more in chapter 4. This does not mean that regulations and policies do not influence business practices in various ways, both positive and negative. It is important to frame this discussion within a broader definition of regulation, one that moves past the narrow notion of restrictions exercised by public agencies over various activities. Robert Baldwin and Martin Cave make the distinction between "red light" regulations, ones that restrict behavior and prevent the occurrence of undesirable activities, and "green light" regulations, ones that are enabling or facilitative.[14] Within this definition, one can include all deliberate state actions designed to influence industrial and social behavior. Such decisions do not occur in isolation, as the choices made reflect the dominate ideas and ideologies of a historic period and become a unique pattern of political intervention in business activities.

This broader definition of regulation expands the range of policies that influence the production and distribution of motion pictures and television programs. Tax breaks and other economic incentives are a focal point in the current decade. Much is made of so-called "runaway production" in which U.S.-based companies produce films or television programs in Canada, Australia, or other countries to realize lower labor costs and take advantage of various economic inducements. In 2004 and 2005, there were extensive discussions at the federal and state levels about a suitable response, with California Governor Arnold Schwarzenegger among those campaigning for the antirunaway provisions. In the first half of 2004 alone, state legislatures from Utah to South Carolina, Pennsylvania to Florida, New Mexico to Georgia discussed or passed tax and other economic incentives for film and television production. While such deliberations were ongoing in state houses, Congress passed legislation in the fall of 2004 that included incentives to support films and television production. One clause of the Jumpstart Our Business Strength (JOBS) Act made films and television programs eligible for tax credits on productions with budgets up to $15 million, providing that 75 percent of wages expended were for services rendered in the United States.

These incentives for U.S.-based productions were almost afterthoughts in the midst of the JOBS Act, designed to address broader issues related to multinational corporations. In 2002, the World Trade Organization (WTO) ruled that long-standing tax breaks given to U.S.-based corporations operating abroad were an unfair subsidy. The "foreign sales corporations" system allowed companies with a foreign presence, including the corporations that owned the major motion picture studios, to exempt between 15 and 30 percent of their export income from U.S. taxes. After appeals of the ruling were exhausted, the WTO gave the European Union permission to slap as much as $4 billion in duties on U.S. goods starting in March 2004, with increases each month. The JOBS Act originated to address these violations and assist companies that manufacture products in the United States, but it evolved into a much broader framework to aid, among others, Hollywood. In addition to the specific assistance discussed above, the mere fact that films were classified as manufacturing products alongside computer software, oil and gas refining, and engineering services made the studios eligible for various tax breaks and revealed the lobbying power of the industry.

The WTO and its predecessor, GATT, ruled time and again that various schemes to provide tax relief for export earnings is little more than an illegal subsidy, which is quite significant to this discussion, since the U.S. government has long fought against various subsidies for film and television production. These objections, fought on behalf of the Motion Picture Association (MPA), the international arm of the Motion Picture Association of America (MPAA), focused on direct production subsidies, common in Australia, Canada, and across much of Europe, as well as national or regional content quotas. The importance of these policies was most evident during the Uruguay Round of GATT negotiations that concluded in 1993. One of the final obstacles of the entire international trade agreement, still contested after agriculture issues were settled, was over European initiatives to place quotas on audiovisual texts. One focal point was the "Television Without Frontiers" protocol, approved by the European Community in 1989, which mandated that a "majority proportion" of broadcast time in the twelve member states be reserved for programs of European origination.

With MPAA head Jack Valenti putting pressure on the White House, the United States made repeated attempts to have the culture industries incorporated into the 117-nation agreement that resulted from the Uruguay Round, but in the end it was unsuccessful. Much of the debate boiled down to a battle between the United States and France. The French claimed a cultural exemption for audiovisual texts based on an argument of national sovereignty and identity, believing that creative content is altogether different from other products. The Americans countered that such creative content—film, television, and recorded music—should be treated like other industries, with open markets and an elimination of subsidies. In the end, the United States backed down and agreed to drop the audiovisual provision in order to reach agreement on what President Clinton called a "historic victory to open foreign markets to American products." Jack Valenti called the European position "blatant protectionism unmasked."[15]

The Uruguay Round of GATT was not the lone example of the media industries factoring into international trade policies. Among the most contentious issues in negotiations between the United States and Canada over the North American Free Trade Agreement (NAFTA) were Canadian quotas and protections for its culture industries. In 1992, U.S. Trade Representative Carla Hills acquiesced to a "cultural exclusion" that enabled Canada to maintain content restrictions and incentives in the film and television industries. It is important to note that the United States took exemptions to protect other industries within NAFTA. At the end of the decade, an agreement between the United States and China to advance the latter's admission into the WTO in 1999 was predicated in part on concessions made for greater media access. These included an increase in the quota on foreign films allowed into China and opportunities for foreign investment in the construction, operation, and ownership of cinemas in China.

Another area of regulation is quite important in the discussion of media industries. The wave of mergers and acquisitions that involved the motion picture studios and broadcast networks and began in the 1980s occurred within a new ideological framework relative to antitrust regulation and vertical and horizontal integration. Prior to this period, antitrust laws and similar legislation were based not just on economic theories but also upon concerns about the control and power over industrial sectors by a few individuals or corporations. One of the motivations was a fear that "excessive concentration tends to promote antidemocratic tendencies in the society as a whole."[16] Because of this, merger analysis in the 1960s and 1970s was most concerned with the structure of industries, with the Department of Justice arguing that the main role of merger enforcement was to "preserve and promote market structures conducive to competition" because the "conduct of the individual firms in a market tend to be controlled by the structure of the market."[17]

It was in the 1960s that the government was successful in its attempt to block International Telephone and Telegraph's acquisition of ABC, with the objections based in part on the political strand of antitrust policies. There were no such concerns raised within the federal government over General Electric's purchase of NBC in the 1980s. The actions of the Federal Trade Commission and Department of Justice during the Reagan Administration were based on a faith in economic analysis over other principles and a belief that the economic welfare of consumers was the appropriate objective of antitrust regulation rather than other social concerns. The impact of these ideas and ideologies are evident in changes in the merger reviews in this period. An important component of the Reagan doctrine was a move away from cases based on vertical and share monopoly theories and a refocusing on traditional horizontal restraint-of-trade matters. The 1984 Merger Guidelines were the articulation of these principles.

This proved to be a seminal moment, as the analysis of mergers since the mid-1980s start from a narrow definition of market power and a total focus on horizontal integration. There is little question that this was a historical period in which new ideas and ideologies became dominant. The Reagan era came on the heels of a period of new social regulation, within which a "public lobby regime" moved to the fore and environment and consumer regulations were prominent. Richard Nixon, Gerald Ford, and Jimmy Carter all attempted to control regulators, but each embraced the New Deal principle that federal programs were a needed response to socioeconomic problems. President Reagan, on the other hand, believed that new social regulation was "inconsistent, even antithetical, to the American notion of liberal democracy." This was the historical context for the wave of conglomeration discussed below.

THE MAJOR MOTION PICTURE STUDIOS

The roots of most of the major motion picture production and distribution companies, best known as the major studios, can be traced to the 1920s, the period in which the production, distribution, and exhibition of motion pictures first assumed true industrial characteristics. Adolph Zukor laid the basis for this structure with the creation of Paramount in 1919. It was from this foundation that the industry evolved and developed the organizational structure that would characterize it for the next two decades. It began to resemble a typical American industry, with the production, distribution, and exhibition branches corresponding to the manufacturing, wholesaling, and retailing activities in a typical industry.[18] At the end of the 1920s, the industry had developed into a mature oligopoly, with five integrated, diversified, and worldwide corporations—Warner Bros. Pictures, Loew's Incorporated, Paramount Pictures, Radio-Keith-Orpheum Corporation (RKO), and Fox Film Corporation—in control of 77 percent of the first-run theaters and the production and distribution of 50 percent of the feature films in the United States.[19] Just below the big five were the little three, Universal Pictures, Columbia Pictures, and United Artists.

Important dimensions of this transformation were initiatives to take advantage of economies of scale. The profits from a single film were magnified with an increase in the number of available outlets, and each major corporation created a network for worldwide distribution and large chains of domestic theaters. In their theaters, the companies adopted business methods developed in large chain store retailing. While these practices resulted in increased profits, they also gave the companies more power and control, and that, in turn, attracted investors, which led to the integration of the film industry into the American economic system.

This integration is most evident in the involvement of banks and other financial institutions in the production and distribution of motion pictures.

Banks funded much of the horizontal and vertical expansion that occurred in the 1920s, which led to these financial institutions wielding effective control over the studios.[20] The best example of this was Fox Film Corporation. William Fox bought his first movie theater in 1906 and was a true pioneer, but he began to lose control of the corporation that bore his name in the late 1920s, as expansion in various areas required more and more capital. In 1929, Fox acquired control of Loew's Incorporated, the parent corporation of MGM, for a short time. The combination of Fox and Loew's would have created the largest motion picture conglomerate in the world, but William Fox assumed substantial short-term debt in the process.[21] With the panic that surrounded the collapse of the stock market in 1929, Fox needed funds to cover margins on his Loew's stock, and his pursuit of those funds led to the sale of his interest in Fox Film Corp. in April 1930 and the eventual control over both Fox and Loew's landed in the hands of Chase National Bank.[22] The remnants of Fox combined with Twentieth Century in 1935 to create Twentieth Century Fox.

The post-World War II period was one of transition and reorganization for the film industry in the United States. The period began with high expectations, predicated on record box office receipts in 1946. Dreams of continued success were dashed, however. Between 1946 and 1956, annual box office receipts declined 23 percent, from $1.692 billion to $1.298 billion, and the combined profits of the ten largest corporations declined 74 percent, from $121 million to $32 million. There were many reasons for these changes, including the dawn of the baby boom, the enrollment of World War II service men in educational institutions, and the penetration of automobiles, appliances, and other commodities, all of which turned attention and disposable income away from motion pictures. Another factor, of course, was the advent of broadcast television.

There were also important structural changes. In 1938, the federal government filed suit charging the five major motion picture companies—Paramount, Loew's, RKO, Warner Bros., and Twentieth Century Fox—with "combining and conspiring to restrain trade unreasonably and to monopolize the production, distribution and exhibition of motion pictures and to monopolize such trade in violation of the Sherman Act."[23] Three smaller companies—Columbia, Universal, and United Artists—were charged with "combining with the five majors to restrain trade unreasonably and to monopolize commerce in motion pictures." The case reached the Supreme Court in 1948, and it affirmed most of the lower court rulings: block booking, uniform systems of runs and clearances, uniform admission prices, and other trade practices were illegal. The Supreme Court, however, set aside the lower court ruling on divestiture between distribution and exhibition and remanded it back to the District Court for further consideration. Worn out after a decade of litigation, Paramount and RKO chose to enter into negotiations with the Department of Justice and both signed consent decrees in 1949. The other three majors soon followed.

The Paramount decrees mandated that the motion picture companies cease all unfair distribution practices, with contracts written on a theater-by-theater, picture-by-picture basis. What made this feasible was that the companies were also required to break ties between their production and distribution operations and the theatrical exhibition of motion pictures, and divest of theaters operated in pools with other companies. The decrees were designed to make it easier for nonmajors to enter the market, since Paramount and other studios could no longer demand block booking and other monopolistic business practices. There was an increase in independent film production after the signing of the decrees, since these producers now had access to first-run theaters, but there was also an increase in the number of films that failed, which had a deleterious impact on small producers.[24]

The decline in theater attendance that began in 1947 made capital more difficult to procure. Financial institutions demanded that a film producer have a distribution contract before funding production, so power and control remained with the majors. The banks, moreover, were reluctant to fund a project that was of a "controversial nature from the religious, racial or ideological point of view."[25] Tino Balio argues that independent film production became "assimilated by the majors as an alternative to the studio system of production," with the majors functioning as "bankers supplying financing and landlords renting studio space."[26] These realities point to the central role distribution assumes in this process and deemed to be where true control lies. Without a distribution agreement, a producer oftentimes cannot obtain the financing needed for a film.

Conglomeration of the Major Motion Picture Production and Distribution Companies: 1960–1984

The period between 1960 and 1984 was one of considerable change for the major motion picture production and distribution companies, as each underwent conglomeration in which activities unrelated to motion pictures were drawn under the same corporate umbrella. In some instances, such as Disney, this diversification occurred under the same general ownership, but in other cases, ownership and control transferred to larger, more diversified corporations. Table 2.1 documents the major ownership changes. What is most important is to draw a distinction between the mergers and acquisition that occurred between 1960 and 1984, and those that have taken place since then, with the News Corp. purchase of Twentieth Century Fox in 1985 indicative of a significant change.

The bulk of the changes in control that occurred between 1960 and 1984 involved corporations that did not have extensive investments in media industries. In 1966, Gulf + Western Industries, Inc. purchased Paramount Pictures for $130 million. Gulf + Western was the quintessential conglomerate of the mid-1960s, as Charles Bluhdorn spearheaded the acquisition of over ninety

Table 2.1.   Transfers in the Ownership and Control of the Major Motion Picture Studios, United Artists, and MGM, 1960–1984

1961	Universal Pictures	Music Corp. of America, a Chicago-based talent agency better known as MCA Inc., absorbs Decca Records and its subsidiary, Universal Pictures.
1966	Paramount Pictures	Gulf + Western Industries Inc. acquires Paramount Pictures Corporation for $130 million.
1967	United Artists	Transamerica Corporation acquires United Artists.
	Warner Bros.	Seven Arts Productions acquires Warner Bros.
1969	Warner Bros.	Kinney National Services and Steven Ross acquire Warner Bros. from Seven Arts.
	MGM	Financier Kirk Kerkorian acquires MGM for the first time.
1972	Warner Bros.	Steven Ross restructures Kinney National Services and becomes Warner Communications, Inc.
1981	United Artists	Transamerica Corporation sells United Artists to Metro-Goldwyn-Mayer.
	Twentieth Century Fox	Oil baron Marvin Davis acquires Twentieth Century Fox.
1982	Columbia Pictures	Coca-Cola Co. purchases Columbia Pictures Industries, Inc. for $750 million.
1983	Paramount Pictures	Gulf + Western divests its industrial properties but retains Paramount Pictures, Simon & Schuster, and Madison Square Garden.
1984	Walt Disney	The Bass family acquires a controlling interest in The Walt Disney Co., and Michael Eisner and Frank Wells assume managerial control.

smaller companies between 1958 and 1969.[27] Most of those properties were in manufacturing sectors, which is where Gulf + Western traced its roots, although the corporation did obtain interests in book publishing (Simon & Schuster, Inc.) and theatrical exhibition (Famous Players Ltd. in Canada). It also owned the New York Knicks of the National Basketball Association and New York Rangers of the National Hockey League through Madison Square Garden Corp.

The second domino to fall was United Artists, which became a wholly owned subsidiary of Transamerica Corporation in 1967.[28] Transamerica was a "multi-market service organization" with its roots in insurance and business services, as well as investments in the car rental and airline businesses.[29] The third to fall was Warner Bros. It sold out to a smaller production company, Seven Arts Productions, in 1967, a sale that bankers Serge Semenenko and Charles Allen orchestrated. The combination lasted just a short time, however, and Kinney National Services, Inc., a real estate and financial services concern headed by Steven Ross, acquired Warner Bros. in 1969 for $400 million. At the time, Kinney National Service was most prominent in car rentals, parking lots, construction, and funeral homes, although it did hold interests in publishing and creative talent management.[30]

While these diversified corporations had vast holdings outside of the entertainment and media industries, what drew them to the film companies, and what became of them, is quite important. Gulf + Western was attracted to Paramount not so much for the movies it was producing at that time, but for the vast film library that it owned.[31] The control of content would become a recurring theme in mergers and acquisitions. Kinney National Services provides another important example. When that corporation restructured and became Warner Communications, Inc. in 1972, Ross had already begun the expansion into related media industries. In 1970, the corporation bought Sterling Publications, the publisher of various movie and television fan magazines, Coronet Communications, the publisher of paperback books that was later renamed Warner Books, and Elektra Corporation, the popular music manufacturer and distributor that became the foundation of the Warner Music Group. In 1971, Kinney acquired three large cable television systems, which later became the heart of Warner Cable.

There were other changes in the first half of this period. In 1969, Kirk Kerkorian, a financier with holdings in the hotel and airline industries, gained beneficial ownership of close to 50 percent of Metro-Goldwyn-Mayer and assumed control of the corporation. In 1973, he orchestrated the opening of the MGM Grand in Las Vegas, a gambling mecca with a reported cost of $125 million.[32] What made this of interest was the use of the MGM brand equity to foster the development of a hotel and casino. That same year, Kerkorian dismantled the distribution arm of MGM and signed a deal to have United Artists distribute the films produced within MGM.

The conglomeration of the major motion picture studios continued after the spate of transactions between 1966 and 1970, although there was not a major change in ownership until the 1980s.[33] In 1981, oil baron Marvin Davis acquired Twentieth Century Fox, and in 1982, Coca-Cola purchased Columbia Pictures for $750 million. The latter was one of two investments in 1982 that involved Coca-Cola. The second was the creation of TriStar Pictures, which began as a partnership between CBS Inc., the Home Box Office division of Time Inc., and the Columbia Pictures division of Coca-Cola.[34] These groups represented interests in broadcast television, cable television, and motion pictures, which was a preview to the type of conglomeration that was to follow.

Paramount and Disney also experienced significant change prior to 1985, although these related more to the shifts in focus and corporate control than outright sales. In 1983, Gulf + Western divested its industrial properties but retained Paramount Pictures, Simon & Schuster, and Madison Square Garden as it continued the transformation from a diversified conglomerate into one focused on media industries. The changes within Disney were subtler. In the fall of 1984, Sid Bass and his brothers gained effective control of The Walt Disney Co. with ownership of close to 25 percent of the common stock and placed Michael Eisner and Frank Wells in managerial control of the Magic Kingdom. While the Disney focus remained entertainment, the creation of Touchstone Pictures earlier in the year signaled the start of the evolution of Disney from a purveyor of family fare into a modern media conglomerate.

Conglomeration of the Major Motion Picture Production and Distribution Companies: 1985–2000

The cover of *Newsweek* announced the purchase of Columbia Pictures in 1989 in a most dramatic fashion: "Japan Invades Hollywood" was the headline that accompanied a drawing of the Statue of Liberty clad in a Japanese kimono.[35] In the words of *Newsweek*, the $3.4 billion transfer of Columbia Pictures Industries, Inc. from The Coca-Cola Co. to Sony Corp. did not represent the mere sale of another building but the purchase of "a piece of America's soul."[36] Another sentence in the article sketched an image of what the magazine felt was at stake: "The Sony deal marks the biggest advance so far in a Japanese invasion of Hollywood."[37] The Japanese purchase of Columbia, in the eyes of *Newsweek*, was nothing short of cultural warfare.

The arrival of Sony Corp. in Hollywood did represent something akin to an "invasion," but that had nothing to do with its roots in Japan. Rather, the sale of Columbia Pictures and TriStar Pictures represented the conglomeration of entertainment and media holdings into a small cadre of integrated corporations, with the Hollywood majors at the center of the map. The acquisition also reflected the importance that the culture industries placed on the control of content, "software" that can be distributed across vast empires that span the globe. Sony did not represent vertical integration in the traditional sense: a motion picture distributor that owns theaters, broadcast network, or cable channels; a broadcast network that owns local stations; a cable systems operator that owns cable channels. This case did represent vertical integration, however, as the stated purpose of the purchase of Columbia, as well as CBS Records that Sony acquired in 1988, was to create synergies between the corporation's hardware and software activities and to control entertainment software to feed its hardware products.[38]

The need to control content was born out of the Betamax experience of the 1970s. In 1975, Sony introduced the first home video recorder, the Betamax, but some Japanese companies refused an offer to produce a standardized format, and JVC and Matsushita developed the VHS. While the Betamax was a superior product, and remained the standard in professional video production for years, VHS became dominant in the United States and distributors refused to market motion pictures on Beta. The ownership and control of software, Sony believed, would prevent a repeat with new consumer products.

These factors signaled a sea change in the nature of conglomeration. The studios were no longer the show ponies of diversified industrial conglomerates but rather the content producers for media conglomerates. The transfer of Columbia and TriStar to Sony was just one of numerous mergers and

Table 2.2.   Transfers in the Ownership and Control of the Major Motion Picture Studios, United Artists, and MGM, 1985–2005

1985	20th Century Fox	News Corp. acquires Twentieth Century Fox Film Corp. from Marvin Davis.
1986	MGM/UA	Turner Broadcasting Systems acquires MGM/UA for $1.5 billion, keeps the film libraries, and sells the rest back to Kirk Kerkorian.
1989	Columbia Pictures	Sony Corporation acquires Columbia Pictures and TriStar for $4.9 billion from The Coca-Cola Company.
	Warner Bros.	Time Inc. and Warner Communications Inc. merge to form Time Warner Inc., which includes Warner Bros.
	Paramount Pictures	Gulf + Western Industries divests its financial services division and changes its corporate name to Paramount Communications.
1990	Universal Pictures	Matsushita Electric Industries Co. acquires MCA Inc., which includes Universal Studios, for $6.6 billion.
1992	MGM/UA	French bank Credit Lyonnais acquires MGM/UA after a series of owners.
1994	Paramount Pictures	Viacom Inc. acquires Paramount Communications.
1995	Universal Pictures	Seagram Co. Ltd. acquires 80 percent of MCA Inc., including Universal, for $5.7 billion, while Matsushita Electric Industries Co. retains the other 20 percent.
2000	Universal Pictures	Vivendi SA acquires Seagram Co. Ltd., including Universal, for $34 billion.
2001	Warner Bros.	Time Warner Inc. and America Online merge to create AOL Time Warner.
2004	Universal Pictures	The merger of NBC and Vivendi Universal Entertainment creates NBC Universal, with General Electric holding an 80 percent interest.
2005	MGM/UA	Consortium led by Sony Corp. acquires the assets of MGM/UA for $4.8 billion.

acquisitions that altered the structure of the motion picture industry and created vertical and horizontal integration of unsurpassed dimensions. And while most of these conglomerates were adding media assets, one was shedding its nonmedia holdings. Just months prior to Sony's move into Hollywood, Gulf + Western announced that it would sell its financial services subsidiary, Associates First Capital Corp., and change its name to Paramount Communications Inc. to reflect its focus on media industries. Table 2.2 documents significant ownership changes between 1985 and 2005.

The transformation of Twentieth Century Fox from a major studio into the engine for a global chain of media outlets was one of the first moves down this road. In 1985, News Corp. purchased a 50 percent interest in Twentieth Century Fox Film Corp. from Marvin Davis in March for $250 million, then acquired the remaining 50 percent in September for $325 million. At the time, News Corp. owned a terrestrial broadcast network in Australia, Network Ten, and satellite service in Europe, Sky Channel. Rupert Murdoch recognized the power, and wealth, that the control of content could bring. When the Fox network launched in 1986, it programmed less than fifteen hours per week so that Twentieth Century Fox could hold an ownership interest in shows on the network and still conform to the Financial Interest and Syndication Rules (Fin/Syn).[39] This content, in turn, could also be distributed on Sky Channel and Network Ten and syndicated to local Fox stations.

The benefits of vertical integration were also evident in the combination of Time and Warner in 1989. With this merger, a corporate link was established between Warner Bros. and premium cable channels Home Box Office and Cinemax, not to mention the second largest cable operator that resulted from the combination of the cable households controlled within Warner (Warner Cable) and Time (American Television and Communications Corp.). The vertical connections evident in the creation of Time Warner were also a factor in the Viacom acquisition of Paramount. In the 1980s, Viacom created Showtime and The Movie Channel with American Express and Warner Communications, and Viacom retained control of the channels at the end of the decade. In 1994, it acquired Paramount Communications and Blockbuster Entertainment. While the latter raised concerns on Wall Street, the vertical integration these acquisitions created meant that a motion picture produced within Paramount Pictures could be shown on Showtime and rented at Blockbuster.

Three other significant transfers between 1985 and 2000 involved Universal Pictures. In 1990, months after the Time Warner merger and the Sony purchase of Columbia, Matsushita Electric Industries Co. acquired MCA Inc., the corporate home of Universal. While this transaction created vertical integration between Matsushita's consumer electronics products and Universal, its next two transfers were throwbacks to the earlier period when classic diversification was common. In 1995, The Seagram Co. Ltd., with extensive holdings in spirits and wine and fruit juices and beverages, acquired an 80 percent interest in MCA from Matsushita. While that purchase did not reflect either horizontal or vertical integration, subsequent ones did. In 1998, for example, Seagram's acquired PolyGram N.V., which included the production and distribution outlets owned by PolyGram Filmed Entertainment, PolyGram Pictures, and Gramercy Pictures. That was not what Seagram head Edgar Bronfman Jr. cherished, however, as the PolyGram record labels, including PolyGram Records, A&M Records, Island Records, and Motown, were the main impetus for the acquisition. This, too, represented horizontal integration, since Seagram's acquired MCA Records and Geffen Records in the acquisition of MCA Inc.

The marriage of Seagram and Universal Pictures proved to be a troubled one, and after just five years the studio, and Seagram, was sold to Vivendi S.A. in 2000. The French conglomerate traced its roots to the 1850s when it was founded to irrigate farmland and provide water to towns. Prior to its purchase of Seagram, Vivendi was the world's largest water company, providing water and wastewater services to over one hundred million people. It also had media investments, including stakes in satellite television services, Canal+ and BSkyB, and a publisher, Havas. The $34 billion acquisition of Seagram and the portion of Canal+ that it did not own left the renamed Vivendi Universal with crippling debt, and it posted a loss of approximately $25 billion in 2002, a record for a French corporation. It also cost the architect of the move into media his job, as Jean-Marie Messier was replaced as chairman in the summer of 2002. His successor, Jean-Rene Fourtou, argued that it was "illusory" to think Vivendi could manage a United States-based empire from Paris and put most of its entertainment assets on the auction block.

The marriage of a major motion picture studio and a corporation that excelled in water treatment might have seemed odd, but the combination of the largest traditional media producer, Time Warner, with the largest Internet service provider, America Online, appeared to be a match made in "new media" heaven. This proved, at least in the short term, not to be the case. When the creation of AOL Time Warner was first announced in January 2000, it was valued at $165 billion, the largest merger in history. When the FCC gave its approval and the deal was completed 12 months later, the value had been reduced to just $106 billion. Within three years, the value of the combined corporation was a fraction of that amount; the engineers of the deal, Stephen Case and Gerald Levin, had lost control; and AOL had been stripped from the name of the corporation as it reverted to Time Warner Inc.

The one major motion picture production and distribution company that did not change hands between 1960 and 2000, at least not in a formal sense, was Disney. As discussed earlier, there was a fundamental change in this period, however, as the Bass brothers of Texas, in an alliance with Roy E. Disney, bought a controlling interest in the company in 1984 and installed Michael Eisner and Frank Wells at the corporate helm. The once moribund film division of Disney, which went from 50 percent of the company's revenues in 1970 to under 20 percent in 1980, was revitalized, and the company expanded to a dramatic degree, with the acquisition of Capital Cities/ABC Inc. in 1996 the defining moment.[40] Table 2.3 details the ownership of the major studios in 1980, 1990, and 2000.

Conglomeration of the Major Motion Picture Production and Distribution Companies: 2004–2005

The ownership and control of the motion picture production and distribution companies in the middle of the decade, and the oligopolistic market structure these companies represent, is rather simple. The major studios that continue to dominate the production and distribution of motion pictures fall under the umbrella of six of the largest corporations in the world. The final piece of the puzzle was put in place in the spring of 2004 when General Electric and Vivendi Universal received final approval for the creation of NBC Universal, with General Electric holding beneficial ownership of approximately 80 percent of the new corporation. NBC Universal combined most of the entertainment assets of Vivendi Universal, including Universal Pictures and USA Network, with those of General Electric, including the NBC Television

Table 2.3.   Corporate Ownership and Major Shareholders of Major Motion Picture Studios, as of 1980, 1990, and 2000

	1980	1990	2000
Columbia Pictures	Columbia Pictures Industries, Inc. Kirk Kerkorian (25.3%) Philipp Kreuzer (5.04%)	Sony Corp. Morita & Co. (6.4%)	Sony Corp. No one with beneficial ownership of more than 10%
Paramount Pictures	Gulf+Western Industries, Inc. American Financial Corp (7.87%) Charles Bluhdorn (5.17%)	Paramount Communications Co. Gabelli Funds Inc. (6.11%)	Viacom Inc. Sumner Redstone (68.1%)
Twentieth Century Fox	20th Century Fox Film Corp. Chris Craft Industries Inc. (18.9%)	News Corp. Rupert Murdoch (43.3%)	News Corp. Rupert Murdoch (30.0%)
Universal Pictures	MCA Inc. Jules Stein (16.39%) Lew Wasserman (8.41%)	Matsushita Electric Industries Co. No one with beneficial ownership of more than 10%	Vivendi Universal S.A. Edgar Bronfman (3.3%) Edgar Bronfman Jr. (3.5%)
Walt Disney Pictures	Walt Disney Productions The Group (5.97%) Roy E. Disney (4.96%)	The Walt Disney Co. Sid R. Bass & Other Inv. (18.62%)	The Walt Disney Co. Strong Capital Man. (9.22%) Waddel & Reed Asset (8.79%)
Warner Bros	Warner Communications, Inc. Marsh & McLennon Co. (6.27%) Putnam Advisory Co. (5.03%)	Time Warner Inc. The Capital Group Inc. (6.6%)	Time Warner Inc. R.E. Turner (9.6%) Janus Capital Corp. (7.7%) FMR Corp. (7.7%) Capital Research Man. (5.0%)

Note: Ownership is derived from Proxy Statements (Schedule 14-A) filed with the Securities and Exchange Commission. The specific dates vary given the schedule of shareholder meetings.

Network and its owned and operated stations and cable channels such as CNBC, MSNBC, and Bravo.

Universal Pictures was the one major motion picture studio to trade hands between 1995 and 2005, although the creation of AOL Time Warner did have an impact on Warner Bros. The nature of conglomeration, however, evolved to a dramatic degree over the course of this period. The weakening of federal ownership regulations fueled many of these changes. The expiration of the Financial Interest and Syndication Rules (Fin/Syn) in 1995, to be discussed in greater detail in chapter 5, opened the door to the common ownership of broadcast networks and motion picture studios. The Fin/Syn rules did not prohibit such ownership, but the limitations placed on the corporate parents of broadcast networks from holding a financial interest in programming were an enormous hurdle.

The elimination of the Fin/Syn rules removed the final barrier to vertical integration between the studios and networks. The rules expired on November 1, 1995, three months after Disney announced its $19 billion acquisition of Capital Cities/ABC. That placed Walt Disney Pictures and the powerful Touchstone Television production group under the same corporate umbrella as the ABC Television Network. The next network transfer followed a similar pattern, with the parent corporation of a major studio purchasing a broadcast network. In September 1999, Viacom announced the $36 billion acquisition of CBS Inc. Once again, deregulation opened the door to this deal. While the expiration of the Fin/Syn rules eliminated one obstacle, the duopoly rules that prohibited the ownership of two television stations in the same local market presented another as both Viacom and CBS owned large local station groups. In August 1999, the FCC voted to allow such ownership in large markets, and just a month later Viacom announced the deal to acquire CBS.

The General Electric acquisition of a majority interest in Universal Pictures followed the opposite path, with the parent corporation of a broadcast network adding a major studio, but the vertical integration that it created was much the same. The end result of this period of conglomeration is also rather clear as the parent corporations of five of the six major motion pictures studios owned at least one broadcast network, and all six of these corporations ranked among the largest corporations in the world. In the *Forbes* rankings for 2004, based on a composite score for sales, profits, assets, and market value, all six placed within the top 110 companies across the globe: No. 2 General Electric, No. 42 Time Warner, No. 61 Viacom, No. 82 Sony, No. 85 Walt Disney, and No. 110 News Corp.

Ownership and Control

The ownership of these corporations is also quite important to consider. Some have argued that there is a separation of ownership and control in modern corporations, with control transferred to a managerial class that represents the capitalist class. Much has been made of this alleged separation. Adolph Berle and Gardiner Means argued in the 1930s that the dissolution of the "old atom of ownership" into two parts, control and beneficial ownership, destroyed the "very foundation" upon which the economic order had rested for three centuries.[41] The central tenet of an economic order based on private enterprise was that the self-interest of the property owners was tantamount.[42] The ownership interests of those who controlled modern corporations in the twentieth century was so minimal, it was argued, that the "return from running the corporation profitably accrue to them in only a very minor degree" so corporations would no longer be beholden to the bottom line.[43] Berle and Means argue that a new motivation would rule corporations and that serving the community interests would become tantamount, and that it "remains only for the claims of the community to be put forward with clarity and force."[44] Such a shift would be quite significant with media conglomerates, if these predictions were accurate, of course.

The ownership of these conglomerates, and individuals and groups with beneficial ownership of more than 5 percent of one of the parent corporations at the start of 2005, is detailed in table 2.4.[45] An important dimension of ownership that is most evident in these cases is that in two of the six, there are individuals who own a controlling interest of the parent corporation and exercise operational control of its motion picture studio. News Corp. had beneficial ownership of 82 percent of Fox Entertainment Group, the legal parent of Twentieth Century Fox, and there was little question that Rupert Murdoch remained involved in the day-to-day operations of Fox. The same was true of Sumner Redstone, who had beneficial ownership of 71 percent of Viacom, which, in turn, owned Paramount Pictures. In each instance, the ownership was through other companies, the shares of News Corp. that Cruden Investments held in the case of Murdoch and the shares of Viacom that National Amusements held in the case of Redstone.

General Electric and Disney provide a more traditional model, with no individual or group claiming beneficial ownership of more than 5 percent of the outstanding shares of common stock. This does not mean, however, that there has been a separation of ownership and control in a real sense or that these corporations are no longer beholden to the bottom line. When Jack Welch stepped down as the chairman of General Electric in 2001, he was ranked among Forbes's four hundred wealthiest Americans, with an estimated wealth of $680 million. Much of this was based on ownership of just under ten million shares of General Electric common stock. That same year, Michael Eisner also ranked among the four hundred wealthiest, with an estimated wealth of $720 million. This, too, resulted in large part on the ownership of corporate stock.

The case of Eisner is important to this discussion. In 1999, Forbes ranked him as the highest paid chief executive officer in the United States, with a

Table 2.4. Ownership of Major Motion Picture Studios and Beneficial Ownership of Parent Corporation, January 2005

Studio	Ownership Group	Parent Corporations	Ownership of more than 5% of Common Stock or Notable Parties under 5%
Columbia Pictures	Sony Pictures Enter.	Sony Corp.	No Person or Group with Ownership of more than 5% of the common stock
Paramount Pictures	Paramount Pictures	Viacom Inc.	Sumner Redstone (71.2%)[a] Gabelli Asset Management (6.8%)
Twentieth Century Fox	Fox Entertainment Group	News Corp. (82%)	Rupert Murdoch (30%)[b] Liberty Media Corp. (9%) FMR Corp. (7%)
Universal Pictures	NBC Universal	General Electric (80%)	No Person or Group with Ownership of more than 5% of the common stock
		Vivendi Universal (20%)	No Person or Group with Ownership of more than 5% of the common stock
Walt Disney Pictures	Walt Disney Studios	The Walt Disney Co.	No Person or Group with Ownership of more than 5% of the common stock
Warner Bros.	Warner Bros. Enter.	Time Warner Inc.	Capital Research & Man. (7.2%) Comcast Corp. (2.9%)

[a] Sumner Redstone controlled his shares through National Amusements, Inc.
[b] Rupert Murdoch controlled his shares through Curden Investments.

total compensation package of over $589 million for the year. Most of his compensation, just under $570 million, came from the exercising of stock options granted over a series of years. Corporations give options with a preset price at which the shares can be purchased, so an increase in the share price of the common stock makes these options more valuable. A decline in the stock price makes the options worthless. While a rise in stock price benefits all shareholders, it also renders nonsensical the argument that the separation of ownership and control had eliminated the focus on the bottom line since running a corporation in a profitable manner would no longer result in financial gain. This was not the case with Eisner, who translated two decades of stock options into ownership of 13.9 million shares of The Walt Disney Co., 1.7 percent of the outstanding shares, with another 21 million exercisable stock options as of December 2004.[46]

Time Warner presents a different example of ownership, but the result is similar. When AOL and Time Warner announced the merger in 2000, Ted Turner held an ownership interest of approximately 9.6 percent in Time Warner and had considerable influence of the business decisions of the corporation. After the completion of the merger in 2001, his ownership stake in AOL Time Warner was just 3.8 percent of the common stock, and his influence over the merged corporation was minimal.[47] Between 2001 and 2005, Turner sold almost 120 million shares and reduced his beneficial ownership of Time Warner to less than 1 percent. The largest shareholder within Time Warner at the start of 2005 was Capital Research and Management Company, with beneficial ownership of 7.2 percent of the common stock.[48] It was Capital Research and Management that led the fight to oust Stephen Case in 2003 that resulted in a no-confidence vote of 22 percent and his subsequent departure as chairman. While there was a range of issues within Time Warner, the impact that the America Online unit was having on the bottom line of the corporation was at the top of the list, so there is no question that running the corporation in a profitable manner remained of utmost importance.

"Independence" in an Age of Conglomeration

There is a second dimension of the ownership of motion picture production and distribution companies in this age of conglomeration that is quite important. As discussed at the beginning of this chapter, there has been a great deal of discussion about the prominence of the "independents" and a sense that these companies have turned the studio system on its head. This was most evident when the four films produced and distributed outside of the major studios, *The English Patient, Shine, Fargo,* and *Secrets & Lies,* received best picture nominations for the Academy Awards in 1997. The distributors of those films—Miramax, Fine Line Features, Gramercy Pictures, and October Films—were heralded as "independent" studios that had sent "a signal to Hollywood."[49] The question one must ask is how independent were these companies?

The quartet raises a series of questions about independence and provides clear examples of what conglomeration and horizontal integration has meant to the motion picture business. As discussed earlier, production of the *The English Patient* began within Fox Searchlight before it migrated to Miramax where the Disney-owned corporation contributed $27 million to the production of the film before spending millions more on its distribution. As such, *The English Patient* fails the most basic test of independence, the source of its financing. The same is not true of *Shine*. The Australia Film Finance Corp., South Australian Film Corp., and Film Victoria as well as Pandora Cinema and the British Broadcasting Corporation financed its production, so it qualifies as an independent on that count. *Shine* was a sensation at the 1996 Sundance Film Festival and ignited a bidding war between Fine Line Features and Miramax for the North American distribution rights, which the former won for $2.5 million. By the time Fine Line released *Shine* in November 1996, its independence was questionable, as it had become a subsidiary of Time Warner through its acquisition of Turner Broadcasting Systems Inc.

Fargo presents a more complicated case. It was financed and distributed by Gramercy Pictures, which began in 1992 as a joint venture of Universal Pictures and PolyGram Filmed Entertainment. Universal was instrumental in the development of Gramercy until PolyGram acquired Universal's 50 percent interest in the company in January 1996. This transaction, however, came after Gramercy had acquired *Fargo*, so the link to Universal is undeniable. The break from Universal and the existence of Gramercy Pictures both proved to be brief. In 1998, Universal's parent company, Seagram, acquired PolyGram for its music labels and reclaimed Gramercy in the process. That placed Gramercy under the same corporate umbrella as October Films, the distributor of *Secrets & Lies*. In April 1997, Seagram had purchased a 51 percent interest in October Films just weeks after the Academy Awards. As such, October Films was an independent production and distribution company when it released *Secrets & Lies*. In 1999, Universal folded both Gramercy Pictures and October Films into USA Films to create a new "independent" wing of the studio. It was later renamed Focus Features.

It is valuable to consider a definition of independence often used with motion pictures: "The independent producer may be defined as a corporate organization controlled as to ownership and management by one or more individuals who obtain the needed financing and arrange for the distribution of the pictures under their supervision."[50] When applied to the motion picture industry, some established producers, Walt Disney, Sam Goldwyn, David Selznick, and others, who arranged distribution through the major companies and sometimes even received financial support from these same companies, were independent.[51] These producers, however, "maintained their own organizations, separate from (and outside of) the major studios."[52] Under such a definition, production and distribution companies that exist within the corporate structure of a major motion picture studio and use that corporation to finance films would not qualify as an independent.

There are a range of definitions that are now utilized with motion picture production and distribution. The definition above—independence defined in terms of the source of financial backing—remains prominent. Some argue that the size of a production budget is critical, with anything under $20 million viewed as an independent work. Other definitions are qualitative. One position argues that the nature of the material is determinant, with nonmainstream fare earning the independent title, while another reduces the question to one's state of mind, "If you believe you work as an independent, you are."[53] It seems ludicrous to equate a film financed through one of the major media conglomerates with one funded through individual sources because all involved think of themselves as independent producers. Sidebar 4.1 discusses the meaning of independence in more detail.

Corporate Cousins

The tales of conglomeration that the distribution companies behind the 1997 best picture nominations represent are symptomatic of a business in which true independence is rare. One of the defining characteristics of the motion picture industry since the 1980s has been horizontal integration within the major studios and their corporate parents. The incentives to integrate are clear, as it enables companies to extend their control within a particular sector of production or distribution. The corporate parents of the majors have followed two basic tracks in the quest for horizontal integration: the acquisition of independent companies and the creation of specialized units within their own studios.

Disney has followed both of these tracks. Disney started down the road to horizontal integration in 1984 with the creation of Touchstone Pictures, a name chosen to distance the new unit from the Disney image. Touchstone became the adult arm of the studio, and the first film it released, *Splash*, featured brief nudity. It also generated $6,174,059 at the box office in its first weekend, which set a record for Walt Disney Studios, surpassing the $5,951,801 opening weekend for the reissue of *Snow White and the Seven Dwarfs* in 1983.[54] Two years later, Touchstone's *Down & Out in Beverly Hills* became the first motion picture produced within Disney to be distributed with an R rating, and in 1988 the studio created another label, Hollywood Pictures, to create more mature fare. It was under the Touchstone name that Disney even released a film about a prostitute, *Pretty Woman*. Sidebar 2.2 addresses the financial impact of these changes on the Disney bottom line.

The tale of Julia Roberts' character is tame compared to some of those linked to Disney through its acquisition of Miramax. The Weinstein brothers, Bob and Harvey, founded Miramax in 1979 in New York and soon earned a

Sidebar 2.2
From the Magic Kingdom to the Media Behemoth

The 1980s were a time of remarkable change for the major studios. Columbia Pictures began the decade as the heart and soul of a corporation focused on making movies and ended it within a Japanese conglomerate that viewed films as little more than software to feed its hardware. It spent seven years in the middle, moreover, within one where soft drinks were king. The Coca-Cola acquisition of Columbia Pictures in 1982 and the subsequent sale of the film group to Sony Corp. in 1989 might have made for the strangest corporate bedfellows, but other mergers and acquisitions defined the era. After all, this was the decade in which News Corp. acquired Twentieth Century Fox, the merger of Time Inc. and Warner Communications changed things at Warner Bros., and Gulf + Western was dropped from the corporate parent of Paramount. The name that remained more or less constant was Walt Disney's, but that did not mean it was not a tumultuous time within the Magic Kingdom.

At the dawn of the 1980s, Disney was a corporation focused on "family entertainment" that derived the bulk of its revenue from its theme parks and merchandise. The domestic and foreign box office for its motion pictures contributed just 15.5 percent of total revenue in 1980, with home video accounting for an additional 1.2 percent on sales of $10.6 million.[1] And these box office numbers were records for Walt Disney Productions. The worst was still to come as combined box office receipts dropped to $82.5 million in 1983, just 6.3 percent of total revenue. The bulk of the $38.6 million that Disney generated at the domestic box office came from the reissue of two classics, *Peter Pan* in December 1982 and *Snow White and the Seven Dwarfs* in July 1983. Most remarkable is that the studio had just three new theatrical releases in the 1983 fiscal year.[2]

Its transformation over the decade that followed was remarkable. In the first quarter of the 1993 fiscal year, *Aladdin* alone generated over $100 million at the box office in less than two months. At the end of the fiscal year, the filmed entertainment division of Disney had generated $3.673 billion in revenue and grossed more than the theme parks for the first time. The corporation that distributed *Aladdin* was altogether different from the one that reissued *Peter Pan* a decade earlier. This was most evident in the 1993 annual report, which hailed what *Aladdin* did for Disney and defined the watchword of the Michael Eisner era in terms of the animated hit:

> SYNERGY: The inspiration of a classic movie like *Aladdin* to serve as an unparalleled catalyst to move the entire Disney Company to new heights of cooperative energy. In one year, *Aladdin* inspired thousands of new products in every conceivable category including genie and camel dolls and an exciting interactive video game for Sega Genesis, a dramatic new ice show touring the world, and major new parades and characters at Disney parks.[3]

The film grossed over $200 million at the domestic box office, but "because one plus one equals three at The Walt Disney Company, *Aladdin* became a great deal more than a hit movie." In the words of Disney, the audience "wanted to read it, wear it, listen to it and play with it . . . and Disney's many operating units made those things happen."

(Continued)

The arrival of Eisner from Paramount Pictures and Frank Wells from Warner Bros. in 1984 is often cited as the transformative moment in the Magic Kingdom, and the importance of that shift in leadership cannot be overstated. For the film division, however, change began before the arrival of Eisner and Wells. In June 1983, the company created Walt Disney Pictures as a separate unit with the task of developing a "boldly diversified program of films aimed at significantly broadening the Disney audience."[4] The need to broaden the Disney audience was clear and the plan was aggressive. In the first quarter of 1984, Touchstone debuted with the release of *Splash,* which went on to earn a Disney record of $69 million at the box office. The creation of Touchstone enabled the conglomerate to produce films intended for "mature audiences" without sullying the Disney name. President Ronald Miller was a realist, arguing, "It was clear that we were in never-never land. Yet we wouldn't let ourselves go. If we were going to make movies for a broad audience, we needed a second distribution label."[5]

The creation of Touchstone Films proved to be just the start. Disney created Hollywood Pictures in 1988 and acquired Miramax Films in 1993. Even without the addition of Miramax, there was a significant increase in the number of Disney films in theaters, from a half dozen per year in the first half of the 1980s to eighteen in both 1988 and 1989 and twenty-seven in 1992. These increases made Disney a major force in the motion picture business. Between 1979 and 1985, the Disney share of North American theatrical film rentals hovered between 3 and 4 percent. That changed between 1986 and 1988, when Disney moved from ninth in 1985 with a 3.5 percent market share to third in 1986; second in 1987; and first in 1988, with shares of 10.1 percent, 14.0 percent, and 19.4 percent, respectively. The slate of films that contributed to that box office crown in 1988 represented the advantage of the new model. Three Disney films topped the $100 million mark for the calendar year, and two of these featured content that broke the Disney mold. *Good Morning, Vietnam* included military violence, while *Three Men and a Baby* featured a child born out of wedlock and a drug smuggling subplot. The third was *Who Framed Roger Rabbit.*

While the horizontal integration of motion picture production and distribution companies was step one in the Disney expansion, diversification into other media sectors was step two. The defining moment came in 1996 with the completion of the acquisition of ABC. The impact of that deal was evident in the 2004 fiscal year, when Disney generated revenue of $30.752 billion, almost twenty times what it did in 1984. The Media Networks segment accounted for 38.3 percent of total revenue and 48.3 percent of operating income, with most of that coming from the cable networks. The production and distribution of motion pictures had once again taken a back seat to another division, although television hits produced within Touchstone Television such as *Desperate Housewives* and *Lost* contributed to the revitalization of the ABC Television Network in 2004–2005. The Studio Entertainment segment contributed 28.3 percent of total revenue but just 14.8 percent of operating income.

Such financial figures and the connection to such enterprises are buried deep within the Disney corporation. When one opened its website, Disney Online, in the summer of 2005, there were icons for its theme parks and resorts, as well as Walt Disney Pictures and cable channels and children's programming. And there were easy links to purchase toys and games, movies and music, clothes and accessories. In a sense, the Disney website reflected the corporation that struggled through the first half of the 1980s, one with a clear focus on family entertainment. Disney in the first half of the 2000s, however, was an altogether different beast, with ownership of a broadcast network and an array of cable services, as well as motion picture companies that featured films with content that might have turned Walt's face as red as Mickey's famous pants. Such endeavors were not prominent on Disney Online, but they were critical to the bottom line of the major media conglomerate Disney had become.

NOTES

1. September 30 is the end of the fiscal year at Disney, so these figures represent sales from October 1979 through September 1980. Annual Report, Walt Disney Productions, Inc., 1980.

2. The three films were *Tex, Trenchcoat,* and *Something Wicked This Way Comes.* Annual Report, Walt Disney Productions, Inc., 1993.

3. Annual Report, The Walt Disney Co., 1993.

4. Annual Report, Walt Disney Productions, Inc., 1983.

5. Quoted in "Problems in Walt Disney's Magic Kingdom," *Business Week,* 12 March 1984, 50.

reputation for spotting "art" films, foreign and domestic, that could attract a large American audience. From 1988 to 1991, a Miramax distributed film received the foreign-language Oscar in four consecutive years.[55] *Sex, lies and videotape,* a Miramax release in 1989, set the box-office record for a specialty film, a mark that was broken three years later by another Miramax release, *The Crying Game.*

Miramax lost its true independence in 1993, however, when it moved under the corporate umbrella of Disney. Trade journals and newspapers continued to call Miramax an independent in many instances and, in theory, it was set up as an "autonomous division" under Disney's distribution arm, Buena Vista Pictures.[56] When the deal was announced, Harvey Weinstein proclaimed that the studio would have "complete freedom to operate as we always have."[57] Miramax fails a crucial measure of independence, however, as the most important component of the acquisition agreement was that Disney would finance all future Miramax films. The original deal also stipulated that Miramax could not release films that carried an NC-17 rating, so the complete freedom that Weinstein spoke about was missing.

New Line Cinema Corp. is another prominent example. New Line was founded in New York in 1976 and became successful in the distribution of low budget and offbeat films that were popular with teenagers, such as *A Nightmare on Elm Street* and *Teenage Mutant Ninja Turtles.* In 1991, New Line created another division to handle films that catered to an older audience, Fine Line Features. New Line became a wholly owned subsidiary of Turner Broadcasting Systems Inc. in 1993 and became a part of Time Warner with the completion of its merger with Turner in 1996.

Miramax and New Line are the biggest names under the same corporate umbrella as a major studio, but each of the majors has created or acquired additional production and distribution labels over the last decade. Table 2.5

Table 2.5. Corporate Ownership and Studio Alignment of Prominent Specialty Production and Distribution Companies, as of June 2005

Corporate Parent	Major Studio	Production/Distribution Company	Year Acquired or Created	Notes
General Elec.	Universal	Focus Features	2002	Created within Universal Pictures through the consolidation of Universal Focus, USA Films, and Good Machine
	Universal	Good Machine	2002	Acquired by Universal Pictures
	Universal	Universal Focus	1999	Created within Universal Pictures
	Universal	USA Films	1999	Created within USA Networks Inc. through the consolidation of October Films, Gramercy Pictures, Polygram Films, and Propaganda Films (Seagram held 45% interest in USA)
	Universal	Gramercy Pictures	1998	Part of Seagram's acquisition of Polygram
	Universal	October Films	1997	Acquired by Universal Pictures
News Corp.	20th Century Fox	Fox Searchlight	1994	Created by Twentieth Century Fox
	20th Century Fox	Fox 2000	1994	Created by Twentieth Century Fox
	20th Century Fox	20th Century Fox Animation	1994	Created by Twentieth Century Fox

Corporate Company	Major Studio	Production/Distribution Company	Year Acquired or Created	Notes
Sony Corp	Columbia Pictures	Screen Gems	1998	Created by Sony Pictures Entertainment
	Columbia Pictures	Sony Pictures Classics	1990	Created by Sony Pictures Entertainment
Time Warner	Warner Bros.	Newmarket Films	2005	Acquired by New Line Cinema and HBO Films within Time Warner
	Warner Bros.	Warner Independent Pict.	2003	Created within Warner Bros.
	Warner Bros.	HBO Films	2003	Created within Time Warner unit
	Warner Bros.	Fine Line Features	1996	Part of the Time Warner acquisition of Turner Broadcasting
	Warner Bros.	New Line Cinema	1996	Part of the Time Warner acquisition of Turner Broadcasting
Viacom	Paramount Pictures	Paramount Classics	1998	Created by Paramount Pictures
Walt Disney	Walt Disney Pict.	Miramax Films	1993	Acquired by The Walt Disney Co.
	Walt Disney Pict.	Dimension Films	1993	Part of the Disney acquisition of Miramax
	Walt Disney Pict.	Hollywood Pictures	1988	Created within Walt Disney Pictures
	Walt Disney Pict.	Touchstone Pictures	1984	Created within Walt Disney Pictures

ıese companies. News Corp. pursued a different tact in its main efforts
ate. In 1994, it created three additional production and distribution
arms to complement Twentieth Century Fox: Fox 2000, Twentieth Century
Fox Animation, and Fox Searchlight Pictures. The business model for Fox
2000 is to produce motion pictures for mainstream audiences, while Twentieth
Century Fox Animation focuses on feature-length animated motion pictures.
Fox Searchlight Pictures is the specialty division of Fox Filmed Entertainment,
what the company calls the "independent arm" of Twentieth Century Fox.[58]

Viacom and Sony followed similar paths. Viacom created Paramount Classics in 1998 to distribute specialty films alongside Paramount Pictures. Sony
did much the same in 1990 when it launched Sony Pictures Classics and later
added Sony Pictures Repertory to reissue films from the Sony Pictures Entertainment libraries. In 1998, Sony turned to a name from the past when it created Screen Gems to distribute midsize films that fall between the mainstream
releases of Columbia Pictures and the low-budget fare of Sony Pictures Classics. For the fiscal year ending March 31, 2005, Sony Pictures Entertainment
was scheduled to distribute fifty-one films, including thirteen from Columbia,
seven from Screen Gems, and nineteen from Sony Pictures Classics, as well
as four Revolution Studios releases and eight films cofinanced with MGM.[59]

As one might suspect for a studio that had four different corporate parents over the course of a decade, Universal Pictures has links to a number
of different specialty production and distribution companies. The trail is a
complicated one. As discussed earlier, Universal created Gramercy Pictures
with PolyGram in 1992, sold its interest in 1996, and then purchased October
Films in 1997. Seagram's acquisition of PolyGram in 1998 not only brought
Gramercy back into the Universal fold but also gave it ownership of PolyGram Films, Interscope Communications, and Propaganda Films. In 1999,
these companies were sold along with October Films to Barry Diller's USA
Networks, Inc., which created USA Films. At that time, Seagram held a 45
percent equity interest in USA Networks so there was still a link to Universal.
That connection became direct again in 2002 when Vivendi Universal Entertainment combined the entertainment assets of USA Networks and Vivendi
Universal.

Such links come with a price. In 1998, Seagram and Universal Pictures
blocked October Films from releasing *Happiness*, a film that garnered acclaim
at the Cannes International Film Festival but included subject matter, such as
pedophilia, that October's corporate parents could not stomach.[60] In 1999,
Disney stopped Miramax from releasing Kevin Smith's *Dogma* when the
Catholic League promised a holy war against the film, a comedy that satirized the Catholic Church and starred Ben Affleck and Matt Damon as fallen
angels. That same year, the Dimension Films unit of Miramax was scheduled
to release Tim Blake Nelson's *O*, a modern-day telling of Othello set in a
high school that ends with the deaths of the main characters in a shooting.
Dimension delayed the release after the killings at Columbine High School in

1999, and subsequent release dates came and went amid speculation of corporate pressure from Disney for Dimension not to distribute the film. Lions Gate Films eventually released it.

True Independence

The motion picture production and distribution companies one cannot connect to the corporate parents of one of the major studios are quite rare. The fabled Metro-Goldwyn-Mayer entered 2004 without a link to one of the majors, but its fate was sealed before the year was over. Marcus Loew created MGM in 1924 through the combination of Metro Pictures Corp., Goldwyn Pictures Corp., and Louis B. Mayer Pictures Corp. and it remained independent eight decades later. In the spring of 2004, a Sony led consortium of investors entered into exclusive negotiations for a deal for the studio and its four thousand-film and ten thousand-television episode library, which included *Gone With The Wind*, *The Wizard of Oz*, and the James Bond series. There was a point in the negotiations when it appeared as though MGM/UA might slip through Sony's fingers, and into the hands of Time Warner, but at the last minute, the Sony group raised its bid and claimed the prize. The final piece of the puzzle was an agreement with Comcast to create a series of cable channels that feature films from the MGM/UA library. The deal was completed in the spring of 2005, with most of the MGM/UA employees losing their jobs and the rest moving to the Sony Pictures Entertainment lot to operate a scaled down version of the studio.

The corporation that embodied the image of independence best was Newmarket Films, the distribution arm of Newmarket Capital Group, which was created to finance and produce films. Its move into distribution began when the investment group could not find someone willing to handle the release of *Memento*. Newmarket hired Bob Berney to distribute the film, *Memento* grossed $24 million in 2000, and Newmarket Films was born. It gained further prominence with Charlize Theron's Oscar-winning performance in *Monster* and then released Mel Gibson's *The Passion of the Christ* after Twentieth Century Fox decided not to release the film. That attention came with a price, however, as New Line Cinema and HBO Films purchased Newmarket in the spring of 2005, and it became part of Time Warner.

Some independent production and distribution companies remained prominent in 2004 and 2005. Lions Gate Entertainment rose in stature with the acquisition of Artisan Entertainment in the latter stages of 2003, a deal that was built around Artisan's ownership or long-term distribution rights to thousands of titles, including *Total Recall*, *Dirty Dancing*, *Basic Instinct*, and *On Golden Pond*. The success of *Fahrenheit 9/11* in 2004 and two films that grossed over $50 million in the first half of 2005, *Crash* and *Diary of a Mad Black Woman*, raised the profile of Lions Gate. Magnolia, ThinkFilm, and IDP Distribution were three others that remained nonaligned in 2005. Still others were often deemed to be independent but have clear connections to the majors. Revolution Studios, for example, was promoted as a new independent studio when it was created by Joe Roth in 2000, but the bulk of its financing came from Sony Corp., News Corp., and Liberty Media with Sony Pictures Entertainment distributing its films.

The tale of DreamWorks SKG is more complicated. With the backing of Steven Spielberg, Jeffrey Katzenberg, and David Geffen, not to mention $500 million from Paul Allen, the Hollywood press hailed DreamWorks as a studio that could remain self-reliant in an era of concentration when it opened its doors in 1994. The critical acclaim of *American Beauty* and financial windfall of *Shrek* and *Shrek 2* are success stories that DreamWorks wrote on its own. But such independent moments were rare, even for DreamWorks. Three of its best known films, best picture Oscar winners *A Beautiful Mind* and *Gladiator* as well as *Saving Private Ryan*, were coproductions with major studios, the first two with Universal Pictures and the third with Paramount Pictures. Even the limited independence of the live action studio of DreamWorks was fleeting. The studio entered into exclusive negotiations with NBC Universal on a possible takeover in the summer of 2005, but when General Electric failed to pull the trigger in the fall, Viacom moved in and a $1.6 billion deal was announced in early December for DreamWorks to become part of Paramount Pictures. The deal would also give Paramount the right to distribute the releases of DreamWorks Animation SKG Inc., the computer-generated features division that went public in October 2004.

The Production of Television Series and Serials

The production and distribution of motion pictures for theatrical exhibition is the first pursuit of the major studios and accounts for a significant portion of their revenues. The same motion pictures released in theaters, moreover, generate additional revenue through home video rentals and sales and exhibition on broadcast and cable television. Another connection between these companies and the broadcast networks and cable channels, however, does not receive the same degree of attention. Since the 1970s, following the enactment of the Fin/Syn rules, the major motion picture studios have also been the dominant producers of prime time programming for the broadcast networks.

The roots of this involvement in television program production are found in the 1950s. While the Paramount decrees forced the integrated majors to divorce themselves from their theaters, the advent of television provided them with another outlet. The major studios saw it as a threat to their business, and while it would be inaccurate to argue that they jumped into television without reservation, there were scattered attempts to become involved in the new medium. Television provided various avenues for the studios: the broadcast of films in the studio vaults, production of made-for-television movies, production of television shows, and ownership of television stations.

Columbia was not the most prominent studio in the 1950s, but it was the first in Hollywood to venture into television production when it converted Screen Gems, a subsidiary that produced short films, into a television department in 1949.[61] Its vision was rewarded in 1954 when *Father Knows Best* debuted. Columbia's involvement in television production became its salvation, as it provided a more stable base of revenue than films. The same year that *Father Knows Best* debuted, Disney entered into a contract with ABC to produce an hour-long series, and *Disneyland* became the network's first major hit. ABC also invested in the Disneyland theme park.

Disney, of course, now owns ABC, an acquisition that was made possible with the demise of the Fin/Syn rules, and Touchstone Television produced two shows that fueled its revival in 2004–2005, *Desperate Housewives* and *Lost*. The ownership of television programming has become a critical issue. News Corp., for example, owned two of the most prominent shows on the Fox prime time schedule, *The Simpsons* and *24*, as Twentieth Century Fox Television produced both. Such vertical integration of production and distribution was one of the hallmarks of the creation of NBC Universal, since Universal Network Television owned one of the most important assets on the NBC network, *Law & Order*. And on the day the completion of the merger was announced, the new conglomerate also celebrated a deal that would keep the franchise on NBC through 2008.

Given the prominence of television production units, such as Twentieth Century Fox Television, Warner Bros. Television, and Touchstone Television within the major studios, it is not surprising that the conglomeration that has defined the motion picture business since the mid-1980s has also had a huge impact on the production of television dramas and situation comedies and even so-called reality programs. Nor is it unexpected that horizontal integration of television production companies within the conglomerates has followed the same patterns as those of the motion picture production and distribution companies. Some conglomerates, such as Viacom, have grown through the acquisition of established companies, while others, such as News Corp., focused on the in-house creation of production units. Once again, what passes for independence is questionable.

News Corp. provides an important example as it built television production units from within, much as it has with motion picture units. Twentieth Century Fox Television and Twentieth Television predate the News Corp. acquisition of Twentieth Century Fox Film Corp. in 1985, but there are more recent additions. In 1997, the studio launched Fox Television Studios to house small, diverse production units that share business, administrative, financial, and production services. The first unit within Fox Television Studios, The Greenblatt-Janollari Studio, was heralded as the hot new "independent" production unit at the dawn of the 1998–1999 season when it landed three situation comedies on CBS and ABC. The independence claims attributed to Greenblatt-Janollari are unsupportable, however.

When Greenblatt-Janollari opened, News Corp. president Peter Chernin stated that the two executives had the "opportunity to create a Carsey-Werner type company."[62] While it is doubtful whether Greenblatt-Janollari programs will match those of Carsey-Werner, which includes *The Cosby Show, Roseanne, 3rd Rock from the Sun,* and *That 70's Show,* one thing is certain: in terms of structure and ownership, the two companies have nothing in common. Carsey-Werner was a true independent, with Marcy Carsey and Tom Werner taking second mortgages on their homes to finance the company before *The Cosby Show* became a success. Greenblatt-Janollari, on the other hand, was built on the capital of News Corp. Moreover, the president of Fox Television Studios was to "oversee" the new venture and handle its business affairs, which includes syndication rights that belong to News Corp. In spite of these connections, news reports on the formation of the Greenblatt-Janollari Studio stated that it was an "independent mini-studio."[63]

The evolution of Regency Television is different, but the results are quite similar. In 1998, Fox Entertainment Group acquired a 20 percent interest in Monarchy Enterprises Holdings B.V., the parent corporation of New Regency Productions, one of the most prolific and successful independent production companies at the time. In return for that investment, Fox obtained certain rights to distribute New Regency products. An important outgrowth of that deal was the creation of Regency Television, a fifty-fifty joint venture between Monarchy Enterprises and Fox Entertainment Group. As Greenblatt-Janollari was in the fall of 1998, Regency was the hot new "independent" production unit in the fall of 2000.

The evolution of DreamWorks provides another example and raises further questions about the meaning of independence. When it opened shop, DreamWorks was heralded as a new independent studio to challenge the majors, a claim that was questionable in the case of motion pictures given the number of coproduction deals it reached with major motion picture companies. In the case of television, however, it was not even debatable. When DreamWorks created a new television division in 1994, it was a fifty-fifty joint venture between DreamWorks and Capital Cities/ABC. The latter reportedly contributed in excess of $100 million to the deal, with Spielberg, Katzenberg, and Geffen matching that commitment.[64] The two parties received an equal share of revenues generated by the television programs produced within DreamWorks. The television unit of DreamWorks was designed to produce programs for all the broadcast networks, cable, and first-run syndication, and while ABC was not guaranteed a first look at pilots developed within the company, there were "special financial incentives" that favored ABC.[65] The one DreamWorks program that was successful in its first decade aired on ABC, *Spin City.*

The original deal between DreamWorks and ABC expired in the summer of 2002, and the studio signed a new development agreement with NBC.

This agreement gave the network the first look at series developed within the DreamWorks television division, with the network covering the production costs of the shows that moved forward on NBC in exchange for a majority financial interest.[66] DreamWorks could shop shows that NBC did not pick up to other networks, with NBC under no obligation to finance such shows. The deal called on the network to contribute a fee on an annual basis to cover some of the overhead cost associated with the television division of DreamWorks.

SUMMARY

The motion picture studio system that first evolved in the 1920s, featuring vertical integration between production, distribution, and exhibition, has remained intact for close to a century. While the Paramount decrees forced divorcement between distribution and exhibition, the link between production and distribution is the cornerstone of the motion picture business in the United States to this day. There are significant changes that occurred in the nature and scope of the corporations that own the studios, however. When conglomeration first came to the motion picture industry in the 1960s, some of the studios moved under the corporate umbrellas of diversified businesses with holdings in a vast array of sectors, from manufacturing and financial services to car rentals and funeral homes. The link between General Electric and Universal Pictures shows that conglomeration of this type is still evident.

The nature of conglomeration has changed to a dramatic degree, however, as the studios have been engulfed within conglomerates with vast holdings in the motion picture, broadcast television, and cable television industries. In some cases, this evolution included the divestment of nonmedia assets within a corporation, but across the board it featured increased vertical integration through the acquisition or creation of business units at different levels of the production and distribution process, and horizontal integration through the acquisition or creation of additional business units at the same level. This transformation affected not just the motion picture business but most areas of broadcast and cable television as well.

At the end of this period of conglomeration, corporations that ranked among the largest in the world owned the six major motion picture studios. Five of the six studios were under the same corporate umbrella as a major broadcast network, and each of those five owned a general-interest basic cable channel, which afforded them tremendous opportunities to move creative content vertically between the production and distribution levels. And in both the production and distribution of motion pictures and the production of prime time television programming, prominent independent companies were brought within the same corporations as the major studios while additional specialty units were created in-house. In the end, there were few of these companies without links to one of the major studios, which raised serious questions about how much motion picture and television content originates from outside of these conglomerates.

NOTES

1. Andy Marx, "Independents Day for Oscars," *Daily Variety*, 18 February 1993, 1.

2. Quoted in Marx, "Independents Day for Oscars," 1.

3. Sharon Waxman, "Independents Day for Oscar Nominations," *Washington Post*, 12 February 1997, D01.

4. Claudia Eller and John Evan Frook, "Mickey Gets A New Mini: Miramax," *Daily Variety*, 3 May 1993, 1.

5. Quoted in Eller and Frook, "Mickey Gets A New Mini: Miramax," 1.

6. Bernard Weinraub, "Business Match Made in Hollywood," *New York Times*, 30 April 1993.

7. Tino Balio, *The American Film Industry*, revised edition (Madison: University of Wisconsin Press, 1985), 116.

8. John Milton, *Areopagitica* (Folcroft, PA: The Folcroft Press, Inc., 1969), 58–59.

9. Quoted in Leonard W. Levy, *Freedom of the Press from Zenger to Jefferson* (Indianapolis, IN: The Bobbs-Merrill Company, Inc., 1966), 329.

10. *Mutual Film Corp. v. Industrial Film Corp.*, Supreme Court, 35 S. Ct. 387, 1915.

11. Thomas Guback, "Are We Looking at the Right Things in Film?" (paper presented at the Society for Cinema Studies conference, 1978), 2.

12. Guback, "Are We Looking at the Right Things in Film?" 1–3.

13. *Mutual Film Corp. v. Industrial Film Corp.*

14. Robert Baldwin and Martin Cave, *Understanding Regulation: Theory, Strategy, and Practice* (Oxford: Oxford University Press, 1999).

15. Quoted in Daniel B. Wood, "Hollywood Irate Over GATT Export Ban," *Christian Science Monitor*, 17 December 1993, 2.

16. Stephen M. Axinn, "A Lawyer's Response," *Antitrust Law Journal* 52 (1983).

17. Axinn, "A Lawyer's Response."

18. Balio, *The American Film Industry*, 122.

19. Janet Wasko, *Movies and Money: Financing the American Film Industry* (Norwood, NJ: Ablex Publishing Corporation, 1982), 49.

20. Wasko, *Movies and Money*, 49.

21. Wasko, *Movies and Money*, 49.

22. Wasko, *Movies and Money*, 49.

23. Quoted in Michael Conant, *Antitrust in the Motion Picture Industry* (Berkeley: University of California Press, 1960), 94.

24. Quoted in Conant, *Antitrust in the Motion Picture Industry*, 132–133.

25. Balio, *The American Film Industry*, 416.

26. Balio, *The American Film Industry*, 419.

27. Wasko, *Movies and Money*, 184–185.

28. Balio, *The American Film Industry*, 439.

29. Wasko, *Movies and Money*, 182–183.

30. Balio, *The American Film Industry*, 576.

31. Wasko, *Movies and Money*, 185.

32. Wasko, *Movies and Money*, 177.

33. Twentieth Century Fox, for example, purchased a Coca-Cola bottling company, a ski resort, and a savings and loan company; Warner Communications acquired a toy company and a manufacturer of video games; and Columbia purchased a pinball machine manufacturer.

34. Before Coca-Cola sold Columbia and TriStar to the Sony Corp. in 1989, CBS left the partnership, HBO reduced its share, and Columbia became the dominant owner.

35. *Newsweek*, 9 October 1989.

36. John Schwartz, "Japan Goes Hollywood," *Newsweek*, 9 October 1989.

37. Schwartz, "Japan Goes Hollywood."

38. Norio Ohga, the former chairman and CEO of Sony, said, "[s]oftware and hardware are two wheels of the same cart," while Morita has said, "[t]wenty years from now history will prove us right" (Quoted in Richard J. Barnet and John Cavanaugh, *Global Dreams: Imperial Corporations and the New World Order*, New York: Touchstone, 1994).

39. Fox did surpass the fifteen-hour threshold before the demise of the Fin/Syn rules, but the FCC waived the rule.

40. "The Walt Disney Company," *Hoover's Guide to Media Companies* (Austin, TX: Hoover's Business Press, 1996).

41. Adolf A. Berle, Jr. and Gardiner C. Means, *The Modern Corporation and Private Property* (New York: Macmillan, 1933), 8.

42. Berle, Jr. and Means, *The Modern Corporation*, 8.

43. Berle, Jr. and Means, *The Modern Corporation*, 8–9.

44. Berle, Jr. and Means, *The Modern Corporation*, 8–9.

45. There are various theories on how much stock must be owned to control a corporation. Peter Dreier argues that as little as 1 percent is sufficient in some cases. There was a time when the FCC used 1 percent beneficial ownership in its enforcement of the multiple ownership rules, although that percentage has been raised to 5 percent of voting stock or 10 percent of what it calls passive stock, shares that banks and other financial institutions hold.

46. The Walt Disney Co., *Proxy Statement*, 2005.

47. AOL Time Warner, *Proxy Statement*, 2001.

48. Time Warner Inc., *Proxy Statement*, 2005.

49. Sharon Waxman, "Independents Day for Oscar Nominations," *Washington Post*, 12 February 1997, D01.

50. Quoted in Wasko, *Movies and Money*, 106.

51. Quoted in Wasko, *Movies and Money*, 106.

52. Quoted in Wasko, *Movies and Money*, 106.

53. Sharon Swart, "The Independents," *Daily Variety*, 18 August 2003, A1.

54. PR Newswire, 12 March 1984.

55. The four films were, *Pelle the Conqueror*, *Cinema Paradiso*, *Journey of Hope*, and *Mediterraneo*.

56. Bernard Weinraub, "Business Match Made in Hollywood," *New York Times*, 30 April 1993, 39.

57. Quoted in Weinraub, "Business Match Made in Hollywood," 39.

58. Fox Searchlight, "About Us," www.foxsearchlight.com (accessed 16 May 2004).

59. Sony Pictures Entertainment holds equity in Revolution Studios and distributes films produced within Revolution. Sony Corp, *Form 20-F,* 2005.

60. Thom Geier, "'Happiness' Too Hot for October Owner Seagram," *Hollywood Reporter,* 2 July 1998.

61. Balio, *The American Film Industry,* 433.

62. Quoted in Jenny Holtz, "Grant Returns to Head Fox TV Studios," *Variety,* 28 July–3 August 1997, 27.

63. "Freshman Production Company 'The Greenblatt Janollari Studio' Lands Three Television Series for the Fall," *Business Wire,* 27 May 1998.

64. Jane Hall, "'Dream Team,' ABC Plan Joint Venture," *Los Angeles Times,* 29 November 1994, A1.

65. Brian Lowry and John Brodie, "Cast of Three Meets ABC; Troika, Network Link Up to Create New 'TV Studio,'" *Daily Variety,* 29 November 1994.

66. Michael Schneider, "D'Works Finds Nest at Peacock," *Variety.com,* 7 August 2002.

3

❖

Conglomeration in the Broadcast Television Industry

It is a moment that exemplifies what the ownership of broadcast networks, cable and satellite services, and motion picture studios has come to. On September 7, 1998, *ABC's Monday Night Football* opened its twenty-ninth season with the defending Super Bowl champion, Denver Broncos, and the New England Patriots. The debut was the first regular season game under the contract Disney negotiated with the National Football League eight months earlier, which called for a rights fee of $550 million per season for MNF alone.[1] For Disney, there had been few options, as ABC was in the midst of a long slide in the prime time ratings, and *Monday Night Football* was the network's only show in the top ten in the 1997–1998 season. Prime time football was the cornerstone of ABC's rise to prominence in the 1970s, and the Disney brass was betting big bucks that it could steady the ship once again. In the parlance of sports television, signing the deal was a no-brainer.[2]

The moment that defined the season premier, however, occurred long before kickoff. In an effort to improve ratings, *Monday Night Football* began an hour earlier, moving kickoff to around 8:20 p.m. This enabled ABC to schedule a pregame show, *Monday Night Blast*. The show provided time to preview the marquee game of the week, but the network chose to feature Disney properties rather than the Broncos and Patriots. The pregame show originated from the ESPN Zone in Baltimore, the first in a chain of sports bars that featured the cable network's brand.[3] The limited time and commercial obligations created a frenetic pace to the show, but there was time for something that had nothing to do with football and everything to do with media ownership in the modern era. In the midst of the pregame show for one of the most celebrated sports television franchises, ABC broadcast a vignette featuring *Mrs. Munger's Class*.[4] These one-minute interstitials were part of a revitalized two-hour block,

"Disney's One Saturday Morning," that featured Disney children's programs on ABC.

The connections between ABC and ESPN are significant, although the balance of power in the relationship between the two, as well as broadcast and cable in general, shifted over time. At the start of the 1984–1985 season, broadcast television was still king, and ABC remained under the control of Leonard Goldenson. At the same time, the ABC-owned cable outlets—ESPN, A&E, and Lifetime—were en route to a combined loss of $44.6 million for the year.[5] Two decades later, ABC was part of one of the largest media conglomerates in the world, and the Disney cable networks generated over $500 million in operating income.[6] ESPN was the most profitable in this group, and ABC assumed a role in its growth. When ESPN inked a $2.4 billion deal with the National Basketball Association in 2002, an important part of the deal was that the NBA Finals would air on ABC. The broadcast network was little more than another distribution platform for ESPN to utilize, much as it was with properties that ranged from the Stanley Cup Finals in hockey to the X-Games in extreme sports. One must understand how the broadcast networks fit within these behemoths, and how the nature of ownership has changed over time.

The historical evolution and maturation of multifaceted, multinational corporations such as Disney is significant, but what is also critical is the socio-politico-economic structure within which they evolved. This is most important in the evaluation of broadcast and cable television, since changes in the regulation of these industries are often justified and legitimized based on scientific and technical rationale. The "chaos" that resulted from the uncontrolled use of the electromagnetic spectrum justified the need for broadcast regulation in the 1920s. The proliferation in the systems of distribution and the resultant increase in the number of available outlets that satellite and cable technologies create, meanwhile, is the rationale for deregulation since the 1980s. The promotion of such reasoning, with an emphasis on scientific and technical rationale, allows decision-makers to frame changes within "objective" logic. This conceals the active influence that changes in the sociopolitical regime have upon policies and regulations, and the conscious decisions made in the allocation of resources.

THE FOUNDATION OF THE AMERICAN SYSTEM

The decade that ended in 1934 was a watershed period in the evolution of broadcast radio and television in the United States. It is a span that included the last in a series of radio conferences in which broadcasters, advertising agencies, and others promoted a structure that relied on advertising rather than license fees and framed it as the "American System" of broadcasting. This period also encompassed passage of the Radio Act of 1927 and the Communications Act of 1934, two pieces of legislation that were critical in the establishment of the network-dominated, advertiser-supported, privately owned system that remains unchallenged in the United States. The Radio Act of 1927 prompted the reallocation of radio frequencies that favored large commercial broadcasters and marginalized nonprofit broadcasters, while the Communications Act of 1934 locked the structure in place "economically, politically, and ideologically."[7] Robert McChesney argues that this was the "sole instance in which the structure and control of a major mass medium were subject to anything close to legitimate debate in U.S. history," and that such debate has been "off-limits" in public discourse since that time.[8]

There is little question that the debate over the structure of broadcast radio and television in the United States has been off-limits for decades, and that the correctness of a network-dominated, advertiser-supported, private sector-owned system has never faced serious challenge. Advocates of this structure have long contended that it is a fundamental component of democratic societies, most evident in the words of David Sarnoff, the head of the Radio Corporation of America (RCA), in 1938:

> Our American system of broadcasting ... is what it is because it operates in the American democracy. It is a free system because this is a free country. It is privately owned because private ownership is one of our national doctrines. It is privately supported, through commercial sponsorship of a portion of its program hours, and at no cost to the listener, because ours is a free economic system. No special laws had to be passed to bring these things about. They were already implicit in the American system, ready and waiting for broadcasters when it came.[9]

The Sarnoff statement was clear and concise, and it was also inaccurate. From the point when the federal government orchestrated the pooling of patents and the creation of RCA in 1919, people in power, from the halls of Congress to the White House, made conscious decisions in regard to broadcast radio that influenced the allocation of scarce resources to the benefit of certain interests and the expense of others.

There is also an essential truth in the Sarnoff proclamation. The notion that a democratic system dictated private ownership and commercial sponsorship of broadcast stations is questionable, but the sense that it was inevitable rings true given the political, social, and economic stakes. There was extensive discussion about the structure and control of the telegraph and telephone prior to World War I, and their relationship to broadcast radio and television makes this debate critical to later deliberations. One can argue that the struggle over the structure and control of the telephone and telegraph made it clear that public sector ownership of a communication medium was unpalatable, and the elimination of such an option made the outcome of the radio debate predictable.

Control over the tools of communication in the United States—telephone, telegraph, radio, and, in time, television—differed from most of the industrialized world in one significant area as ownership remained in the private sector rather than the public sector. This made the United States an aberration. Public service models were the norm throughout Europe, as well as Canada,

Australia, New Zealand, and Japan. Great Britain provided the most prominent example as the state sponsorship and public service objectives of the BBC
became its calling card. The choice between commercial and public service
models involves more than the source of funding and extends to a fundamental difference in how broadcasters relate to their audiences.[10] This was most
evident in a famous quote from Sir John Reith, the first general director of the
BBC, who in response to a common criticism that the network provided what
the BBC determined the public needed rather than what the public wanted,
once said that, "few know what they want and very few what they need."[11]

Control of Broadcasting in the United States

The debate over the structure and control of broadcast radio in the United
States continued into the 1930s, but decisions made prior to and in the im-
mediate aftermath of World War I had a tremendous impact on the outcome.
The most viable alternative to the advertiser-supported, private sector-owned
broadcast system was marginalized, and the sociopolitical environment that
emerged during the Wilson Administration favored the interests of big business. While it is accurate to argue that the debate over broadcast radio did not
begin in earnest until after World War I, one could predict the outcome based
on decisions that were made relative to the telephone and telegraph prior to
the war and on the general attitude that prevailed relative to big business in
this period.

The public sector ownership of broadcast radio that some advocated appears futile when viewed within the debate over the ownership of the telephone and telegraph. These issues were the focus of constant discussion
between 1866, when Congress enacted legislation on the government acquisition of all telegraph lines, and 1914, when Congress ordered the printing of a
Post Office Department report entitled "Government Ownership of Electrical
Means of Communication."[12] Within this period, at least seventeen different Congressional committees advocated the government ownership of the
telephone and telegraph.[13] Members of Congress drafted numerous bills toward that end, but ownership of the telephone and telegraph remained in
the private sector. The debate included most of the arguments advanced for
public control of broadcast radio. As early as 1844, Henry Clay advocated
government ownership of the telegraph:

> It is quite manifest it is destined to exert great influence on the business affairs of
> society. In the hands of private individuals they will be able to monopolize intel-
> ligence and perform the greatest operations in commerce and other departments
> of business. I think such an engine should be exclusively under the control of the
> Government.[14]

This basic tenet of the argument was furthered in a Senate Committee on Commerce report in 1872, which argued that such a "great and marvelous agent
should be, as far as possible, free from exclusive privilege and monopoly."[15]

There was another important vein within the debate, a contention that the behavior of the private companies that controlled the means of communication was monopolistic in action and intention. The Senate Commerce report also stated that the policy of Western Union had been of a uniform nature: "It has been to ridicule, belittle, cripple, destroy, acquire, consolidate, and absorb all rival lines, until now it virtually controls the telegraph business of the whole country."[16] The report painted the picture of a corporation with extensive power and called on Congress to reel it in:

> With its network of wires covering the face of the land, it holds the incalculable commercial interests of the people of this nation in its grasp, as securely as the spider holds its struggling prey in the meshes of its web. There is no power but in Congress to grapple with this monster monopoly and afford adequate relief to the heavily taxed commercial interests of the country.[17]

Despite such arguments, control of the telegraph remained in the hands of Western Union, and power over the telephone remained with American Telephone & Telegraph (AT&T). While the Senate report provided one side of the argument, the *Commercial and Financial Standard* advanced another in 1882: a government-run telegraph would be "communistic."[18]

The marginalization of public sector ownership as a viable alternative was significant and, when coupled with other historical and sociopolitical factors, contributed to the establishment of a private sector-owned system for broadcast radio. The historical period in which radio developed was critical, with United States involvement in World War I the defining event. Prior to American engagement in the war, control of important patents rested in the hands of various corporations, such as AT&T, General Electric, and American Marconi and, as a result, no single corporation could dominate radio.[19] The best radios combined various technologies, which allowed amateurs to construct devices that oftentimes surpassed commercial models.

American involvement in World War I transformed radio, however. When the United States entered the war, the Navy utilized Presidential power contained within the Radio Act of 1912 to establish legal control over all radio in the name of national security. The Navy banished amateurs from the air and seized their equipment, while it enlisted corporations in the war effort.[20] The Navy also pooled various patents, which accelerated the development of the medium. After the conclusion of the war, the House of Representatives rejected a bill to leave control of radio in the hands of the Navy, a proposal that the State Department endorsed and one for which the Secretary of the Navy, Josephus Daniels, campaigned. Daniels argued that the "commercial interests of the Nation" were best served with radio under the control of a "non-partisan" agent rather than "foreign domination" or a "private domestic monopoly."[21] Central to his argument was the contention that radio was a natural monopoly: "Efficient radio communication required effective control; effective control requires a monopoly and the Government should exercise the control."[22]

While Daniels argued that radio would not flourish in the hands of a "private domestic monopoly," that is what he helped create in 1919. One of the final impetuses for the creation of RCA were negotiations between General Electric and the Britain-based Marconi companies for the sale of transmitters for use in the United States. When Daniels learned of these talks, he enlisted Rear Admiral W. H. G. Bullard to "direct the fight against British monopoly."[23] Bullard encountered a kindred spirit at General Electric, general counsel Owen D. Young, and together they squelched negotiations with Marconi and set in motion the creation of RCA, completed on October 17, 1919.[24] The initial corporation combined the patents that General Electric and American Marconi controlled, with AT&T and Western Electric adding theirs in 1920 and Westinghouse Electric and United Fruit doing likewise in 1921. Over two thousand patents became available to each company, and each staked out areas of dominance so that radio would develop in cooperation rather than in competition.[25]

The creation of a corporate behemoth was inconsistent with the arguments that Daniels presented to Congress, but it was congruous with other developments in the period. The friction between business and government that once existed had dissipated, most evident in an address to Congress that President Woodrow Wilson delivered on January 14, 1914, when he declared that, "The antagonism between business and government is over."[26] Wilson's declaration was one of the clearest endorsements for a period of corporate liberalism, a term that represented not a particular prescription for liberal ends but "reformist ideologies that accepted the large business corporation as a permanent and desirable feature of national life."[27]

There has been a great deal of debate over the Wilsonian embrace of corporate liberalism.[28] While this dispute is not germane to this discussion, it is clear that Wilson believed that corporations were "indispensable to modern business enterprises" and that "big business in the modern world" was inevitable.[29] What is also evident is that Wilson accepted the "fact" that large corporations had replaced individual entrepreneurs and small production units as the dominant feature of modern capitalism.[30] Martin Sklar argues that the acceptance of such a change had an important influence on his thinking: "the adjustments to be made, in Wilson's mind, involved not an attempt to restore the entrepreneurial competition of by-gone days nor the dissolution of large corporations, but on the contrary, 'the task of translating law and morals into terms of modern business'."[31] The basic problem was simple: "Our laws are still meant for business done by *individuals*; they have not been satisfactorily adjusted to business done by great *combinations*, and we have to adjust them."[32] This is a critical point, since radio went from a medium in the hands of entrepreneurs to one in the hands of corporations in the Wilson era.

The regulatory regime that Wilson established became that within which radio evolved in the 1920s. Herbert Hoover was prominent in this process as he administered a series of four radio conferences as Secretary of Commerce and selected the first members of the Federal Radio Commission before he was elected president in 1928. Hoover envisioned a superior socioeconomic order, one in which "America could benefit from scientific rationalization and social engineering without sacrificing the energy and creativity inherent in individual effort."[33] He called the redefined relationship between business and government an "associative state," which made a clear distinction between constructive and undesirable activism.[34] Central to this "American System" was the development and proper use of cooperative institutions, trade associations, and professional societies in particular, organizations that could contribute to the government apparatus "needed for an assured transition to an American utopia."[35] One of the trade associations that became prominent in this period was the National Association of Broadcasters (NAB), which formed in 1922.

The Commercialization of American Broadcasting

The creation of a network-dominated, advertiser-supported, private sector-owned broadcast system in the United States was consistent with the historical period in which the medium emerged, which undermines the perception that the structure created in the United States was the lone configuration that was suitable for democratic societies. The prominence of large corporations in broadcast radio was consistent with corporate liberalism; the role of the NAB was consistent with the concept of the associative state; the reliance on advertisers was consistent with a historical period in which a consumer culture was born and the pursuit of business became the creation of customers as well as products.[36] There was debate over the future of broadcast radio in the late 1920s and early 1930s, as McChesney documents, but it was not an equal battle.[37] The conflict pitted educational institutions, labor organizations, religious groups, and other entities that endorsed a public service role for radio against the large corporations that manufactured receivers and operated local stations and national networks. The rise of commercial radio stations and the demise of educational and religious stations in the latter stages of the 1920s were dramatic. The number of educational radio stations in the United States, for example, declined from 121 in the mid-1920s to 77 in 1929 to just 53 in 1931.[38]

An important topic within this debate was over the reliance on advertising to fund broadcast radio. In 1922, the trade journal *Radio Broadcast* proposed various sources of funds for broadcast radio, a list that included endowments, municipal financing, state financing, and others, but did not mention advertising. Such sources of funding were consistent with public statements by Hoover that "radio communication is not to be considered as merely a business carried on for private gain, for private advertisement, or for entertainment of the curious."[39] While Hoover made such pronouncements, he also believed that the radio industry should resolve the issue with the "approval of its listeners and without government interference."[40] Thus, the battle for radio became not so much a debate over policies as a public relations campaign. In the end, the creation of an "American System" with a reliance on advertising rather than license fees was presented as the natural extension of capitalist economies and the lone scheme compatible with democratic societies.[41] What is most notable about this development is that it resulted from a conscious campaign by commercial broadcasters, advertising agencies, and other promoters of broadcast advertising to present such a system as natural and inevitable.

The role of the NAB was critical in this period. Leaders in the organization believed that it "fathered" the Radio Act of 1927 through its influence in Congress, and the organization provided various "informal services" to the Federal Radio Commission.[42] The importance of the NAB was most evident in the months prior to passage of the Communications Act of 1934. In 1932, Congress called upon the Commission to report on the use of radio facilities for commercial advertising purposes. The NAB stated in public that the Senate request was "an opportunity to demonstrate to the American people the superiority of our system of broadcasting," but in private, the organization launched a fund-raising program to cover the cost of "providing the broadcasting stations with materials designed to present to the American public the real facts."[43] Those who advocated radio reform could not challenge the resources that the NAB and commercial broadcasters could marshal, and the Communications Act of 1934 did not challenge two fundamental components of the system, broadcast advertising and radio networks. An amendment to reallocate 25 percent of all frequencies to nonprofit groups died in Congress. The structure that the Communications Act codified became the foundation for broadcast television when it emerged in the post-World War II era.

POLICY AND REGULATORY FRAMEWORK

The ideas and ideologies prominent in the 1920s had a profound impact on the structure of broadcast radio. The same is true of the 1980s when the federal government transformed broadcast regulation, although the ideas and ideologies of the day were quite different. The inauguration of Ronald Reagan in 1981 was the clearest statement that a new political era had arrived in the United States, with restrictions on business a focal point. The basic tenet of the Reagan doctrine was evident in his inaugural address when he declared, "Government is not the solution to our problem, government is our problem."[44] His ascension came on the heels of a period of new social regulation, within which environmental and consumer regulations were prominent.[45] In the 1970s, Richard Nixon, Gerald Ford, and Jimmy Carter attempted to control regulators but each embraced the New Deal principle that federal programs were a needed response to socioeconomic problems.

Reagan, however, embraced a different ideological framework. A deep-seated belief that the new social regulation was "inconsistent, even antithetical, to the American notion of liberal democracy" was at the heart of the Reagan doctrine.[46]

This was a critical point in the regulation of the broadcast television, cable television, and motion picture industries, and it is important to consider the policies and regulations the federal government enacted in a broader histori-cal framework. An important dimension of the Reagan approach was the ap-pointment of loyal and determined policy officials to departments and agen-cies, with the Federal Communications Commission and the Federal Trade Commission as two focal points. The appointment of Mark Fowler as the chair of the FCC was an example of this as he brought to the Commission a deep and abiding commitment to regulatory relief. The links between Fowler and the industry were extensive, dating to his high school years in Florida when he worked part-time at local radio stations. He strengthened those ties while an attorney in the communication practices of prominent Washington law firms, organizations that promoted the causes of commercial television and radio before the government. Most important, however, were his ties to Reagan, as Fowler served as the communications counsel for the Reagan for President Committee in the primaries and filled a similar role in the general election.

Fowler was a devoted advocate of the Reagan doctrine. He preached the merits of the marketplace, and argued that the "public interest" is whatever the public wants, and the market should be the judge of that. Fundamental to his words and actions was a belief that broadcast regulation should mir-ror other industrial sectors, that the power of television and radio to shape the news and information marketplace and to celebrate dominant values and offer models of thought and behavior did not demand a different level of reg-ulation. In his statement that accompanied the Report and Order that raised television station ownership limits in 1984, Fowler made a clear statement on his position:

> Bigness is not necessarily badness, sometimes it is goodness, sometimes it is just bigness and nothing more. But without a good reason to forbid growth, this Commission should not just utter the magic word "Television" and treat the industry differently.[47]

In this statement, Fowler makes clear that the unique nature of television did not demand more consideration than other industries. This was evident in another Fowler statement when he compared a television to a toaster with pictures.

Regulation of Media Industries

Broadcast television is at the heart of federal regulation of media indus-tries. Ever since the Radio Act of 1927 established the premise that broadcast licensees must serve the public interest, convenience, and necessity, there has been some degree of political intervention, in theory, to stop broadcasters from gaining or abusing excessive market power and ensure that broadcasters contribute to the political discourse and other social goals. The First Amendment prohibits Congress from making laws that abridge the "freedom of speech or of the press," and this protects newspapers and magazines from most government intervention. The Supreme Court extended the same protection to films in 1952, arguing that motion pictures were "a significant medium for the communication of ideas" and the fact that films "entertain as well as inform" did not lessen their importance in this regard.[48] In spite of these protections, the Commission enacted the Financial Interest and Syndication Rules in 1970 and the Newspaper/Television Cross-Ownership Prohibition in 1975. While some argue that such regulations limited First Amendment rights, both withstood legal challenges since federal power to grant broadcast licenses in the advancement of the public interest, convenience, and necessity was at their foundation.

The courts have affirmed the legal foundation for such regulation on a repeated basis. In 1943, the Supreme Court addressed the power of the FCC to regulate the relationship between broadcast networks and their affiliates through its Chain Broadcasting Regulations, concluding that it was within the Commission's authority to structure the business arrangements between them.[49] In that case, NBC argued that the Chain Broadcasting rules abridged its right to free speech. Justice Felix Frankfurter wrote in the majority opinion:

> Freedom of utterance is abridged to many who wish to use the limited facilities of radio. Unlike other modes of expression, radio inherently is not available to all. That is its unique characteristic, and that is why, unlike other modes of expression, it is subject to governmental regulation. Because it cannot be used by all, some who wish to use it must be denied.[50]

Had the FCC based its decision to grant or reject a license application on "political, economic or social views" then the issue, in the words of Frankfurter, would be "wholly different." Since Congress established the "public interest, convenience and necessity" as the licensing standard, however, the Supreme Court ruled that the rejection of a license to individuals who engaged in certain network practices was not a denial of free speech.

This position addresses one of the rationales for granting broadcasters limited First Amendment protection: spectrum scarcity. Another is the belief that broadcasters are trustees of the airwaves that the public owns. In the Red Lion case in 1969, the Supreme Court upheld a basic tenet of the Fairness Doctrine that required broadcasters to provide reasonable right-to-reply opportunities to individuals attacked during the presentation of a public issue or to political opponents of those candidates for public office who received the endorsement of a broadcaster.[51] Justice White argued that "Where there are substantially more individuals who want to broadcast than there are frequencies to allocate, it is idle to posit an unabridgeable First Amendment right to broadcast comparable to the right of every individual to speak, write, or publish."[52] This portion of the decision is consistent with the scarcity rationale in *NBC v. United States*. Justice White also made a connection with public service objectives: "It is the purpose of the First Amendment to preserve an uninhibited marketplace of ideas in which truth will ultimately prevail, rather than to countenance monopolization of that market, whether it be by the government itself or a private licensee. . . . It is the right of the public to receive suitable access to social, political, esthetic, moral, and other ideas and experiences which is crucial here."

The pervasiveness of broadcast radio and television and the fact that it comes into the home over the air, free of charge, is another rationale for limited First Amendment protection. This has become a prominent issue as broadcast networks push the envelope to compete with cable channels, which are not held to the same standard since cable subscribers, unlike over-the-air viewers, can choose "targeted blocking" of unwanted channels.[53] While the First Amendment protects indecent speech, the courts have supported FCC attempts to limit such material on broadcast outlets during certain times of day, including the safe harbor hours between 6:00 a.m. and 10:00 p.m., when it is reasonable to expect children to be in the audience. This was the rationale for fines imposed on CBS for the Janet Jackson "wardrobe malfunction" at the Super Bowl in 2004, just as it was when radio station WBAI broadcast George Carlin's "Filthy Words" monologue on a Tuesday afternoon in 1973. The Supreme Court upheld the power of the FCC to sanction the licensee of WBAI, Pacifica Foundation, in 1978.[54] Justice John Paul Stevens argued that, "the broadcast media have established a uniquely pervasive presence in the lives of all Americans. Patently offensive, indecent material presented over the airwaves confronts the citizen, not only in public, but also in the privacy of the home, where the individual's right to be left alone plainly outweighs the First Amendment rights of an intruder."[55] In the eyes of the majority, the fact that broadcast outlets were accessible to children, "even those too young to read," justified the "regulation of otherwise protected expression."[56]

Broadcast Television Regulation

The regulation of broadcast television has assumed different forms and served different functions. Much of the public deliberation in the first half of the 2000s focused on content regulation that addressed the broadcast of indecent material. The Parents Television Council fueled much of this debate and orchestrated the filing of countless complaints with the FCC, which saw such filing increase from 111 in 2000 to 1.4 million in 2004.[57] In 2004 and again in 2005, Republican Fred Upton introduced the Broadcast Decency Enforcement Act in the House, which would increase the fines for "obscene, indecent or profane" broadcasts from a maximum of $32,500 per violation, per licensee to a maximum of $500,000.[58] Outside of a brief uproar in the summer of 2003, structural regulations produced far less traction, both inside and outside of the federal government. While Congress and the FCC assailed Viacom for the halftime show at the Super Bowl in 2004, each of them passed legislation or wrote regulations that allowed it to engulf CBS and expand into a media behemoth with little regard for serving the public interest, convenience, and necessity. These structural regulations are central to this discussion.

The federal government addresses broadcast ownership at two different levels, both of which are quite important. National ownership rules address and restrict undue market power at that level. Such statutes limit the ownership of multiple broadcast networks and the potential reach of a corporation or individual through the ownership of broadcast stations. The local ownership regulations inhibit the concentration of market power in individual communities. These rules limit the ownership of multiple television and/or radio stations in a single market as well as the cross ownership of a newspaper and television station in the same market. The Commission examined all these regulations in its 2002 Biennial Regulatory Review and scheduled all but the dual network rule for relaxation or elimination before Congress and the U.S. Court of Appeals for the Third Circuit stepped into the fray.

Critical to this discussion of ownership is the concept of localism, which has been a cornerstone of broadcast regulation for decades. The foundation of localism is a simple concept: local concerns take precedent over national ones and individuals and institutions should resolve such issues at the local level. The connection between this concept and broadcast radio and television ownership is basic, albeit problematic. The FCC grants a license for a radio and television station at the local level and mandates that licensees serve the needs and interests of that community. The FCC has been centrally concerned with the relationship between networks and affiliates since it promulgated the Chain Broadcasting rules in 1941, although it has a strange way of showing this unease at times. It was not until after the Commission voted in favor of wholesale changes in its television ownership rules in 2003, ones that could have further empowered the networks and large station groups, that Michael Powell created the Localism Task Force to examine how the FCC could better promote localism.

Broadcast Television Regulation: National Ownership Rules

Regulations to limit the reach of broadcast station groups have existed since before United States involvement in World War II, when television was in its infancy. In 1941, the FCC imposed a national ownership cap of three stations per company, a limit it increased to five in 1944. The FCC advanced the clearest argument for the national ownership limit in 1953 in its defense of the five-station cap: "The purpose of the multiple ownership rules is to promote diversification of ownership in order to maximize diversification of program and service viewpoint as well as to prevent any undue concentration of economic power contrary to the public interest."[59] In 1954, the Commission adopted the "Seven Station Rule" when it raised the limit from five stations to seven, with no more than five being on the more powerful VHF frequencies.[60] The objective behind the two-station increase was the promotion of the UHF band.

The "Seven Station Rule" held firm for four decades, prohibiting a corporation or individual from holding a cognizable ownership position in more than seven AM and seven FM radio stations and no more than seven television stations. In the last two decades, however, the rules have come under a full-scale frontal assault. In 1984, the FCC raised those limits to allow ownership of twelve AM and twelve FM radio stations and twelve television stations; it also repealed the rules subject to a six-year transition period.[61] The justification for such changes was the "explosive growth and change" that had occurred in media markets.

What is most important about the arguments that the FCC presented is the reliance on quantitative changes in the marketplace, not on the issue of power that was at the core of the Sherman Act and other antitrust regulations. The Commission argued that local markets included a "wide variety of active, energetic organs in the dissemination of ideas" and that on a national level the "growth in the number of programming sources is a significant factor that supports the abolition of the rule."[62] The conclusion was simple: the "elimination of the Seven Station Rule poses no threat to the diversity of independent viewpoints in the information and entertainment markets."[63] Congress blocked the implementation of the 1984 Report & Order and forced the FCC to reconsider. The Commission maintained the twelve-station limit and added a prohibition on ownership of stations that reached more than 25 percent of television households nationwide.

While the seven-station cap stood for forty years, the twelve-station limit remained in place for just over a decade. In the mid-1990s, the tide of deregulation crested anew and Congress undertook the first comprehensive rewrite of the Communications Act of 1934. Among the stated goals of the Telecommunications Act of 1996 was to increase competition in the telephone and cable sectors, and new rules for local and long distance phone service allowed greater access while those for cable encouraged more facilities-based competition. The National Television Station Ownership (NTSO) Rule was little more than a blip on the radar, but the broadcast television networks capitalized on the legislative moment, thanks to friends in high places.

Senate Commerce Committee chair Larry Pressler authored the bill, and a draft version included a total repeal of the ownership rule. The version that made its way through the Senate eliminated the numerical station limit and increased the ceiling for national reach from 25 percent to 35 percent. The National Association of Broadcasters was on the sidelines through much of the debate, split between the networks who favored the increase and other affiliated station groups that opposed it, fearful that such an increase would make the networks too powerful. The owners of the smaller station groups mobilized some opposition, and the Senate passed an amendment to retain the 25 percent limit in June 1995.[64] Majority leader Bob Dole stepped into the breach,

convinced a handful of Republicans to switch their votes, and the amendment was defeated moments later. The 35 percent ownership limit became law
when President Clinton signed the Telecommunications Act in February 1996.

A second provision of the Telecommunications Act of 1996 further influenced the station ownership rule. Section 202 (h) of the act mandated that the
FCC conduct biennial reviews of its ownership rules and repeal or modify any
regulation it determines "to no longer be in the public interest."[65] In the 1998
Biennial Regulatory Review, the FCC opted to retain the NTSO rule, arguing
that it needed to observe the impact of changes in local ownership rules and
the increase in the national limit from 25 percent to 35 percent with an eye
toward preserving the power of local affiliates in their negotiations with the
broadcast networks. The failure of the Commission to remove or increase the
35 percent ceiling prompted the Fox Television Stations and others to file suit
in federal court.[66] Central to the Fox argument was the FCC position in 1984
that the rule should be repealed since it focused on national rather than local
markets and competition had made the rules unnecessary. Fox also argued
that the ownership limit violated its First Amendment rights since it could
not speak directly to 65 percent of the potential U.S. television audience. The
U.S. Court of Appeals for the DC Circuit concluded that the rule was not
unconstitutional but that the Commission's decision to retain the rule was
"arbitrary and capricious" because it failed to give adequate reason for its
decision and sent it back to the Commission for further consideration.

The Court of Appeals handed that decision down in June 2002, which set
the table for the upcoming Biennial Regulatory Review. The battle lines were
much as they were in 1996. The television networks pushed for an increase in
the ownership limits, arguing that their survival depended on it, and affiliate
station groups fought for the retention of the 35 percent cap, contending that
it was vital to the preservation of local community responsiveness. The NAB
was more prominent in these discussions than it had been earlier, and for good
reason. It no longer represented the interests of the networks. CBS, Fox, and
NBC terminated their memberships in the organization in 2002, and ABC did
likewise in 2003. The networks were once again victorious, at least in round
one, as the FCC voted to raise the NTSO limit to 45 percent in June 2003.
Sidebar 3.1 discusses the review process in more detail.

This was not the end of the story, however. In May 2003, even before the
Commission issued its Report & Order, identical legislation was introduced
in both houses of Congress to maintain the national audience reach at 35
percent, but the bill made little progress in either chamber.[67] Congress reen-
tered the debate days after the FCC released the new rules in June 2003,
and the Senate passed legislation to retain the 35 percent limit in September
2003. President Bush threatened to veto legislation that included such a rollback, however, and the Republican leaders ensured that the House never
voted on the Senate bill. That was not the end either, as a Senate-House
conference committee added the 35 percent limit to the $820 billion Con-
solidated Appropriations Act of 2004.

Sidebar 3.1
The Battle for Airwaves: 2002–2003

The debate over media ownership has made for some strange bedfellows. In June 2003, the right-leaning National Rifle Association and left-leaning National Organization for Women raised their voices as one to protest the Federal Communications Commission (FCC) decision to relax a wide range of ownership rules. The Prometheus Radio Project, a Philadelphia-based nonprofit group that promoted low-power radio stations, became the standard-bearer in the case that went before the U.S. Court of Appeals for the Third Circuit. In one of the great David versus Goliath tales, the Court of Appeals prevented the FCC from enacting its new rules in September 2003 and then sent most of them back for further consideration in June 2004, concluding that it had not justified the changes. Twelve months later, the Supreme Court declined to hear an appeal. While that decision sent the FCC back to square one, the regulatory process behind the review remains quite important.

Chairman Michael Powell called the 2002 Biennial Regulatory Review the most "exhaustive and comprehensive review of our broadcast ownership rules ever undertaken."[1] In certain regards, that was an accurate assessment. When the review began in September 2002, the Commission opted to examine six different ownership rules rather than focus on one or two.[2] The review encompassed national ownership rules as well as local rules.[3] In other respects, however, the review was far from exhaustive, and the outcome appeared to be a forgone conclusion. Commissioner Michael Copps questioned whether the "timing and tone" of the review notice suggested that the outcome was "prejudged" in favor of deregulation and called for a series of public hearings around the country to discuss the rules and assess the impact of ownership in diverse local markets.[4] That series of hearings never materialized.

The FCC held just one official public hearing over the course of the proceedings, in Richmond, Virginia, in February 2003. Powell stated on a repeated basis that one hearing was sufficient and that individuals could file written comments, but others argued that public discussions and debates were critical to achieving the proper balance in the ownership rules. The most outspoken commissioner on this front was Copps, who organized a series of forums to discuss the ownership rules. What was striking about these meetings was the refusal of the Republican commissioners, including Powell, to participate. In mid-May, Copps and fellow Democratic commissioner Jonathan Adelstein called for a delay in the vote on the ownership rules and reiterated their pleas for additional public hearings, appeals that numerous members of Congress echoed. Powell refused those requests and the Commission adopted the Biennial Regulatory Review on June 2, 2003, by a 3–2 vote along party lines.

The absence of public discussions over the proposed changes in the rules was a focal point in the uproar that followed the FCC decision. The criticism came from most points on the political spectrum. Conservative columnist William Safire asked in the *New York Times* whether broadcasters and other media outlets were not obligated to call attention to "the arrogance of a regulatory commission that will not hold extended public hearings on the most controversial decision in its history?"[5] Jeffrey Chester, the executive director of the Center for Digital Democracy, also focused on the shortcomings of Powell's approach: "He refused to conduct [adequate] public hearings, he refused to have 30- or 60-day debates on the rules, he has been unwilling

(Continued)

to reach out to the public. If Saddam Hussein had stayed in business, Powell might have made a great minister of information."[6]

The behind closed-door approach to regulation is now quite common within the FCC. The Government in the Sunshine Act mandates that federal agencies such as the FCC conduct the public's business in public, and there was a time when it did. Between 1978 and 1981, the Commission conducted more than 80 percent of its votes at regular open hearings.[7] This percentage stands in sharp contrast to later figures, as one study found that between 1986 and mid-1995 the Commission held more than 80 percent of such votes in private. Not just votes have moved behind closed doors. In 1978 and 1979, the FCC met at least once a week in public session; during Powell's chairmanship, the Commission met just once a month in public hearings.[8] What makes such practices questionable is that it helps obscure the individuals and organizations that gain access to commissioners to argue for or against a particular position.

This was a prominent issue over the eight months the FCC conducted its 2002 Biennial Regulatory Review. A study conducted by the Center for Public Integrity found that the nation's top broadcasters met behind closed doors with FCC officials more than seventy times, compared to just five meetings between officials and representatives of two prominent consumer and public interest advocates, the Consumers Union and Media Access Project.[9] Executives of ABC and Disney topped that total on March 11, 2003, alone with six different sessions with eighteen FCC officials. Powell was involved in just four private sessions as the Commission constructed its proposals, but the schedule included face-to-face meetings with Rupert Murdoch of News Corp., Mel Karmazin of Viacom, Robert Wright of NBC, and Doug McCorkindale of Gannett.

Under most circumstances, hiding the decision-making process behind closed doors would raise concerns, but such trepidation becomes more intense when one tracks the infusion of money into the political process. Little noted in the mainstream media are the dollars media conglomerates spend to affect election outcomes and influence legislation before Congress and the White House and rulemaking within the FCC and other agencies. One investigation into campaign contributions, lobbying expenditures, and other spending found that the communications industry spent $1.1 billion between 1998 and mid-2004 to influence the process in some form or fashion.[10] This total included the three communication sectors, broadcasting, cable television, and telecommunications, so much of this was not related to the ownership rules before the FCC in 2002 and 2003. The totals, however, were quite significant. The broadcast group alone spent over $220 million lobbying the federal government in this period and contributed another $25.5 million to federal candidates and lawmakers.[11]

The impact of this influence was most evident within Congress. Within days of the completion of the FCC Report and Order, Congressional committees initiated hearings to address the changes in ownership rules. One of the focal points within Congress was the national television ownership limit, which the FCC raised from 35 percent to 45 percent of television households nationwide. The Senate passed a joint resolution in September 2003 to roll the limits back to 35 percent, but House Majority Leader Tom DeLay said the bill was "dead on arrival," and it never reached the House floor for a vote. There was still widespread support in both houses of Congress, and a Senate-House conference committee added the rollback to an omnibus appropriations bill in November, despite repeated threats of a presidential veto. The White House did not retreat, however, as it orchestrated a backroom deal with the Republican chair of the Senate Appropriation Committee, Ted Stevens, to set the ownership limit at 39 percent. Much as it did when in 1934 Senator Clarence Dill undermined a bid to reserve part of the radio spectrum for nonprofit broadcasters, the major media conglomerates had friends in high places when it needed them most.

NOTES

1. Michael Powell, "Press Statement of Chairman Michael Powell," in the matter of 2002 Biennial Regulatory Review, Federal Communications Commission, 2 June 2003.

2. The Telecommunications Act of 1996 mandated that the FCC reconsider its ownership rules on a biannual basis and repeal or modify any regulation it determined to no longer be in the public interest.

3. The following ownership rules were examined within the Biennial Review: (1) Newspaper/broadcast cross-ownership ban, passed in 1975. (2) Local radio ownership, adopted in 1941. (3) National TV ownership, also adopted in 1941, capping ownership of stations to reach no more than 35 percent of national audience. (4) Local TV multiple ownership, passed in 1964. (5) Radio/TV cross-ownership restriction, adopted in 1970. (6) Dual TV network rule, passed in 1946.

4. Michael Copps, "Concurring Statement of Commissioner Michael J. Copps," in the matter of 2002 Biennial Regulatory Review, Federal Communications Commission, 2 June 2003.

5. William Safire, "The Great Media Gulp," *New York Times*, 22 May 2003, 33.

6. Quoted in Tom Shales, "Michael Powell and the FCC: Giving Away the Marketplace of Ideas." *Washington Post*, 2 June 2003, C1.

7. Doug Halonen, "FCC's Public Record Of Private Votes," *Electronic Media*, 13 November 1995.

8. What is curious about the move away from such meetings is that the Sunshine Act prohibits private communication between three or more commissioners at once, so an open meeting is the one forum when all the commissioners can engage in discussion and debate. The commission, however, now conducts much of its business in private and resolves issues on "circulation," a process through which debates and votes are conducted through assistants and via paper and e-mail.

9. Bob Williams, "Behind Closed Doors: Top Broadcasters Met 71 Times with FCC Officials," publicintegrity.org (accessed 25 June 2005).

10. John Dunbar, Daniel Lathrop, and Robert Morlino, "Networks of Influence: The Political Power of the Communications Industry," *The Center for Public Integrity*, 28 October 2004 (accessed 25 June 2005).

11. Robert Morlino, "Broadcast Lobbying Tops $222 Million," *The Center for Public Integrity*, 28 October 2004 (accessed 25 June 2005).

The television networks and their allies rose to the occasion once again. Before the final vote on the appropriations bill, Senate Appropriations Committee chair Ted Stevens and the White House negotiated a backroom "compromise" to set the limit at 39 percent. This was a significant number, since it allowed Viacom and News Corp. to retain the stations each owned in excess of the 35 percent limit. The Court of Appeals ruled in *Fox Television Stations, Inc. v. FCC* that the Commission decision to maintain the NTSO rule was arbitrary and capricious, meaning that there was an absence of a rational connection between the facts found and the choice made. In the case of the 39 percent ownership cap, the connection between the facts and the choice was clear and Senator John McCain put the question in simple terms: "Why did they pick 39 percent? So these two conglomerates could be grandfathered."[68]

The 39 percent ownership cap, moreover, is not a hard one, and Viacom and News Corp. were among the station groups that exceeded this limit at the start of 2005.[69] Under FCC rules, when determining the reach of a broadcast group, markets in which the group owns a UHF station receive a 50 percent discount. News Corp., for example, owned WFLD and WPWR in Chicago at the start of 2005, but since both are UHF stations, the market counted just 1.576 toward the 39 percent limit, rather than 3.152, which was the percentage of television households nationwide that were in the Chicago designated market area in 2004–2005. Since the UHF signal is weaker than the VHF signal, the FCC created the UHF discount to foster growth in the band in an era when most households received television over the air.

The development of cable and satellite systems has made such households quite rare, with around 85 percent receiving at least some form of basic service via such services. This has minimized the differences between UHF and VHF since carriage on such services eliminates the power discrepancies between the two bands. The "must-carry" rules, moreover, allow UHF stations to demand carriage on local cable systems and the Satellite Home Viewer Improvement Act of 1999 extended these provisions to satellite services. In spite of these changes in the delivery of such channels, the FCC opted to retain the UHF discount following the 2002 Biennial Regulatory Review. With Congress raising the ownership limit to 39 percent, the UHF discount means a single individual or corporation could own local stations that reach 78 percent of television households nationwide.

Broadcast Television Regulation: Local Ownership Rules

The changes in the National Television Station Ownership Rule extended the reach of the networks and other large groups at the national level, but the biggest impact from changes in the rule might be at the local level. The core argument in support of the NTSO rule is that local stations with ownership ties to a broadcast network or other large group will be more responsive to the wants and needs of their corporate parents than to the communities they are licensed to serve. This would compromise localism, the advancement of which has been an objective of broadcast regulation since the 1930s. A second goal has been the promotion of diversity at the national and local levels, based on the notion that a vibrant marketplace of ideas is the foundation of democratic societies. As part of its 2002 Biennial Regulatory Review, the Commission voted to maintain the Dual Television Network Rule, which prohibits common ownership of two of the four major broadcast networks, but local restrictions designed to promote diversity have been relaxed over the last decade.

The first to fall were long-standing rules that prohibited common owner-ship of more than one television station per market, the so-called duopoly rules. The Commission allowed common management of local television sta-tions through the 1990s, known as Local Marketing Agreements (LMA), and eliminated rules that prohibited ownership of more than one AM and one FM radio station in a market in 1992. The Telecommunications Act of 1996 allowed greater concentration in ownership of radio stations at the local level and called upon the FCC to conduct a rulemaking to determine whether to retain, modify, or eliminate the television duopoly rules.[70] That process con-cluded in 1999 when the FCC relaxed the rules to allow dual ownership in markets where there were at least eight independently owned television sta-tions, provided only one was among the four top-rated stations in the market. In 2003, the FCC attempted to lower the threshold to allow common owner-ship in markets with five or more stations and permit the ownership of three stations in markets with eighteen or more stations.

The issue that generated more headlines after the FCC issued its Report & Order in 2003 was the decision to eliminate restrictions on the ownership of newspapers and television stations in the same market. The Commission insti-tuted its Newspaper/Broadcast Cross-Ownership Prohibition in 1975 in a bid to enhance program and viewpoint diversity in local communities, although it did not force divesture of existing cross-ownership in most cases. While such ownership continued to exist in numerous communities, including the common ownership of the *Tribune* and WGN in Chicago, the cross-ownership ban stood firm until 2003. That does not mean that there were not members of Congress who wanted it eliminated. In 2001, Representative Billy Tauzin, the powerful chair of the House Energy & Commerce Committee, said that if the FCC did not repeal the rule, then Congress would.

The FCC attempted to do just that in 2003. The revisions in the newspa-per/broadcast rules were among the most lobbied components of the FCC review, and the Commission voted to eliminate the cross-ownership prohi-bition in markets with nine or more television stations.[71] These provisions would have allowed for newspapers-television cross-ownership in all but the smallest markets and became a focal point of the firestorm that followed. The reinstatement of the cross-ownership rules was in the bill that received bipartisan support in the Senate in September of 2003, but the bill never re-ceived a hearing in the Tauzin-controlled Energy and Commerce Committee and died in the House. A spokesperson for Tauzin said, "We have absolutely no intention of taking up the Senate bill. This has become a political soap opera, and given the chance Chairman Tauzin intends to cancel its run."[72]

Tauzin long stood as one of the strongest advocates for the media conglom-erates, and among his corporate friends and donors was the Tribune Co., among the most active in the campaign to rewrite the cross-ownership rules. In the spring of 1997, Harry Caray "interviewed" Tauzin during a Cubs broad-cast, a visit to the booth that was repeated in 1998 with Caray's grandson, Chip.

While WGN-TV labeled the visit as an interview, it is difficult to comprehend why baseball fans in Chicago would care about the opinions of a Republican from Louisiana. The connections to the corporate interest of the Tribune Co. were easier to discern. When the Tribune Co. acquired the Times-Mirror Co. in 2000, it added newspapers in New York, Los Angeles, and Hartford where it owned local television stations, WPIX, KTLA, and WTIC, respectively.[73] When the deal was consummated, Tauzin was among those who repeated his demand that the FCC eliminate the cross-ownership rule, saying "It's time for the FCC to recognize that the world has changed since those rules were put in place."[74] The Tribune does not have to confront the cross-ownership issue until the licenses for the stations come up for renewal, beginning with KTLA in December 2006. The FCC rewrite of the cross-ownership rules would have eliminated all obstacles in these markets, but those rules were among the ones that the U.S. Court of Appeals for the Third Circuit sent back to the Commission for further consideration, leaving the Tribune Co. in a state of limbo.[75]

PATTERNS OF OWNERSHIP: BROADCAST TELEVISION

When Ronald Reagan and his troops within the FCC launched their offensive against federal regulations of television and radio in the 1980s, the broadcast landscape was far different than it is today. The "Seven Station Rule" limited a single corporation to the ownership of seven television stations, seven AM and seven FM radio stations nationwide, while the duopoly rule limited them to one of each in a given market. The Financial Interest and Syndication Rules, moreover, all but precluded the common ownership of a broadcast network and motion picture studio, while the cross-ownership rule prohibited the combination of television stations and newspapers at the local level. Fast-forward two decades and the landscape is altogether different. At the start of 2005, Viacom Inc. owned and operated 39 broadcast television stations and 183 radio stations, and in Los Angeles alone it controlled two local television stations, KCBS and KCAL, and seven radio stations. It owned two broadcast networks, CBS and UPN, both of which were under the same corporate umbrella as a motion picture studio, Paramount Pictures. All that was missing was a newspaper.

There is little doubt that the media scene has also changed to a dramatic degree since the 1980s, and the broadcast networks and local stations are not as dominant as they once were. These outlets, however, remain critical in the dissemination of news and information on the national and local levels, command a significant share of the television audience on a day-to-day basis, and are home to common social and cultural experiences such as the Super Bowl and Academy Awards. Just as significant is the role these networks and stations assume in the vast media conglomerates that produce and disseminate cultural products. While cable networks have claimed half of the television audience, much of the content on these channels originates, and builds a following, on the broadcast networks. In 2005, for example, three current or former broadcast mainstays—*Everybody Loves Raymond, Friends,* and *Seinfeld*—were the foundation of the TBS schedule, while *Law & Order* anchored the TNT schedule. At the same time, *Law & Order: Special Victims Unit* and *Law & Order: Criminal Intent* provided the foundation for the prime time schedule on USA Network, and *CSI: Crime Scene Investigation* was driving a ratings upswing for the Viacom-owned Spike TV.

The examination of distribution in broadcast television requires analysis at two different levels: the broadcast networks and the local stations. From a financial perspective, there are important distinctions to be made between the two, as the stations are veritable cash cows while the networks struggle to control costs and earn even a meager profit, at least on paper. This has fueled campaigns for an increase in local station ownership, which the networks claim is critical to the survival of free-to-air television. Local station groups not integrated into networks counter that the station limits are an important buffer against the power of the networks, and the NAB and Network Affiliated Stations Alliance fought increases in the 35 percent cap on these grounds. This conflict raises another related issue: the power of local stations to respond to the wants and needs of their local communities, rather than making decisions based on the best interests of their corporate parents, whether they are network owners or large station group operators. This once again points to the importance of an analysis at both levels.

Broadcast Networks

The ownership and control of the broadcast networks has undergone dramatic change since the mid-1980s. For over three decades, control of the three broadcast networks—ABC, CBS, and NBC—rested in the hands of Leonard Goldenson, William Paley, and David Sarnoff. Goldenson became involved with ABC in 1953 when United Paramount Theaters Inc., separated from Paramount Pictures after the signing of the Paramount decrees, acquired the broadcast network. This made Goldenson a veritable interloper, as Paley and Sarnoff were center stage in the formation of CBS and NBC in the 1920s and guided these broadcast networks for the better part of the five decades. What is important is the culture that permeated these companies. The networks operated within private corporations in which the bottom line was important but not the sole determinant of success. When CBS considered offers to sell in the mid-1980s, the board rejected various overtures because the directors believed that it was imperative for CBS to remain independent. Paley advanced the basic argument in favor of independence: "CBS is a public trust and should remain independent. I don't believe it can carry out its mission if it were part of another company."[76]

CBS turned back the challenges from Coca-Cola, Ted Turner, and others, but the mid-1980s became a time of remarkable change for the networks. In a ten-month period from the start of 1986, ownership and control of each of the three networks changed hands, while a fourth debuted. In January 1986, Capital Cities Communications completed its $3.5 billion acquisition of ABC Inc., which integrated ABC into a prominent media corporation with ownership of newspapers, television and radio stations, and cable systems. In June, the federal government approved the General Electric acquisition of RCA Corp. for $6.2 billion, which coupled NBC News with one of the Pentagon's largest contractors. In September, Laurence Tisch and Loews Corp. gained effective control of CBS with a 24.9 percent share of the corporation. And on October 9, 1986, Twentieth Century Fox launched the Fox network. After these ten months, broadcast television would never be the same.

The mergers and acquisitions that occurred in 1986 represented different patterns of conglomeration, including horizontal and vertical integration and diversification, but each occurred within a laissez-faire era of regulation. The FCC decision in 1984 to raise the multiple station ownership limits from seven to twelve fueled the combination of Capital Cities and ABC, as the former owned seven local stations, four of which were ABC affiliates. The General Electric acquisition of RCA was a more traditional form of diversification, although General Electric did own the NBC affiliate in Denver. The timing was significant, however, as review of the transfer of the NBC station group licenses occurred around the time the FCC adopted a much narrower "character" qualification required of broadcasters, limiting the discussion and disregarding most misconduct unrelated to broadcast operations.[77] General Electric completed the purchase of NBC less than twelve months after it pleaded guilty to 108 federal counts of fraud in its business practices with the Pentagon.

The impact of this transfer of control was evident from the beginning. Lawrence Grossman, the president of NBC News, believed that the networks were a public trust; Jack Welch, the chairman of General Electric, believed that the same public trust applied to making an air conditioner as running a broadcast network.[78] For Welch, the main obligation was not to the public who owned the airwaves, as Grossman believed, but to the shareholders who owned General Electric stock. Less than a year after it took control of NBC, a team of "management consultants" began an examination of the operations of NBC News looking for waste and inefficiencies.[79] Grossman left the network in the summer of 1988.

The rise of Loews and Tisch within CBS was a more traditional change in ownership, but the FCC still assumed a role. When Tisch assumed power and ousted CBS chairman Thomas Wyman in 1986, members of Congress and others argued that an unauthorized transfer of control had occurred when Tisch upped his ownership stake from 12.2 percent in March to 24.9 percent in September and became the new chief executive officer. At the time, Commissioner James Quello said, "There's no doubt, with a 25 percent interest, he's going to call the shots. It's hard to deny there's been a transfer of control."[80] The FCC, however, ruled a month later that control remained with the hands of the shareholders so it did not constitute an illegal transfer of licenses. Among those representing the interests of CBS and Tisch before the Commission were two former FCC chairmen, Richard Wiley and Newton Minow, who was also a member of the CBS Board of Directors.

What was clear during this period was that the Fowler-chaired FCC would take almost any action, whether in the writing of new rules or the interpretation of old ones, to allow media consolidation to occur. The creation of the fourth major broadcast network, Fox, provides an example of this. The Metromedia chain of local stations provided the foundation for the Fox network, including New York, Los Angeles, Chicago, Dallas, Washington DC, and Houston, but under FCC foreign ownership restrictions, Murdoch's Australia-based News Corp. could not own more than 25 percent of a local station. The FCC granted the transfer of the Metromedia stations in November 1985 based on the premise that Murdoch had become a naturalized U.S. citizen and that he provided the capital for the purchase. That was not the case, however.

In the mid-1990s, in the midst of an FCC investigation, Murdoch revealed that News Corp. had provided 99 percent of the financing to acquire Metromedia, a clear violation of FCC rules. In the spring of 1995, the FCC ruled that the News Corp. ownership of the Fox stations was a violation of foreign ownership rules. Despite a recommendation from its Mass Media Bureau and Office of General Counsel that News Corp. be forced to change its ownership structure, the Commissioners granted News Corp. a permanent waiver of the rules based on the argument that the network served the public interest. That decision came two years after the FCC granted Murdoch a permanent waiver of the Newspaper/Broadcast Cross-Ownership Prohibition and allowed ownership of the *New York Post* and WNYW. It was also four years after it rewrote the Financial Interest and Syndication Rules to allow Fox to continue as is without adhering to the rules.

The second burst of ownership transfers began in the mid-1990s. Once again, Congress and the FCC made a critical contribution to these changes. The elimination of the numerical limit on station ownership and increase in the national market penetration limit to 35 percent codified in the Telecommunications Act of 1996 opened the door for the merger between Westinghouse and CBS. What is significant about this combination is that it occurred even before the Telecom Act became law. The combination of Westinghouse and CBS gave the new corporation ownership of sixteen television stations with a national reach of 32 percent. The FCC approved the transfer of the CBS station licenses to Westinghouse in November 1995, granting a series of temporary waivers of its ownership rules in the process. As is often the case, Westing-house and CBS gambled that the ownership rules would change or that the government would waive compliance of such limitations.[81]

While the relaxation of the national ownership rule fueled many combinations over the decade that followed, the expiration of the Financial Interest and Syndication Rules in 1995 had the biggest impact on network ownership. ABC was the first to fall in 1996 when Disney completed its acquisition of Capital Cities/ABC for $19 billion. This created vertical integration between ABC and the Disney studios, including Touchstone Television. CBS followed suit in 2000 when the FCC approved its merger with Viacom, valued at $46 billion, which formed a vertical bond between the network and Paramount Pictures. In 2004, NBC and Universal Pictures combined under the mantle of NBC Universal, with General Electric holding an 80 percent interest in the new corporation. With these combinations, the big three networks and their corporate brethren could capitalize on the benefits of vertical integration, much as Fox did from its launch in 1986, and UPN and The WB did from their debuts in 1995. While the advantages of integration to the networks and studios are clear, the implications are quite serious. Chapter 5 explores the impact of this integration on prime time program ownership.

The speed with which the media conglomerates responded to changes in ownership rules is quite remarkable. The FCC issued its Report & Order on television duopolies in August 1999, allowing for ownership of two stations in markets with at least eight independently owned stations. Viacom and CBS needed that change to unite, and they announced their merger just one month later in September 1999. The combination of the Viacom and CBS station groups created duopolies in six cities, including four of the ten largest markets: Philadelphia, Boston, Dallas, and Detroit. The FCC did not modify its dual network rule to allow common ownership of one of the big four networks and an emerging network until the spring of 2000, which removed the final barrier for CBS and UPN to reside together under the Viacom umbrella. Once again, a corporation moved forward, confident that Congress or the FCC would change the rules to accommodate their needs.

The impact that federal deregulation and market consolidation had on the ownership of broadcast networks is clear. In 1984, when the onslaught began, there were six major motion picture studios and three broadcast networks, and nine different corporations owned these studios and networks. Two decades later, there were three more broadcast networks, but these additions did not result in more voices in the marketplace. With the integration of Universal Pictures and NBC under the mantel of NBC Universal in the spring of 2004, there were six major studios and six broadcast networks within just six integrated and diversified media conglomerates. Table 3.1 details the ownership of these corporations at the start of 2005. Control varies a great deal, from General Electric, with ownership dispersed and no executive or member of the board owning more than one-tenth of one percent of the outstanding

Table 3.1. Ownership of Major Television Networks and Beneficial Ownership of Parent Corporations, as of January 2005

Network	Ownership Group	Parent Corporation(s)	Beneficial Ownership of more than 5% of Common Stock or Notable Parties under 5%.
ABC	ABC, Inc.	The Walt Disney Co.	No Single Person or Group has Beneficial Ownership of more than 5% of the common stock.
CBS	CBS Broadcasting Inc.	Viacom Inc.	Sumner Redstone (71.2%)[a] Gabelli Asset Management Inc. (6.8%)
Fox	Fox Entertainment Group Inc.	News Corp. (82%)	Rupert Murdoch (30%)[b] Liberty Media Corp. (9%) FMR Corp. (7%)
NBC	NBC Universal, Inc.	General Electric (80%)	No Single Person or Group has Beneficial Ownership of more than 5% of the common stock.
		Vivendi Universal (20%)	No Single Person or Group has Beneficial Ownership of more than 5% of the common stock.
UPN	United Paramount Network	Viacom Inc.	Sumner Redstone (71.2%) Gabelli Asset Management Inc. (6.8%)
WB	WB Television Network	Time Warner Inc. (78%)	Capital Research & Management (7.2%) Comcast Corp. (2.9%)
		Tribune Co. (22%)	R. McCormick Tribune Found. (13.32%) The Chandler Trusts (11.61%) Vanguard Fiduciary Trust Company (6.93%)

[a] Sumner Redstone controlled his shares through National Amusements, Inc.
[b] Rupert Murdoch controlled his shares through Cruden Investments.

shares, to Viacom, with Sumner Redstone controlling over 70 percent of the outstanding shares and wielding both allocative and operational control over the corporation.

The rewrite of FCC rules that spurred the integration of the major studios and broadcast networks also impacted secondary and Spanish-language networks. Just one week after Viacom and CBS consummated their merger in 1999, NBC announced that it was acquiring a 32 percent interest in Paxson Communications and the fledgling PaxNet for $415 million. The deal included an option for NBC to obtain total control of Paxson and the two companies later signed joint sales agreements in twelve markets with NBC-owned and-operated stations.[82] Since NBC held a non-voting interest in a corporation with a single majority shareholder, Lowell "Bud" Paxson, and its interest remained below 33 percent, the Pax stations did not count against the 35 percent national cap or the revised local ownership limits. This enabled NBC to acquire the Spanish-language Telemundo network and its 10 owned and operated local stations in October of 2001 for $1.98 billion. Unlike the deal with Paxson in which it remained at arms length, NBC folded Telemundo into its overall operation.

The ownership of the leading Spanish-language network, Univision, remained outside the reach of the dominant U.S. media conglomerates, but that did not mean there were not ownership issues.[83] In 2002, Univision followed the dual-network model that Viacom forged with CBS and UPN and created a second broadcast network designed to attract the 18–49 Hispanic audience, Telefutura. The relaxation of the local ownership rules fueled the expansion of the new network as Univision Communications went from ownership of twelve full-power and seven low-power local stations at the end of 1999 to a juggernaut with thirty-seven full-power stations and twenty-four low-power stations at the start of 2005.[84] This group included multiple stations in five of the ten largest markets—New York, Los Angeles, Chicago, San Francisco, and Dallas—as well as four others with prominent Hispanic communities: Phoenix, Miami, Sacramento, and Fresno. Univision also held a 30 percent non-voting interest in Entravision Communications, which owned and operated forty-seven full-power and low-power stations at the start of 2005, with all but four affiliated with either Univision or Telefutura.[85] Entravision owned and operated duopolies in a number of prominent Hispanic markets, including Albuquerque, San Diego, and Harlingen and El Paso, Texas, and combined with Univision-owned stations to complete virtual duopolies in Boston, Washington DC, Tampa, and Orlando.[86] The dominance of Univision in the Spanish-language market was almost complete.

Broadcast Television Stations

The integration of the established broadcast networks into vast entertainment empires drew what little attention was devoted to issues related to broadcast ownership prior to the summer of 2003. What went unnoticed was the tremendous consolidation in ownership of local television stations. This is a critical issue, since "localism" has been an ideal in broadcast regulation in the United States since the advent of radio. The notion that broadcast stations should be licensed in local communities so that they respond to local wants and needs and reflect local tastes, not the political, social, and economic agendas of vast corporations, is of utmost importance, although one can argue that true localism does not and cannot exist at a network affiliate in the modern era. As mentioned earlier, the connection between ownership and localism was even lost on Michael Powell, who created his Localism Task Force after an uproar in Congress and the public at large greeted the Commission's revised ownership rules in 2003.

The ownership of local television stations, while often overlooked, is quite significant, since local stations are the financial lifeblood of the national networks. In fiscal 1997, for example, the CBS network lost $107 million on $2.8 billion in revenues, compared to a profit of $325 million on $836 million in revenues for CBS's fourteen owned and operated stations.[87] The financial troubles of the network were numerous, but it was attributable in large part to higher program costs and lower audience levels in desired demographic groups. The revenues that local affiliates generate prompted the established networks to argue that the FCC or Congress must raise or eliminate the ownership limits so that free-to-air television can survive. That was the battle cry of network executives in their discussions with the FCC over the course of the 2002 Biennial Regulatory Review, but it was not a new argument. Bob Iger, then president of ABC, made a similar appeal in the summer of 1998 before the Senate Judiciary Committee. He argued that without a further relaxation of the ownership limits, the television networks would cease to exist.

The desire to own more local stations was not the only change Iger believed broadcast networks needed to survive. At the NAB convention in 1998, he argued that, "We need to re-examine our entire business, and nothing should be sacrosanct."[88] Among his targets in that speech was one of the most venerated of all relationships in broadcast television, that between the broadcast networks and their affiliates.[89] The connection between networks and their affiliates is unique: the networks spend millions of dollars to develop and produce programs and then deliver them to their affiliates, free of charge. For decades, moreover, the networks provided financial compensation to their affiliates to air programs in their local communities, a practice that dates back to the 1920s when NBC paid $50 for each hour of network-sponsored programming aired.

The commercial nature of broadcast television in the United States dictates that such a structure must exist. National advertisements provide the main revenue stream for the broadcast networks, and the size of the audience determines the price of commercial units. The difference between successful shows and also-rans is significant. In 2003–2004, for example, *Advertising Age* reported the price of a thirty-second commercial for *Friends* on NBC at $473,500, while ABC generated just $66,375 in the same time block for *Threat*

Matrix. This makes the "clearance" of a program, the decision of a local station to place it on its schedule, essential for the success of a network since a program cannot generate big numbers unless it receives ratings in markets nationwide. While a local station would clear shows such as *Seinfeld*, the networks oftentimes struggle to obtain clearances for low-rated shows and in other day-parts: soap operas, and talk shows in the afternoon and sports and news programs on the weekends. When David Letterman first switched from NBC to CBS, in fact, the ratings for his show were lower than projected, and the percentage of clearances was one factor.[90] The failure to clear a program has a deleterious impact on its ratings and, in turn, the rates the networks can charge for national spots, as well as the ability of a program to generate momentum and build an audience.

Federal regulations prohibit a network from forcing an affiliate to broadcast a program, although, as discussed in sidebar 3.2, the Commission was slow to respond when the Network Affiliated Stations Alliance argued that the networks were doing just that in 2001. Local stations can decline to broadcast a network program for various reasons, including a determination that the content is inconsistent with contemporary community standards. To induce local stations to clear their programs, ABC, CBS, and NBC long provided financial compensation to their stations. In the 1990s, the cost was in the neighborhood of $200 and $300 million for each of the networks, a total divided among two hundred or so affiliates.[91] This model has been under assault over the last decade, with the networks working hard to reduce affiliate fees. In 2000, Gannett and NBC reached a new six-year agreement for thirteen stations, including affiliates in Atlanta, Minneapolis, and Phoenix, that reportedly reduced network compensation from $25 million to $10 million per annum.[92] The previous year, ABC affiliates agreed to reverse compensation that totaled $45 million per annum to help the network cover the rights fee for *ABC's Monday Night Football*, with ABC also receiving the right to repurpose 25 percent of its prime time entertainment programming on cable or other platforms.[93]

The Fox network has followed a different path. It has long received reverse compensation from its affiliates, reported to total $1 million to $1.2 million per month for the network, and negotiated a cost-sharing agreement with its affiliates to help cover its NFL contract in 2003.[94] There is little question that the Fox business model is different than the older networks, with fewer prime time hours and the absence of a nightly news program, late-night programming, and afternoon soap operas. There was another important difference, however, as the Fox station group long included more affiliated stations than the other established networks. In the historic 2004–2005 season in which Fox claimed the season-long contest for the 18–49 demographic, the network owned and operated twenty-five of its affiliates, which reached just under 45 percent of television households nationwide. This group included Fox affiliates in nine of the ten largest markets, with San Francisco-Oakland the lone exception, and sixteen of the top twenty. The ownership of these stations

Sidebar 3.2
The Major Networks and Their Affiliated Stations: A Marriage on the Rocks

It is somehow appropriate that *Married by America,* a reality-based program on Fox that trivialized matrimony, revealed the tension that exists in the marriage between the major broadcast networks and their affiliated stations.[1] The April 7, 2003, episode of the show featured explicit scenes from bachelor and bachelorette parties in a hotel in Las Vegas, which the FCC later ruled included material that was "patently offensive as measured by contemporary community standards for the broadcast medium, and is therefore indecent."[2] The FCC proposed a $7,000 fine for each Fox station that broadcast the episode, including the affiliates that the network did not own, arguing that it was a taped show and, as such, the affiliated stations could have preempted it. While federal regulations give an affiliate the right to reject network programs it believes to be "unsatisfactory or unsuitable or contrary to the public interest," the realities of the network-affiliate relationship are quite different.[3]

In its announcement, the FCC focused on the fact that one Fox affiliate rejected the episode of *Married by America* that contained the actionable material. Capitol Broadcasting pulled the series from WRAZ-TV in Raleigh after the first episode, stating that the show "did not reflect prevailing standards of good taste" and was "clearly demeaning to the institution of marriage."[4] That is what the right to reject rules are all about, giving local stations the power to broadcast what is most appropriate for their communities. While the networks insist that affiliates are free to make such decisions, others argue that there is a huge gap between the letter of the law and the realities of everyday life.

Pappas Telecasting was among the companies fined for the broadcast of the *Married by America* episode, thanks to the ownership of Fox affiliates in Sioux City, Fresno, Lincoln, and Omaha. Harry Pappas painted a different picture of the network-affiliate relationship at one of the FCC localism hearings in 2004:

> Today, local affiliates have been virtually stripped of any right to receive network programming in advance and to evaluate its content. An affiliate is now asked to pay compensation, and even risks losing its affiliation, if it preempts more than a specified number of hours of Big Four network programming. And as the result of unduly relaxed federal oversight, the Big Four networks are in a position to effectively deny local stations the ability to reject network programs that may simply be unsuitable for their markets, or to substitute programs of greater local interest or importance.[5]

Pappas operated a large group of local stations affiliated with CBS, ABC, UPN, and WB in addition to Fox, so he was familiar with the realities of the network-affiliate relationship.

This marriage has long been tumultuous, but the situation has taken a decided turn over the last decade. The connection is based on simple economics: networks need to broadcast in all local markets to sell national advertising, while affiliates need popular programming to attract audiences and sell local advertising of their own. While the basic structure has remained constant, the balance of power between the two parties has changed. In the three decades between the mid-1950s and mid-1980s when the FCC limited group ownership to just seven stations, the networks

(Continued)

were more reliant on their nonowned and operated affiliates and paid significant affiliate fees to maintain connections with prominent stations. The steady increase in national ownership rules has allowed the networks to own more of their affiliates. In addition to aiding the bottom line of their parent corporations, this also altered the relationship between the networks and their nonaligned affiliates.

The relaxation of the ownership limits has the potential to undermine two of the cornerstones of localism. In its 2002 Biennial Regulatory Review, the Commission argued that affiliates promote localism in two manners: the preemption of network programming by individual stations to provide something better suited for local audiences and collective negotiations to influence the programming that the networks provide. While owned and operated stations maintain the same right to reject programs as nonaligned affiliates, it is folly to think that the manager of such a station would preempt network programming deemed to be inappropriate and remain in a decision-making position for very long.[6] The more stations that the government allows the networks to own, the fewer that might preempt a program for cause. These increases also alter the balance in collective negotiations with the networks, since discussions over the merits of a given program change when networks hold the votes of larger blocks of stations.

Married by America provides an example of these issues. The FCC found the licensees of 169 Fox-affiliated stations had broadcast indecent material, including twenty-five stations that News Corp. owned and operated through the Fox Entertainment Group. This total included stations in nine of the ten largest markets, and sixteen of the top twenty. The potential audience of those sixteen stations alone was over 37 percent of the national total and the combined reach of the Fox-owned and -operated stations was just under 45 percent of all television households nationwide. None of the Fox-owned and -operated stations preempted *Married by America,* including KSTU in Salt Lake City, UT. This stands in sharp contrast to KSL, the NBC affiliate in the same market, which does not broadcast *Saturday Night Live* and preempted *Coupling* in 2003, responding to "abnormally high" complaints from viewers to a promotional campaign that focused on the sexual content of the show. While one could attribute these decisions to the fact that the Mormon Church operates KSL, one could also argue that local ownership was responding to the contemporary community standards in Salt Lake City.

The response of the FCC to the rising power of the broadcast networks over their affiliates has been quite limited, which stands in sharp contrast to the Commission's reaction to the dominance of the NBC and CBS radio networks prior to World War II. In the 1930s, the FCC became concerned with the power of the radio networks and affiliate contracts that limited the range within which licensees could program their stations. The FCC issued the Report on Chain Broadcasting in 1941 and while it is best remembered for forcing the separation of the two NBC networks, it also established parameters for the business relationship between networks and their affiliates that were consistent with the "public service" obligations of broadcasters.[7] NBC fought these regulations in court, but in 1943 the Supreme Court ruled that it was within the authority of the Commission to issue regulations pertaining to the business relationships between networks and their affiliates.

The reaction of the FCC some six decades later was altogether different. In 2001, the Network Affiliated Stations Alliance (NASA) petitioned the FCC to institute an inquiry into whether certain practices of the top four television networks were "consistent with the Commission's network rules, the Communications Act and the public interest."[8] The FCC did not even issue a notice on the NASA petition for over three years, during which it attempted to raise the station ownership cap and allow the networks to acquire more local stations. The FCC did not rule on the matter before Michael Powell stepped down as chair in March of 2005. A few weeks earlier, the four networks urged the FCC to reject the NASA request for the Commission to provide further guidance on affiliate and network agreements contending, "The Commission appears to recognize that the government generally should avoid influencing the outcome of private disputes."[9] While the disputes were indeed private, the airwaves in question were public, and the FCC had a statutory obligation to ensure that the networks were not abusing their power.

NOTES

1. In *Married by America* five couples were engaged, sight unseen, based on votes from the viewing audience. A panel of judges eliminated one couple each week, until the final episode when the two remaining couples were to be married, with the one voted most compatible receiving a $500,000 wedding gift.

2. Federal Communications Commission, "Notice of Apparent Liability for Forfeiture," "In the Matter of Complaints Against Various Licenses Regarding Their Broadcast of the Fox Television Network Program 'Married by America' on April 7, 2003," FCC 04–242.

3. "Affiliation Agreements And Network Program Practices," Code of Federal Regulations, 47 C.F.R. 73.658.

4. Quoted in Adrienne Johnson Martin, "Raleigh, MC Fox Affiliate Pulls Network Program from Its Lineup," *News & Observer*, 11 March 2003.

5. Harry J. Pappas, "Statement of Harry J. Pappas, Federal Communications Commission Broadcast Localism Hearing," Federal Communications Commission, 21 July 2004.

6. It is important to note that the Commission requested that the networks provide data that compares preemptions between owned and operated affiliates and nonaligned affiliates, but the networks withheld that information.

7. These regulations included affiliate rights to reject programs and broadcast programs from multiple networks and limitations on network influence over affiliate advertising rates and power to option time from local stations.

8. Federal Communications Commission, "Comment Sought on 'Petition for Inquiry into Network Practices,'" FCC 01-1264, 22 May 2001.

9. "Leave Relations Between Networks, Affiliates to Them, Big 4 Tell FCC," *Television A.M.*, 1 March 2005.

placed considerable power in the hands of Fox executives, who did not need to fret about clearances for programs such as *Married by America*. The concentration of such decision-making is one reason that the examination of station ownership is so important.

Consolidation in Ownership of Broadcast Television Stations

The relaxation of FCC rules that limit the ownership of multiple broadcast stations in a local market had a huge impact on the television and radio landscape. What were once large station groups have become vast empires that span the nation, while the number of midsize, oftentimes regional station groups has declined to a dramatic degree. True local ownership of television and radio stations, long presented as a critical component of broadcast regulation in the United States, has all but disappeared. To be certain, there are television and radio stations in major markets that have local ownership. In 2005, longtime Miami resident Edmund Ansin continued to own the Fox affiliate in that market, WSVN, a station he purchased for $185,000 in 1967. Even the largest broadcast chains, moreover, have historic roots in some region of the nation where the parent corporation oftentimes owns stations with a local connection. Belo Corp., which is the oldest continuously operated business in the state of Texas, began 2005 as the dominant force in Dallas with control of the *Dallas Morning News* and ABC affiliate WFAA, with additional ownership of CBS affiliates in Houston and San Antonio and the ABC affiliate in Austin.

There are far more television and radio stations, however, which are owned and controlled by corporations with little or no connection to the communities in which most of their broadcast stations operate. The changes in multiple ownership rules in the Telecom Act ushered in a period of unparalleled broadcast license transfers. In 1996, the total price of television and radio station sales in the United States reached $25.4 billion, a 204 percent increase over 1995.[95] This sum surpassed $22.7 billion in both 1997 and 1998, raising the three-year total to $71.6 billion, more than the four previous decades combined. The impact was most evident in the radio marketplace, as Congress eliminated all national limits on radio stations and allowed for the local ownership of up to eight stations in markets with forty-five or more stations. These changes resulted in an unprecedented period of horizontal integration. The merger of three of the most prominent radio groups in the nation, which occurred with the combination of Westinghouse and CBS in 1995 and subsequent acquisition of Infinity Broadcasting in 1996, prompted the most headlines, but there were many others. Clear Channel owned sixteen AM and twenty FM stations at the start of 1996, but those totals reached 367 AM and 822 FM stations at the start of 2005.[96]

Television station groups were not as large as those in radio, but the speed and scope of acquisitions followed the same pattern. The 1996 Act removed the numerical limit on the number of television stations under common ownership and raised to 35 percent the percentage of television households nationwide a station group could reach, based on the designated market area of those stations.[97] The speed with which the large station groups responded to the changes in the FCC rules was remarkable. As discussed earlier, the FCC approved the merger of Westinghouse and CBS before the 1996 Act even cleared Congress, and there were numerous other deals in the months that followed its signing in February 1996. In a six-month period between April and September, there were four deals valued at over $1 billion each that involved station groups that remain prominent: Sinclair and River City Broadcasting; News Corp. and New World Communications; Tribune Co. and Renaissance

Communication; and Belo and The Providence Journal Co. These changes had a profound impact on the television landscape, in terms of social, political, and economic power on the national level and in terms of the relationship between broadcast stations and the communities served at the local level.

There has been dramatic change in the size and scope of local station groups since 1996. The decision to remove the numerical limit on stations under common ownership and raise the national ceiling to 35 percent of television households, and the subsequent change to allow ownership of multiple stations in local markets, transformed local television. The impact of these rule changes is most evident in table 3.2, which outlines the twenty largest station groups at the start of 2005. The cornerstones of the Viacom and News Corp. empires were huge station groups that reach just under 45 percent of television station households nationwide. The prominence of these two groups exceeded this percentage, however, as it does not account for a combined total of eighteen duopolies that the two operate in major markets. The focal points of the two station groups were the CBS and Fox affiliates, but what is most interesting is that either Viacom or News Corp. owned the UPN affiliate in each of the top ten markets. This raises obvious questions about the degree to which the media conglomerates are true competitors and whether the emergence of new broadcast networks has increased the diversity of voices in local communities.

The White House and Congress settled on a national ownership cap to 39 percent in 2004, which was significant since it was the lowest number at that time that would not force Viacom or News Corp. to sell stations, as both were just below that number when the FCC utilized the UHF discount.[98] These station groups were not the only ones to eclipse the 39 percent barrier in real terms at the start of 2005, however. Paxson Communications took full advantage of the discount to build the Pax TV Network, owning fifty-three UHF stations that reached over 63 percent of television households nationwide. What is significant about the Paxson model is that it acquired less powerful stations and then utilized the FCC's must-carry provisions to force cable operators to include its stations in their basic tiers, which mitigated the relative weakness of the UHF signal. Univision Communications took a similar approach and the combination of the Spanish-language Univision and Telefutura station groups gave Univision a total reach of 43.42 percent. The Tribune Co. also exceeded 39 percent with a collection that included at least one station in eight of the top ten markets and sixteen of the top twenty-five. NBC Universal was just below the number, without counting its ownership stake in Paxson Communications.

The other numbers that are striking in table 3.2 is the size of the modern station group. Viacom, News Corp., Tribune, and NBC Universal built their lineup around stations in major markets and owned or operated between twenty-six and thirty-six stations less than a decade after the FCC limit stood at twelve. Just as significant are corporations that have come to dominate

Table 3.2. Largest Station Groups Based on Common Ownership and/or Operation and Ranked by Total Households Reached, as of January 2005

Station Group & Ownership	Total Stations Owned & Operated [a]	Stations in Top 25/50 Markets	FCC Coverage [b]	Total Coverage
Paxson Communications Paxson Communications Corp.	53	22/38	31.65%	63.30%
Viacom Television Stations Group Viacom, Inc.	36	26/33	38.75%	44.64%
Fox Television Stations News Corp. (82%)	35	27/33	37.85%	44.48%
Univision & Telefutura Groups Univision Communications	36	26/30	22.63%	43.42%
Tribune Broadcasting Tribune Co.	26	18/25	29.91%	40.13%
NBC Universal Television Stations General Electric (80%) Vivendi Universal (20%)	29	19/26	33.62%	38.65%
Trinity Broadcasting Network Trinity Broadcasting Network	23	11/16	16.92%	33.83%
ABC TV Station Group The Walt Disney Co.	10	6/7	23.30%	23.54%
Sinclair Broadcast Group Sinclair Broadcast Group, Inc.	62	8/33	13.53%	22.74%
Scripps Howard Broadcasting The E.W. Scripps Co.	15	9/14	13.99%	21.85%
Hearst-Argyle Television Hearst-Argyle Television, Inc.	28	8/20	16.51%	18.17%
Gannett Broadcasting Gannet Co., Inc.	20	9/12	17.69%	17.86%
Belo Television Group Belo Corp.	20	8/14	13.11%	13.83%
Entravision Communications Univision Comm. (32%)	36	10/20	6.61%	13.13%
Clear Channel Clear Channel Communications	40	2/10	9.02%	13.08%
Pappas Telecasting Pappas Telecasting Co.	20	3/4	7.68%	12.41%
Raycom Media Raycom Media Inc.	33	2/6	7.66%	10.20%
Cox Television Cox Enterprises Inc.	15	7/9	10.02%	10.15%
Meredith Broadcasting Group Meredith Corp.	14	4/9	7.65%	9.26%
Media General Television Division Media General Inc.	22	1/5	7.14%	8.06%

[a] These totals include low-power stations that are affiliates with a network but not satellite stations.

[b] The FCC attributes half of the market size for stations using UHF frequencies under the "UHF Discount."

midsize and smaller markets through vast chains. Sinclair Broadcast Group and Clear Channel Communications are the best examples of this trend, with control of sixty-two and forty stations, respectively, at the start of 2005, with just ten of these stations in top ten markets.[99] Other groups that did not rank among the top twenty in terms of total reach acquired a significant number of stations. The stated goal of Nexstar Broadcasting is to acquire stations in medium-sized markets, and it owned and operated twenty-eight stations and managed another seventeen stations at the start of 2005.[100] Perhaps most significant is the fact that Nexstar operated multiple stations in fifteen of the twenty-seven markets, including three in the Wichita Falls, Texas-Lawton, Oklahoma market where it owned the NBC affiliate and also operated the Fox and UPN stations.

It is difficult to generalize about the nature of ownership of local stations since most markets have unique characterizations and combinations, with Wichita Falls-Lawton an example of this. There are clear trends, however. In 2005, the four big broadcast networks combined—ABC, CBS, Fox, and NBC—owned twenty-nine of their forty affiliates in the top ten markets, including all of them in the four largest markets: New York, Los Angeles, Chicago, and Philadelphia.[101] While the big four have focused on the largest markets, other station groups looked elsewhere to extend their reach. The Mobile-Pensacola market provides a vivid example of what this has done to the local television landscape. Sinclair Broadcast Group, Emmis Communication, and Clear Channel Communications each owned a station affiliated with one of the big four networks in Mobile-Pensacola. What is most significant, however, is the fact that each of these conglomerates also owned and operated a second station in this market, the UPN affiliate in the case of Clear Channel, the WB affiliate in the case of Emmis, and an independent station in the case of Sinclair, giving the market three active duopolies. Media General owned the CBS affiliate. That meant that corporations located in Maryland, Virginia, Indiana, and Texas exercised almost total control over a television market located on the Gulf of Mexico.

The death of local ownership and demise of regional station groups over the last two decades is evident in countless cities. In the mid-1980s, the Seattle television market featured three stations with strong local ownership, while a fourth, KIRO-TV, was one-half of the two-station Bonneville International group.[102] KOMO-TV, the ABC affiliate, remained under the control of the descendents of O. D. Fisher, who launched his first radio station in Seattle in 1926 and ventured into television in 1953. That was five years after Dorothy Bullitt opened the doors of KING-TV, which she ran with a strong public service commitment until her death in 1990.[103] The third member of the local triad was Robert E. Kelly who operated an independent station, KCPQ, through Kelly Television Co. Two decades later, the Seattle television scene is altogether different. In 2005, the Tribune Co. owned the Fox (KCPQ) and WB (KTWB) affiliates, while Belo Corp. controlled the NBC affiliate (KING), the most prominent independent station (KONG), and a regional cable news channel. The UPN affiliate (KSTW) was part of the Viacom group, while Cox Enterprises owned the CBS affiliate, KIRO. Clear Channel operated an independent television station (KVOS) but was more prominent in radio with the ownership of five local stations. There are far more television outlets in Seattle than there were decades earlier, but diversified media conglomerates ruled where local families were once dominant, and KOMO was the one local voice that remained.

The station groups that are prominent in Mobile-Pensacola and Seattle have contributed to a remarkable occurrence: the number of local television stations has increased over the last fifteen years, with 25 percent more VHF and UHF stations and almost three times as many low-power stations, but the number of individuals and corporations owning stations has decreased in prominent areas. This is a significant change. The creation of giant station groups translates into social, political, and economic power on the national level, but it also raises serious doubts about whether local stations are responding to the wants and needs of their communities or some other authority. The mandate within the Sinclair Broadcast Group that its stations broadcast a program that included several minutes from a controversial documentary, *Stolen Honor: Wounds That Never Heal,* in the weeks leading up to the 2004 general election raises serious concerns. So does the decision of all News Corp.-owned and-operated Fox affiliates to broadcast *Married by America.* Sidebar 3.3 addresses the Sinclair case in more detail.

Consolidation in the local television marketplace in the 1980s and 1990s was profound and attributable to Congressional action in 1984 and again in 1996. The number of individuals and corporations that owned a local station affiliated with ABC, CBS, or NBC in the fifty largest markets decreased 44.0 percent between 1982 and 1998, 38.2 percent between 1994 and 1998 alone. The ownership figures for these three networks, detailed in table 3.3, indicate that much of this consolidation occurred in markets outside the top ten where local ownership was once more common. For example, the number of corporations that owned a station affiliated with one of the three long-established networks in the five largest markets at the time—New York, Los Angeles, Chicago, Philadelphia, and San Francisco—did not change to a dramatic degree between 1982 and 1998. There was also little variation in the top ten as a whole, with a decrease from a high of seventeen different corporations in 1986 to fourteen corporations in 1998. Where the most profound change came was in markets eleven through fifty, as numerous smaller station groups, as well as most stations that stood alone in the portfolio of an individual or corporation, merged into larger groups. The number of individuals or corporations that owned an ABC, CBS, or NBC affiliate in one of the twenty-five largest markets decreased from forty-three to twenty-four (44.2 percent) between 1982 and 1998, while the decrease in the top fifty markets was from seventy-five to forty-two (44 percent) in the same period.

Sidebar 3.3
The Abuse of Ownership: Sinclair Broadcast Group and the
Public Airwaves

It was one of the polarizing stories of the 2004 presidential campaign. A month before the general election, the *Los Angeles Times* reported that the Sinclair Broadcast Group intended to broadcast a documentary critical of John Kerry, *Stolen Honor: Wounds That Never Heal,* on its local television stations. Sinclair controlled the largest station group in the nation, with sixty-two stations spread across thirty-nine markets, and several were located in critical battleground states. In Ohio alone, it operated the WB affiliate in Cincinnati and both the ABC and Fox affiliates in Columbus and Dayton as well as the Charleston-Huntington market in West Virginia that served over one hundred thousand television households in the southern part of the state. A Sinclair representative argued that the documentary was newsworthy because Kerry had "made his Vietnam service a foundation of his presidential campaign" and because it had not been out in the "news marketplace."[1] Six months earlier, the ABC affiliates in Columbus, Dayton, and Charleston were among the Sinclair stations that preempted an installment of *Nightline* in which Ted Koppel read the names of U.S. soldiers killed in Iraq, with the conglomerate arguing that it was a political statement "disguised as news."[2]

The *Stolen Honor* revelation created a firestorm, with much of the reaction along party lines. The Democratic National Committee filed a complaint with the Federal Election Commission, arguing that the film was an illegal in-kind contribution, while a group of Democratic senators sent a letter to the Federal Communications Commission (FCC) asking it to investigate whether the broadcast of a "blatantly partisan attack in lieu of regular programming" was improper use of the public airwaves. FCC chairman Michael Powell argued that it would be prior restraint to block a program before it was broadcast, and such action would be unconstitutional. More significant than the backlash in political circles was the impact on its bottom line. The Sinclair stock price dropped after news of *Stolen Honor* broke, and public interest groups launched campaigns to pressure companies to pull their advertisements from Sinclair stations. In the end, excerpts from *Stolen Honor* aired in a one-hour program titled *A P.O.W. Story: Politics, Pressure and the Media* on one Sinclair station in each market.[3]

Lost in the partisan wrangling over *Stolen Honor* were important questions: to what degree did broadcast deregulation that allowed Sinclair to expand from control of eleven stations in 1995 to sixty-two stations in 2005 contribute to its decision-making, and what are the implications for the communities in which it operates. As discussed in sidebar 3.2, the Commission has long maintained the right of affiliated stations to reject network programs and provide something better suited for local audiences. Similar issues arise when a group owner mandates that stations in diverse communities respond to the political, social, or economic agenda of their parent corporations rather than serve their local audience as their license demands. Commissioner Michael Copps argued, "it is proof positive of media consolidation run amok when one owner can use the public airwaves to blanket the country with its political ideology—whether liberal or conservative. . . . It is a sad fact that the explicit

(Continued)

public interest protections we once had to ensure balance continue to be weakened by the Federal Communications Commission while it allows media conglomerates to get even bigger. Sinclair, and the FCC, are taking us down a dangerous road."[4]

The order to preempt prime time programming to air *A P.O.W. Story*, as well as the decision to stop its ABC affiliates from broadcasting *Nightline* in April 2004, is consistent with how David D. Smith and his brothers run Sinclair. In 2002, Sinclair launched a centralized news operation that originated from its corporate headquarters in Hunt Valley, Maryland. "News Central" was promoted as a means to increase local news programming in underserved markets, but in numerous cases Sinclair fired entire news operations at local stations before or after the introduction of "central casting."[5] In addition to the financial incentives behind "News Central," there is also a political motive. In the midst of the *Nightline* and *Stolen Honor* controversies, the daily feed included commentaries from Mark Hyman, Sinclair's vice president for corporate relations, called *The Point*. In a September 2004 edition of *The Point*, Hyman argued that "The terrorist leaders would dearly love to see President Bush replaced with Senator Kerry who has a weak Senatorial record when it comes to national defense and fighting terrorism."[6]

In addition to the political leanings of the Smith brothers, there was another reason the Sinclair news operation was supportive of the Bush campaign. Duopolies and Local Marketing Agreements were the foundation for expanded Sinclair prominence in twenty-one of thirty-nine markets at the start of 2005, and President Bush supported the further relaxation of the multiple station ownership rules that the corporation had long championed. In 2002, the Court of Appeals for the DC Circuit remanded the rules to the FCC for further consideration in response to a Sinclair petition for review that argued that limiting common ownership of television stations to markets with eight independent voices was arbitrary and capricious.[7] In 2003, the FCC opened the door for further Sinclair expansion as it voted to allow television "triopolies" in markets with eighteen stations or more and duopolies in markets of seventeen or fewer. That door closed, at least for the time being, when the Court of Appeals for the Third Circuit remanded the rules to the Commission for further consideration. Sinclair petitioned the Supreme Court to overturn that decision, but the Court refused to hear the case.

Sinclair has long used various tactics to circumvent FCC limitations. In 1991, it acquired the Fox affiliate in Pittsburgh, WPGH-TV, from Renaissance Communications. To conform with FCC rules that limited television station ownership to one per market, Sinclair sold WPTT-TV to one of its employees, Eddie Edwards, and continued to operate the station under a Local Marketing Agreement.[8] This became a model for future acquisitions, albeit with a twist. In 1993, Edwards acquired WNUV-TV in Baltimore through Glencairn, Ltd., a corporation in which his main partner and financial backer was Carolyn Smith, the mother of the brothers who controlled Sinclair. Since the Sinclair flagship station, WBFF, was located in Baltimore, it could not purchase WNUV-TV, but it could operate the station under Glencairn ownership. Sinclair repeated this pattern as it expanded into new markets and increased its presence in existing ones.

At the start of 2005, the successor to Glencairn, Cunningham Broadcasting Corp., owned six stations and Sinclair operated each of them. Carolyn Smith had transferred her ownership of the corporation to trusts for her grandchildren, the children of the brothers who own Sinclair. In spite of this connection, the FCC held that these stations were not under common ownership and that Sinclair was not in violation of the multiple ownership rules. The lengths the Republican-controlled FCC went to protect Sinclair was most evident in 2001. In its review of the transfer of the Sullivan Broadcasting stations to Sinclair and Glencairn, which other station groups and civil-rights organizations challenged, the Commission concluded that Sinclair did exercise de facto control of Glencairn and that there had been unauthorized transfers of control in violation of FCC rules. Rather than blocking the sale of the fourteen Sullivan stations or stripping Sinclair of other licenses, the three Republicans on the Commission concluded that there was no intent to deceive, issued a $40,000 fine, and approved the deal.

NOTES

1. Quoted in Jim Rutenberg, "Broadcast Group to Pre-empt Programs for Anti-Kerry Film," *New York Times*, 11 October 2004, 19.

2. Quoted in Michele Greppi, "Sinclair Plans Review of Show Pre-emption," *Television Week*, 10 May 2004, 7.

3. Two of those markets were the largest in Iowa, Des Moines and Cedar Rapids, where George W. Bush carried the state by just 10,059 votes.

4. Michael J. Copps, "FCC Commissioner Copps Criticizes Sinclair Corporate Decision to Preempt Local Stations for Political Broadcast," Federal Communications Commission, 11 October 2004.

5. In 2001, Sinclair closed the news operation of KDNL, the ABC affiliate in St. Louis, which made it the lone ABC, CBS, Fox, or NBC affiliate in a top twenty-five market without a local newscast.

6. Quoted in "Sinclair and the Public Airwaves: A History of Abuse," *Free Press*, 11 October 2004.

7. *Sinclair Broadcast Group, Inc. v. Federal Communications Commission*, 350 U.S. App. DC 313 (2002).

8. The terms were quite favorable, as Edward is reported to have purchased the station with a $10 down payment and a $7 million loan from Sinclair.

Table 3.3. Individuals and Corporations with Ownership of Television Stations in the 50 Largest Markets Affiliated with the ABC, CBS, or NBC Television Networks, 1982–1998

	1982	1986	1990	1994	1998
Individuals & Corporations with Network Affiliates in Top 5 Markets	6	6	5	5	4
Individuals & Corporations with Network Affiliates in Top 10 Markets	16	17	16	16	14
Individuals & Corporations with Network Affiliates in Top 25 Markets	43	39	33	32	24
Individuals & Corporations with Network Affiliates in Top 50 Markets	75	69	70	68	42

Note: Ownership based on data in *Broadcasting & Cable Yearbook.*

Table 3.4. Individuals and Corporations with Control of a Television Station in the 50 Largest Markets Affiliated with the ABC, CBS, FOX, or NBC Television Networks, 1990–1998

	1990	*1994*	*1998*
Individuals & Corporations with Network Affiliates in Top 5 Markets	8	8	6
Individuals & Corporations with Network Affiliates in Top 10 Markets	19	20	15
Individuals & Corporations with Network Affiliates in Top 25 Markets	46	42	26
Individuals & Corporations with Network Affiliates in Top 50 Markets	93	83	49

Note: Ownership based on data in *Broadcasting & Cable Yearbook*.

The FCC and other federal agencies long argued that the creation of additional broadcast networks would increase the diversity of voices in the television marketplace, but based on ownership alone that is not the case. The evolution of the Fox network over its first two decades provides an important measure of whether additional broadcast networks, given federal regulations that allow for increased ownership at the national and local levels, promote marketplace diversity or not. Table 3.4 documents the period between 1990 and 1998, with the Fox totals included with those of ABC, CBS, and NBC. To be certain, when the network first became prominent, there were a number of new owners in the marketplace. In 1990, News Corp. owned the Fox affiliates in seven of the ten largest markets, but sixteen different corporations controlled the Fox stations in the other top twenty-five markets. Some of those affiliates had strong connections to the communities in which those stations were located, as the aforementioned Edmund Ansin owned the Fox affiliate in Miami, while Malrite Communications Group and Sinclair Broadcast Group owned Fox affiliates in their corporate homes, Cleveland and Baltimore, respectively. Such examples were even more common in markets twenty-six through fifty.

The launch of the Fox network did increase the number of individuals and corporations that owned stations affiliated with one of the broadcast networks, but there was a clear decrease between 1994 and 1998. The number of corporations that owned big four affiliates in the five largest markets decreased slightly between 1994 and 1998, and the same occurred in the top ten markets. News Corp. contributed to this consolidation, acquiring its affiliates in Philadelphia, Boston, and Detroit. It acquired WTXF in Philadelphia from Paramount Communications and WFXT in Boston from Boston Celtics L.P, while the Detroit station was one of ten Fox affiliates that News Corp. gained through its purchase of New World Communications in 1996.

The decline is constant as the number of markets measured increases from ten to twenty-five to fifty. Forty-two individuals or corporations owned stations affiliated with one of the four networks in the top twenty-five markets in 1994, but only twenty-six remained at the start of 1998. For the top fifty markets, the number decreased from eighty-three to forty-nine over the same period. What is most evident in this analysis is that the presence of the Fox network did not increase the diversification of ownership of network affiliates, at least not in the fifty largest markets. There were more stations affiliated with a major broadcast network, but this did not translate into actual diversification. Numerical diversity in this case did not equal voice diversity.

Station Ownership in Local Markets: 2004–2005

The local station feeding frenzy that greeted passage of the 1996 Act slowed somewhat between 1999 and 2004 as owners awaited clarification from Congress and the FCC. Viacom and News Corp. were confident enough in their power to persuade that the two conglomerates moved forward with their expansion plans and acquired CBS Inc. and Chris Craft Industries, respectively, which put both well over the 35 percent audience cap. Other station group owners were more cautious, waiting for the ruling of the Court of Appeals for the DC Circuit in *Fox Television Stations, Inc. v. FCC* and the outcome of the FCC's 2002 Biennial Regulatory Review. The Court of Appeals refused to set aside the ownership limit, and the FCC rulemaking brought Congress into the battle. The 39 percent ownership limit gives most groups room to grow, but left unresolved were the prohibition on newspaper/television cross-ownership and ownership of three television stations in large markets.

While this uncertainty slowed some of the dominant station groups, there was still further consolidation in the first half of the decade and the changes since the mid-1990s have been profound. This is evident in table 3.5. There were decreases at each level in the number of individuals and corporations that owned local stations affiliated with one of the big four networks between 1994 and 2005. The reductions in the top ten markets were attributable, in large part, to major mergers and acquisitions. The Viacom Television Stations Group in 2005 included the remnants of the CBS, Westinghouse, and Paramount groups from 1994, and the creation of Hearst-Argyle Television combined two prominent station groups, Hearst Corp. and Argyle Television Holding. The major networks also moved to control more of their most prominent affiliates. NBC, for example, acquired KXAS in Dallas and shifted its affiliation in San Francisco after purchasing KNTV.[104]

The more significant changes occurred outside of the top 10. The number of individuals and corporations that controlled a station in the top twenty-five markets dropped from forty-two in 1994 to twenty-three in 2005, while those in the top fifty markets dropped from eighty-three to forty. News Corp. alone contributed a great deal to this decrease, growing from eight big four affiliates in the top fifty markets in 1994 to twenty-three in 2005. The NBC station group more than doubled, from six to fourteen in this period, while those

Table 3.5.   Individuals and Corporations with Control of a Television Station in the 100 Largest Markets Affiliated with the ABC, CBS, FOX, and NBC Television Networks in 1994 and 2005, and UPN and The WB in 2005

	Big Four 1994	Big Four 2005	Big Six 2005
Individuals & Corporations with Network Affiliates in Top 5 Markets	8	6	7
Individuals & Corporations with Network Affiliates in Top 10 Markets	20	13	15
Individuals & Corporations with Network Affiliates in Top 25 Markets	42	23	27
Individuals & Corporations with Network Affiliates in Top 50 Markets	83	40	51
Individuals & Corporations with Network Affiliates in Top 100 Markets	145	83	109
Individuals & Corporations with Ownership of a Single Big Four Affiliate in Top 100 Markets	89	30	—
Individuals & Corporations with Ownership of a Single Big Six Affiliate in Top 100 Markets	—	—	49

Note: Ownership for 1994 is based on data in *Broadcasting & Cable Yearbook*. Ownership in 2005 is based on station ownership disclosure forms filed with the Federal Communications Commission.

with direct connections to CBS also increased from six to fourteen. There was also a huge drop in ownership and control in the top one hundred markets, which represented over 85 percent of television households nationwide in the 2004–2005 season. There were 145 distinct owners of these affiliates in 1994, but just eighty-three were in control of stations in these markets in 2005.

Much of the overall change is attributable to a dramatic decrease in the number of individuals or corporations that owned just one station affiliated with the four networks, which dropped from eighty-nine in 1994 to just thirty in 2005. The architects of the movement from local or regional ownership to national chains are the station groups that focused on midsize markets. Raycom Media did not even exist in 1994, but it owned nineteen stations affiliated with ABC, CBS, Fox, or NBC in the top one hundred markets in 2005. Clear Channel Communications more than doubled, from seven to fifteen, while Sinclair Broadcast Group increased from three big four affiliates in these markets in 1994 to thirty in 2005. This underrepresents the prominence of these station groups, as Sinclair owned or operated at least one additional station in fifteen of the top one hundred markets in which it owned a big four affiliate.

The evidence makes clear that the evolution of a fourth broadcast network did not increase the diversity of voices in local communities, a promise the FCC advanced on numerous occasions as it waived ownership rules for News

Corp. There was a time when Fox affiliates were more diverse than those from ABC, CBS, and NBC, but that is no longer the case. In 1994, there were fifty-one distinct owners of Fox affiliates in the one hundred largest markets, but in 2005 membership in the group was down to twenty-seven. News Corp. and Sinclair Broadcast Group alone accounted for forty-two Fox affiliates in the top one hundred markets that reached over 53 percent of television households. With the addition of the Fox affiliates from four of the dominant station groups—Tribune, Raycom, Clear Channel, and Emmis—six corporations controlled sixty-four stations that reached over 67 percent of television households. The fate of WMSN in Madison, Wisconsin, is representative of how local ownership disappeared. A limited partnership with eighty-five owners controlled the Fox affiliate until 1996 when Nashville-based Sullivan Broadcasting purchased it for $26.5 million. Just two years later, the station was part of the Sinclair Broadcast Group acquisition of Sullivan.

The UPN and WB networks did not debut until 1995, so it is not possible to make a similar comparison, but there is nothing to suggest that these two networks increased the number of voices in local communities before CBS and Time Warner announced plans to merge the networks in 2006. Table 3.5 also documents the total number of individuals or corporations in control of network affiliates when UPN and WB are added to the totals. There was some increase at each level between the four network and the six network totals, but these are quite modest given the potential for two hundred new network affiliates, one hundred for UPN and one hundred for The WB. Most evident is the almost total lack of new voices in top ten and top twenty-five markets, which speaks to the creation of these two networks within the major media conglomerates. The Tribune Co., one of the two corporations that created The WB, owned and operated its most prominent affiliates from its launch, and Viacom and Chris Craft Industries did likewise in the case of UPN. The subsequent sale of Chris Craft to News Corp. in 2000 made the latter an important contributor to the growth of UPN, but these conglomerates are so prominent that it would be implausible to argue that these stations, in terms of ownership, increased diversity in any meaningful way.

The lack of a significant increase in individuals and corporations that controlled stations affiliated with these broadcast networks was testament to the prominence of the major conglomerates. In 2005, in the top ten markets, the lone additions from the four-network group were The Tribune Co. and Granite Broadcasting, owner of WB affiliates in San Francisco and Detroit. UPN did not contribute any new owners, as either Viacom or News Corp. owned each of its affiliates in the ten largest markets. The duopoly rules contributed a great deal to this lack of diversity, as either the UPN or WB affiliate had common ownership with the ABC, CBS, Fox, or NBC affiliate in eighteen of the top twenty-five markets, including nine of the top ten. The same was true in twelve of the markets ranked between twenty-six and fifty, while in five of the other markets a single corporation owned both the UPN and WB affiliates.

SUMMARY

A great deal has changed since the early days of radio in the United States, but in some respects things remain much the same. The network-dominated, advertiser-supported, privately owned system for broadcast radio that evolved in the 1920s and was locked in place with the Communications Act of 1934 provided the foundation for the development of broadcast television in the 1940s and 1950s. And that basic structure remains in place in the new millennium. Broadcast television features more local stations and national networks than ever before, but the diversity of voices in the marketplace has diminished over the last two decades, much as it did in broadcast radio between the mid-1920s and the mid-1930s. Based on its rulemaking in 2003, the Federal Communications Commission would like to allow further conglomeration and concentration.

Federal deregulation that the Reagan Administration launched in the mid-1980s has continued almost unchecked and the impact on broadcast television at both the national and local levels is profound. For the broadcast networks, the expiration of the Financial Interest and Syndication Rules in 1995 resulted in the greatest change, as the vertical integration of the networks with major motion picture studios occurred with the combinations of Disney and ABC, Paramount and CBS, and Universal and NBC. The three upstart broadcast networks—Fox, UPN, and The WB—featured such a link from the outset. The other dramatic change is in the size of station groups. Prior to 1984, common ownership was limited to just seven stations, but Congress removed the numerical limit in 1996 and raised the total allowable reach to 39 percent in 2004, even higher through the UHF discount. The lowering of this ceiling fueled the consolidation of ownership of local stations from large markets to small ones.

The increase in the size of station groups has altered power dynamics in broadcast television, with networks such as CBS and Fox in control of more of their local stations and less reliant on nonowned and operated affiliates. This change raises serious concerns about localism, the ideal that broadcast stations are more responsive to local wants and needs than to corporate interests. Changes in regulations have also contributed to the concentration of ownership at the local level. The relaxation of the one-to-a-market rule has allowed for common ownership of multiple stations in all but the smallest markets. This has further increased the true power of the large station groups.

These changes have also undermined the potential for new broadcast television networks to contribute to greater diversification of the voices in the marketplace, at both the national and the local levels. Without question, there has been a quantitative increase, but actual diversification has not occurred as more and more of the voices emanate from a small cadre of corporations. Most of these corporations have ownership ties to the major motion picture production and distribution companies, vertical integration that was all but prohibited prior to 1995. The parent corporations of the major motion picture companies now control all six major broadcast television networks. These networks, in a real sense, have become just another outlet for the "software" that is produced by vast corporations.

NOTES

1. The Disney total was $9.2 billion for eight seasons, with the ESPN contract for a Sunday prime time package valued at $600 million.

2. It is interesting to note that in 2005, with the network in better shape with first-season hits such as *Desperate Housewives*, *Lost*, and *Grey's Anatomy*, Disney and ABC chose not to renew the NFL deal.

3. In October 1998, Disney announced that it would build an ESPN Zone in Times Square in Manhattan, and that restaurant became a regular home for various ABC Sports studio shows. At the start of 2005, there were eight across the nation: Anaheim, Atlanta, Baltimore, Chicago, Denver, Las Vegas, New York, and Washington, DC.

4. *Mrs. Munger's Class* brought to life the yearbook pictures from a class in 1975 from Woodbridge Middle School in Virginia. Five former students and the teacher of the class filed a defamation suit against Disney in December 1998, and the network dropped the interstitials.

5. Richard W. Stevenson, "ABC, Once A Laggard, Rose to Prominence," *New York Times*, 19 March 1985, D1.

6. Geraldine Fabrikant, "Profits Are Up 24% at Disney And So, It Says, Is Teamwork," *New York Times*, 19 November 2004, C5.

7. Robert W. McChesney, *Telecommunications, Mass Media and Democracy: The Battle for the Control of U.S. Broadcasting, 1928-1935* (New York: Oxford University Press, 1994), 3.

8. McChesney, *Telecommunications, Mass Media and Democracy*, 3.

9. Quoted in McChesney, *Telecommunications, Mass Media and Democracy*, 243.

10. Ien Ang uses "audience-as-consumer" and "audience-as-public" to mark this difference, with the audience positioned as a potential consumer of both programs and advertisers in the former, while in the latter the audience is viewed as citizens who must be "reformed, educated, informed as well as entertained—in short, 'served'— presumably to enable them to better perform their democratic rights and duties."

11. Quoted in Willard D. Rowland, Jr. and Michael Tracy, "Worldwide Challenges to Public Service Broadcasting," *Journal of Communications* 40 (1990), 22.

12. Committee of the Post Office, *Government Ownership of Electrical Means of Communication*, 63rd Cong., 2nd. sess., 1914.

13. House of Representatives, Honorable David J. Lewis of Maryland, Extension of Remarks on The Postalization of the Telephone, 63rd Congress, 3rd sess., *Congressional Record*, 1915.

14. Committee of the Post Office, *Government Ownership of Electrical Means of Communication*, 18.

15. Senate, Committee on Commerce, *Telegraph System of the United States*, 42nd Cong., 2nd sess., 1872, Committee Report 223.

16. Senate, Committee on Commerce, *Telegraph System of the United States*, 4.

17. Senate, Committee on Commerce, *Telegraph System of the United States*, 4.

18. Quoted in Richard B. DuBoff, *Accumulation & Power: An Economic History of the United States* (Armonk, NY: M. E. Sharpe, Inc., 1989).

19. In the period just prior to World War I, AT&T and other large corporations snatched up most of the important patents from individuals such as Reginald Fessenden and Lee DeForest, which all but eliminated entrepreneurs from the field.

20. Thomas Streeter, *Selling the Air: A Critique of the Policy of Commercial Broadcasting in the United States* (Chicago: The University of Chicago Press, 1996), 82.

21. Josephus Daniels, "Views of Navy Department on Radio Communication," *Congressional Record*, 66th Cong., 1st sess., 1919, 165.

22. Daniels, "Views of Navy Department on Radio Communication."

23. Quoted in Barnouw, *A Tower in Babel*, 57.

24. Owen D. Young became the chairman of the board of RCA with Bullard the representative of the government. That position was guaranteed in the articles of incorporation, which stated that a non-U.S. citizen could not hold a seat on the board and that there would be a government representative with the "right of discussion and presentation in the board of the Government's views and interests concerning matters coming before the board." Quoted in Barnouw, *A Tower in Babel*, 59.

25. Barnouw, *A Tower in Babel*, 60.

26. Woodrow Wilson, "Trusts and Monopolies," in *The New Democracy: Presidential Messages, Addresses, and Other Papers*, vol. 1, no. 3 (New York: Harper & Brother Publishers, 1926).

27. Ellis W. Hawley, "The Discovery and Study of a 'Corporate Liberalism'," in *Business History Review*, vol. 52, no. 3 (1978).

28. See Martin J. Sklar, "Woodrow Wilson and the Political Economy of Modern United States Liberalism," *Studies on the Left*, vol. 1, no. 3 (1960); Alan L. Seltzer, "Woodrow Wilson as 'Corporate-Liberal': Toward a Reconsideration of Left Revisionist Historiography," *The Western Political Quarterly*, vol. 30, no. 2 (1977).

29. Seltzer, "Woodrow Wilson as 'Corporate-Liberal,'" 196.

30. Sklar, "Woodrow Wilson and the Political Economy," 22.

31. Sklar, "Woodrow Wilson and the Political Economy," 22.

32. Quoted in Sklar, "Woodrow Wilson and the Political Economy," 22.

33. Ellis W. Hawley, "Herbert Hoover, the Commerce Secretariat, and the Vision of an 'Associative State,' 1921-1928," *The Journal of American History*, vol. 61, no. 1 (1974).

34. Hawley, "Herbert Hoover, the Commerce Secretariat."

35. Hawley, "Herbert Hoover, the Commerce Secretariat," 120.

36. Stuart Ewen, *Captains of Consciousness* (New York: McGraw-Hill Book Company, 1976).

37. McChesney, *Telecommunications, Mass Media, & Democracy*.

38. Susan Smulyan, *Selling Radio: The Commercialization of American Broadcasting, 1920–1934* (Washington, DC: The Smithsonian Institution Press, 1994), 130.

39. Quoted in Sydney W. Held, *Broadcasting in America* (Boston: Houghton Mifflin, 1972), 420.

40. Smulyan, *Selling Radio*, 71.

41. Smulyan, *Selling Radio*, 71.

42. Quoted in Smulyan, *Selling Radio*, 142.

43. Quoted in Smulyan, *Selling Radio*, 146.

44. Quoted in Richard A. Harris and Sidney M. Milkis, *The Politics of Regulatory Change*, 2nd ed. (New York: Oxford University Press, 1996), 5.

45. Representative of this new social regulation were federal initiatives in environmental policy, occupational safety, public health, consumer affairs, and equal opportunity that were adopted in the 1970s.

46. Harris and Milkis, *The Politics of Regulatory Change*, 8.

47. Federal Communications Commission, *Amendment of Section 73.3555 (formerly Sections 73.35, 73.240, and 73.636) of the Commission's Rules Relating to Multiple Ownership of AM, FM and Television Broadcast Stations*, 100 F.C.C. 2nd 17 (1984), 58.

48. *Joseph Burstyn, Inc. v. Wilson, Commissioner of Education of New York, et al.*, 77 Sup. Ct. 777 (1952).

49. *National Broadcasting Co., Inc. et al v. United States et al*, 63 S. Ct. 997 (1943).

50. *National Broadcasting Co., Inc. et al v. United States et al.*

51. *Red Lion Broadcasting Co., Inc., et al v. Federal Communications Commission et al*, 89 S. Ct. 1794 (1969).

52. *Red Lion Broadcasting Co., Inc., et al v. Federal Communications Commission et al.*

53. *United States et al v. Playboy Entertainment Group, Inc.* 120 S. Ct. 1878 (2000).

54. *Federal Communications Commission v. Pacifica Foundation et al.* 98 S. Ct 3026 (1978).

55. *Federal Communications Commission v. Pacifica Foundation et al.*

56. *Federal Communications Commission v. Pacifica Foundation et al.*

57. In a pair of decisions handed down in 2005, the FCC rejected complaints that the PTC lodged against thirty-six different programs—from *Friends* to *The Simpsons*—that aired between October 2001 and February 2004.

58. Broadcast Decency Enforcement Act of 2005, 109 H.R. 310.

59. Federal Communications Commission, *Amendments of Section 3.35, 3.240 and 3.636 of the Rules and Regulations Relating to the Multiple Ownership of AM, FM and Television Broadcasting Stations*, 18 FCC 288 (1953).

60. Federal Communications Commission, *Amendment of Multiple Ownership Rules*, 43 FCC 2797 (1954).

61. Federal Communications Commission, *Commission's Rules Relating to Multiple Ownership of AM, FM and Television Broadcast Stations* (1984).

62. Federal Communications Commission, *Commission's Rules Relating to Multiple Ownership*, 27–29.

63. Federal Communications Commission, *Commission's Rules Relating to Multiple Ownership*, 30–31.

64. Mike Mills, "Bell Companies Score Win with Senate Vote; Amendment Would Curb Justice Dept. Oversight," *Washington Post*, 14 June 1995, F1.

65. *Telecommunications Act of 1996*, 104th Cong., 1st sess., S. 652.

66. *Fox Television Stations, Inc. v. Federal Communications Commission*, 280 F.3d 1027.

67. Preservation of Localism, Program Diversity, and Competition in Television Broadcast Service Act of 2003, H.R. 2052 (9 May 2003) and S. 1046 (13 May 2005).

68. Quoted in Bill McConnell, "New Ownership Cap Fits Fox, CBS Perfectly," *Broadcasting & Cable*, 26 January 2004, 5.

69. At the time, News Corp. was at 44.97 percent and Viacom Inc. was at 43.35 percent.

70. The Telecommunications Act included a clear delineation of how many stations an individual or corporation could own in a given market based on the total number of stations in the market but left undefined what constituted a market. The end result is that radio groups collected stations in various markets that far exceeded the levels that Congress mandated.

71. In markets with between four and eight television stations, one could own a newspaper, television station, and up to half of the radio station limit for that market or a newspaper and the total radio station limit for the market but no television station.

72. Susan Crabtree, "Re-Reg Roadblock," *Daily Variety*, 20 June 2003, 1.

73. The Tribune Co. created another cross-ownership challenge in South Florida in 1997 when it acquired WBZL from Renaissance Communications Corp. The Tribune Co. already owned the Sun-Sentinel in Ft. Lauderdale. In 2002, the FCC allowed the Tribune Co. to merge the operations of the two units pending completion of its review of cross-ownership rules.

74. Quoted in Jon Lafayette and Doug Halonen, "Tribune Deal to Test Print-TV Cooperation," *Electronic Media*, 20 March 2000, 3.

75. The Tribune Co. was among the petitioners in *Prometheus Radio Group v. Federal Communications Commission*.

76. Quoted in Ken Auletta, *Three Blind Mice* (New York: Vintage Books, 1992), 173.

77. Policy Regarding Character Qualifications In Broadcast Licensing, 102 FCC 2nd 1179.

78. Auletta, *Three Blind Mice*, 19.

79. Peter J. Boyer, "Fiscal Experts to Look at NBC News Operation," *New York Times*, 9 January 1987, C25.

80. Quoted in Bill McCloskey, "Tisch CBS Holdings May Raise Regulatory Issue," *Associated Press*, 12 September 1986.

81. There was little public debate before the FCC granted its approval. On November 21, 1995, two days prior to the Thanksgiving Day holiday, the Commission announced an open meeting to "consider the applications of CBS Inc. and Westinghouse Electric Corporation for the transfer of control of the CBS broadcast stations to Westinghouse." While the announcement of such a meeting was appropriate, and the need for an open discussion great, the Commission meeting in question was scheduled for the next morning. Under the Sunshine Act, such open hearings are to be announced one week in advance, but the FCC claimed that, "The prompt and orderly conduct of Commission business requires that the meeting be held with less than 7-days notice." What the notice failed to mention was that the merger of Westinghouse and CBS had been announced close to four months earlier. Given such a timetable, it is difficult to defend a decision to hold a meeting on such a merger with less than twenty-four hours notice.

82. The NBC investment in Paxson did not go well. The main purpose from an NBC perspective was to give the network another distribution arm for its programming, but the financial parameters within Paxson made such a deal difficult to complete. In 2001, Bud Paxson attempted to block the NBC acquisition of Telemundo since it made it all but impossible for NBC to activate its option to purchase control of Paxson, since that would have placed the combined group well over the FCC ownership limits. In

2003, NBC exercised its right to terminate its ownership and force Paxson to reacquire its stake or allow NBC to sell to a third party, but two years later this battle was still in court.

83. While the major American conglomerates do not have a stake in Univision, Mexican television powerhouse Televisa did hold a 10.8 percent interest at the end of 2004.

84. The stations were split more or less equally into the Univision Station Group and the Telefutura Station Group.

85. As part of an agreement with the Department of Justice, the Univision stake in Entravision must not exceed 15 percent after 26 March 2006 and 10 percent after 26 March 2009. (Form 10-K, Entravision Communications Corp.)

86. In each of these markets, Entravision operated both stations under Local Marketing Agreements.

87. It is now difficult to find such figures since the financials for the broadcast networks and stations are lumped within large divisions. The ABC Television Network and its stations, for example, are combined with ESPN and the other Disney cable networks within a "Media Networks" group for reporting purposes.

88. Kyle Pope, "ABC Official Urges Sweeping Change Such as Fees for Some Network Fare," *Wall Street Journal*, 7 April 1998.

89. Each of the big three established networks, ABC, CBS, and NBC, have just over two hundred affiliated stations across the country, while Fox is just below that number.

90. There were a number of CBS affiliates that shifted the program thirty minutes later so they could broadcast off-network sitcoms between 11:30 p.m. and 12:00 midnight.

91. The network compensation formula takes various factors into consideration: the number of commercial minutes in an hour, the size and demographics of the audience, the size of the market, the strength of the station, and the time allocated to the program. Howard J. Blumenthal and Oliver R. Goodenough, *This Business of Television*, 2nd ed. (New York: Billboard Books, 1998).

92. Michael Schneider, "Peacock Slashes Compensation to Gannett," *Variety*, 6 March 2000, 60.

93. Jon Lafayette, "ABC Deal 'Fair' Say Affiliates," *Electronic Media*, 5 July 1999, 3.

94. Michele Greppi, "Fox Net, Affils Settle NFL Tab," *Television Week*, 20 October 2003, 1.

95. Broadcasting & Cable Yearbook 2000 (New Providence, NJ: R.R. Bowker, 2000), A-109.

96. Form 10-K, Clear Channel Communications Inc., 29 March 1996 and 3 March 2005.

97. The 35 percent limit was not a true one, however. When the FCC calculates the designated market area for a station, it discounts the coverage of a UHF station, which counts for just 50 percent of its market area.

98. Viacom surpassed the 35 percent limit with its merger with CBS in 1999, while News Corp. did the same with its acquisition of Chris Craft Industries in 2000. In both cases, the FCC did not force the conglomerates to get back under the cap as it pondered changes in the rules.

99. These totals include stations owned as well as those operated through Local Marketing Agreements.

100. Form 10-K, Nexstar Broadcasting Group, Inc., 15 March 2005.

101. In these four markets, either News Corp. or Viacom also owned the UPN affiliate.

102. The Church of Jesus Christ of Latter-day Saints owned KIRO and KSL in Salt Lake City and operated the stations through Bonneville International. Gaylord Broadcasting Co., based in Nashville, owned KSTW in Tacoma.

103. Emmett Watson, "Dorothy Bullitt Placed King-TV In a Class by Itself," *Seattle Times*, 26 August 1990, B1.

104. There were some changes in the markets ranked in the top five and top ten. Boston moved from sixth to fifth, displacing San Francisco in the top five, while Atlanta moved into the top ten in 2005, dropping Houston to eleventh.

4

❖

Patterns of Ownership in Motion Picture Distribution

There was a time when one could associate the major motion picture production and distribution companies with the individuals who created them: Adolph Zukor and Paramount; Mary Pickford, Charlie Chaplin, Douglas Fairbanks, and D. W. Griffith and United Artists; and Walt Disney, William Fox, and the four Warner brothers with the studios that bore their names. Such ties to an individual with ownership and control are far less common with the corporate conglomeration of the motion picture studios in the current era, although such links do exist. Rupert Murdoch and Sumner Redstone wield operational control over Twentieth Century Fox and Paramount Pictures, for example, but the role these media moguls assume in the operation of these studios is quite different than in the cases of William Fox and Adolph Zukor. While the links between Murdoch and Twentieth Century Fox and Redstone and Paramount are clear, these companies are mere properties—albeit important ones—in vast media conglomerates, corporations that demand a different kind of leader than the motion picture companies did generations ago.

While there are oftentimes not owners linked to some of these major motion picture companies, the individual continues to command the headlines in the culture industries. Since Zukor lured Pickford to Famous Players in 1914, the prominence of actors in motion pictures and then television is undeniable. Zukor fostered the development of a motion picture system built upon "stars" and Pickford became one of the first actors to become an independent producer and earn profit participation.[1] Actors remain the focal point in the motion picture business, and many of these "stars" command a percentage of the profits, as Pickford did over eight decades ago. The marquee names can even command a percentage of the total gross before the studios recoup their costs. According to the trade journals, the standard deal for Tom Cruise at one point included no up-front fee but 22.5 percent of gross receipts, starting with the first dollar earned at the box office.[2] While it is natural to focus on the glitter and gold, an industrial structure supports the motion picture business, and it is critical that the attention on the "stars" does not distract one from the true bases of power.

The preeminence of the individual and the hidden role of the corporations were most evident at the 70th Academy Awards, held in March 1998 and watched in one in three American television households. The evening became a celebration of the various individuals who contributed to the success of *Titanic*, the epic production that grossed over $600 million in theaters in the United States and Canada, and over $1.2 billion in theaters in the rest of the world. Cinematographers, composers, film editors, set and costume designers, and sound and special effects specialists earned Oscars for their work on *Titanic*. And, above all else, it was the coronation of James Cameron, who captured Oscars for directing and film editing, then proclaimed, "I am the King of the World" after *Titanic* was named best picture. There is little question that Cameron was a force in the production of *Titanic*, but, alas, there were powers even greater than he, contributors who were little mentioned as the Oscar avalanche gained speed.

Titanic won eleven Oscars to equal the record held by *Ben-Hur*, released close to four decades earlier in 1959. While *Titanic* and *Ben-Hur* came from different eras, the two motion pictures had much in common. Both were quite long, three hours and fourteen minutes for *Titanic*, three hours and thirty-two minutes for *Ben-Hur*, and unlike numerous best picture recipients of the past, neither earned an Oscar for best original screenplay nor best adapted screenplay. Most significant, however, were the costs incurred in the production of these two films. MGM produced *Ben-Hur* for $15 million, an almost unspeakable budget for that time. *Variety* estimated that it would have cost $200 million to produce *Ben-Hur* in 1998, equal to the approximate costs incurred in the production of *Titanic*.

Titanic stands as one of the most expensive motion pictures ever produced, but the corporations that financed production and marketing were little mentioned during the Oscar presentations. Twentieth Century Fox bankrolled the development of *Titanic*, but as costs soared, it solicited assistance from its would-be competitors, other major motion picture companies. Twentieth Century Fox found its savior in Paramount Pictures, which in exchange for domestic distribution rights, agreed to contribute a reported $60 million.[3] The production costs for *Titanic* exceeded $200 million, which meant that Twentieth Century Fox was still on the hook for over $140 million. Of course, it proved to be a sound investment, with the foreign gross for *Titanic* exceeding $1 billion.

The focus on the artisans rather than the corporations is not surprising in a nation that has embraced the notion of individualism since the drafting of the Constitution and Bill of Rights. This is also common in numerous examinations of the culture industries, which oftentimes ignore the degree to which oligopolies control the production and distribution of motion pictures and other products—artifacts that present values, ideas, and ideologies. To understand the impact of two decades of consolidation and concentration in the motion picture and television industries, however, one must trace these creations through the structure that dominates the business. The two previous chapters located the ownership of the major motion picture studios and broadcast networks in six diversified conglomerates. This chapter will address the degree to which these corporations control the distribution of motion pictures in the United States. Distribution is the nexus of power in the motion picture business so these are important questions. How concentrated is the distribution of motion pictures in the United States and how did this change over time? Has the prominence of "independent" motion picture distributors decreased the degree of corporate concentration?

The examination of motion pictures is an appropriate starting point for the discussion of the production and distribution of film and television content. Theatrical exhibition of motion pictures generated just under $10 billion in 2004, and films accounted for the bulk of the $24 billion in home video sales for the year. Just as significant for the purposes of this analysis is the importance of these same motion pictures to broadcast and cable television. Much of the growth in cable television, in particular, comes from the development of multichannel premium services such as HBO and Showtime, as well as pay-per-view and video-on-demand services. Motion pictures, new and old, also litter the schedules of the most prominent basic cable services, such as TNT and USA Network, in addition to their prominence on niche channels, such as AMC, Fox Movie Channel, and Turner Classic Movies. This connection was most evident in the Sony-led acquisition of Metro-Goldwyn-Mayer/United Artists (MGM/UA) when the impetus for the winning bid was an agreement between Sony and Comcast to create cable channels that utilized the content from the film libraries the MGM/UA controlled.

POLICY AND REGULATORY FRAMEWORK

Ronald Reagan's first tenure as president of the Screen Actors Guild coincided with the hearings before the House Committee on Un-American Activities, and he testified before that committee in 1947. Fifteen years later, he was a witness before a federal grand jury concerning a Department of Justice probe of the relationship between the Screen Actors Guild and MCA, the talent agency that represented him. Perhaps his experiences with the Guild inspired the proclamation in his 1981 inaugural address: "Government is not the solution to our problem, government is our problem." As discussed in the previous chapter, this mantra guided a period of deregulation that had a profound impact on the structure of broadcast television in the United States. The influence such ideas and ideologies had upon the production, distribution, and exhibition of motion pictures was more subtle, but no less significant. The Reagan Doctrine preached an emphasis on economic efficiencies in the enforcement of antitrust laws, with an insistence on the primacy of consumer welfare concerns and subsequent exclusion of other social and political factors. Attorney General William French Smith articulated this approach when he argued that, "We must recognize that bigness does not necessarily mean badness, and that success should not automatically be suspect...Efficient firms should not be hobbled under the guise of antitrust enforcement."[4]

An important dimension of the Reagan Doctrine was a move away from antitrust cases based on vertical and shared monopoly theories and a refocus on traditional horizontal restraint-of-trade matters. In the 1960s and early 1970s, the Department of Justice believed that its main role in merger enforcement was to preserve and promote market structures that were favorable to competition, arguing the structure of the market tends to dictate the conduct of individual firms. This focus began to shift with the rise to prominence of the "free market" libertarianism of the so-called Chicago School, which became dominant during the Reagan Administration. Under revised merger guidelines issued in 1982 and amended in 1984, the Department of Justice placed an emphasis on efficiencies, technological change, and other factors that mitigated the anticompetitive effects of mergers. The guidelines also clarified market definitions and promoted the rigorous application of economic measurements, including market shares and levels of concentration. This reflected an emphasis in antitrust enforcement based on the economic welfare of consumers rather than social welfare and other concerns, such as fears that excessive concentration tends to promote antidemocratic tendencies in societies.

The movement away from vertical and shared monopoly theories was significant for the motion picture business, since such concerns were at the heart of the consent decrees, known collectively as the Paramount decrees, which the government signed with the major motion picture studios after the Supreme Court ruled in 1948 that their activities violated the Sherman Act.[5] While the courts addressed various business practices that it deemed to be anticompetitive, the Supreme Court did not rule that such vertical integration was illegal per se. It was the Paramount decrees that forced the studios to divest their ownership in theater chains between 1949 and 1952. The Reagan Administration undertook an examination of all such consent decrees in its first term, and while the Department of Justice announced in 1984 that it would not eliminate the Paramount decrees, it signaled that it was amenable to their demise and would support petitioners that sought their termination. The Justice Department, moreover, made it clear that it would not challenge such vertical combinations.[6] The reaction of the studios was swift. In 1986 alone, MCA Inc., the parent of Universal, acquired a 50 percent interest in Cineplex Odeon, the largest theater chain in North America, while Gulf +

Western, the parent of Paramount, collected around 500 screens in three different transactions, including 360 operated by Mann Theaters.[7] In turn, Gulf + Western sold a 50 percent interest in those theaters to Warner Communications in 1987.[8]

The decade that followed the studio return to exhibition was one of tremendous growth. The number of indoor screens in the United States increased over 66 percent in the 1990s, from 21,907 at the start of 1990 to 36,448 at the end of 1999.[9] Much of this growth occurred between 1995 and 2000, a period in which the number of theater sites actually declined, a clear indication that much of the screen growth was in large-chain multiplexes that came to dominate the business. The major studios were in the middle of both the expansion and consolidation. In 1998, the Loews Theater Exhibition Group and Cineplex Odeon Corp. merged to create Loews Cineplex Entertainment, which brought together the theater assets of Sony Corp., the parent of Columbia Pictures, and Seagram, the parent of Universal. Loews Cineplex controlled 9.3 percent of the theater screens in North America, but in short order it came to represent the poor business model that theater ownership had become. The rapid expansion in the 1990s left most chains with tremendous debt, and Loews Cineplex filed for bankruptcy in 2001, the eleventh theater chain to do so in an eighteen-month period. Universal sold its 25.6 percent share in Loews Cineplex for $1.

The most prominent integration of distribution and exhibition in the mid-2000s belonged to Viacom Inc. The connection between Viacom and Paramount Pictures is clear, as was its ownership of Famous Players, one of the most prominent theater chains in Canada that Viacom sold in the summer of 2005. Not as evident is the link between Viacom and National Amusements, the sixth largest theater operator in the nation at the start of 2005. Sumner Redstone wielded total power within Viacom, thanks to an ownership interest of over 70 percent. Redstone owned much of this through National Amusements, the family business that evolved from his father's collection of nightclubs and drive-in theaters. National Amusements was the only major theater chain with a clear connection to a major studio, but in another respect, it was representative of this group.

The eight largest theater chains in the United States at the start of 2005 accounted for just under 50 percent of all indoor screens, with the four largest chains—Regal Entertainment, AMC Entertainment, Cinemark USA, and Carmike Cinemas—owning over 38 percent of the total screens. What is most interesting about these figures is that the prominence of the large chains in the development of multiplex theaters is most evident. While the four largest chains accounted for 38.72 percent of total screens, these same four owned just 22.33 percent of total sites. This level of concentration increased with the announcement in June 2005 of the AMC Entertainment Group acquisition of Loews Cineplex Entertainment Corp., which would push ownership

within the top four to over 40 percent. Perhaps more significant, Regal Entertainment and AMC Entertainment/Loews Cineplex would control around
30 percent of indoor screens in the United States.

There is little doubt that the nature of theater ownership has changed since
the 1980s, but one must question whether the Reagan Administration mantra
that "bigness" does not equate to "badness" held true. Critical to this discussion is whether the concentration of ownership in exhibition coupled with the
dominance of the major studios in distribution has made it impossible for independents on either end of the sequence to compete. In 1999, the Department
of Justice launched an investigation into two practices that were prominent
in the Paramount case: block booking and clearances. Block booking is the
practice of studios selling films in packages to theaters on an all-or-nothing
basis, forcing theaters to feature numerous less desirable films in order to gain
access to marquee films. Clearances occur when theaters receive an exclusive
first-run engagement of a particular film in a protected area. The Supreme
Court ruled that both of these practices were illegal, but consolidation on
both ends of the distribution-exhibition process renewed such concerns.

The Justice Department investigation lost its impetus, perhaps in the han-
dover from the Clinton Administration to the Bush Administration, but other
legal actions point to the advantages of bigness in the motion picture marketplace. In 2004, Mel Gibson's Icon Distribution, Inc. filed suit against Regal
Entertainment Group in Los Angeles Superior Court over revenues from *The
Passion of the Christ*. Icon alleged that Regal reneged on a deal to disburse
gross box office revenue in a 55 percent to 45 percent ratio in favor of the
distributor, what Icon called "studio terms." Instead, according to the lawsuit, Regal offered just 34 percent of gross revenues.[10] Some in the business
pointed out that "studio terms" did not mean 55 percent of the box office in
each instance, but no one questioned the basic idea that studios get a much
better deal from theater chains and that independent distributors are at a
decided disadvantage.

At the other end of the distribution and exhibition process, the Attorney
General for the state of California, Bill Lockyer, launched an antitrust investigation into Century Theaters in 2005 to determine whether the chain was
using its market power to negotiate clearances for marquee films. The Camera 12 in San Jose was one of the independent theaters that rallied support
for the examination. In the summer of 2004, Century allegedly requested
clearance from DreamWorks of *The Terminal* for one of its theaters five miles
away from the Camera 12 and declined to exhibit the film when DreamWorks
refused to honor the demand.[11] One of the issues at the heart of the California investigation was whether clearances were a reasonable business practice
or an attempt to eliminate competition, but unquestioned was the fact that
"bigness" in exhibition resulted in market power for the large chains and
imperiled independent theaters.

THE DISTRIBUTION OF MOTION PICTURES

The preeminence of the director in motion pictures is as old as the medium itself. What D. W. Griffith, Cecil B. DeMille, Orson Welles, Frank Capra, and John Ford were to their generations, Steven Spielberg, Robert Zemeckis, Martin Scorsese, and Oliver Stone are to theirs. Under the studio system of the 1910s, 1920s, 1930s, and 1940s, it was rare for directors such as Griffith, DeMille, Welles, Capra, and Ford to rise above the actors, and even the studio. This became more common in the post-World War II period with the decline of the studio system, which fueled the emergence of the director as the acknowledged star of countless films. When one thinks of *Jaws, Close Encounters of the Third Kind, ET: The Extra-Terrestrial, Jurassic Park*, and *Schindler's List*, Spielberg is more apt to come to mind than the lead actors in those films: Roy Scheider, Richard Dreyfuss, Henry Thomas, Sam Neill, and Liam Neeson. In the case of the *Indiana Jones* trilogy and *Saving Private Ryan*, Spielberg does no worse than share top billing with Harrison Ford and Tom Hanks, respectively.

There is little question that directors such as Spielberg are true craftsman, but the focus on the individual distracts one from the corporations that bankroll these expensive, albeit artistic, creations. This was most evident in the summer of 2003. In a three-month period from May through July, the six major studios released eight big-event, action/adventure films with production budgets estimated in excess of $95 million.[12] The average for the eight films was $135 million, ranging from *Terminator 3: Rise of the Machines* at $200 million to *Lara Croft Tomb Raider: The Cradle of Life* at $95 million, with another $40 million on average for marketing and distribution. While this collection did not include a Spielberg film, there is little question that he contributed to the dramatic increase in production costs. His first hit, *Jaws*, cost an estimated $8.5 million to produce but generated $260 million in domestic box office gross after it opened in 1975.[13] *Jaws* had a profound impact on Spielberg and on Hollywood, as it ushered in the era of summer blockbuster movies. *Raiders of the Lost Ark, ET: The Extra-Terrestrial*, and *Jurassic Park*, three of the all-time box office champions, can be viewed as descendants of *Jaws*.

What is critical about the Spielberg collection is that he created each of them with capital from the major motion picture companies. *Jaws* and *ET: The Extra-Terrestrial* were produced within Universal Pictures, while *Close Encounters of the Third Kind* was produced within Columbia Pictures. Paramount Pictures financed *Raiders of the Lost Ark* and the other films in the Indiana Jones series. Universal Pictures backed two of his award-winning films of the 1990s, *Jurassic Park* and *Schindler's List*, while *Saving Private Ryan*, the most prominent film produced under the banner of his much-heralded company, DreamWorks SKG, was a coproduction with Paramount Pictures, with the two splitting the $70 million production budget. What is most interesting about this group is that the estimated $70 million for *Saving Private Ryan* was the highest estimated production costs for one of these films.[14] That was not the case with *The War of the Worlds*, released in the summer of 2005, which was a coproduction of Paramount and DreamWorks with a reported production budget of $130 million.

The prominence of companies such as Columbia Pictures, Paramount Pictures, and Universal Pictures as the financial backbone of Spielberg projects over the last three decades is undeniable. While Spielberg's unmatched success in this period gave him the cachet to seek financial investors elsewhere, and he did obtain outside investors in the creation of DreamWorks, the most available source of capital remains the major corporations. The majors do not produce all of the motion pictures in the United States, but for generations they have dominated the distribution of motion pictures, which allows them to wield significant control over the films that find wide distribution in the United States and the rest of the world.

The distribution of motion pictures is the linchpin of the entire industry. The distributor can be seen as an intermediary between the producer and the exhibitor, but the major motion picture companies are far more than middlemen, for they have the means to influence what is produced and who produces it. Their control assumes various forms. The majors have lines of credit with financial institutions, so the studios become sources of capital for film development and production. Moreover, it is rare for financial institutions to invest in the production of a film unless the producer has procured a distribution agreement. The central role of the distributor predates the introduction of sound. In 1921, John E. Barber of the First National Bank of Los Angeles and the L.A. Trust and Savings wrote:

> As in other industries, the distribution or marketing of pictures is of far more importance commercially than production. Pictures do not sell on their intrinsic excellence alone. They require to be skillfully sold by wholesalers, called 'distributors' to retailers called 'exhibitors'.[15]

Motley Flint, who was also associated with L.A. Trust and Savings, was even more emphatic when he wrote that unless 100 percent distribution can be assured, "a bank cannot be expected to loan to the independent producer."[16]

This financial dimension has become even more significant with the dramatic increase in the average cost to produce and distribute films in the United States. In 1980, the average negative cost for a film from a Motion Picture Association of American member company was $9.38 million, which included production costs, studio overhead, and capitalized interest.[17] Adjusted for inflation, this average cost would have been $21.5 million in 2004. As detailed in table 4.1, the average negative cost for MPAA member companies was three times the adjusted cost, $63.6 million. What is most striking about these numbers is the fact that the combined production and distribution costs for the average MPAA film was over $100 million in 2003 and just under that benchmark in 2004. And that was the average cost

Table 4.1.   Average Theatrical Costs for Motion Picture Association of America Members and Subsidiaries, 1984–2004

	MPAA Member Company[a] Average Theatrical Costs			MPAA Member Subsidiary/Affiliate[b] Average Theatrical Costs		
	Negative Cost	Marketing Cost	Total Cost	Negative Cost	Marketing Cost	Total Cost
1984	$14.4	$6.7	$21.1			
1994	$34.3	$16.1	$50.3			
2000	$54.8	$27.3	$82.1	$21.5	$10.1	$31.6
2001	$47.7	$31.0	$78.7	$31.5	$9.5	$41.0
2002	$58.8	$30.6	$89.4	$34.0	$11.2	$45.2
2003	$63.8	$39.0	$102.9	$46.9	$14.7	$61.6
2004	$63.6	$34.4	$98.0	$28.2	$11.4	$39.6

Source: Motion Picture Association of America, "US Entertainment Industry: 2004 MPA Market Statistics," 2005.
[a] The members of the MPAA include the major studios as well as some of the prominent independents: Buena Vista Pictures Distribution (Walt Disney), Sony Pictures Entertainment Inc., Metro-Goldwyn-Mayer Studios Inc., Paramount Pictures Corporation, Twentieth Century Fox Film Corporation, Universal City Studios LLP, and Warner Bros. Entertainment Inc.
[b] The subsidiary/affiliate group includes the "classic" divisions within the studios such as Sony Pictures Classics, Paramount Classics, and Fox Searchlight, as well as once independent companies that are now under the same parent corporation of the major studios, such as Miramax Films and New Line Cinema.

for 199 films and not the high water mark or the mean for the box office champions. In 1994, the average negative cost for new feature films from MPAA companies was $34.3 million, but just ten years later the average cost for marketing, which included prints and advertising, was $34.4 million.

The second group of companies is also quite significant. The MPAA member subsidiary and affiliate group includes the in-house distribution units that the major studios created, such as Focus Features, Fox Searchlight, Paramount Classics, Sony Pictures Classics, and Warner Independent Pictures, as well as the companies that the parent corporations of the studios acquired, such as Miramax Films and New Line Cinema. These so-called "independent" companies have garnered countless headlines over the last decade, but under the traditional definition scores of films would not earn the independent label. Sidebar 4.1 addresses this question in more detail. What the figures in table 4.1 indicate is the degree to which these companies use the financial resources of the major media conglomerates to produce and distribute films in a manner that is quite similar to the studios. In 2003, for example, the average negative cost for films that the MPAA subsidiary/affiliate group released was $46.9 million, $1 million less than the average for the MPAA member companies just two years earlier.

The increase in the production and marketing budgets of films forces one to refocus on the financial dimension of motion picture production, distribution, and exhibition. Film did not evolve in the United States as a forum for public communication, or as an art form, but rather as a commercial, profit-oriented activity. As discussed earlier, the Supreme Court ruled in 1915

Sidebar 4.1
The Meaning of Independence in a Studio-Dominated World

The nominations for the twentieth IFP Independent Spirit Awards said a great deal about the state of independence in the motion picture business in the 2000s. Filmmakers established the Independent Feature Project (IFP) to champion the cause of independent films and support artists who "embody diversity, innovation, and uniqueness of vision."[1] Most of the finalists for the best feature crown for films released in 2004—*Sideways, Baadasssss!, Kinsey, Maria Full of Grace,* and *Primer*—had something significant in common with more mainstream productions, however, as the distributor of four of the five films shared a corporate parent with a major studio.[2] Such a connection did not preclude consideration for the Independent Spirit Awards, although selection criteria included the percentage of independent financing and the total production budget and individual compensation. Nevertheless, there is little doubt that the power driving Fox Searchlight's *Sideways* was far mightier than that behind a ThinkFilms movie, *Primer.*[3]

Hollywood bandies about the independent label, but few of those who adopt the title would make the grade under the classic definition. In a traditional framework, the financing of a film is the first measure of independence. As such, films financed by the "art house" or "independent" divisions of the major motion picture studios, such as Fox Searchlight, Sony Pictures Classics, and Paramount Classics, would not qualify as independents. The same would hold true for the once independent distributors that are now under the same parent of a major studio, such as Disney's Miramax and Time Warner's New Line and Fine Line, since the source of capital to produce and distribute films is the same as their more renowned corporate cousins. Access to such capital was the impetus for the original sale of Miramax to Disney and an ongoing source of tension between the Weinstein brothers and Michael Eisner, most evident when corporate headquarters would not green-light the *Lord of the Rings* trilogy.

Strict adherence to this definition of independence would eliminate a significant number of films nominated for the Independent Spirit Awards for 2004. The much heralded *Sideways*, which also collected five Academy Award nominations including one for Best Picture, is a clear example of such connections. Producer Michael London offered the project to the Universal Pictures specialty division as part of his first-look deal with Focus Features; he then shopped the film to Paramount, DreamWorks, and Fox Searchlight when Focus balked at the budget.[4] London signed a deal with Fox Searchlight before shooting began in the fall of 2003. HBO Films had a similar impact on *Maria Full of Grace,* a Spanish-language film about a Columbian woman who uses her body to transport drugs to New York. Director/writer Joshua Marston had completed the original script for *Maria* a half decade earlier, but nothing came of the project until he teamed with Paul Mezey and they convinced HBO to finance the film. HBO Films did not forecast a theatrical release, but plans changed after *Maria* received acclaim at the Sundance Film Festival, and HBO opted to distribute the film through another Time Warner unit, Fine Line Features. The journey for *Kinsey* was far more difficult, as over eighty studios and production companies rejected producer Gail Mutrux over close to a decade before London-based Qwerty Films and Fox Searchlight agreed to finance the film in the summer of 2003.

While the source of financing is one measure of independence, other definitions rose to prominence as the studios and their corporate parents extended their tentacles into each level of distribution. In a special section on the state of independent filmmaking in 2003, *Daily Variety* addressed this topic and advanced a collection of definitions that encompass a wide range of productions:[5]

- The "financial pedigree": nonstudio funding of production was the first test of independence.
- The size of the budget: the $20 million mark was the ceiling for an independent film.
- The nature of the material: films with nonmainstream content qualified at independents.
- Your state of mind: In the words of *Daily Variety*, "If you believe you work as an independent, you are."

Viewed within this context, one could categorize all five of the nominees for the Independent Spirit Awards best feature prize for 2004 as independent films. *Daily Variety* embraced the notion that independence was a state of mind, which ignores the power and influence six corporations hold over the distribution of motion pictures in the United States and the degree to which once independent distributors have come to function in a fashion quite similar to the major studios.

The prominence of New Line and Miramax in 2003 spoke volumes about the state of independence in the current era. These two distributors, with the inclusion of New Line's Fine Line Features and Miramax's Dimension Films, combined for 18.17 percent of the domestic box office that year. In addition to the obvious links to the financial resources of Time Warner and Disney, most of this market share was attributable to films that violated other definitions of independence. In the New Line total, 86.39 percent of its box office revenue came from nine films with production budgets of over $20 million, while in the Miramax total, 89.96 percent came from eleven films that surpassed that same threshold.[6] The nine New Line films had an average estimated production budget of $43.78 million, while the eleven Miramax films averaged $44.54 million. Moreover, these figures do not include marketing budgets for these films, which averaged an estimated $24 million for the twenty films included in the above totals.

In addition to their financial pedigree and production budgets, the New Line and Miramax collections of 2003 ran afoul with other definitions of independence. These films violated another often-used measure of independence, the scope and pace of a film's rollout. When Twentieth Century Fox released the final installment of the *Star Wars* serial in May 2005, it debuted on 3,661 screens. This was similar to the openings for the two blockbuster summer films of 2004, DreamWorks's *Shrek 2* and Sony Picture's *Spider-man 2*, which debuted on 4,163 and 4,152 screens, respectively. Such rollouts had long been a trademark of the major studios, but once upon a time independent distributors did not have the financial capital required to support a widespread debut.[7]

All of this changed in October 1994 when *Pulp Fiction* opened on 1,338 screens nationwide, thanks to the financial resources that Miramax could access after it became part of Disney.[8] A decade later there was oftentimes little to distinguish the

(Continued)

release patterns of distributors such as Miramax and New Line from their corporate cousins. In 2003, New Line's *The Lord of the Rings: Return of the King* opened on 3,703 screens, more than the opening weekend for the highest grossing Warner Bros. film of the year, *The Matrix Reloaded*, and four other New Line films debuted on more than 3,000 screens.[9] The Miramax slate included three films that debuted on more than 3,000 screens, and both *Spy Kids 3-D: Game Over* and *Scary Movie 3* had wider opening weekends than Disney's *Pirates of the Caribbean: The Curse of the Black Pearl*. In the end, with mainstream capital, multimillion dollar production and marketing budgets, and widespread releases, the so-called independents are little more than scaled down major studios.

NOTES

1. Independent Feature Project, "Independent Spirit Awards," www.ifp.org/content/pdf (accessed 06 June 2005).

2. Fox Searchlight distributed two of the films, *Sideways* and *Kinsey*, while Sony Pictures Classic handled *Baadasssss!* and Time Warner's Fine Line released *Maria Full of Grace*.

3. It is interesting to note that both *Sideways* and *Primer* opened on just four theater screens. While *Primer* topped out at thirty screens nationwide and grossed under $500,000, *Sideways* reached a peak of 1,786 screens and grossed over $70 million.

4. Zorianna Kit, "Payne Signs Up for 'Sideways,'" *The Hollywood Reporter*, 2 July 2003.

5. Sharon Sweat, "The Independents," *Daily Variety*, 18 August 2003.

6. The collection of nine New Line Cinema films does not include *Lord of the Rings: Fellowship of the Rings*. That film had a production budget of an estimated $93 million, but it was in release for just two weeks on 126 screens in 2003. It earned around $1.4 million more at the box office.

7. Distributors need financial resources for marketing and promotion as well as to make thousands of prints of their films.

8. The fall opening was a trademark of Miramax, but Disney dollars enabled it to be far more aggressive. *The Crying Game* and *The Piano* claimed the cherished slot in 1992 and 1993, respectively, but both opened on less than ten screens. *The Piano* did not surpass five hundred screens until Christmas, its seventh week in release, while *The Crying Game* did not reach that modest number until late February, the weekend after Oscar nominations were announced.

9. *The Matrix Reloaded* opened on 3,603 screens for Warner Bros.

that, "the exhibition of motion pictures is a business pure and simple, originated and conducted for profit." For that reason, it is critical to understand film as a commodity and not as "autonomous creations, independent of economic institutions."[18] Rather, one must consider the industrial mechanism that "produces and disseminates our culture," since this system impacts on the selection and development of content, relationships within the industry, and the ownership and control of the productive apparatus.[19] There is little question that distribution is the most critical step in this process, more so now than ever, since these companies distribute films not just to theaters but also to broadcast and cable television networks as well as the home video market.

Concentration in the Distribution of Motion Pictures

The dominance of a small group of companies in the distribution of motion pictures in the United States is not a new phenomenon. In the 1930s, the "Big Five" (Metro-Goldwyn-Mayer, Paramount, RKO, Twentieth Century Fox, and Warner Bros.) and the "Little Three" (Universal, Columbia Pictures, and United Artists) collected about 95 percent of all film rentals.[20] That was the general state of competition prior to World War II when the federal government began the antitrust action that led to the Paramount decrees. There have been clear shifts over time, however, periods when the impact of motion pictures distributed outside of the major studios was greater than at others. In 1987, for example, distributors such as Orion Pictures, Tri-Star Pictures, MGM/UA, New World Pictures, Vestron Pictures, New Line Cinema, De Laurentiis Entertainment Group, Cannon Group, and New Century/Vista Film Co. claimed at least 1.0 percent of the domestic box office share, with the top three combining for over 20 percent market share. Just eight years later, a headline in *Variety* asked, "Where have all the independents gone."[21]

The *Variety* article raises important questions about the decade that followed. Leonard Klady argues that the mergers and acquisitions that occurred in the first half of the 1990s represented a "cyclical scenario: Whenever independent films find an audience, mainstream forces attempt to replicate that success. And if history repeats itself with increasing precision, the majors will phase out their interest in specialty films within two or three years."[22] There is no question that replication is something that Hollywood does well, on the big screen and the small screen. Far less certain is the prediction that the major studios would "phase out" of specialty films within a matter of years. As discussed in chapter 2, the corporate parents of the major studios have continued to collect production and distribution companies of various shapes and sizes. This suggests a significant change in the nature of conglomeration, with the horizontal integration of specialized units into the major studios being part of a business model predicated on control over as much of the market as possible rather than a whim.

It is important to understand how this change in tactics influences the distribution of motion pictures in the United States. Scholars have examined concentration in the distribution of motion pictures in both historical and political economic contexts, and there is no need for a detailed examination of distribution in this analysis.[23] Given the apparent change in the mid-1990s, this study requires a review of the distribution of motion pictures between 1970 and 1995 and then a more focused examination on the decade that followed. This mirrors the measurement of prime time broadcast television program ownership that follows.

Motion Picture Distribution in the United States: 1970–1995

The prominence of the major motion picture production and distribution companies remained somewhat constant between 1970 and 1995, although there were some ebbs and flows. Table 4.2 details the average annual market share of box office revenues for the six major studios as well as MGM/UA

Table 4.2.   Domestic Market Share of Six Major Motion Picture Production and Distribution Companies and Metro-Goldwyn-Mayer/United Artists by Percent, 1970–1995

	1970–1974	1975–1979	1980–1984	1985–1989	1990–1995
Columbia Pictures[a]	9.5	11.1	13.2	7.1	15.4
Disney (Buena Vista)	7.1	5.4	3.8	12.2	17.2
Paramount Pictures	13.8	13.9	15.6	16.3	11.7
Twentieth Century Fox	13.9	13.9	14.8	9.0	11.1
Universal Pictures	10.4	16.3	17.0	11.5	12.5
Warner Bros.	14.4	14.8	15.7	13.7	16.3
Six Studio Average	69.1	75.4	80.1	69.8	84.2
MGM/United Artists	14.7	14.0	8.9	6.6	2.9

Source: The annual figures used to calculate the numbers are from *Variety*, 15 January 1975, 18 January 1978, 28 January 1981, 18 January 1984, 9 January 1985, 6 January 1988, 10 January 1990, 3 January 1994, 24 January 1994, 3 January 1995, and 2 January 1996.
[a] The total for Columbia Pictures includes both Columbia Pictures and TriStar Pictures for the six years from 1990 through 1995. Sony Corp. owned TriStar Pictures throughout this period, and the two units were placed under the common banner of Sony Pictures Entertainment in 1991.

in half-decade blocks. The dominance of these six studios over this period is clear. In each of the sample periods, the majors combined for an average market share of at least 69.1 percent and surpassed 80 percent in two of these periods, from 1980 through 1984 (80.1 percent) and again from 1990 through 1995 (84.2 percent). The market share for the top four firms is also quite high in these two periods, averaging 63.1 percent and 61.4 percent, respectively. The four-firm ratio (CR4) is a traditional measure of concentration, and these ratios gravitate toward a high level of concentration and point to a "tight" oligopoly, which suggests that collusion would be relatively easy. It is important to remember that such complicity was at the heart of the Paramount consent decrees.

What these market shares indicate is that six companies collected around 75 percent of the domestic box office revenues on average between 1970 and 1995. There were other studios active in this period, including Orion Pictures and the mercurial Metro-Goldwyn-Mayer/United Artists, which operated as both a single corporation and two different companies over this span.[24] The success of these two companies influenced the market share of the six studios that remain prominent. In the first half of the 1970s, for example, the market share of United Artists alone ranged from a low of 7.4 percent in 1971 to a high of 15.0 percent in 1972. This corresponded to the lowest five-year average for the six major studios, 69.1 percent. The majors built their market share through the 1970s and into the 1980s, growing from an average of 69.1 percent between 1970 and 1974 to 75.4 percent between 1975 and 1979 and to 80.1 percent between 1980 and 1984. What is interesting in this period is the decline of The Walt Disney Co. In 1970, Disney had a market share of

9.1 percent, but that percentage dropped over the course of the decade to 4.0 percent in 1979 and was no higher than that through 1985.

Independent distributors reached their apex in the last half of the 1980s. Between 1985 and 1989, the market share of the six major studios dropped back below 70 percent, with a five-year average of 69.8 percent. The high water mark might have been 1987, when Orion Pictures, MGM/UA, and TriStar Pictures combined for a 20.8 percent market share and the major share was just 66.6 percent.[25] Orion alone had a market share of 10.4 percent, which placed it fourth behind Paramount, Buena Vista, and Warner Bros. *Platoon* was the engine behind that drive, ranking second at the box office behind *Beverly Hills Cop 2*, but Orion had eight films that ranked among the top one hundred at the box office. What was most significant about 1987 is that eleven different distributors outside of the six majors had at least one film in that group, including five with films in the top twenty-five: Orion, Vestron, MGM/UA, New Line, and TriStar. In 1988, MGM/UA, Orion, and TriStar combined for a market share of 22.7 percent, but the major share was back above 70 percent and the integration of TriStar into Columbia signaled a change in tactics for the parent corporations of the major studios.

The first half of the 1990s witnessed the resurrection of the major studios. What is significant about this period is that it was the first after a series of mergers and acquisitions that altered the financial footing of some of the majors, including the integration of Warner Bros. into Time Warner and Columbia/TriStar into Sony. Another important change was the transformation of Disney from a studio that focused on content for children and families into a diversified studio with Touchstone Pictures and Hollywood Pictures. The value of this approach was most evident in 1992 when Buena Vista released three of the top ten grossing films, including *Sister Act* from Touchstone, *Aladdin* from Walt Disney, and *The Hand That Rocks the Cradle* from Hollywood. Buena Vista ended 1992 with a market share of 19.4 percent, second behind Warner Bros. (19.8 percent). The combined share for the top four in 1992—Warner Bros., Columbia/TriStar, Buena Vista, and Twentieth Century Fox—was a staggering 72.5 percent.[26]

The rising dominance of the six major studios in this period is clear, with an increase in average market share from 69.8 percent to 84.2 percent between the last half of the 1980s and the first half of the 1990s.[27] The highest single year total came in 1992, with a 94.1 percent market share, but it never dropped below 78 percent. This average, moreover, does not include the subsidiaries of the major studios or their parent corporations such as Miramax, which Disney acquired in 1993. The most dominant distributors in this period were Buena Vista and Warner Bros., with average shares of 17.2 percent and 16.3 percent, respectively. What is most striking, however, is the demise of the independents at the other end of the spectrum. The market share for MGM/UA topped three percent just once in this period, 6.2 percent in 1995, while Orion Pictures was a nonfactor after filing for bankruptcy protection in December 1991.

MOTION PICTURE DISTRIBUTION IN
THE NEW MILLENNIUM

The arrival of the new millennium coincided with what some proclaimed to be a prescient moment for the motion picture business. The financial success of *The Blair Witch Project* in 1999, fueled in large part from the buzz generated through a web-based marketing campaign, led some to predict the dawn of a new age. One Internet executive proclaimed, "It totally changed the economics and power structure of the business in one weekend," while another stated that, "for the first time controlling distribution is not important."[28] A trade journal made clear what was at stake, proclaiming that, "Digital video and the Web are coming together to change the rules of Hollywood moviemaking."[29] There is no question that *The Blair Witch Project* was something altogether different. One of the first films to utilize extensive digital video footage and edited on a nonlinear system, *Blair Witch* grossed just under $150 million at the domestic box office after being produced for less than one-tenth of one percent of that amount. A half-decade down the line, however, one must question whether anything really changed and whether *Blair Witch* was little more than an aberration.

The consolidation of motion picture distribution companies within a handful of corporations began long before the release of *The Blair Witch Project* and continued long after its startling success at the box office. The casualties of this quest for dominance include the independent distributor that handled *Blair Witch*, Artisan Entertainment, which became part of Lions Gate Entertainment in late 2003. In the months that followed, larger corporations engulfed other prominent independent distributors. In September 2004, a Sony-led consortium acquired the longest-standing independent distributor, MGM/UA, for close to $5 billion after a protracted bidding war with Time Warner. In March 2005, Time Warner overcame that setback and acquired Newmarket Films, a fresh new face in the distribution game that made headlines the previous year with the box office success of *The Passion of the Christ* and the Oscar for Charlize Theron for *Monster*. In December 2005, Viacom's Paramount Pictures acquired the live-action division of DreamWorks SKG.

The integration of Newmarket into one of the major media conglomerates put an appropriate period to a decade of consolidation in the motion picture business. Two Time Warner subsidiaries, New Line Cinema and HBO Films, acquired Newmarket to distribute some of their films, with the new company, Picturehouse, also financing additional films with modest budgets. The acquisition came nine years after Time Warner completed its merger with Turner Broadcasting, which included New Line Cinema and Fine Line Features, and two years after Warner Bros. created Warner Independent Pictures to distribute cheaper, more artistic films from "independent" filmmakers. The result is that Time Warner had a stable of distributors—Warner Bros., New Line Cinema, Fine Line Features, Warner Independent Pictures, and Picturehouse—to handle films of various genres and budgets, a classic example of horizontal integration. As discussed in chapter 2, the parent corporations of all of the major studios mirrored the Time Warner approach to one degree or another.

It is important to place these different independent studios within the structure of the corporations that own them. When News Corp. created Fox Searchlight in 1994, for example, it was one of four divisions within Fox Filmed Entertainment: Twentieth Century Fox, Fox 2000 Pictures, Fox Animation Studios, and Fox Searchlight. What is significant about this structure is that Bill Mechanic, the chairman and chief executive officer of Fox Filmed Entertainment at the time, oversaw each of these divisions, so operational control of Fox Searchlight resided in the same hands as Twentieth Century Fox, and funds came from the same corporate coffers. The same was true with the creation of Sony Pictures Classics in 1990. It was part of Columbia TriStar Motion Picture Group, which also included Columbia Pictures and TriStar Pictures. The management of Sony Pictures Classics answered to the same corporate executives as Columbia Pictures, one of the oldest majors.

The connections within Time Warner and Disney were not as direct but are nonetheless significant. As discussed above, Time Warner acquired New Line when it merged with Turner Broadcasting in 1996. As such, New Line Cinema was a wholly owned subsidiary of Time Warner, while Warner Bros. at that time was part of Time Warner Entertainment, in which Time Warner held a 74.49 percent interest. Disney acquired Miramax in 1993, and it remained a wholly owned subsidiary in the "creative content" area of the Disney corporate structure. While both Miramax and Buena Vista answered to Michael Eisner, which is significant, the two operated independently of one another. There is little question, however, that the financial capital that Disney brought to the table benefited Miramax.

Whether Miramax qualifies as a true independent is not the real question. The critical issue becomes what difference it makes. In 1997, Miramax announced that it acquired the sequel rights to *Rambo* and *Total Recall*, big event motion pictures that have been the hallmark of the major studios, not the independents. The reaction of a Miramax spokesperson speaks volumes: "The thinking is it [*Rambo*] is a great opportunity. These are pre-proven, pre-sold commodities. Not only domestically but overseas these properties performed enormously."[30] The open discussion of films as commodities is quite significant, and suggests that "independent" distributors, most of which now derive their capital from and deliver revenues to the same corporations as the majors, look at their medium in the same way as the majors. Sidebar 4.2 addresses the case of Miramax and Disney in further detail.

Motion Picture Distribution: 1996–2004

There is little question that the approach to achieving market dominance by the major studios has shifted since the 1930s. Prior to the signing of the

Sidebar 4.2
Miramax Films and Walt Disney: The Financial Ties That Bind

The end of the turbulent twelve-year marriage between The Walt Disney Company and the founders of Miramax Films, Harvey and Bob Weinstein, featured something of a Hollywood ending in the spring of 2005. While the Weinstein brothers agreed to leave Miramax after a contentious public spat with Michael Eisner and others, they did so with an agreement from Disney to finance and distribute future films produced under their new banner, Weinstein Co., albeit at the discretion of Disney. In fact, at the time of their divorce, Disney committed to cofinance six films, including *Scary Movie 4*.[1] No matter how acrimonious relationships become in Hollywood, it seems difficult to walk away from the deep pockets of the major media conglomerates. And there is no doubt that the Weinsteins thrived while writing checks from the Disney bank account.

The Weinstein brothers founded Miramax in 1979 and soon earned a reputation for spotting "art" films, foreign and domestic, which could attract an American audience. From 1988 to 1991, a Miramax distributed film received the foreign language Oscar for four consecutive years.[2] *Sex, lies and videotape*, a Miramax release in 1989, established a box office record for a specialty film at just under $25 million, a mark that was broken three years later by another Miramax release, *The Crying Game*, with over $60 million. *The Crying Game* was significant for other reasons as well, as it became the first in a series of Miramax releases to receive an Oscar nomination for Best Picture for 1992. It is also representative of "independent" films of this period as it was financed through outside sources, with an estimated budget of $5 million, and Miramax did not enter the picture until it acquired North American distribution rights for the finished product.

Miramax lost its true independence when Disney acquired it in 1993. Trade journals and newspapers continued to call Miramax an independent in many instances and, in theory, it was set up as an "autonomous division" under Disney's distribution arm, Buena Vista Pictures Distribution.[3] In the announcement of the deal, Harvey Weinstein proclaimed that the studio would have "complete freedom to operate as we always have."[4] Miramax failed a crucial measure of independence, however, as the most important component of the acquisition agreement was that Disney would finance all future Miramax films. The impact of this relationship was evident in Miramax's third consecutive Best Picture nomination, *Pulp Fiction*.[5] While the budget for the Quentin Tarantino production was estimated at a modest $8.7 million, it was quite different from its predecessors in that Miramax financed the film and produced it in-house. More significant was the impact the Disney dollars had on distribution, as *Pulp Fiction* opened nationwide on 1,338 screens in the fall of 1994 with a promotion and marketing budget estimated at between $5 and $9 million.[6] That was what the Disney deal was all about, giving Miramax what Bob Weinstein called, "the backbone and financial resources to back our bets and our instincts. Obviously, we would not have been able to go out and do this without their help."[7]

Miramax had its hands in seventeen different Best Picture nominations between 1992 and 2004. Some were low budget, nontraditional films such as *The Crying Game* and *The Piano*, while others were big budget, mainstream films such as *The Aviator*. Miramax's first Oscar triumph in the Best Picture category came for *The*

English Patient, which cost an estimated $27 million to produce, while its second Oscar came for *Shakespeare in Love,* which tipped the production budget scales at an estimated $85 million. The production costs for the third winner, *Chicago,* fell in between, at an estimated $45 million. *Gangs of New York, The Aviator,* and *Cold Mountain* represent the high profile projects that Miramax was able to pursue with Disney funds. The budgets for *Gangs of New York* and *The Aviator* topped the $100 million mark, with *Cold Mountain's* estimated at $79 million. All three featured big-name actors and all benefited from widespread distribution.[8]

Disney bankrolled Miramax to the tune of $700 million per year to produce or purchase films and then promote and distribute them, but there was a limit to the largesse. In 1997, Harvey Weinstein was the first to back Peter Jackson's quest to bring *The Lord of the Rings* to the big screen. Weinstein had a relationship with both Jackson and Saul Zaentz, who owned the film rights to the J. R. R. Tolkien work. Weinstein convinced Zaentz to sell the film rights to Miramax and funneled over $10 million to Jackson to develop the project. Jackson envisioned a multifilm series, and the projected budget was high enough to require Disney approval. Weinstein pitched a two-film package with a combined budget at a reported $180 million to Disney, but Eisner and Co. opted to walk away.[9] Jackson shopped the project to other studios, and New Line Cinema agreed to finance the trilogy.[10] New Line reimbursed Miramax for its costs, while Harvey and Bob Weinstein retained an executive producer credit and Miramax collected a percentage of the gross. The worldwide box office receipts for the *Lord of the Rings* series surpassed $2.9 billion, so the film padded the Disney bottom line, but it could have done much more.

Other complications came with the financial resources that Disney provided. The original deal stipulated that Miramax could not release films that carried an NC-17 rating, so the complete freedom that Harvey Weinstein spoke about was missing. This contingency was an issue from the beginning. In 1994, Miramax dropped plans to distribute Martin Lawrence's *You So Crazy* after it received an NC-17 rating. In 1995, Miramax used Disney funds to acquire *Kids* at the Sundance Film Festival, but it could not release the film after it received an NC-17 rating. The Weinstein brothers created an independent unit, Shining Excalibur Pictures, to distribute the film without a rating and then closed Shining Excalibur when its theatrical run was completed. Miramax faced a similar challenge in 1999 with *Dogma,* a satire on organized religion that featured Ben Affleck, Matt Damon, Salma Hayek, and Chris Rock. Although *Dogma* received an R rating, the controversial subject matter led the brothers to buy the rights back from Miramax and distribute the film through Lions Gate Films.

The final chapter in the Miramax-Disney saga revolved around political intrigue rather than excessive violence, inappropriate language, or religious content. In 2004, Disney prohibited Miramax from distributing Michael Moore's *Fahrenheit 9/11.* The conflict began in the spring of 2003 when word leaked that Miramax was bankrolling a film that explored links between the families of George W. Bush and Osama bin Laden. Disney sent letters stating that Miramax could not release the documentary, but the Weinsteins continued to finance Moore, believing that it was within its contractual rights since the $6 million budget was well below the level that required Disney approval.[11]

(Continued)

When the film was finished in the spring of 2004, Harvey Weinstein invited Michael Eisner, Bob Iger, and others at Disney to screen the film, but the senior executives declined the request and remained steadfast in their position. Following the pattern established with *Dogma*, the Weinstein brothers bought back the rights and distributed the documentary through Lions Gate Films. Less than a year later, the Weinsteins were out, Disney was in total control of Miramax, and one could only wonder who remained to distribute films that address controversial issues.

NOTES

1. Richard Verrier and Claudia Eller, "Weinsteins Face Life After Disney," *Los Angeles Times*, 30 March 2005, C1.

2. The four films were *Pelle the Conqueror, Cinema Paradiso, Journey of Hope,* and *Mediterraneo.*

3. Bernard Weinraub, "Business Match Made in Hollywood," *New York Times*, 30 April 1993, 39.

4. Quoted in Weinraub, "Business Match Made in Hollywood," 39.

5. The consecutive Best Picture nominations were for *The Crying Game, The Piano,* and *Pulp Fiction.*

6. Steve Brennan, "New Juice for 'Pulp Fiction,'" *Hollywood Reporter*, 19 October 1994.

7. Quoted in Brennan, "New Juice for 'Pulp Fiction.'"

8. The headliners included Leonardo DiCaprio in *Gangs of New York* and *The Aviator* and Nicole Kidman and Renee Zellweger in *Cold Mountain.*

9. James B. Stewart, *Disney War* (New York: Simon & Schuster, 2005), 303–304.

10. The production costs of the *Lord of the Rings* trilogy reached an estimated $281 million, plus an estimated $145 million in marketing and distribution costs.

11. Stewart, *Disney War*, 429–430.

Paramount decrees, the ownership of theaters was a critical tool in controlling the marketplace. While some of the majors have dabbled in theater ownership since the mid-1980s, the modern-day approach to market control through vertical integration is with the ownership of broadcast networks and cable and satellite programming services, including premium services such as HBO and Showtime, basic networks such as TNT and USA Network, and pay-per-view services such as InDemand. The fragmentation of the marketplace has required another modification. There was a time when the Hollywood studios could take a "one size fits all" approach to distribution, but that is no longer the case. The creation of in-house units, such as Fox Searchlight and Sony Pictures Classics, and the acquisition of independent distributors, such as New Line Cinema and Miramax Films, are testament to this more nuanced tactic. This also mandates a more sophisticated method of analysis.

In at least one sense, the prominence of the major studios declined over the last half of the 1990s and the first half of the 2000s. After an average year-to-year market share of 84.2 percent from 1990 through 1995, the majors dropped to an average of 76.2 percent between 1996 and 1999 and then 68.6 percent between 2000 and 2004. Table 4.3 outlines the market share for each of the studios between 1996 and 2004. With the exception of 1998, when the

Table 4.3. Domestic Market Share for Six Major Motion Picture Production and Distribution Companies by Percent, 1996–2004

	1996	1997	1998	1999	2000	2001	2002	2003	2004
Columbia/TriStar (Sony)	10.38	20.51	10.96	8.76	8.91	9.00	17.12	13.09	14.19
Disney (Buena Vista)	21.05	14.31	16.27	17.13	14.65	10.89	13.02	16.68	12.45
Paramount Pictures	12.82	11.97	15.89	11.52	10.55	10.97	7.48	7.11	6.79
Twentieth Century Fox	12.61	10.38	10.70	10.68	9.89	10.41	10.14	8.25	9.85
Universal Pictures	8.45	9.92	5.67	12.80	14.60	11.74	9.47	11.37	9.90
Warner Bros.	15.78	10.93	11.02	14.33	11.91	15.14	11.71	12.66	13.08
Major Studio Totals	81.09	78.02	70.51	75.22	70.51	68.15	68.94	69.16	66.26

Note: Market share estimates are measured through weekly box office figures in *Variety* and the database in *Variety.com*. All films included on the weekly box office charts are included. The year begins with the first week after New Year's Day.

combined market share for the majors dropped to 70.51 percent, the six-studio total ranged between 75.22 percent and 81.09 percent between 1996 and 1999. The market share for the majors was quite consistent between 2000 and 2003. In each of these years, they combined for between 70.51 percent and 68.15 percent of the U.S. market share from ticket sales at theaters. Each of the studios experienced ups and downs over this period. Three different studios claimed annual honors for the highest total market share at least once: Warner Bros. in 2000 and 2001, Sony Pictures Entertainment in 2002, and Buena Vista in 2003. Four studios ended a given year with the highest grossing film: Universal and *Dr. Seuss' How the Grinch Stole Christmas* ($255,327,115) in 2000, Warner Bros. and *Harry Potter and the Sorcerer's Stone* ($294,474,009) in 2001, Sony and *Spider-man* ($403,706,375) in 2002, and Buena Vista and *Finding Nemo* ($339,714,978) in 2003. Despite these shifts in fortunes, the combined total for the major studios remained constant.

Two thousand and four, at least at face value, appeared to be different. The market share for the six major studios dropped to just 66.26 percent and the highest grossing film of the year, *Shrek 2* ($436,721,703), came from DreamWorks. That marked the first time in over a decade that the box office crown went to a film from outside of the major studios.[31] The apparent decline in the market share of the major studios is more suspect, however. The third highest grossing film of 2004 was *The Passion of the Christ*, which grossed over $370 million at the U.S. box office alone. Mel Gibson's Icon Productions financed and produced the film outside of the studio system, but as part of a first-look deal it signed with Twentieth Century Fox in 2002, the studio had the right to distribute the film in the United States. After protestors marched outside the News Corp. offices in New York City in the summer of 2003, claiming the film was anti-Semitic, Fox opted not to distribute the film and it ended up with independent Newmarket Films. With revenue from *The Passion of the Christ* included in the total, the major studio share would have jumped to 70.2 percent, right in line with the previous four years. Twentieth Century

Fox, moreover, did make money from the film, since the studio exercised its first-look rights and distributed *The Passion* to the home video market.

The dominance of the major studios in the distribution of motion pictures remains just one aspect of this story, however. As discussed in detail in chapter 2, the corporate parents of the studios used horizontal integration to extend their reach throughout the motion picture business through the creation or acquisition of specialty production and distribution companies. The impact of this is evident in table 4.4. For example, while Warner Bros. generated over $1 billion at the box office in all five years, New Line made substantial contributions to the Time Warner coffers as well, with gross box office revenues ranging from just under $400 million in 2000 to just over $925 million in 2003. New Line was the most successful of the mini-majors in this period and bettered two of the major studios in both 2002 and 2003, Universal and Paramount in the former and Twentieth Century and Paramount in the latter. Miramax also bettered Paramount in 2003 with a market share of 7.92 percent and was a consistent contributor to Disney over this period, with a market share over 6.4 percent in four of nine years.

An analysis of the major studios that takes into account their subsidiaries and affiliates paints a truer picture of the dominance of a handful of major media conglomerates. While the market share of the majors did decline in

Table 4.4. Domestic Market Share for Distributors Owned by the Major Motion Picture Studios or Parent Corporations by Percent, 1996–2004

	1996	1997	1998	1999	2000	2001	2002	2003	2004
Sub Total (Major Studios)	81.09	78.02	70.51	75.22	70.51	68.15	68.94	69.16	66.26
Columbia/TriStar Sony Classics & Rep.	0.74	0.37	0.66	0.47	0.74	1.69	0.27	0.36	0.45
Disney (Buena Vista) Miramax & Dimension	4.48	6.80	5.77	4.47	6.42	7.53	4.14	7.92	4.34
Paramount Paramount Classics	—	—	—	0.03	0.22	0.28	0.08	0.10	0.06
Twentieth Century Fox Fox Searchlight	0.36	0.80	0.45	0.52	0.26	0.55	1.47	1.34	1.87
Universal Pictures Focus/USA Films/ October	—	0.29	2.66	1.08	1.20	1.74	0.89	1.15	1.32
Warner Bros. New Line & Fine Line[a]	5.14	6.20	7.99	4.17	5.32	7.15	9.62	10.25	4.71
Sub Total B (Affiliated)	10.72	14.46	17.53	10.74	14.16	18.94	16.41	21.12	12.75
Total	91.81	92.48	88.04	85.96	84.67	87.09	85.35	90.28	79.01

Note: Market share estimates are measured through weekly box office figures in *Variety* and the database in *Variety.com*. All films included on the weekly box office charts are included. The year begins with the first week after New Year's Day.

[a] The New Line & Fine Line figure in 2004 includes the market share of 0.138 for Warner Independent Pictures.

the latter half of the 1990s and again in the first half of the 2000s, much of that shift in market share was attributable to the distribution companies that fall under the same corporate umbrellas and utilize the same financial resources. Between 1996 and 2004, these subsidiaries and affiliates combined for a market share ranging from a low of 10.72 percent in 1996 to a high of 21.12 percent in 2003. In four of the nine years, the market share was 16.41 percent or higher. Time Warner's combination of New Line and Fine Line alone surpassed a 6 percent share five times, while Disney's combination of Miramax and Dimension did so four times.

When one combines these figures with those of the major studios, the market share of the six conglomerates between 1996 and 2003 ranged from 84.67 percent in 2000 to 92.48 percent in 1997. The totals for each year are included in table 4.4. The most dominant year in the new millennium was 2003, when the six major conglomerates accounted for nine out of ten dollars spent at the box office in the United States. Disney and Time Warner alone combined for a market share of just under 50 percent (47.51 percent). Seven of the ten highest grossing films of the year came from these two corporations, but what is most significant is that two of the films were from New Line (*Lord of the Rings: The Return of the King* and *Elf*) and one was from Miramax (*Chicago*). The four-firm concentration ratio was 73.48 percent with the combined market shares for Disney (24.60 percent), Time Warner (22.91 percent), Sony (13.45 percent), and Vivendi Universal (12.52 percent). That was the highest of this period and was the result of four years of growth.

As discussed above, 2004 was an unusual year, and the total market share for the major corporations dropped to just 79.01 percent. *The Passion of the Christ* was not the lone big revenue generator to slip through the fingers of the majors and mini-majors in 2004. As discussed in sidebar 4.2, Miramax provided Michael Moore with $6 million to produce *Fahrenheit 9/11*, a documentary that was critical of the actions of the Bush Administration before and after the attacks of 9/11. Disney, however, barred its subsidiary from releasing the film. In a complicated deal, Miramax founders Bob and Harvey Weinstein bought the distribution rights back from the corporate parent, financed the rest of the film on their own, and then released it through Lions Gate Films and IFC Films. *Fahrenheit 9/11* grossed over $119 million in U.S. theaters and accounted for 1.27 percent of the domestic box office for 2004. Without *The Passion of the Christ* and *Fahrenheit 9/11* included in the totals, the majors and mini-majors dropped to 79.01 percent combined. The inclusion of *Fahrenheit 9/11* alone pushes that percentage back over 80 percent and 2004 begins to look a great deal like every other year.

The performance of the nonaffiliate distribution companies was far more sporadic. Table 4.5 illustrates the market shares for the most prominent distributors within this group. To be certain, there were years when some of the smaller companies were quite successful and eclipsed a market share of 2 or 3 percent, but most of the time such peaks were attributable to a single

Table 4.5. Domestic Market Share for Prominent Nonaffiliated Production and Distribution Companies by Percent, 1996–2004

	1996	1997	1998	1999	2000	2001	2002	2003	2004
Major Studio Totals	81.09	78.02	70.51	75.22	70.51	68.15	68.94	69.16	66.26
Affiliated Totals	10.72	14.46	17.53	10.74	14.16	18.94	16.41	21.12	12.75
Artisan Entertainment	—	0.27	0.49	2.60	0.98	0.17	0.60	0.26	—
DreamWorks	—	1.54	6.92	4.54	10.27	4.93	5.41	2.84	9.86
Gramercy[a]	1.48	1.23	—	—	—	—	—	—	—
IFC Films	—	—	—	—	0.00	0.04	2.63	0.22	0.09
Lions Gate Films	0.06	0.11	0.13	0.69	0.42	0.66	0.76	0.60	3.22
MGM/UA	5.14	2.67	2.90	4.17	1.38	5.52	4.02	4.19	2.14
Newmarket Films	—	—	—	—	—	0.32	0.06	0.24	4.33
Orion	0.64	0.10	—	—	—	—	—	—	—
Polygram[b]	—	0.78	—	—	—	—	—	—	—
Others	0.87	0.82	1.52	2.04	2.28	1.27	1.17	1.37	1.35
Nonaffiliated Totals	8.19	7.52	11.96	14.04	15.33	12.91	14.65	9.72	20.99

Note: Market share estimates are measured through weekly box office figures in *Variety* and the database in *Variety.com*. All films included on the weekly box office charts are included. The year begins with the first week after New Year's Day.

[a] Gramercy totals are included in the specialty unit of Universal starting in 1998.

[b] Polygram totals are included in the specialty unit of Universal starting in 1998.

film. As discussed above, this was the case with Artisan Entertainment and *The Blair Witch Project* in 1999, and the pattern repeated itself with IFC and *My Big Fat Greek Wedding* in 2002 and Newmarket Films and *The Passion of the Christ* in 2004. In the other years, each of these companies was below 1 percent, and oftentimes well under that modest threshold. Lions Gate is a more complicated case. *Fahrenheit 9/11* accounted for close to 40 percent of its box office total in 2004, but even without that documentary, its market share would have been a relatively robust 1.95 percent. With the acquisition of Artisan Entertainment in 2003, Lions Gate was one of the few independent producers looking to expand in the mid-2000s.

That was not the case with MGM/UA. As addressed in chapter 2, 2004 marked the end of its storied and turbulent run when the Sony-led consortium acquired the studio. What was most significant about that purchase is that this group was not interested in the production or distribution capabilities of MGM/UA. Rather, the focal point was its vast libraries. MGM/UA experienced modest success between 1996 and 2004, with its market share bouncing between 1.38 percent and 5.52 percent. Its demise is significant, since it leaves few prominent independent distributors in the marketplace. With Lions Gate swallowing Artisan Entertainment and the New Line Cinema/HBO Films combo doing likewise with Newmarket Films, DreamWorks and Lions Gate Films were about all that remained in the summer of 2005, and DreamWorks's days as an independent were numbered. It engaged in takeover discussions with NBC Universal that summer and fall before Viacom swooped in and snatched up the studio in December.

DreamWorks raised additional issues. The much-ballyhooed independent studio posted some strong results since its debut in 1997, most notably in 2000 (10.27 percent) and 2004 (9.86 percent) when its market share hovered around 10 percent. DreamWorks also suffered through some down periods, however, including 2003 when its market share dropped below 3 percent. The high points from a critical perspective were back-to-back Oscars for Best Picture for *American Beauty* for 1999 and *Gladiator* for 2000 and one for Steven Spielberg for directing *Saving Private Ryan* for 1998. Despite these headlines, the most successful arm within DreamWorks from a financial standpoint was the animation unit that created *Shrek* and *Shrek 2*, which grossed over $700 million combined at the domestic box office and almost as much at the foreign box office. Seven of the twenty-five highest grossing films distributed by DreamWorks between 1997 and 2004 were from its animation group. This success prompted the transition of DreamWorks Animation SKG into a publicly traded company.

There is a second subset within that group that is of interest and further illustrates the influence of the major studios. Of the remaining eighteen films in the top tier released under the DreamWorks banner, a major studio cofinanced seven of them. This group includes two of its most successful films, *Saving Private Ryan* in 1998 and *Gladiator* in 2000. DreamWorks and Paramount split the production budget for *Saving Private Ryan*, while Universal agreed to share the up-front costs for *Gladiator* after DreamWorks grew concerned with the financial exposure from a budget that surpassed $100 million. In the case of *Gladiator*, Universal handled the foreign distribution of the film as well as home video sales, but the two parties split the worldwide proceeds on a fifty-fifty basis.[32] In 2000, Twentieth Century Fox cofinanced two other DreamWorks released films, *What Lies Beneath* and *The Legend of Bagger Vance*. The three films accounted for 48.68 percent of the $765.9 million that Dream-Works collected at the box office total for 2000. As such, it owed a portion of its record 10.27 percent market share to the major studios. At the same time, Twentieth Century Fox released a DreamWorks produced film, *Cast Away*, so there was cash moving in both directions, although it was far more common for the majors to handle the foreign and home video distribution of Dream-Works films.

SUMMARY

The distribution of feature films has stood as the least noticed but most powerful position in the process from production to exhibition since the studio system took root and a cause for concern for almost as long. In the 1930s, films distributed from eight studios, the "Big Five" and the "Little Three," accounted for 95 percent of the box office receipts in the United States. The Paramount consent decrees, which forced the studios to sell their theater chains and prohibited block booking and forced clearances, addressed the market power that the studios wielded. More than a half-century later, the major motion picture studios have not moved back into the ownership of theaters to a significant degree, but the power of the majors remains as a prominent issue.

The major studios are not as dominant as they once were, at least not at first glance. Between 2000 and 2004, the six majors accounted for between 70.51 percent and 66.26 percent of the domestic box office gross, significant numbers to be certain but well below the golden age of the studio system. Hollywood is different than it was generations ago, however. The studios once took a "one size fits all" approach to distribution, but that is no longer the case. The horizontal integration of once independent motion picture distributors into the same corporations as the major companies, and the creation of such distribution outlets, is the most significant development of the last two decades. The Disney creation of Touchstone Pictures and Hollywood Pictures in the 1980s and subsequent acquisition of Miramax is the most dramatic example, since it helped transform the house that Walt built into a diversified media conglomerate. With the addition of the corporate cousins of the major studios, the share for six corporations soared as high as 90.28 percent between 2000 and 2004.

This degree of concentration in the distribution of motion pictures becomes more serious when placed within a broader context. The motion picture industry has long functioned within an oligopolistic market structure, with high levels of concentration. What is new, however, is that these are no longer simple film companies, although their quest for market domination was never innocent. Instead, they are critical cogs within vast media conglomerates. In January 2005, one of the corporations that owned the six major motion picture production and distribution companies also owned each of the major broadcast networks, and most have vast collections of cable networks. This changes the story. Measured next is the degree to which these same corporations dominate the production of prime time television programming, the second important piece of the cultural content pie.

NOTES

1. Tino Balio, "Stars in Business," *The American Film Industry*, revised ed. (Madison: The University of Wisconsin Press, 1985), 159.

2. Claudia Eller, "Cruise Agrees to 3rd 'Mission'," *Los Angeles Times*, 8 June 2005, C2.

3. Todd McCarthy, "Spectacular 'Titanic' a Night to Remember," *Variety*, 3–9 November 1997, 7.

4. Quoted in Robert Pear, "Justice Dept. on Antitrust: 'Bigness' is Not 'Badness,'" *New York Times*, 25 June 1981, D1.

5. *United States v. Paramount Pictures, Inc. et al*, 68 S. Ct. 915 (1948).

6. "Justice Department decides not to seek modification of Paramount antitrust consent decrees," *Entertainment Law Reporter* 6, no 9 (1985).

7. Jennifer Holt, "In Deregulation We Trust," *Film Quarterly* 55, no. 2 (2001), 22–29.

8. Under the consent decree Warner Bros. signed in 1951, it was required to request modifications of that agreement before acquiring ownership of theaters. The Justice Department did not challenge the request, but in 1988 Judge Edmund J. Palmieri found that the court was not presented with an adequate record to base a long-range decision, so he ordered that Warner hold separate its interest in Cinamerica Theatres and that the court review its practices at the end of 1989. Judge Palmieri died of cancer in June 1989, and the U.S. Court of Appeal granted Warner ownership without restrictions two months later.

9. National Association of Theater Owners, "Number of U.S. Movie Screens," www.natoonline.org (accessed 28 May 2005).

10. Icon Distribution Inc. and Regal Entertainment Group settled the dispute out of court, with the lone acknowledgment coming in Regal filings with the SEC that amended its year-end financial data to decrease net income by $8.3 million. Regal Entertainment Group, Form 8-K, 1 March 2005.

11. Gabriel Snyder, "The Probe of the Century," *Daily Variety*, 14 April 2005, 1.

12. The eight films were *X2: X-Men United, The Matrix Reloaded, Hulk, Charlie's Angels: Full Throttle, Terminator 3: Rise of the Machines, Pirates of the Caribbean: The Curse of the Black Pearl, Bad Boys II,* and *Lara Croft Tomb Raider: the Cradle of Life*.

13. "All-Time B.O. Champs," *Variety*, 2–8 March 1998.

14. Two of Spielberg's more recent films, *A.I. Artificial Intelligence* with Warner Bros. and *Minority Report* with Twentieth Century Fox, crossed the $100 million barrier.

15. Quoted in Janet Wasko, *Movies and Money: Financing the American Film Industry* (Norwood, NJ: Ablex Publishing Corporation, 1982), 26.

16. Wasko, *Movies and Money*, 27.

17. Gary Arnold, "Film Notes," *Washington Post*, 26 February 1981.

18. Thomas Guback, "Are We Looking at the Right Things in Films?" (paper presented at the conference of the Society for Cinema Studies, 1978).

19. Guback, "Are We Looking at the Right Things in Films?"

20. Balio, "Stars in Business," 254.

21. Leonard Klady, "Where Have All the Independents Gone," *Variety*, 23 January 1995, 13.

22. Klady, "Where Have All the Independents Gone," 13.

23. See Balio for a historic discussion; Thomas Guback, "Theatrical Film," in *Who Owns the Media?* (White Plains, NY: Knowledge Industry Publications, Inc., 1982); and Janet Wasko, *Hollywood in the Information Age* (Austin: University of Texas Press, 1995).

24. The ups and downs of MGM/UA were remarkable over these two and a half decades. It ranked second among the studios in 1976 and 1977 with market shares of 16 percent and 18 percent, respectively. It gradually lost ground to the majors over the next decade and had a market share of just 4.2 percent in 1987.

25. While Coca-Cola owned part of TriStar Pictures from the beginning, it did not merge with Columbia Pictures until December 1987, so one can include TriStar in this group.

26. Sony Corp. created Sony Pictures Entertainment to combine Columbia Pictures and TriStar Pictures in 1991. SPE ranked third at 19.1 percent with Twentieth Century Fox fourth at 14.2 percent.

27. The 1990 through 1995 average includes six years rather than five. This resulted in a slight decrease in the average, from 85.3 percent to 84.5 percent, for this period.

28. Jonathan Talpin and Henry T. Nicholas quoted in Laura Randall, "'Blair Witch,' Broadband Makes Hollywood Rethink Web," *Newsbytes*, 3 August 1999.

29. Stephen Porter, "Changing the Rules for Movies," *Video Systems*, August 1999.

30. Quoted in Sharon Waxman, "Miramax Buys Some Hollywood Muscle; Does Move Make Studio Less 'Independent'?" *Washington Post*, 30 May 1997, B1.

31. TriStar Pictures distributed *Terminator 2: Judgement Day*, which claimed the box office crown for 1991 after grossing over $200 million at the box office. TriStar became part of the Sony empire in 1989, but it was not fully integrated into Columbia Pictures until the summer of 1991 when both became part of Sony Pictures Entertainment.

32. Andrew Hindes and Chris Petrikin, "U suits up for D'Works' 'Gladiator,'" *Daily Variety*, 13 November 1998, 1.

5

❖

Patterns of Ownership in Prime Time Network Programming

It was a tumultuous and telling six months, a time that made clear the importance of ownership of not just creative content but also outlets for distribution over broadcast and cable television. The first headline came in the summer of 2001 with the flameout of the Artists Television Group, the television production arm of the independent company that Michael Ovitz launched two years earlier. A second came a few months later when Sony Pictures Entertainment announced that it planned to shutter its network television production division, Columbia TriStar Television, five decades after Columbia created Screen Gems and become the first studio to move into the television business. Within days of that announcement, The Walt Disney Co. completed its $5.2 billion acquisition of Fox Family Worldwide, which gave Disney a general-entertainment basic cable channel, the renamed ABC Family, to go with its broadcast network, ABC. These were two outlets that neither Artists Television Group nor Sony Corp. controlled, which changed the dynamics of program production and distribution.

The changes that occurred in the later half of 2001 point to the importance of ownership in the production of prime time programming and the impact of conglomeration on the television business. Those who speak in grandiose terms about a five hundred-channel cable universe and pontificate about the demise of the broadcast networks would argue that the examination of patterns of ownership of prime time programming on the broadcast networks is no longer relevant. That is not the case, however. While the audience for the broadcast networks dropped in dramatic fashion over the last three decades, they remain the lone outlets that create shared cultural experience such as the Super Bowl, Academy Awards, or the final episode of *Seinfeld*, which attracted an audience estimated at 76.3 million.[1] Even in the aftermath of the attack on the World Trade Center in 2001, CNN and Fox News Channel reached an audience just a tenth of that size at its peaks.[2]

The flow of programming from the broadcast networks to cable channels is also quite significant. The highest rated channels on basic cable feature countless programs that built their viewer base on the broadcast networks. Much was made of the ratings that basic cable networks garnered in the February 2005 sweeps, a first ever win for basic cable over the broadcast networks in prime time.[3] The four highest rated channels in that sweeps period—TNT, USA Network, TBS, and Spike TV—all built the foundation for their prime time schedules around off-network programs. The battle between TNT and USA Network for top billing was one between different editions of the *Law & Order* franchise, with the original *Law & Order* on TNT and *Law & Order: Special Victims Unit* on USA Network. Spike TV countered with another off-network standout, featuring multiple editions of *CSI: Crime Scene Investigation*. The TBS approach was different but at the same time similar, as it opted for comedies rather than dramas but remained reliant on off-network shows such as *Friends, Seinfeld,* and *Everybody Loves Raymond.*

The connection between *Law & Order* and USA Network is an important one. When NBC and Studios USA discussed a long-term renewal of the original *Law & Order* in 1999, it was the third highest rated drama on television and a critical component of the NBC schedule.[4] That put Studios USA head Barry Diller in a strong position and in addition to a fee of over $2.5 million per episode for *Law & Order*, the studio also received the green light for a second edition of the Dick Wolf produced serial, *Law & Order: Special Victims Unit*. What was most interesting about the deal was that it allowed Studios USA, later folded into Universal Network Television and then NBC Universal Television Studios, to "repurpose" *Law & Order: SVU*. In the old days, prime time programs would not appear on cable until syndication began after four or five seasons, but episodes of some programs now appear on cable within days of their debut on the broadcast networks. And the cable outlet Studios USA chose for *Law & Order: SVU* was its corporate cousin, USA Network. The parties followed the same pattern in 2000 when NBC ordered a third installment, *Law & Order: Criminal Intent*.

Such negotiations are now much easier with NBC, NBC Universal Television Studios, and USA Network all under the same corporate umbrella. This was most evident in December 2004 when NBC Universal announced a then record price of around $2 million per episode for the syndication rights to *Law & Order: Criminal Intent*. What was unusual about the deal is that NBC Universal passed over traditional broadcast platforms and sold the entire package to cable. What was predictable was that the cable channels that acquired the rights, USA Network and Bravo, shared a corporate parent with the program producer. The deal for *Law & Order: Criminal Intent* broke the off-network record that *CSI: NY* set the month before. Corporate ties ruled the day in that deal as well, with the coproduction of CBS

Productions and Alliance Atlantis making the short trek within Viacom from CBS to Spike TV.

The stories of *Law & Order: Criminal Intent* and *CSI: NY* point to the importance of "software" within modern media conglomerates. The first two installments of *Law & Order* helped make TNT and USA Network the top two cable networks in the first quarter of 2005, and NBC Universal made certain that some of that positive karma was reserved for Bravo. What an off-network hit can do for a cable channel was also evident when the prime time ratings for Spike TV increased 33 percent in the first sweeps month of 2005 behind *CSI: Crime Scene Investigation*. Such programs can also improve the fortunes of local broadcast stations, most evident in the syndication of *The Simpsons* to the Fox-owned and -operated stations a decade earlier. Taken together, these cases make clear the importance of the examination of ownership and control of prime time programming to the understanding of how the motion picture and television industries work.

REGULATORY AND POLICY FRAMEWORK

The basic tenet of federal ownership rules in broadcast television was once the promotion of a diversification of ownership to maximize "program and service viewpoints" and to prevent undue "concentration of economic power."[5] In adopting the Financial Interest and Syndication Rules and Prime Time Access Rule in 1970, the FCC argued that "the public interest requires limitation on network control and an increase in the opportunity for development of truly independent sources of prime time programming" and "diversity of program ideas."[6] Such ideas remain part of the debate over program ownership. In the spring of 2002, Senators Ernest Hollings, Herb Kohl, and Mike DeWine called on the FCC to conduct a thorough examination of television program production before broadcast ownership regulations were relaxed, stating that, "Diversity of voices and opinions is vital to competition as well as the discourse of our democracy."[7]

The history of the Financial Interest and Syndication (Fin/Syn) Rules illustrates the power of the networks and studios within Congress and the FCC. In 1965, the FCC proposed the creation of new regulations related to the financial interests of networks with the expressed desire to increase the competitive sources of prime time programs.[8] The Commission addressed three areas in which network control was excessive and advanced the following goals:

> (1) eliminating networks from domestic syndication and from the foreign syndication of independently (nonnetwork) produced programs; (2) prohibiting networks from acquiring additional rights in programs independently produced and licensed for network showing; and (3) limiting to approximately 50 percent (with certain programs exempted) the amount of network prime time programming in which networks could have interests beyond the right to network exhibition.[9]

This framework became the foundation for the Fin/Syn rules, but the networks were able to delay the implementation until 1970. One reason that networks were able to do so was that the studios did not yet see television production as a market to exploit.

The dominance of the three national networks—ABC, CBS, and NBC—in the 1960s was clear. The network incursion into production and syndication took various forms, with in-house production in an owned and operated unit one option. Far more prominent, however, was a network interest in programs obtained from independent producers, shares that ranged from a percentage of profits from first-run network broadcast to a percentage of profits from syndication. One FCC report indicated that network financial interest in prime time programs increased from 67.2 percent in 1957 to 96.7 percent in 1968.[10] The overall change did not come from an increase in network productions, as the percentage of such programs decreased from 28.7 percent to 16.3 percent. What did increase was the percentage of prime time programs in which the networks obtained an interest in first-run broadcast and/or syndication.

The imposition of the Fin/Syn rules changed the ownership pattern in prime time programming. The rules restricted the number of program hours a week a network could self-produce and prohibited the networks from having a financial interest in the syndication of programs. The rules also prohibited the networks from syndicating off-network shows. The imposition of Fin/Syn did open the marketplace for prime time program production, at least for a while. In 1975, independent producers accounted for fifteen and a half hours of prime time programming compared to just four hours for the broadcast networks.[11] Most significant, however, was that seven motion picture production and distribution companies had stepped into that void and produced twenty-six hours of prime time programming. The prominence of these companies continued in the 1980s, as the major studios accounted for twenty-two and a half of fifty-two hours of prime time programming in 1982.[12]

The longevity of the Fin/Syn rules is remarkable and speaks to the power of the major motion picture studios. The Department of Justice once stated that, "the willingness of producers to spend large amounts of money to keep the rules suggests that significant wealth transfers may be involved."[13] In 1983, the FCC concluded that the financial interest rule was neither necessary nor desirable and could be eliminated without adverse consequences to the public.[14] Such a relaxation of the rules did not occur, however. In 1991, the departments of Justice and Commerce as well as the Federal Trade Commission all argued that the FCC should abolish Fin/Syn, but the Commission voted to relax but not eliminate the rules.

The Commission added two significant new components to the Fin/Syn rules in 1991. For the first time since 1970, networks could hold a financial interest in programs that were part of their prime time schedules, but could produce no more than 40 percent of their shows in-house. The networks, however, could not even discuss a financial interest in a program until thirty days after signing a license agreement with the producer. This prevented the networks from demanding a financial interest in a program from an independent producer or major studio in exchange for one of the coveted spots on a prime time schedule. The networks challenged these new rules in court, and in 1992 the Court of Appeals ordered the Commission to either change the rules or justify them more thoroughly.[15] In 1993, the FCC voted to eliminate the final components of the rules and set them to expire on November 1, 1995.

Seven years later, as the FCC began its biennial review, concerns over the power of the networks in the program marketplace had reemerged, most evident in the call for caution from Senators Hollings, Kohl, and DeWine. In the Notice of Proposed Rulemaking that set in motion the 2002 Biennial Regulatory Review, the FCC advanced four aspects of diversity that were the guiding principles of its multiple ownership rules that are central to this discussion: viewpoint diversity, outlet diversity, source diversity, and program diversity. The definition of source diversity related to the "availability of content to consumers from a variety of content producers," which speaks to the issues that have reemerged since the expiration of Fin/Syn.[16] In spite of the recognition that the public needed access to programming from multiple content providers, the Commission did not address the ownership of prime time programming after the demise of Fin/Syn. Instead, it attempted to push through the most widespread rewrite of federal ownership rules ever.

OWNERSHIP IN A CHANGING BUSINESS

When the FCC adopted the Financial Interest and Syndication Rules in 1970, the television business was quite different than it is today. The three broadcast networks programmed all the prime time hours, from 7:00 p.m. through 11:00 p.m., with local or national news most often as bookends, so the local market for syndicated programming was more limited. There were far fewer commercial television stations nationwide, so there were also fewer local outlets in search of programming. And there were no basic cable channels in the marketplace looking to fill a twenty-four-hours-a-day, seven-day-a-week schedule. These all influenced the market for off-network content. The two-and-a-half decades that Fin/Syn endured witnessed dramatic changes in this landscape: 7:00 p.m. to 8:00 p.m. became the most lucrative syndication window for local stations, there were almost twice as many local commercial stations in 1995 as in 1970, and there were countless cable channels searching for content.[17]

The television marketplace changed to a more dramatic degree in the first decade in the post-Fin/Syn world. In this period, the three long-standing broadcast networks—ABC, CBS, and NBC—aligned with a major motion picture studio, duplicating the structure that existed with Fox. Paramount and Warner Bros. also launched new networks, UPN and The WB, respectively. The corporate parent of each of them also acquired or created a general-entertainment basic cable channel to complement their broadcast network and in some cases placed them under common management: ABC with ABC

Family, CBS and UPN with Spike TV, NBC with USA Network, Fox with FX, and The WB with TNT and TBS.

These changes intensified the quest for ownership and control of creative content. For the broadcast networks, three distinct but related issues prompt the demand for an ownership interest. First, the control of prime time programs allows corporations to steer such content to in-house cable channels through either repurposing or off-network syndication. Second, an ownership interest ensures that the networks will share in the financial windfall when a program made popular in the prime time window is also successful in off-network syndication. Third, control of programs enables networks to reduce their vulnerability and better control the market when the time comes to renew license agreements with program producers. Sidebar 5.1 explores one of the implications of such control.

The perils of program procurement without ownership and control are substantial. *ER* was the surprise hit of the 1994–1995 season, but NBC rebuffed offers from its producer, Warner Bros. Television, to finalize an extended license agreement for the show during its first two seasons.[18] As the time approached to negotiate at the end of the initial four-year agreement, Warner Bros. found itself in a favorable position. *ER* continued to do well in the ratings, executives from other networks expressed interest in the show and valued it at $10 million per episode, and Jerry Seinfeld announced that 1997–1998 would be the last season for *Seinfeld*. Faced with losing two of the anchors from its powerful Thursday night franchise, NBC signed a new license agreement with Warner Bros. for $13 million per episode in 1998. NBC and Warner Bros. signed another four-year agreement for between $8 million and $9 million an episode in 2000.

The *ER* experience had a profound impact on NBC. In the fall of 1998, the heart of the development period for the 1999–2000 season, the network attempted to rewrite the rules of the business. In its negotiations with program producers, NBC demanded either an ownership interest in new serials or perpetual license fees that extended for the entire life of a show. The major studios balked at these demands and an unofficial boycott of NBC ensued for the better part of a year. Under the standard license agreement, a network obtained the right to broadcast an episode twice in exchange for a fee, with further distribution rights for the program, including syndication, reverting to the producer. The standard agreement covered four seasons, after which the producer could shop the show to other networks.

What strains the financial relationship between program producers and networks is the fact that license fees in the standard agreement often cover a mere fraction of the actual production costs of a show and contribute nothing to the general overhead of a studio. The program producers deficit finance the show over the first few seasons in the hopes of reaping higher license fees upon renewal and, most importantly, generating millions of dollars in off–network syndication. There are few shows, however, that last the four seasons needed

Sidebar 5.1
Television Program Ownership and Profit Participation

Creative accounting and disputes over profits have been around almost as long as the major studios. A common component of contracts between production companies and actors, directors, and writers is for the creative talent to receive a percentage of the profits, but collecting such back-end earnings can prove elusive. The financial books often suggest that motion pictures that gross hundreds of millions of dollars at the box office never break even. There have been scores of lawsuits filed over such accounting practices. In the summer of 2003, the original producer of *My Big Fat Greek Wedding*, MPH Entertainment, filed suit against actress/writer Nina Vardalos and others over a 3 percent share of the net profits from the film. Although the film grossed over $360 million at the box office and an estimated $240 million more in home video sales, and the original budget was just $5 million, the distributors claimed *My Big Fat Greek Wedding* had lost $20 million.

Box office icons such as Tom Hanks and Steven Spielberg can command a percentage of gross profits, and the *Los Angeles Times* reported that each of them received 17.5 percent of the first-dollar gross profits for *Saving Private Ryan*. Collecting a percentage of gross receipts provides some protection from studio shenanigans with the books, but even these covenants are not flawless. In February 2005, *Lord of the Rings* director Peter Jackson filed a lawsuit against New Line Cinema. The central claim was similar to countless other lawsuits: New Line owed Jackson as much as $100 million. What is interesting about this case is that Jackson was a gross participant, so his percentage, reported to be 20 percent, came off the top. In his lawsuit, however, Jackson claimed that New Line "self-dealing" with other units of Time Warner, such as Warner Books and Warner Music, diminished the gross revenues for the trilogy.

The stakes are much the same in television, where back-end syndication sales can generate billions. The conglomeration of the motion picture and television industries has complicated the issues and made self-dealing a prominent term in television disputes as well. Some of the accounting issues prominent in legal battles over motion picture profits are also evident with television programs, but vertical integration has introduced other flash points. The most contentious issues relate to the renewal of license agreements between in-house production companies and broadcast networks and the off-network syndication of programs to local stations or cable channels.

All these issues were evident in a single lawsuit between David Duchovny and Twentieth Century Fox. In 1996, the star of *The X-Files* negotiated profit participation in an extension of his deal with the studio. In 1999, he filed a lawsuit alleging that Twentieth Century Fox Television had reduced revenues for the program through the renewal of the series with its own network, Fox, and the sale of syndication rights to its own cable network, FX, and its own group of local stations, Fox Television Stations. Duchovny estimated that Fox shortchanged him at least $25 million in profits. The two parties settled the suit in 2000 when Duchovny agreed to participate in an eighth season of the series with a large increase in his per episode fee.

One of the most prominent cases in this area involved Steven Bochco and Twentieth Century Fox. The capital to create Steven Bochco Productions included $40- to $45 million from Twentieth Century Fox in exchange for which the studio obtained the

(Continued)

syndication rights to shows he produced on the Fox lot, including *NYPD Blue*. Bochco moved to Paramount in 2000 with an exclusive five-year agreement. Before he left Fox, however, Bochco filed a $15 million lawsuit accusing the studio of self-dealing the cable rights of *NYPD Blue* to the News Corp.-owned FX network for below market value. FX acquired the rights to *Blue* with a "pre-emptive bid" of $400,000 per episode in 1995, which was a record for basic cable at the time but was eclipsed within a matter of months. Bochco argued that News Corp. had sold the rights to FX in a "sweetheart deal" to boost the viewership and distribution of the cable network.[1]

The difference between the $400,000 per episode fee FX paid and the $700,000 fee that Bochco's lawyers argued was the fair market value for the cable rights was significant, since he received a 60 percent share of the syndication rights. Fox and Bochco settled out of court on the eve of trial in 2001, with the FX network granting an early release of its rights to *NYPD Blue*. Time Warner orchestrated the new deal, with Court TV, in which Time Warner held a 50 percent interest, gaining prime time and weekend rights, while TNT, another Time Warner channel, controlled other day parts. TNT and Court TV bought the rights for a combined total of around $700,000 for older *NYPD Blue* episodes that had aired on FX and $1 million for newer episodes that had not aired in syndication.[2]

While the *NYPD Blue* case involved the sale of the syndication rights, there have also been multiple suits involving the renewal of prime time series and serials from program producers that fall under the same corporate umbrella as the broadcast networks. When *Home Improvement* debuted on ABC in 1991, there was no connection between the network and the show creator, Wind Dancer Productions, or production company, Touchstone Television. That changed in 1996 with the merger between Disney and Capital Cities/ABC. Just one year later, the show creators filed a lawsuit alleging that Disney had forced a renewal with ABC rather than shopping *Home Improvement* to other networks or providing a license agreement at market value. Once again, the two parties settled on the eve of the trial.

A more recent case involved *Will & Grace*. Series creators David Kohan and Max Mutchnick signed a three-year, multimillion-dollar development deal with NBC Studios in 1996, and *Will & Grace* was the first show to earn a slot on the network schedule under that agreement in 1998. In January 2002, NBC Studios began discussions with NBC over a new license agreement and two months later signed a three-year deal worth between $4 and $5 million per episode. That made *Will & Grace* the fourth most expensive show on NBC behind *ER*, *Friends*, and *Frasier*. Fourth must not have been good enough for the show creators, however, as Kohan and Mutchnick filed a lawsuit in December 2003 claiming that the license fee was well below fair market value. NBC Studios countersued a few months later, claiming that the show creators had not participated in renewal discussions and had "hatched a plan driven by greed to squeeze every last dollar for themselves."[3]

Such litigation is becoming quite rare. That is not because the issues involved have dissipated but because producers and other profit participants are forced to sign agreements that preclude legal action. Most studios and networks have dropped language that they must seek "fair market value" and conduct "arm's length negotiations" when selling off-network syndication or repurposing rights for a show. The standard language in post-*Will & Grace* contracts at NBC Studios stipulated that, "(NBCS) is under no duty or obligation to attempt to maximize the amount of Modified Adjusted

Gross Receipts, Gross Receipts or Participant's participation in the Program."[4] The standard contract, moreover, stated that NBC Studios had no obligation to shop the show to other networks. Such agreements strengthen the hand of the broadcast networks and studios. And there are few options for show producers and actors, since the slots on prime time schedules are so limited.

NOTES

1. Cynthia Littleton, "Fox, Bochco Cuff 'NYPD' Lawsuit," *Hollywood Reporter.com*, 9 April 2001.
2. "Bochco's 'NYPD' Rights Cuffed at Court TV, TNT," *Hollywood Reporter.com*, 27 April 2001.
3. Quoted in "Courthouse Steps," *Entertainment Law & Finance*, 8 April 2004, 5.
4. Leslie Ryan, "Suit Cites Conflict of Interest; 'Will & Grace' Creators Say NBC's Vertical Integration Prompts Self-Dealing," *Television Week*, 15 December 2003, 1.

to generate one hundred episodes, the usual minimum for syndication. A Warner Bros. study found that only 13 percent of 428 situation comedies launched on the networks over a fourteen-year period lasted four years or more, and just 11 percent made it to syndication.[19] And a mere handful of those shows were considered to be true off-network hits.

For program producers, the numbers can be daunting. In one estimate, the average one-hour drama in the 2002–2003 season cost $1.6 to $2.3 million per episode to produce, but the average license fee was between $1 million and $1.6 million per episode.[20] The differences for multicamera situation comedies were similar, with average production costs between $850,000 and $1.2 million and license fees between $600,000 and $900,000. Program producers can recoup some costs through international distribution, but a deficit usually remains. The studio or production company will sometimes negotiate a higher license fee from a network, but the program producer must often give a percentage of the back-end profits in return, which reduces the windfall that comes from the megahit that can finance a series of failures.

The case of *CSI: Crime Scene Investigation* is an important one. Touchstone Television developed the original *CSI* for CBS, but when push came to shove, Disney did not believe it was a sound business arrangement and decided not to move forward. The estimated production costs were $2.4 million per episode, and CBS was offering a fee of just $1.1 million.[21] Moreover, dramatic series and serials often struggle in overseas markets.[22] When Touchstone walked away, CBS moved the show to its in-house unit, CBS Productions, as part of a coproduction with Alliance Atlantis. The *CSI* franchise added *CSI: Miami* for the 2002–2003 season and *CSI: NY* in 2004–2005. Not surprisingly, the original *CSI* made its first off-network run on the Viacom-owned Spike TV in 2004.

The other complicating factor is the financial reward that can await in off-network syndication for successful shows. The NBC experience is once again insightful. The peacock network broadcast four of the most successful sitcoms in history: *The Cosby Show*, *Cheers*, *Seinfeld*, and *Friends*. All of these shows began in the Fin/Syn era, and NBC did not have a financial interest in any of them. As such, it could not benefit from the profits the shows generated in off-network syndication. In the case of *Seinfeld*, projections are for the third run from 2008 through 2011 to push the value of that show in syndication alone to close to $3 billion.[23] *Friends* topped the $1 billion mark in its first syndication cycle, 1998 through 2004, and was expected to approach $3 billion in fees and barter advertising over three cycles.[24] In reaction to such success stories, the networks want a financial interest in shows on their prime time schedules in order to benefit from the financial windfall that awaits a handful of shows in syndication.

The Production and Ownership of Prime Time Programming: The 1970s

The production of prime time programming was quite different in the mid-1970s than it is at the dawn of the twenty-first century, but so too was the television marketplace. In the seventies, there were just three broadcast networks and there were far fewer independent local stations. The latter fact was significant, since it limited the available outlets for off-network syndication of prime time programs. There was another difference. When ABC, CBS, and NBC announced their new prime time schedules in the spring of 1976, just two cable networks had made inroads, Home Box Office and WTBS. While HBO relied on the output of the Hollywood motion picture studios, WTBS was the first cable network that transmitted off-network programs (i.e., reruns) to a national audience. The emergence of cable television as a programmer, and not just as the retransmitter of broadcast signals, had an untold impact on the production and distribution of prime time programs.

The Fin/Syn rules were put in place to minimize the power of the broadcast networks, and for a time the rules were effective. Table 5.1 lists the

Table 5.1. Independent Production Companies with Multiple Prime Time Shows, 1976–1977 Season

	Programs Produced	Hours Produced
Komack Co.	3	1.5
Lorimar Productions	2	2.0
MTM Enterprises	6	3.0
Quinn Martin Productions	3	3.0
Spelling-Goldberg Productions	3	3.0
T.A.T. Communications Co.	4	2.0
Tandem Productions	4	2.0

independent producers who had more than one show on the air in the fall of 1976. Some of the most heralded programs of that era originated with independent producers, classics such as *All In the Family* (Tandem Productions); *The Waltons* (Lorimar Productions); *Barney Miller* (Four D Productions); and *The Mary Tyler Moore Show* (MTM Enterprises), not to mention *Charlie's Angels* and *Starsky and Hutch* (Spelling-Goldberg Productions). What is also notable about this period is that the featured actors were more diverse, and many of these shows came from independent producers, such as *Good Times* and *Sanford and Son* (Tandem Productions), *Chico and the Man* (Komack Co. and Wolper Productions), and *The Jeffersons* (T.A.T. Communications).[25]

There were also independent shows that addressed topics that were new to prime time television. *The Mary Tyler Moore Show*, for example, focused on an idealized career woman, Mary Richards, and she came to symbolize independent women in a medium that created *The Adventures of Ozzie and Harriet, Father Knows Best,* and *Leave it to Beaver.* While Mary Richards was a television producer, Ann Romano was a divorcee raising two daughters in a small apartment on *One Day at a Time.* That show delved into topics all but ignored on prime time programs, and it too had independent roots, as Norman Lear produced it through T.A.T. Communications.

The range of programs that emanated from independent production companies, and the topics that such producers were willing to address, becomes quite evident when compared to the prime time slate from one of the major studios. Universal Television produced fourteen hours of prime time programming in the fall of 1976, but there was a remarkable sameness to many of the programs. That was most evident with *The Six Million Dollar Man* and *The Bionic Woman*, but there was a third show, *Gemini Man*, that followed a similar theme. In *The Six Million Dollar Man*, Steve Austin, an American astronaut, was injured when an experimental moon-landing craft crashed. Doctors replaced certain human parts with atomic-powered electromechanical devices, and he became a secret agent for the government's "Office of Scientific Information." In *The Bionic Woman*, Jaime Sommers, a tennis professional, was injured in a skydiving accident. She received electromechanical devices from the same doctors and became a secret agent for the same federal agency. In *Gemini Man*, Sam Casey was a secret government agent affected by the radiation from an underwater explosion and rendered invisible, which made him an even more effective agent.

The sameness of the Universal programs is most evident when one considers the collection of police and detective dramas that it produced, with at least one on each of the three broadcast networks. The Universal slate included four hour-long police or detective dramas, *The Rockford Files, Delvecchio, Kojak,* and *Baretta*, as well as the *NBC Sunday Mystery Movie*, an umbrella title for a ninety-minute program that featured four programs of the same ilk: *Columbo, McCloud, McMillan,* and *McCoy.* While the *NBC Sunday Mystery Movie* provided the audience with police and detective dramas on Sunday night from 8:00 p.m. until 9:30 p.m., CBS countered with programs of much the same genre with *Kojak* at 9:00 p.m. and *Baretta* at 10:00 p.m. on the same night. Universal provided a total of four and one half hours of programming on the average Sunday night that fall, as *The Six Million Dollar Man* aired at 8:00 p.m. on ABC. And there were weeks when the Universal total was even higher, as motion pictures produced within Universal Pictures aired on both *The Big Event* on NBC and the *Sunday Night Movie* on ABC.

The Universal dominance on Sunday night in the fall of 1976 would be common in the current marketplace, but it was somewhat atypical at the time. Once again, the strength of the independent producers was evident in this regard. The ABC lineup on Thursday night that season featured *Welcome Back, Kotter*, *Barney Miller*, *The Tony Randall Show*, *The Nancy Walker Show*, and *The Streets of San Francisco*. These shows experienced various levels of success, ranging from *Barney Miller*, which aired for eight seasons and received an Emmy Award for Outstanding Comedy Series, to *The Nancy Walker Show*, which was canceled before the end of 1976. What these shows had in common was that each came from an independent producer, albeit from different ones: Komack Co. and Wolper Productions (*Welcome Back, Kotter*), Four D. Productions (*Barney Miller*), MTM Enterprises (*The Tony Randall Show*), T.A.T. Communications (*The Nancy Walker Show*), and Quinn Martin Productions (*The Streets of San Francisco*).[26] A network prime time schedule with such an ownership pattern is unthinkable in the current marketplace.

The Production and Ownership of Prime Time Programming: 1976–2000

The production and ownership of prime time programs has changed to a dramatic degree since the mid-1970s. This is most evident in table 5.2, which details prime time program sources for the broadcast television networks in various years between 1976–1977 and 2000–2001. The percentage of program hours produced within the frameworks of the major motion picture studios remained relatively constant for the prime time schedules at the start of the 1976, 1980, and 1984 seasons, with the contribution from the major studios a low of 30.8 percent in 1980–1981 and a high of 39.6 percent in 1976–1977. The same is true of the broadcast networks, which held a financial interest in between 9.8 percent and 12.5 percent of the shows that aired in prime time at the start of each season. As such, the contribution from independent producers also remained more or less constant, with a range from 48.1 percent in 1976–1977 to 57.7 percent in 1980–1981.

The contribution that independent producers made in this period was quite significant. Prominent shows originated not within the major conglomerates but rather within independent production houses, including *Lou Grant*, *St. Elsewhere*, and *Hill Street Blues* (MTM Enterprises), *Cagney & Lacey* (Orion Television), and *The Cosby Show* (Carsey-Werner Productions), as well as the aforementioned *The Jeffersons*, *Barney Miller*, and *The Waltons*. In eight

Table 5.2. Attributable Ownership of Prime Time Programming on Fall Schedules of the Broadcast Networks, Various Seasons between 1976–77 and 2000–2001

	1976–1977	1980–1981	1984–1985	1988–1989	1992–1993	1996–1997	2000–2001
Total Hours	66.0	66.0	66.0	71.5	80.0	94.0	104.0
Attributable Hours[a]	53.0	52.0	56.0	60.5	68.0	82.0	88.0
Major Studio Total Hours	21.0	16.0	21.0	23.0	34.5	44.0	63.0[b]
% of Attributable Total	39.6%	30.8%	37.5%	38.0%	50.7%	53.7%	71.6%
Broadcast Network Total	6.5	6.0	5.5	9.5	19.0	22.0	27.0
% of Attributable Total	12.5%	11.5%	9.8%	15.7%	27.9%	26.8%	30.7%
Additional Hours with Link to Corporate Parent of Major Studio or Broadcast Network	0.0	0.0	0.0	0.0	2.5	12.5	5.5[c]
% of Attributable Total	—	—	—	—	3.7%	15.2%	6.3%
Major Studio, Broadcast Network and Corporate Parent Total	27.5	22.0	26.5	32.5	56.0	76.0	86.5
% of Attributable Total	51.9%	42.3%	47.3%	53.7%	82.4%	92.7%	98.3%
Nonaffiliated Hours	25.5	30.0	29.5	28.0	12.0	6.0	1.5
% of Attributable Total	48.1%	57.7%	52.7%	41.3%	18.4%	7.3%	1.7%

Source: Derived from *Variety* listings for each season.
[a] This number represents the total number of prime time hours programmed by the six broadcast networks, minus the hours in which there is no attributable ownership, hours that feature movies that have been released to theaters and those that have been produced for television.
[b] Figure includes two sitcoms that were coproductions of two major studios; *The P.J.'s* (Touchstone Television and Warner Bros. Television) and *Just Shoot Me!* (Universal Network Television and Columbia TriStar Television). These shows are counted only once in the total.
[c] Viacom Inc. folded its various television production companies under Paramount Network Television in 1999. As such, Spelling Television, Big Ticket Television, and Viacom Productions are included in the totals for the major studios.

consecutive seasons (1978–1979 through 1985–1986), a program produced outside the major studios received the Emmy Award for outstanding drama series. The drama that broke this streak was *L.A. Law,* Steven Bochco's first show after he left MTM Enterprises and set up shop at Twentieth Century Fox.

The prominence of the independent producers in the period was most evident in the 1984–1985 season as shows produced outside the major studios and broadcast networks dominated the Emmy Awards. The categories that went to independents included outstanding drama series (*Cagney & Lacey*/Orion Pictures), outstanding comedy series (*The Cosby Show*/Carsey-Werner Productions), best actor in a drama series (William Daniels, *St. Elsewhere*/MTM Enterprises), best actor in a comedy series (Robert Guillaume, *Benson*/Witt-Thomas Productions), best actress in a drama series (Tyne Daly, *Cagney & Lacy*/Orion Pictures), and best actress in a comedy series (Jane Curtain, *Kate & Allie*/Alan Landsburg Productions).[27] Independents also produced eleven of the twenty highest rated programs, a list that included *Dynasty* (Aaron Spelling Productions), *Dallas* (Lorimar Productions), *The Cosby Show* (Carsey-Werner Productions), *The A-Team* (Stephen J. Cannell Productions), *Knots Landing* (Lorimar Productions), *Falcon Crest* (Lorimar Productions), *Hotel* (Aaron Spelling Productions), *Riptide* (Stephen J. Cannell Productions), *Newhart* (MTM Enterprises), *Kate & Allie* (Alan Landsburg Productions), and *Highway to Heaven* (Michael Landon Productions).

The climate began to change in the mid-1980s, however. The program hours in which the major motion picture studios and broadcast networks produced, coproduced, or held a financial interest increased from twenty-six and a half hours in 1984–1985 to thirty-two and a half hours in 1988–1989, an increase from 47.3 percent to 53.7 percent. This increase is significant because the period saw the creation of Fox. The FCC and others argued that the introduction of a fourth broadcast network would increase the diversity of not only program genres but also program sources in the television marketplace.[28] It was this argument that led the FCC to ignore various ownership regulations that News Corp. violated, arguing that the creation of Fox served the public interest.

The Turning Point: The 1990s

The 1990s witnessed a substantial escalation in the level of concentration evident in the production of prime time programs on the broadcast networks. In 1992, the major motion picture companies, the broadcast networks, and their parent corporations held a financial stake in 82.4 percent of the program hours broadcast in prime time, an increase of just under 30 percentage points since 1988. The major motion picture companies held an interest in 50.7 percent of the programs, while the broadcast networks held an interest in 27.9 percent. What is critical about these figures is that 1992 was the year in which Congress passed the Cable Television Consumer Protection and Competition Act and the United States Court of Appeals for the Seventh Circuit called on the FCC to either eliminate the Fin/Syn rules or provide better justification. Nowhere within these discussions was the level of concentration evident in the production of prime time programming addressed or acknowledged.

The climate changed even further after the demise of Fin/Syn. The figures for 1996 reflect an even higher level of concentration, not just in the hands of the motion picture companies and the broadcast networks, but also in the corporations that own and control these companies. While the programs produced within the major studios increased slightly between 1992 and 1996, and the percentage of program hours with attributable ownership to the broadcast networks decreased, the percentage of program hours that were produced under the parent corporations of the major motion picture studios and the broadcast networks increased from 82.4 percent to 92.7 percent. The percentage of hours attributable to the major media conglomerates would increase even more if one included the motion pictures and made for television movies broadcast in the twelve hours allocated for such entities in both the 1992 and 1996 fall schedules.

Various changes occurred in the television marketplace that contributed to the level of concentration evident in these figures. The most discussed was the expiration of the Fin/Syn rules in 1995, and efforts by the broadcast networks to hold a financial interest in programs that they included in their prime time schedules. This will be discussed in detail later concerning the broadcast network schedules for the 2002–2003, 2003–2004, and 2004–2005 seasons, but the signs were most evident in the 1996–1997 schedule. The four established networks produced or held a financial interest in over 25 percent of the hours broadcast on those networks in the fall of 1996. The earlier relaxation of the Fin/Syn rules set in motion network involvement in the production of prime time programs outside of news and sports, and the 1996–1997 schedule revealed the inroads the networks started to make in this area.

The CBS Television Network was the most aggressive and held a financial interest in nine hours of programming. This total included two shows from CBS News, *60 Minutes* and *48 Hours*, but the remainder came from its in-house production unit, CBS Productions. Its credits included some of the most popular shows on the network, including *Dr. Quinn, Medicine Woman*, *Walker, Texas Ranger*, and *Touched by an Angel*. What is most remarkable, however, is that CBS Productions also produced one program that was quite successful on NBC, *Caroline in the City*. This raises obvious questions as to whether these conglomerates are competitors or collaborators, or as Barry Diller once put it, "enabling each other."[29]

Mission Accomplished: The 2000–2001 Prime Time Schedule

The trends that were evident in the mid-1990s accelerated with vertical and horizontal integration, and total domination was complete with the announcement of the 2000–2001 prime time schedules at the up-front presentations in the spring of 2000. Just twenty-four months earlier, the announcement of the new slate of prime time programs for the 1998–1999 season had been greeted with cries of horror from the major motion picture studios. The focal points were the schedules of CBS and NBC, the two broadcast networks without ownership links to a motion picture studio at that point in time. In what *Daily Variety* called an "unprecedented demonstration of network clout," CBS had been able to negotiate a financial interest in six of the seven programs it added to its prime time schedule.[30] NBC held a financial stake in three of the six programs it added to its schedule and extracted an interest in a returning series, *NewsRadio*, from Brillstein-Grey Entertainment in exchange for what NBC claimed to be the last open spot on the network's prime time schedule.[31]

The heavy-handed approach reviled in the spring of 1998 had become commonplace just two years later. When the networks announced their prime time schedules for the 2000–2001 season, demands for an ownership interest were so ingrained in the system that *Electronic Media* spoke of a "new spirit of cooperation."[32] This was in spite of the fact that the networks held an ownership interest in a record number of new shows.[33] Then again, the number of broadcast networks not under the same ownership umbrella as a major motion picture production and distribution company had dwindled to just one with the Viacom acquisition of CBS. The television networks and motion picture production and distribution companies were closer than ever.

The total domination of the major media conglomerates was almost complete at the dawn of the 2000–2001 season. The percentage of hours in which the major studios held a financial interest increased from 53.7 percent to 71.6 percent between 1996 and 2000, while the percent of hours attributable to one of the broadcast networks showed a similar increase, from 26.8 percent to 30.7 percent. When one accounts for other subsidiaries and investments, 98.3 percent of the program hours were traceable to seven corporations. The only shows without such a link were three sitcoms from Carsey-Werner Productions: *That 70's Show* and *Normal, Ohio* on Fox and *3rd Rock from the Sun* on NBC.

The Production and Ownership of Prime Time Programming: 2002–2003 through 2004–2005

The production and ownership of prime time programming for the mid-2000s was the result of a decade of unprecedented vertical and horizontal integration among the major media conglomerates and raised serious doubts about the degree to which prime time programming represented a diversity of voices and viewpoints. When Senators Hollings, Kohl, and DeWine called on the FCC to examine the production of programming in the spring of 2002, they raised some basic concerns. The first issue was the extent to which the largest distributors controlled the program production market and whether that changed over the previous decade. The second was the degree to which distributors of programming had a substantial economic interest in the programming distributed.[34]

The answers to these questions are complicated and often confusing, and one must examine the production of programming in a multitude of layers. One could define the largest distributors of programming as the six broadcast networks and the percentage of programming in which those networks hold a financial interest is significant. The shares for the debut schedules for the 2002–2003, 2003–2004, and 2004–2005 seasons are detailed in table 5.3 and when combined with the results from the 2000–2001 season, a clear pattern is evident. Over this three-season period, the broadcast networks held a financial interest in about one-third of their attributable prime time hours compared to one-quarter a decade earlier. There were clear differences between the networks, from CBS, which held a financial interest in numerous hours of programming, to UPN and WB that held a financial interest in almost none. But this is just one part of the story.

The case of CBS is an important one. As discussed earlier, CBS was quite aggressive in obtaining a financial interest in programs on its prime time schedule in the post-Fin/Syn world, creating numerous coproductions between CBS Productions and outside companies. At the start of the 2004–2005 season, these included programs shared with the television units of three of the major studios—Sony Pictures Television, Twentieth Century Fox Television, and Warner Bros. Television—as well as Alliance Atlantis. When combined with programs produced within CBS News, including *60 Minutes, 60 Minutes II,* and *48 Hours Mysteries,* there was a clear and direct link to fourteen hours of programming on CBS. So in terms of the "largest distributors" alone, CBS had a stake in 70 percent of the attributable prime time program hours on the network in 2004–2005.

While the prominence of broadcast companies such as CBS increased, what is also evident in table 5.3 is that the dominance of the broadcast networks and major studios continued at an alarming rate. In the 2002–2003 through 2004–2005 seasons, the group had an ownership interest in no less than 93.9 percent of the attributable prime time program hours on the six networks. The reason that the figures for 2004–2005 were a little lower is that the media conglomerates are still searching for a syndication market for reality-based programming, which accounted for five of the six nonaligned hours. This is also changing. In 2003, when NBC signed a new license agreement with Endemol USA for a fifth season of *Fear Factor,* it also acquired syndication rights to the program. In the summer of 2005, moreover, two reality-based programs in which Viacom holds a financial interest, *Survivor* and *The Amazing Race,* made their second-run debuts on cable channels, Outdoor Life Network and GSN, respectively.

Table 5.3. Attributable Ownership of Prime Time Programs on the Big Six Broadcast Television Networks, 2002–2003, 2003–2004, and 2004–2005

	2002–2003		2003–2004		2004–2005	
	Programs Produced or Coproduced	Hours Produced or Coproduced	Programs Produced or Coproduced	Hours Produced or Coproduced	Programs Produced or Coproduced	Hours Produced or Coproduced
Total Program Hours		104		104		104
Attributable Hours		92		97		99
Columbia Pictures	4	3.0	3	2.5	2	1.5
Paramount Pictures	18	13.0	18	14.0	10	8.5
Twentieth Century Fox[a]	22	16.5	24	17.5	15	10.5
Universal Pictures	9	8.0	8	7.5	6	5.5
Walt Disney	12	10.0	12	9.0	13	11.5
Warner Bros.	19	15.0	29	21.5	25	20.5
Major Studio Total	82[b]	64.5	92[c]	70.5	71	58.0
% of Attributable Total		70.1%		72.7%		58.6%
ABC Television Network	4	5.0	6	7.0	7	8.0
CBS Television Network	19	13.0	16	14.5	17	14.5
Fox Television Network	2	1.0	3	2.0	5	4.0
NBC Television Network	11	9.5	10	8.0	10	9.5
United Paramount Network	0	0.0	0	0.0	0	0.0
The WB Network	0	0.0	0	0.0	1	0.5

Broadcast Network Total	36	28.5	35	31.5	40	36.5
% of Attributable Total		31.0%		32.5%		36.9%
Additional Hours thru Subsidiaries or other financial Interest[d]	5	5.0	3	2.5	8	7.0
% of Attributable Total		5.4%		2.6%		7.1%
Studio, Network & Corp. Total	108	89.0	116	93.0	109	93.0
% of Attributable Total		96.7%		95.9%		93.9%
Non-Affiliates Hours	4	3.0	4	4.0	6	6.0
% of Attributable Total		3.3%		4.1%		6.1%

a The totals for Twentieth Century Fox include 20th Century Fox Television and Twentieth Television.

b This total includes two programs that are coproductions of major studios, Columbia TriStar Television and Universal Television in the case of *Just Shoot Me* and Twentieth Century Fox Television and Universal Television in the case of *The Grubbs*.

c This total includes two programs that are coproductions of major studios, Touchstone Television and Paramount Network Television in the case of *It's All Relative* and Touchstone Television and Spelling Television, a division of Paramount, in the case of *10-8*.

d The hours listed on this row include those that are not counted in the studio or broadcast totals.

There was a time when this level of analysis would have been sufficient to answer the questions that Senators Hollings, Kohl, and DeWine posed in 2002, but that is no longer the case. When one discusses "largest distributors" in the current setting, one must look at the corporate level rather than at the network level. In the 2002–2003 and 2003–2004 seasons, five of the six broadcast networks fell within the same corporate structure as one of the major motion picture studios: ABC and Disney, CBS and UPN and Paramount Pictures, Fox and Twentieth Century Fox, and WB and Warner Bros. The lone network not aligned with a major studio at that time was NBC, but the creation of NBC Universal completed the vertical integration of the networks in 2004. The integration of CBS into Viacom created vertical connections with a range of program producers such as Paramount Network Television and Spelling Television and there are other connections buried in subsidiaries and other investments. Sidebar 5.2 discusses these connections in more detail. Even in the case of CBS, where the network held a financial interest in a number of programs, the concentration of ownership looks much different when viewed at the corporate level.

The stories of News Corp., Disney, and Time Warner are similar and at the same time different. The corporate breakdowns for the 2004–2005 season are delineated in table 5.4. In each instance, the dominant producer in each conglomerate is the television division of its major motion picture studio, Twentieth Century Fox Television, Touchstone Television, and Warner Bros. Television, respectively. There are significant differences, however, ones that reflect the evolutions of the different conglomerates. News Corp. founded the Fox Television Network and created various production companies to support the network, including Fox Television Studios and Fox Television Stations Productions. Time Warner is the result of numerous mergers and acquisitions, and it possesses production companies from some of the major contributors to Time Warner: Warner Communications (Warner Bros.), Lorimar (Telepictures Productions), Time Inc. (HBO Independent Productions), and Turner Broadcasting (New Line Television). The Disney story is more similar to that of News Corp., since it did not experience mergers prior to its acquisition of Capital Cities/ABC.

In the end, however, what News Corp., Disney, and Time Warner had in common is more important, and it is something that these three conglomerates shared with Viacom: ownership of both a major motion picture studio and a broadcast network. While Viacom had an interest in twenty-seven hours of prime time programming, the various subsidiaries of News Corp., Disney, and Time Warner combined to give each of the parent corporations a financial interest in over fifteen hours of programming: twenty-one and a half hours for Time Warner, twenty-one and a half hours for Disney, and fifteen and a half hours for News Corp. When one accounts for coproductions, these four conglomerates alone held a financial interest in seventy-eight and a half hours of prime time programming in 2004–2005, 79.3 percent of the attributable hours programmed on the six broadcast networks.

Sidebar 5.2
What A Web: Program Production within the Viacom Empire

The contrasts between the CBS and UPN television networks are as distinctive as the differences between the white and black in the traditional "CBS EYE," the logo that first branded the television network in 1951. CBS traces its evolution to the dawn of television, while UPN took root in the mid-1990s; CBS broadcasts a full slate of programming, including news, sports, and soap operas, while UPN programs just ten hours a week; CBS affiliates rank among the strongest stations in most local markets, while the UPN affiliates are among the weakest. The biggest differences, however, are with the programs that the networks broadcast and the audiences that they reach. The heart of the CBS schedule in 2004–2005 was the *CSI* trilogy, *CSI: Crime Scene Investigation, CSI: Miami, and CSI: NY*, and its audience skewed older and Caucasian. The UPN schedule, on the other hand, was built around situation comedies and featured eight of the ten highest rated shows among African-Americans in the 18–49 demographic in the fourth quarter of 2004.[1] In the end, however, despite these differences, the two networks had one very important thing in common: Viacom owned them and Les Moonves managed them.

When it comes to ownership, things are not always as they would appear. This is true in the case of CBS and UPN and evident as one begins to unravel the programs included in the prime time schedules of these two networks. The challenge stems from the evolution of Viacom. It was created to handle the syndication rights CBS controlled when the FCC instituted the Financial Interest and Syndication Rules in 1970. Long before it acquired Paramount and CBS, Viacom was involved in prime time program production through Viacom Productions, which opened its doors in the mid-1980s. The expansion began in earnest in 1994 when it acquired Paramount Pictures, which included Paramount Network Television. In the process of completing that purchase, Viacom also merged with Blockbuster Entertainment Corp., which held a controlling interest in Spelling Entertainment. That corporation included a pair of television production units: Spelling Television and Big Ticket Television. Viacom reorganized these production companies in 1999 and all are now part of Paramount Television Group.

The Paramount wing of the Viacom armada includes a number of different production companies, and so too does the CBS group. CBS News became the first news division to produce a prime time magazine in 1968 with the debut of *60 Minutes*. The news group continued to provide prime time programming in 2004–2005, with *60 Minutes, 60 Minutes II,* and *48 Hours Mystery* on the fall schedule. When the Financial Interest and Syndication Rules were first relaxed, CBS was the most aggressive in obtaining a financial interest in programs on its prime time schedule, most often through CBS Productions. The common structure of such deals is a coproduction with a major studio, and CBS Productions had shows linked with Twentieth Century Fox Television, Sony Pictures Television, and Warner Bros. Television at the start of the 2004–2005 season. In most cases, the shows were shot on the major studio lots.

The merger of CBS and Viacom, completed in May 2000, gave the latter attributable ownership of two broadcast networks, which was a violation of the FCC's dual network rule. The FCC granted Viacom a temporary waiver of that rule when it approved

(Continued)

the merger and eliminated the rule relative to the UPN and WB networks in 2001. Later that year, Viacom announced that operating control of UPN would shift from Paramount Pictures to CBS, placing two networks under the control of CBS president Moonves. And one sign of that consolidation was evident in a sitcom on the UPN schedule that debuted in the fall of 2003, *Half and Half,* which came from Eye Productions, a unit within CBS Productions.

The power of conglomeration is evident within this group. CBS ranked first in total viewers for the 2004–2005 season, and Paramount Television Group, CBS Productions, and CBS News accounted for seventeen of twenty hours with attributable ownership on the network at the start of the season. There were two more programs with such a link to Viacom, however. The one area where the networks have not been as aggressive in demanding an ownership interest is with reality-based programs because of the absence of a proven back-end syndication market, but this is not the case with Viacom and CBS. While the *Survivor* and *The Amazing Race* franchises were developed outside of CBS (Castaway Television Productions in the case of *Survivor* and Touchstone Television in the case of *The Amazing Race*), the copyrights for the programs belong to subsidiaries of Viacom, Survivor Productions and Amazing Race Productions, respectively.[2] Another Viacom subsidiary, Pottle Productions, held the copyright to *America's Next Top Model,* which aired twice a week on UPN in the fall of 2004–2005.

When *Survivor* and *The Amazing Race* are added to the Viacom total, nineteen of the twenty attributable hours on the CBS network at the dawn of the 2004–2005 season had an ownership link to its parent corporation. The interlopers were two situation comedies on Monday night, *Everybody Loves Raymond* from HBO Independent Productions, Inc. and Worldwide Pants Inc. and *Two and a Half Men* from Warner Bros. Television. When the Financial Interest and Syndication and Prime Time Access rules were put in place in 1970, the FCC argued that, "the public interest requires limitation on network control and an increase in the opportunity for development of truly independent sources of prime time programming" and "diversity of program ideas."[3] When the FCC allowed the rules to expire in 1995, it argued that the networks were no longer in a position of sufficient power to demand an ownership interest and that the marketplace would ensure that there was a diversity of program ideas. While the flood of crime scene series and serials would challenge the latter belief, the Viacom ownership of 95 percent of the attributable program hours on CBS in 2004–2005 raises doubts about the former argument as well.

NOTES

1. Kevin Downey, "UPN's Year-Round Appeal," *Broadcasting & Cable* 7 February 2005, 23.

2. In the case of *The Amazing Race*, both Touchstone Television and Amazing Race Productions are copyright holders.

3. Federal Communication Commission, "In the matter of Amendment of Part 73 of the Commission's Rules and Regulations with Respect to Competition and Responsibility in Network Television Broadcasting," 23 FCC 2d 382 (1970).

Table 5.4 Attributable Financial Interest of Prime Time Programs for Six Media Conglomerates, 2004–2005 Fall Schedule

	Programs Produced, Coproduced, or with Financial Interest	*Hours Produced, Coproduced, or with Financial Interest*
NBC UNIVERSAL[a]		
Studio: Universal Pictures		
Universal Network Television	6	5.5
Network: NBC		
NBC Studios	8	7.5
NBC News	2	2.0
Other Subsidiaries/Investments		
NBC Enterprises	1	1.0
DreamWorks SKG	2	1.5
NBC UNIVERSAL TOTAL[b]	17	15.5
NEWS CORP.		
Studio: Twentieth Century Fox		
20th Century Fox Television	14	9.5
Twentieth Television	1	1.0
Network: Fox		
Fox Broadcasting Co.	3	3.0
Fox Television Stations Prod.	2	1.0
Other Subsidiaries & Investments		
Greenblatt-Janollari Prods.	1	0.5
Regency Television	4	2.0
NEWS CORP. TOTAL[c]	22	15.5
SONY CORP.		
Studio: Columbia Pictures		
Sony Pictures Television	2	1.5
SONY CORP. TOTAL	2	1.5
TIME WARNER INC.		
Studio: Warner Bros.		
Warner Bros. Television	23	18.5
Telepictures Productions	2	2.0
Network: The WB Network	1	0.5
Other Subsidiaries & Investments		
HBO Independent Prods.	1	0.5
TIME WARNER INC. TOTAL	27	21.5
VIACOM INC.		
Studio: Paramount Pictures		
Paramount Network Television	7	5.5
Spelling Television	3	3.0
Network: CBS Network		
CBS News	3	3.0
CBS Productions	13	11.0
Eye Productions	1	0.5

Table 5.4   Attributable Financial Interest of Prime Time Programs for Six Media Conglomerates, 2004–2005 Fall Schedule (*Continued*)

	Programs produced, coproduced, or with financial interest	Hours produced, coproduced, or with financial interest
Other Subsidiaries & Investments		
Amazing Race Productions	1	1.0
Pottle Productions	2	2.0
Survivor Productions	1	1.0
VIACOM INC. TOTAL	31	27.0
WALT DISNEY CO.		
Studio: Walt Disney Studios		
Touchstone Television	12	8.5
Walt Disney Television	1	3.0
Network: ABC		
ABC News	2	2.0
ABC Sports	1	2.0
ABC Entertainment	1	1.0
Greengrass Productions	3	3.0
Other Subsidiaries & Investments		
Diplomatic Productions	2	2.0
WALT DISNEY CO. TOTAL	22	21.5

[a] Universal Network Television and NBC Studios combined with the creation of NBC Universal in the spring of 2004. This was after the development phase of new shows, so programs are attributable to the unit in which they were developed.

[b] There was one program, *American Dreams*, which was a coproduction of NBC Studios and Universal Network Television. It is counted in the figures for each production group but only once in the overall totals. The same is true of a coproduction of NBC Studios and DreamWorks SKG, *LAX*. NBC has a developed deal with DreamWorks Television through which the network holds syndication rights for DreamWorks programs that air on NBC. DreamWorks Animation was listed as the producer of *Father of the Pride*, but NBC held syndication rights for the program.

[c] There are three Fox shows, *Bernie Mac, Method & Red,* and *Malcolm in the Middle,* which were coproduced by Twentieth Century Fox Televsion and Regency Television, in which News Corp. holds a financial interest. The shows are attributed to each production group but counted only once in the totals. There is a fourth show, *Listen Up,* which is a coproduction of Regency Television and CBS Productions. This is not included in the total for Twentieth Century Fox Television.

It is important to compare those four conglomerates to the three that did not feature vertical integration between a broadcast network and a major studio at the start of the 2003–2004 season. As discussed above, Sony announced the closure of its television production unit in the fall of 2001, although it continued to produce three shows for CBS into the 2004–2005 season. NBC was aggressive in obtaining a financial interest in programs on its prime time schedule through NBC Studios, but the overall total was still low because of the absence of a major studio. Vivendi Universal brought its disparate production groups back under one roof, Universal Network Television, after the reacquisition of the Studios USA production group in 2001. And while Universal Network Television accounted for eight programs in 2003–2004, more than a third of those came from the *Law & Order* franchise on NBC. With the creation of NBC Universal, NBC Studios and Universal Network Television merged to create NBC Universal Television Studios and the fifteen and a half hours of program time in which NBC Universal held a financial interest was in line with the four more established network/studio combinations.

What is most striking is the almost total absence of independent productions, shows not traceable back to one of the broadcast networks or major motion picture studios. In 2003–2004, the total count was four out of 121 shows with attributable ownership. The Fox schedule included one sitcom from Carsey-Werner-Mandalbach Productions, *That 70's Show*, and the offshoot of *American Idol* from Freemantle Media, *American Juniors*. Carsey-Werner-Mandalbach had another show on The WB, *Grounded for Life*. The fourth and final show was *WWE Smackdown* on UPN, and there were Viacom connections to that show. When UPN signed the agreement with Titan Sports for carriage of the show, Viacom also took a financial interest in World Wrestling Entertainment, the parent corporation of Titan Sports. That investment ended in the spring of 2003 when WWE repurchased the Viacom shares.

The situation was not much different in 2004–2005. While the number of programs and hours increased, much of this was attributable to reality-based programs such as *The Apprentice* on NBC and *The Next Great Champ* and *The Complex: Malibu* on Fox where there is no identifiable ownership interest as well as the aforementioned *WWE Smackdown* on UPN. There were still only two scripted dramas or situation comedies without such a connection: *That 70's Show* and *Grounded for Life*. In the fall of 2004, The WB opted not to renew *Grounded for Life* for a second thirteen-episode order, so the situation comedy ended its run in mid-season. That was longer than *The Next Great Champ* lasted on Fox, as it moved to Fox Sports Net after just four episodes.

The Evolution of Television Production Companies

Twentieth Century Fox Television ranked as the most prolific producer of prime time programs after the up-front presentations in the spring of 2002 with nineteen shows, the fifth consecutive season in which the Fox production group had led all others. That success was attributable to the myriad of production companies that work under the Twentieth Century Fox Television banner, not to mention those under the Fox Television Studios moniker. The most prominent producer in the Fox camp was David E. Kelley, who claimed a pair of Emmy Awards in 1999 for outstanding drama series for *The Practice* and outstanding comedy series for *Ally McBeal*. Others that signed or extended deals with Fox in 2002 alone included the television wing of Ron Howard and Brian Grazer's Imagine Entertainment, as well as the small-screen unit of Brad Grey's Brillstein-Grey Entertainment.

The relationship between these producers and Twentieth Century Fox Television are a sign of the times. When Marcy Carsey and Tom Werner created Carsey-Werner in 1981, they did not turn to the major production and distribution companies for financing, but, rather, took second mortgages on their homes and worked out of a one-room office above a shoe store.[35] That stands in sharp contrast to the origins of Steven Bochco Productions. Bochco produced *Hill Street Blues* for MTM Enterprises prior to the creation of his own production company, so he had the credentials to attract investment capital from independent sources. In the end, however, the foundation for Steven Bochco Productions was built on a $40 to $45-million investment from Twentieth Century Fox, while the actual offices for Bochco were built on the Fox lot as part of a real estate deal that was also part of that agreement. In exchange, Fox obtained the syndication rights for television programs such as *NYPD Blue*. Bochco moved from Fox to Paramount in 2000 with an exclusive five-year agreement valued at between $45 and $50 million. As discussed in sidebar 5.1, Bochco filed suit before he left Fox accusing the studio of self-dealing the cable rights for *NYPD Blue* to the News Corp.-owned FX network for below market value.

The legal battle between Twentieth Century Fox and Steven Bochco is important to consider, since it illustrates what the control of programming means in a world of diversified media conglomerates for which vertical integration is a mantra. It also reveals the financial dynamics of program production. *NYPD Blue* debuted on ABC in the fall of 1993 and was still on the network roster a decade later, reaping millions of dollars in profits from both the license fees from ABC and the much-discussed off-network syndication on both local broadcast stations and cable networks. The 2002–2003 ABC schedule did not include another Bochco production, *Philly*, which debuted twelve months earlier to critical acclaim but was cancelled in the spring. The up-front dollars to launch *Philly*, which featured former *NYPD Blue* star Kim Delaney, were considerable, but there were no millions in syndication to offset the costs of that program.

It is valuable to revisit the definition of independence often used with motion picture production and distribution companies: "The independent producer may be defined as a corporate organization controlled as to ownership and management by one or more individuals who obtain the needed financing and arrange for the distribution of the pictures under their supervision."[36] These producers, however, "maintained their own organizations, separate from (and outside of) the major studios."[37] When applied to television program production, this definition would strip independence from the various production companies that function within motion picture companies, such as David E. Kelley Productions and Steven Bochco Productions. Other components of this definition are critical to this discussion. The first important point is the notion of "controlled as to ownership and management." Numerous production companies that receive the capital required for program development and production from a motion picture company or broadcast network are called independent. Within this definition, such a claim of independence would be false. The second point is the question of distribution, which is a critical issue when it involves off-network syndication.

Prime Time Programming: Reconsidered

What is ironic about the agreement signed in 2002 between DreamWorks and NBC to produce television programs is that the two engaged in a rather public feud in the spring of 1997. DreamWorks pulled three sitcoms that were in development for NBC, claiming the network demanded a financial interest in two of the programs. That battle shows just how far the networks and studios have come in the post-Fin/Syn era. DreamWorks partner Jeffrey Katzenberg stated, "The world has changed. The networks have a much, much stronger hand and are a much stronger force in the development and production of shows for air. You can stick your head in the sand and ignore that at your own peril. The writing has been on the wall for us for a year."[38]

The new world that producers such as Katzenberg face is one where ownership is critical at every turn. The financial interest in back-end syndication of programs is just one of the issues faced when pilots are in development. Production companies and networks must also address expanded rerun rights, extended license fees, and cable repurposing rights. And in most cases, the power position is that which the broadcast network occupies. That reality became clear in the summer of 2005 when Marcy Carsey and Tom Werner announced that Carsey-Werner Productions, the company responsible for *The Cosby Show, Roseanne, That 70's Show,* and over 2,000 hours of programming, was scaling back on program development and looking for a new business model after twenty-four years. In the words of Werner, "Given the odds of getting on the air, that model had to be thrown up into the air."[39]

The examination of the countless tentacles that tie various production companies back to the conglomerates that own the broadcast networks forces one to revisit the question posed earlier, the degree to which the largest distributors control or influence the marketplace. When the "largest distributors" is defined in a narrow manner as the six broadcast networks, the dominance of prime time programming is significant but not overwhelming, accounting for about one-third of program hours over a three-year period. And a significant portion of that share in each of these years could be attributed to a single network, CBS.

That is a flawed definition of largest distributors, however. True control and influence over these distributors resides not just in the broadcast networks but also in the conglomerates that own them. To disregard the corporate connections would be to ignore the basic tenets of horizontal and vertical integration that drove the mergers and acquisitions that created these behemoths. When ownership is remeasured and the subsidiaries of the corporate parents of the broadcast networks are included, the results were very different and quite dramatic. Table 5.5 documents the dominance of in-corporation productions on each of the broadcast networks.

Table 5.5 Prime Time Programs with Financial Interest Attributable to Network or Parent Corporation of Network, 2002–2003, 2003–2004, and 2004–2005 Fall Schedules

	2002–2003		2003–2004		2004–2005	
	Total Attributable Hours	Hours with Attributable Interest	Total Attributable Hours	Hours with Attributable Interest	Total Attributable Hours	Hours with Attributable Interest
ABC/Walt Disney	19	14.0 (73.7%)	22	16.5 (75.0%)	22	18 (81.8%)
CBS/Viacom	20	17.5 (87.5%)	20	18 (90.0%)	20	19 (95.0%)
Fox/News Corp.	13	11.0 (84.6%)	15	11.0 (73.3%)	15	10.5 (70.0%)
NBC/NBC Universal[a]	19	9.5 (50.0%)	19	9.0 (47.4%)	19	14.5 (76.3%)
UPN/Viacom	8	6.0 (75.0%)	8	4.0 (50.0%)	10	5.0 (50.0%)
WB/TIME Warner	13	6.5 (50.0%)	13	9.0 (69.2%)	13	9.0 (69.2%)

[a] The totals for NBC/NBC Universal include those for NBC Studios, NBC News, and NBC Enterprises for the 2002–2003 and 2003–2004 seasons as well as for those three plus Universal Network Television for the 2004–2005 season.

The percentage of prime time programs on ABC, CBS, NBC, and Fox in which their respective parent corporations held a financial interest at the start of the 2004–2005 season ranged from a high of 95 percent to a low of 70 percent. The road taken varied with the different corporations, but the dominance of home-produced products is overwhelming no matter the approach. Viacom owned a financial interest in a high percentage of its shows through CBS Productions, the network's in-house production company the network created before the Viacom acquisition in 2000 placed CBS and Paramount Pictures under the same roof. On the other hand, Disney completed its acquisition of ABC in the first quarter of 1996, months after the Fin/Syn rules expired, and the dominance of the studio's in-house production company was clear in the 2004–2005 season when Touchstone Television produced nine programs on ABC in addition to *The Wonderful World of Disney*.

SUMMARY

The creation of new broadcast networks was long trumpeted as a guarantor of increased voice and viewpoint diversity in the television marketplace. In 1985, the FCC stated, "communities now have access to such a wide variety of stations that the scarcity doctrine . . . is obsolete."[40] The foundation for the scarcity doctrine was the argument that the scarcity of broadcast channels threatened voice and viewpoint diversity. The proliferation of outlets since that opinion was issued, with an increase in the number of broadcast networks from three to six, should have created access to divergent sources of prime time programming, and, in turn, greater diversification in voices and viewpoints.

That did not occur. With NBC and Universal within the same corporation for the 2004–2005 season, the conglomerates that own the six broadcast networks—as well as five of the six major motion picture studios—had an interest in 93.9 percent of the attributable prime time hours on the six networks, and that share was the lowest in three years. What is perhaps most striking is that prime time program production is right back where it was prior to the creation of the Financial Interest and Syndication Rules. In 1968, the FCC found that the three broadcast networks held a financial interest in 96.7 percent of the shows on their prime time schedules. Now there are six broadcast networks, but that group of networks, coupled with their corporate parents, has returned to a point of dominance. At the start of the 2003–2004 season, there were just four programs total without such a connection. The ABC lineup on Thursday nights at the start of the 1976–1977 season featured five programs, from five different independent producers. Some would argue that the proliferation of cable networks has made these levels of concentration meaningless, but the plot becomes quite different after the examination of ownership of those outlets in the next chapter.

NOTES

1. Brian Lowry, "'Seinfeld's' Finale Ends Up in Sixth Place on All Time," *Los Angeles Times*, 16 May 1998, F2.

2. In prime time on the night of September 11, an estimated sixty million viewers watched the four broadcast networks combined, while CNN and Fox News Channels reached around fifteen million during President Bush's address that evening. *Hollywood Reporter*, 13 September 2003.

3. R. Thomas Umstsead, "Cable Nips a Sweeps Win," *Multichannel News*, 7 March 2005, 31.

4. Stephen Battaglio, "NBC Explains Why 'Law' Went West of the Affils," *Hollywood Reporter*, 17 May 1999.

5. Federal Communications Commission, *Rules and Regulations Relating to the Multiple Ownership of AM, FM and Television Broadcasting Stations* (1953), 292–293.

6. Federal Communications Commission, "In the Matter of Amendment of Part 73 of the Commission's Rules and Regulations with Respect to Competition and Responsibility in Network Television Broadcasting," 23 FCC 2nd 382 (1970).

7. Brooks Boliek, "Senators Urge FCC Media Probe," *Hollywood Reporter.com*, 24 May 2002.

8. Federal Communications Commission, "Notice of Proposed Rulemaking," *Federal Register* 30 (1965): 4065.

9. Federal Communications Commission, "Report and Order," 23 FCC 2nd 382 (1970).

10. Federal Communications Commission, "Report and Order," 389.

11. Thomas H. Guback and Dennis J. Dombkowski, "Television and Hollywood: Economic Relations in the 1970's," *Journal of Broadcasting* 20 (1976).

12. Todd Gitlin, *Inside Prime Time* (New York: Pantheon Books, 1985).

13. Quoted in Federal Communications Commission, Statement of Commissioner James H. Quello, 1991 FCC LEXIS 1763.

14. Federal Communications Commission, "In the Matter of Amendment of 47 CFR 73.658(j)(l)(I) and (ii), the Syndication and Financial Interest Rules," 94 FCC 2nd, 1019.

15. United States Court of Appeals for the Seventh Circuit, *Schurz Communications, Inc., et al. v. Federal Communications Commission and United States of America*, 982 F. 2nd 1043.

16. Notice of Proposed Rulemaking, Federal Communications Commission, FCC 02-249, 33–39.

17. The Prime Time Access Rule prohibited the networks from programming the 7:00 p.m. to 8:00 p.m. window from Monday through Saturday. This became known as the "access hour" and a home for off-network programs on most local stations.

18. Michael Schneider, "Rx for Renewal," *Daily Variety*, 8 May 2003, A1.

19. Steve McClellan, "Does Syndie Kill Net Hits?" *Broadcasting & Cable*, 19 January 2004.

20. Paige Albiniak, "Deficit Disorder: Why Some Good Pilots Never Get Produced," *Broadcasting & Cable*, 5 May 2003, 1.

21. Albiniak, "Deficit Disorder," 1.

22. That did not prove to be the case with *CSI*, as television outlets in 150 territories worldwide carried the show by 2004.

23. Chris Pursell, "Tribune Stations Renew 'Seinfeld' Through 2011," *Television Week*, 1 March 2004, 4.

24. There is something else that *Seinfeld* and *Friends* have in common: revenue generated in syndication contributes to the bank accounts of Time Warner. The *Friends* connection to Time Warner is clear since Warner Bros. Television produced the show. The *Seinfeld* link is more obtuse. Turner Broadcasting acquired Castle Rock Entertainment, the producer of the show, in *Seinfeld's* third full season, which in turn was acquired by Time Warner in its seventh season.

25. Norman Lear owned a pair of production houses in this period, Tandem Productions with Bud Yorkin and T.A.T. Communications Co. with Jerrold Perenchio.

26. Warner Communications, Inc. acquired The Wolper Organization in January 1977, so the true independence of *Welcome Back, Kotter* was fleeting.

27. On a rather remarkable night, independent productions also won for best supporting actress in a drama series (Betty Thomas, *Hill Street Blues*/MTM Enterprises), best writing in a drama series (*Cagney & Lacey*), best writing in a comedy series (*The Cosby Show*), best directing in a drama series (*Cagney & Lacey*), and best directing in a comedy series (*The Cosby Show*).

28. That argument was most evident in a report from the Network Inquiry Special Staff of the Federal Communications Commission, *New Television Networks: Entry Jurisdiction, Ownership and Regulation.*

29. Barry Diller, *Nightline*, ABC Television Network, 28 May 2003.

30. Jenny Holtz, "CBS Gets Eyeful: Web Extracts Stake in 6 of 7 New Shows," *Daily Variety*, 19 May 1998, 1.

31. That is quite significant, since *NewsRadio* debuted as a mid-season replacement in the 1995–1996 season and would be close to the minimum number of programs needed for syndication after the completion of the 1998–1999 season. While NBC did not hold rights to the program prior to 1998, its agreement with Brillstein-Grey gave it a stake in all future syndication.

32. Michael Freeman, "Upfront Harmony," *Electronic Media*, 22 May 2000; Joe Schlosser and Steve McClellan, "Moneyphilia," *Broadcasting & Cable*, 22 May 2000.

33. Freeman, "Upfront Harmony"; Schlosser and McClellan, "Moneyphilia."

34. Brooks Boliek, "Senators Urge FCC Media Probe," *HollywoodReporter.com*, 24 May 2002.

35. Richard W. Stevenson, "The Media Business: 'Cosby' Producers Strike it Rich," *New York Times*, 23 December 1988.

36. Quoted Wasko, *Movies & Money*, 106.

37. Quoted Wasko, *Movies & Money*, 106.

38. Quoted in Michael Schneider, "D'Works Finds Nest at Peacock," *Variety.com*, 7 August 2002.

39. Quoted in Christopher Lisotta, "Carsey-Werner Tinkers With Indie Formula," *Television Week*, 11 July 2005.

40. Federal Communications Commission, "General Fairness Obligations of Broadcast Licensees," *Federal Register* 50 (160), 35418–35455, 1985.

6

❖

Conglomeration in Cable and Satellite Television Systems and Services

When images of the Games of the XVIII Olympiad in Japan traversed the Pacific Ocean via satellite in 1964, it was considered a technological marvel, a "triumph" that was "almost breathtaking in its implications for global communications."[1] The consequences were indeed profound when news outlets transmitted images of demonstrations in Tiananmen Square and along the Berlin Wall via networks of satellites in 1989. The emotions were altogether different when the world watched transfixed as hijacked airplanes crashed into the World Trade Center in New York in 2001 and observed the aftermath of the devastating tsunami that swept across South Asia in 2005. Polish leader Lech Walesa was once asked what caused the collapse of Communism in Eastern Europe. He pointed to a television set and said, "It all came from there."[2]

Much is made of the power of television in the age of communication satellites. It brought global exposure and international pressure to countless domestic conflicts and is now a channel of communication through which hostile governments negotiate. Some believe that global television holds a virtual monopoly over the "construction of world opinion, its agenda of prime concerns, and its main targets of praise or blame."[3] The United States and other Western governments view the flow of information communication satellites provide as the guarantor of Article 19 of the *Universal Declaration of Human Rights*, which extends the right to "seek, receive and impart information and ideas through any media and regardless of frontiers."[4] There are others, however, who point out that such transmissions are decidedly one way, from industrialized countries to developing countries, and argue that this flow exacerbates existing inequalities.

The development of communication satellites influences far more than the relay of news and information across vast distances and national frontiers, although one cannot diminish its significance in that area. Communication satellites also contribute to the spread of motion pictures and television programs around the world. This is evident in the content of multichannel satellite systems such as StarTV in Asia and DirecTV in Latin America as well as program services such as MTV, which includes Viacom-owned regional networks in Europe, Latin America, Asia, and Africa in addition to various joint ventures and licensing agreements at the national level.[5] The prominence of U.S.-based communication and entertainment conglomerates in the dissemination of news and information as well as cultural products raises numerous questions, since the perceived creation of a monolithic global culture is a transformation that some rejoice and others scorn. One must confront the realization that communication technologies that hold tremendous promise also threaten national and personal sovereignties to an unprecedented degree, leaving a dichotomy between "transnational 'rights' of free trade and the free flow of information and the sovereign 'rights' of protectionism, cultural autonomy, and balanced *cum* controlled information flows."[6]

These same technologies transformed television at the national level as well. Communication satellites enable the broadcast networks to transmit programs live from coast-to-coast, but their most profound impact upon television in the United States relates to cable services. Cable television dates to the late-1940s, when it was nothing more than a relay mechanism, a common antenna connected to households via coaxial cable to improve reception of broadcast stations. That is no longer the case, and the development of communication satellites enabled cable television to evolve from a retransmission service to a programming service. This was evident in 1975 when Home Box Office debuted as a national satellite-delivered service and again in 1998 when HBO launched a series of digital services, including HBO Plus, HBO Signature, HBO Family, HBO Comedy, and HBO Zone. The advent of digital compression allowed the transmission of multiple channels via the same satellite transponder space that once supported a single analog channel.

The talk of a five hundred-channel universe promotes the notion that cable television can create such abundance as to guarantee viewpoint, outlet, and source diversity, the core objectives of the Federal Communications Commission ownership rules. This would make cable television quite different from broadcast television, which is limited to a mere handful of national networks through the federal allocation of the electromagnetic spectrum.[7] It is the potential of cable television to promote such diversity, moreover, that has given rise to the widespread deregulation of television, broadcast as well as cable. While technological advances created the potential for an abundance of voices to emanate from cable television, one must question whether the nature of the same technologies would factor against such a transformation.

It is valuable to revisit one of the central arguments that Ithiel de Sola Pool advances in *Technologies of Freedom*: "Freedom is fostered when the means of communication are dispersed, decentralized, and easily available . . . Central control is more likely when the means of communication are concentrated, monopolized, and scarce."[8] This is a critical point, since communication satellites and cable systems are both classic examples of the latter, which promotes central control and reduces freedom. One must question whether even a multitude of conduits can result in a robust range of opinions, values, and ideologies. An evaluation of the ownership of cable programming services becomes an important step toward answering this question.

This chapter explores the evolution of ownership of cable systems and national programming services, beginning in the 1970s and continuing into the 2000s. The detail in this discussion is important, since the narrow focus evident in the FCC's Annual Assessment of the State of Competition in the Market for the Delivery of Video Programming is indicative of the approach often taken in the measurement of national cable and satellite services. Sidebar 6.1 examines how the FCC addresses some of these same questions. It is critical to understand how conglomerates extended their reach from "old media" industries, motion pictures and broadcast television, into "new media" industries, cable and satellite television. It is also important to address the degree to which conglomerates used their market position in the other media sectors to expand their foothold in cable and satellite television and the degree to which federal regulations allow and even encourage this to occur. The basic questions that guided the discussions of motion pictures and broadcast television are also the foundation for the analysis for cable and satellite systems and services: did the proliferation of outlets result in true viewpoint and source diversity or did horizontal integration, vertical integration, and diversification contribute to consolidation and concentration.

REGULATORY AND POLICY FRAMEWORK

The roots of cable television are altogether different from what it is today. The origin of cable television is in the post-World War II period and coincides with the introduction of television to American households. While most homes could receive broadcast signals with the rabbit ears on their sets or antennas on their roofs, those in mountainous or remote areas of the nation could not, and the idea of a community antenna was born. An antenna was placed on a high point and homes connected to that common receiver via coaxial cable, making cable television, in its original form, nothing more than a mechanism for retransmission. These roots are still evident in the acronym often used in discussions of the service, CATV, which stands for community antenna television.

Befitting such a mechanism, the initial federal regulation of cable television related to its impact on broadcast television. In 1958, the FCC ruled in *Frontier*

Broadcasting v. Collier that the Commission had jurisdiction over cable to the degree that it is "reasonably ancillary to the effective performance of the Commission's various responsibilities for the regulation of broadcast television."[9] The regulation of cable television at the national level began in 1962 when the FCC assumed jurisdiction over systems that used microwave to import distant signals, which it later expanded to include all cable systems, a role that the Supreme Court affirmed in 1968.[10] The FCC formulated the first federal regulations in response to broadcast demands that the Commission protect local markets from the encroachment of cable television. Such concerns manifested themselves in strict FCC restrictions on signal carriage, which included a requirement that all local broadcast stations be carried and prohibited the importation of distant signals.[11] While some argue that the Commission responded to the persuasion of the broadcasters, the distant signal prohibition is consistent with the promotion of localism, since such signals would duplicate local service and undermine smaller broadcast stations.

The foundation for federal regulation changed in 1972 when the impetus shifted from the protection of broadcast television to the development of cable television to serve the public interest.[12] The Commission required cable systems that served more than 3,500 subscribers to provide the equivalent of twenty television channels.[13] It also compelled cable operators to provide "access" channels for public, educational, government, and leased-access usage and enacted rules on the acquisition and duration of franchise licenses and rules against cross ownership.[14] The cross ownership rules were important, since the FCC prohibited television networks from the ownership of cable systems and the corporate parents of local television stations from ownership in communities that their broadcast signal reached.

The rationale for regulation shifted again in 1975, when the promotion of the cable industry became the foremost goal. It was an important time in the evolution of cable television, as the development of communication satellites made the transmission of programming services on a nationwide basis a viable option, evidenced by the debut of Home Box Office. The courts assumed an important role in this shift as well. In 1970, the FCC enacted rules that prohibited cable subscribers from paying an additional fee for movies and sports programs that were not available on broadcast channels, but the courts ruled against that position.[15] The U.S. Court of Appeals for the D.C. Circuit also set aside the Commission's access requirements and channel capacity rules in 1978, rulings that the Supreme Court upheld in 1979.[16] The deregulation of various aspects of cable television, coupled with the introduction of services delivered via satellite transmission, fueled a dramatic expansion of cable television in the late 1970s and early 1980s.

Cable Communications Policy Act of 1984

The Cable Communications Policy Act of 1984 codified the general direction that the FCC had followed for close to a decade. The 1984 Act altered the general structure of cable television, both in the ownership of multiple system operators and national programming services. The most discussed aspect of the act was the elimination of local regulation of cable rates. Prior to its passage, local governments could regulate basic fees, but not fees for premium services. The 1984 Act allowed cable operators to increase rates five percent per annum until January 1, 1987, when it eliminated all price restrictions. The deregulation of rates had a profound impact on cable subscribers as rates for basic service more than doubled between 1984 and 1992, from an average of $8.98 per month to an average of $19.08 per month, which translated into an increase in basic revenues for cable operators from $3.534 billion in 1984 to $12.433 billion in 1992.[17]

The 1984 Act, above all else, redefined the relationship between cable operators and their communities. Cable operators functioned under franchise agreements with local governments, which detailed various operational policies, including ownership of systems, provisions of service, and rate structures. There were two justifications for such agreements. The land over which a public road or electric power line passes is considered a public right of way and, as such, falls within the purview of local governments. The fact that cable operators laid coaxial cable under such roads and along such lines validated the need for local franchise agreements.

The second rationale for such agreements was more controversial. Most cable systems functioned as local monopolies, so households in a given area needed to subscribe to a particular system or forego the services offered.[18] The lack of choice inherent in such a relationship supported the rationale that local agencies should control the fees cable operators could charge and to exercise some control over the services offered. All this changed with passage of the 1984 Act, which eliminated rate regulation on the local level and placed strict limits on the areas in which local government could exercise control. Local governments could consider the "quality of the operator's service, including signal quality, response to consumer complaints, and billing practices" in the renewal of such agreements, but they could not address the "mix, quality, or level of cable services or other services provided over the system."[19]

This aspect of the Act altered the relationship between operators and local communities, with the former liberated to choose cable services without concern for local wants and needs. Prior to 1984, as cable television developed and began to realize the potential of the medium to provide nonbroadcast services, local authorities negotiated for the mix of services that best fit the needs of their constituents, or at least what was perceived to be their needs. The 1984 Act prohibited them from assuming such a role, which empowered cable operators to pursue their own interests, and the end of rate regulation provided much of the capital needed for the development of programming services. From that point forward, cable operators underwrote such services in numerous cases. The Discovery Channel, for example, launched in June 1985 with Westinghouse Electric the main backer, but twelve months later four cable operators made financial investments in the network: Tele-Communications,

Inc., Cox Communications, Newhouse Broadcasting, and United Cable Television.

Cable Television Communications and Competition Act of 1992

The Cable Television Communications and Competition Act of 1992 reintroduced some limitations on the amount cable operators could charge on basic services, but such regulations were set to expire and the Telecommunications Act of 1996 placed no limitations on cable operators. Congressional leaders are often critical of the rise in basic cable rates and threaten reregulation, but little has happened. The 1992 Act is important, however, since it reveals how the process works and how it favors the powerful, even amidst complaints about "reregulation" from cable leaders. Congress was concerned about both horizontal and vertical integration, and the 1992 Act compelled the FCC to place limits on the number of cable subscribers a "person" is able to reach and on the number of channels on a cable system that can be "occupied by a video programmer in which the cable operator has an attributable interest."[20] What is critical about this section of the Act is that Congress empowered the FCC to set what it determined to be "reasonable" limits. Sidebar 6.1 addresses another aspect of the 1992 Act in which the Commission application of Congressional mandates is questionable.

The FCC established 30 percent of the national market as the number of cable subscribers an individual or corporation could reach. This was not unreasonable, but the FCC defined the market as the number of households that cable systems pass, not the number of households that subscribe to cable television. The distinction between homes passed and basic subscribers was an important one. In 1998, for example, cable systems passed close to ninety-five million households in the United States, 96.61 percent of total television households.[21] Based on the FCC market definition, a multiple system operator could reach twenty-eight million subscribers as of March 31, 1998. The allowance was close to ten million more subscribers than if the FCC limit was in relation to all basic subscribers, as 30 percent of that total, sixty-five million, would be nineteen and a half million. The calculation of market share based on homes passed was significant since it allowed for a much higher level of concentration.

The limitations on the number of channels in which a cable operator could hold a financial interest was also important, since the Commission established a high threshold and used market definitions that allowed for greater concentration. Cable operators could hold a financial interest in 40 percent of the first seventy-five channels offered, with no limit on additional channels. In the rules, moreover, all channels were included in the overall total, including public, government, and educational access channels as well as local broadcast stations, which enabled operators to hold an interest in more basic, expanded basic, and premium channels. Services in which cable operators

Sidebar 6.1
The Flawed Approach of the FCC to the Measurement
of the Marketplace

When the Federal Communications Commission released the *Annual Assessment of the Status of Competition in the Market for the Delivery of Video Programming* in 2005, chair Michael Powell concluded, "Whether one focuses on distribution or programming, today's video marketplace is the most competitive and diverse in our nation's history."[1] There is little question that the penetration of direct-broadcast-satellite services such as DirecTV and Dish Network increased the available options for distribution of such services. Less certain was whether the proliferation of programming services had also resulted in increased diversity. Commissioners Michael Copps and Jonathan Adelstein were among those who were skeptical, arguing that the annual report served, "mainly as a recitation of the record rather than providing an in-depth analysis of the status of competition."[2] This is most evident in the discussion of programming services.

The annual assessment is a legacy of the *Cable Television Consumer Protection and Competition Act of 1992*, in which Congress called on the FCC to provide annual reports on cable rates and competition in the delivery of video programming. The report evolved from the 1992 Cable Act, but the conclusions were the outgrowth of an FCC bureau that favored deregulation and a trade group that was more than willing to provide the statistical rationale. When named head of the Media Bureau of the FCC in 2001, Kenneth Ferree stated, "I'm a Powell guy." His support for the deregulatory agenda of the chairman was evident throughout his tenure, which included leadership of the bureau that oversees broadcast and cable services and membership on the committee that administered the rewrite of Commission ownership rules in 2003.

Ferree and the FCC found a willing accomplice in the National Cable & Telecommunications Association (NCTA), the trade organization that represents cable interests before the government. Much of the data included in annual assessment comes from the NCTA, including the list of national programming services. Such an incestuous relationship between federal agencies and the industries they regulate dates to the 1920s. Herbert Hoover, the Secretary of Commerce from 1921 to 1928, promoted a structure of self-government known as an associative state. In place of regulation, Hoover believed that trade associations could bridge the public and private sectors, with neutral experts assuming a prominent role in the writing of rules and regulations. Hoover believed that such a relationship was central to the creation of an "American system" and assured the "transition to an American utopia."

The annual assessment of competition in the video programming marketplace is an important document since its findings influence the steps that Congress and other branches of the federal government take in relation to broadcast, cable, and satellite television. A critical examination of the report, however, raises serious questions about the quality of the analysis and, in turn, the conclusions one might reach. Some of the flaws are basic errors. The *Eleventh Annual Report* included various channels that went dark prior to the start of 2004 or did not launch before the end of the year. The Football Channel, for example, debuted with a limited schedule on a handful of systems in the fall of 2003, but it went dark that December and did not transmit in

(Continued)

2004.[3] Telemundo Puerto Rico, also listed as a national programming service, did not launch until 2005 and signed its first carriage agreement with Cablevision Systems Corp. in February of that year.

More problematic are programming services that died long ago but are still included in the FCC report and NCTA database. My Pet TV, a niche network that targeted pet owners, launched with one hour of programming a day in 1997. Most of its carriage was on leased-access cable channels, rather than dedicated outlets.[4] The network shuttered in 1998 when the Federal Trade Commission and Securities & Exchange Commission filed fraud changes against its owners, including Michael Marcovksy, and froze its assets. While the network went dark, it remained on the FCC list of national video programming services six years later. The service was also included in the NCTA database in the first quarter of 2005, listed as an alliance with the Humane Society of the United States that produced programming for veterinary and shelter waiting rooms. The Humane Society confirmed the death of My Pet TV and revealed the existence of Pet Care TV, which did produce programs for such waiting rooms. Pet Care TV, however, distributed its programming via DVD rather than satellite, so it failed the most basic test for inclusion in the FCC list.

There were also channels that the FCC counted multiple times. In the *Eleventh Annual Report*, the Commission reported that there were 388 satellite-delivered national programming networks. Based on Appendix C of the report, this total included thirteen movie channels that were part of the Starz! Super Pack. The so-called Super Pack was nothing more than a marketing tool Liberty Media used to package the Starz! and Encore movie services. The problem arises from the fact that each of the Starz! and Encore channels was listed on its own in addition to the Super Pack, so the FCC counted each of them twice.[5] Another example is the Meadows Racing Network and HorseRacing TV, both of which the FCC report listed as national programming networks. Magna Entertainment, one of the most prominent thoroughbred racetrack operators in the nation, owns and operates HorseRacing TV, which features coverage of races from Magna tracks and others. Meadows Racing Network, on the other hand, is not a viable network, as Magna folded it into HorseRacing TV when the latter launched in 2002.

There are also fundamental issues with the FCC report, which relate to how the Commission addresses integration and what constitutes a national network. HorseRacing TV and Meadows Racing Network illustrate questions on both counts. The connection between production and distribution is clear with HorseRacing TV, since races from Magna Entertainment's most prominent tracks, including Santa Anita Park, Pimlico Race Course, Gulfstream Park, and Laurel Park, provide the heart of its schedule. As such, Magna Entertainment can reap the benefits of vertical integration. The defunct Meadows Racing Network raises another issue. The network was based at The Meadows, a standardbred track outside of Pittsburgh, with carriage limited to less than 1 million homes in Western Pennsylvania and a program schedule that covered no more than half the day. Still, the FCC counted Meadows Racing Network the same as it counted programming networks that reached close to 90 million households and programmed twenty-four hours a day, seven days a week.

These are representative of major flaws in the FCC approach to this topic. The annual assessment limits the discussion of vertical integration to ownership of national programming services by cable operators. In the *Eleventh Annual Report*, the FCC concluded that just 23 percent of national networks, 89 of 388, were vertically integrated with at least one "cable operator" in 2004.[6] Missing from this measurement was the second largest multichannel video programming distributor, DirecTV, vertically integrated with a slew of national programming networks after News Corp. completed the acquisition of the satellite service in 2003. More serious is the failure to examine the implications of horizontal integration. As discussed, the major media conglomerates negotiate carriage of networks in bundles, so the success of ESPN and ESPN2 fueled expanded penetration of ESPNews and ESPN Classic over the last decade. The FCC did not address the use of such market power; nor did it discuss the extent to which broadcasters have used retransmission consent with cable and satellite operators to leverage carriage for programming services.

More remarkable is the fact that the FCC used no apparent standards for inclusion of a programming service in its national total. The question is not about good or bad but rather about a clear distinction between national and regional networks, a minimum benchmark in the number of hours programmed a week, and whether carriage is on dedicated channels or within other programming services and access channels. These questions raise serious doubts about numerous services. For example, just three cable systems carried Celtic Vision at the start of 2003, but it was included in the FCC total. The same was true of Boston Kids & Family TV, a product of WGBH, which even the NCTA database classified as a regional network.[7]

The questions about hours and carriage are often related. There were various networks included in the FCC report that did not program twelve hours per day, let alone twenty-four, which would make it impossible to command dedicated channel space. According to the NCTA, for example, National Jewish Television programmed just three hours per week, which was one more than The Crime Channel, which distributed two hours per week, a mere fraction of the 168 hours per week that the twenty-four-hour cable networks cablecast.[8] It is dubious to equate a service that distributes two hours of programming a week when it can, where it can, to a service that programs 168 hours a week on dedicated channels. Noah's World International, another service that the FCC included on its national list, could not even reach the two hours per week threshold, as it produced a handful of thirty-minute travelogue programs per year for distribution.

The inclusion of a programming service that targets leased access channels, or solicits time on public, educational, or government channels, misrepresents the reach of such content. Without question, these services could expand the marketplace of ideas and serve underrepresented portions of the television audience. Deep Dish TV heralds itself as the first "national grassroots satellite network," one that "distributes creative programming that educates and activates" rather than "homogeneous" programs that present a "one-dimensional view of society."[9] There is little question that Deep Dish TV is unlike the mainstream broadcast and cable networks, but one of the most significant differences is that it distributes just one hour of programming a week to PBS and public access channels.[10] Counting such a service the same as ones that program 168 hours a week and reach close to ninety million cable and satellite households paints an unrealistic picture of the degree of diversity in the programming marketplace and led Congress, the Commission, and others to reach flawed decisions.

(Continued)

NOTES

1. Michael K. Powell, "Separate Statement of Chairman Michael K. Powell," *Annual Assessment of the Status of Competition in the Market for the Delivery of Video Programming,* FCC 05-13, 4 February 2005.

2. Michael J. Copps and Jonathan S. Adelstein, "Joint Statement of Commissioners Michael J. Copps and Jonathan S. Adelstein Concurring," *Annual Assessment of the Status of Competition in the Market for the Delivery of Video Programming,* FCC 05-13, 4 February 2005.

3. The Football Channel signed a definitive agreement with Cornel Capital in February 2005 for an investment of $30 million. It did not announce a timetable for a relaunch at that time.

4. John Carmody, "The TV Column," *Washington Post,* 9 June 1997, D6.

5. The thirteen channels included in the Starz! Super Pack in the fourth quarter of 2004 were Starz!, Black Starz, Starz! Cinema, Starz! Family, Starz! Kids, Starz! Theater, Encore, Encore Action, Encore Love Stories, Encore Mystery, Encore True Stories, Encore WAM!, and Encore Westerns.

6. Federal Communications Commission, *Annual Assessment of the Status of Competition in the Market for the Delivery of Video Programming,* FCC 05-13, 14 January 2005, 145.

7. National Cable & Telecommunications Association, www.ncta.com (30 April 2005).

8. National Cable & Telecommunications Association, *Cable Developments 2004,* vol. 28, no. 1 (Washington, DC, 2004).

9. Deep Dish TV, "About Us," www.deepdishtv.org (30 April 2005).

10. *Cable Developments 2004,* 73 & 135.

held a financial interest prior to the passage of the 1992 Act, furthermore, did not count toward the 40 percent allowance. In the case of Time Warner Cable, this meant that HBO and Cinemax did not count, and neither did most of the Turner networks, including CNN, CNN Headline News, TBS, TNT, and Cartoon Network, since the initial investment in Turner occurred prior to passage of the act.

Much of the public discussion related to the 1992 Cable Act focused on the reregulation of rates for basic services and equipment as well as some of the structural limits discussed above. The component of the bill that was most debated behind the scenes, however, required cable operators to negotiate retransmission consent with local broadcast stations. These deliberations pitted two powerful groups against one another, the National Association of Broadcasters (NAB) and broadcast networks on one side and the National Cable Television Association (NCTA) and cable operators on the other, with a third, the Motion Picture Association of America, against retransmission consent as well since broadcasters rather than program producers would receive compensation. The tone of the debate was clear in 1991 in an advertisement NCTA ran in the *New York Times,* the *Washington Post,* and other major newspapers claiming that broadcasters wanted to "add a 20 percent tax to your basic cable bill" and that money raised would "go right into the broadcaster's pockets."[22] Retransmission consent was not included in the House bill and its inclusion in the 1992 Act was in doubt until the end, when a Senate-House conference committee included the requirement in the final version of the bill. This was not the end of the battle, however, as a presidential veto sent the bill back to Congress, where broadcast interests were able to muster enough votes for the first override of the Bush Administration.

Retransmission consent was one of two components of the Cable Act that addressed carriage. Congress stipulated that either broadcast stations could demand carriage, the so-called "must-carry" provision, or stations could require operators to obtain authorization to retransmit their signal. As is often the case, Congress did not set parameters for such negotiations, stating only that no "multichannel video programming distributor" could retransmit the signal of a broadcast station except, "(A) with the express authority of the originating station," unless the station elected must-carry protection.[23] The task of writing rules for these policies fell to the FCC, which issued a Report and Order in the spring of 1993.[24] The timetable for stations to elect either must-carry or retransmission consent was well articulated, and the Commission defined what local stations were eligible for must-carry status. Outside of stipulating that broadcasters must negotiate rights to their entire signal rather than to individual programs, making a distinction between retransmission and copyright, and refusing to adopt limits on retransmission consent rates, the Commission did nothing to limit what was on the table in such negotiations.

Central themes in Congressional debate prior to passage of the 1992 Act included the contention that broadcast stations faced extinction without carriage fees and that the balance of power between broadcast stations and cable operators needed to be redressed. Representative Jack Fields stated that without retransmission consent, "free, over-the-air TV could go the way of the dinosaur."[25] CBS chairman Laurence Tisch estimated retransmission would be worth $1 billion a year for local stations, but even before the bill passed, John Malone and Tele-Communications, Inc. made clear that the multiple system operators (MSOs) did not intend to pay for retransmission of local broadcast stations. The TCI position was clear: it would not increase basic rates for broadcast stations that consumers could get free without cable. Malone was not against negotiations, however, and in a speech in the first quarter of 1993, he stated that broadcasters had to give cable operators and subscribers something of value to receive a carriage fee, stating, "I don't intend to pay any money. I will scratch backs."[26] That back scratching resulted in retransmission agreements that included carriage for basic cable networks with corporate connections to local broadcast stations. This allowed the owners of large broadcast station groups to extend their reach into cable television.

Telecommunications Act of 1996 and Beyond

Deregulation was the mantra of the 1990s, and the Telecommunications Act of 1996 was the articulation of that campaign. While cable television was not the focal point of the Telecom Act, it was very much in the mix and viewed as one mechanism to advance the "information superhighway." The stated objective of the act was to create competition within and across communication platforms, and the origination of telephone and video services were among the targets. One objective of the act was to create facilities-based competition, a two-wire solution through which cable operators would provide local telephone service and telephone operators would provide video services. This was in addition to the anticipated arrival of satellite television as a viable alternative to cable. To enable cable to compete with satellite providers, all rate regulations outside the basic tier were set to expire in 1999. That was just the beginning.

The more significant development for cable operators was that the 1996 Act offered the encouragement to build broadband networks. According to one analyst, the message from cable and phone companies to politicians was clear: "Give us more incentives and revenue opportunities or the highway will not get built and you will get the blame."[27] The inducement that cable operators needed was the freedom to move into local phone service. An important component of the act from an MSO perspective was that telecommunications services that operators provided were exempt from state and local regulation, which was a step beyond even the modest limits allowed with video services. The response to passage of the Telecom Act in February 1996 was swift, as the investment in the cable infrastructure was estimated at $28.71 billion between 1996 and 1999.[28]

While Congress opened the door for competition in telephone services, it did not define what cable was offering. The 1996 Act placed strict regulations on telecommunications services and classified them as common carriers. Such providers were required to sell access to their networks on a nondiscriminatory basis. Providers for information services, on the other hand, were subject to much less stringent regulation. The act did not stipulate whether new broadband Internet technologies qualified as telecommunications services, information services, or a combination of the two. This was a significant omission, since the "telecommunications service" label would require cable operators to allow competitors to provide services over their systems. The FCC did not take a definitive position in the debate until 2002 when it classified cable modem service as an information service.[29] That was not the end of the road, however, as the U.S. Court of Appeals for the Ninth Circuit ruled in 2003 in *Brand X v. FCC* that cable broadband service was a hybrid of telecommunication and information services and that the FCC could not release such systems from common carrier obligations.[30] That decision was appealed to the Supreme Court, which reversed the lower court ruling, arguing that administrative agencies have the authority to interpret ambiguous statutes.[31]

Like other areas of communication regulation, there were numerous questions left unanswered at the end of Michael Powell's tenure as the chair of the FCC in 2005. Unlike broadcast television, however, this was not as much the result of the 2002 Biennial Regulatory Review but rather of various court decisions, such as the Brand X litigation. The most significant of these was *Time Warner Entertainment v. FCC*, which was the end result of a series of court battles that began after the FCC issued its horizontal and vertical ownership limits following passage of the 1992 Cable Act. [32] In 2000, the Court of Appeals ruled that the FCC did have the authority to promulgate rules that placed limits on ownership, a position that the Supreme Court later affirmed.[33] But that ruling did not last for long.

While the previous case was being appealed to the Supreme Court, Time Warner pursued separate litigation over aspects of the rules. In March 2001, the Court of Appeals ruled that while the restrictions themselves were not a violation of the First Amendment, the actual levels of the limitations were arbitrarily set and insufficiently justified.[34] In the discussion of vertical ownership limits, the court wrote, "the agency must at least reveal a rational connection between the facts and the choice made . . . Yet it appears to provide nothing but the conclusion that 'we believe that a 40 percent limit is appropriate to balance the goals.'"[35] The court remanded the rules to the Commission for better justification. The FCC did not revise those rules in the four years that followed and initiated a second inquiry in the spring of 2005.[36]

PATTERNS OF OWNERSHIP: CABLE AND SATELLITE SYSTEMS

The penetration and expansion of cable and satellite systems has been profound, but just as significant as the increase in the number of television channels available in the average household is how such increases fueled deregulation. In 1980, there were less than twenty million cable households, and the biggest systems offered thirty-five channels. In 2005, over ninety million households received television programming via cable or satellite systems, and the average number of channels in those homes hovered around one hundred. There is little dispute over the increase in the number of television channels in most American households or the range of services available. There are differences of opinion, however, over what it means and how the government should respond.

At the root of divergent positions over the appropriate level of regulation that the television and motion picture industries should encounter are different notions of diversity. As discussed earlier, the promotion of diversity has long been one of the foundations for FCC ownership policies, with the Commission considering four aspects of diversity that are central to this discussion: viewpoint diversity, outlet diversity, source diversity, and program diversity. Michael Powell advanced the notion that sheer volume in the marketplace would ensure diversity, but others have argued that it is possible to increase the number of outlets without a corresponding rise in the range of voices and viewpoints. The launch of Logo in over ten million households in the summer of 2005 provides an example of the issues involved. On one hand, the widespread distribution of a channel that provides entertainment programs for the gay and lesbian community might contribute to viewpoint and program diversity. The fact that Viacom Inc. owns Logo and Tom Freston manages it alongside MTV, Nickelodeon, Spike TV, and others through MTV Networks, however, suggests that it might not enhance outlet diversity, "the control of media outlets by a variety of independent owners" or source diversity, "the availability of content to consumers from a variety of content producers."[37]

Ownership of Cable Systems

Deregulation at the local, state, and federal levels over the last two decades had a profound impact on the basic structure of cable television. It also altered how cable programming services and multiple system operators (MSOs) interact. The dichotomy between big and small in cable television, and the broader entertainment industries, is a prominent issue in these industries. The words of former FCC chairman Mark Fowler, "Bigness is not necessarily badness, sometimes it is goodness," are reminders that legislators and administrators allowed and even encouraged such consolidation. The power that bigness rewards was evident in the merger between Disney and Capital Cities/ABC. When the proposed merger came before the Commission for the transfer of broadcast licenses, the Small Cable Business Association, a group of 350 small cable television operators, filed a petition to block the merger.[38] The group alleged that Capital Cities/ABC had strong-armed small cable operators for carriage of ESPN2 and charged exorbitant rates for other cable networks. It argued that both corporations had "consistently used their market power to deal unfairly with cable operators," and that small operators were charged rates for ESPN, ESPN2, and other networks that were 30 percent to 60 percent higher than the rates charged to large multiple system operators.[39] Those concerns had little impact, and on the say day Bill Clinton signed the Telecommunications Act of 1996, the FCC approved the merger 5–0, with commissioner Rachel Chong saying, "This is no Mickey Mouse deal. This is a merger that makes a lot of sense."[40]

The concerns raised with the merger of Disney and Capital Cities/ABC were similar to those voiced when News Corp. acquired control of DirecTV in 2003 and when Comcast and Time Warner secured the right to carve up Adelphia Communications in 2005. The advantage that Disney holds in its negotiations with cable operators thanks to ESPN is not unlike that which Comcast, News Corp., and Time Warner bring to the table in its bargaining with programming services. It is difficult for such services to reach the thirty million household threshold for national advertising sales without being on the systems these three control. Just as important is the impact of such consolidation at the local level. One advantage of cable television is that it is local in origination, and the potential for content selected or produced for a given community is tremendous. Stephen Godek argues that a basic feature of cable operators who respond to local needs is the presence of some local ownership: "community service is positively related to the extent of local (at least as opposed to out of state) ownership of systems."[41] Moreover, he concludes that local governments should favor smaller multiple system operators, in terms of number of subscribers, over larger ones.[42]

There is little question that local ownership and smaller multiple system operators are not the norm for most television households in the 2000s, but it was not that way in the beginning. As discussed above, cable began as the ultimate local medium, with multiple households connected to a common antenna to improve reception of broadcast signals. The level of concentration began to increase in the 1970s, which coincided with the launch of HBO and introduction of federal policies designed to promote the industry. It was in this period that the horizontal integration of cable systems increased. In 1973, for example, Tele-Communications, Inc. (TCI) and American Television and Communications (ATC) had 737,000 cable subscribers between them, and ranked third and fourth among cable MSOs.[43] A little more than a decade later, those two ranked first and second, and had over five million subscribers combined.

The expansion of the dominant multiple system operators began prior to passage of the 1984 Cable Act and accelerated after it became law. The reach of the four largest MSOs increased from 27.4 percent in January 1984 to 41.1 percent in January 1994, with the market share for the top two firms, Tele-Communications, Inc. and Time Warner Cable, at 31.3 percent in the latter period. These two conglomerates took different paths to market dominance. TCI made a number of different acquisitions through this period, while the scope of Time Warner Cable resulted in large part from one major merger, the combination of American Television and Communications and Warner Amex Cable Communications that occurred with the creation of Time Warner in 1989. Table 6.1 illustrates the growing concentration in the ownership of cable systems in 1984, 1994 and 2004.

The second era of consolidation began in 1995, just prior to passage of the Telecommunications Act of 1996. Most significant in this period were the mergers of large operators, with the transformation of Tele-Communications, Inc. the most telling. At the end of 1995, TCI acquired Viacom Cable Television, the sixth largest MSO at the time with 1.2 million basic subscribers. In 1998, the promise of the digital age enticed AT&T to spend $48 billion to gain access to the 13.9 million cable households that TCI controlled at that time. The renamed AT&T Broadband grew even bigger with the acquisition of MediaOne Group in 1999. The mammoth cable operator did not flourish, however, and AT&T merged with Comcast in 2002 in a deal valued at $47.5 billion. The expansion of Comcast over this period was remarkable, from 2.7 million at the start of 1994 to 21.5 million at the start of 2004.

Table 6.1. Market Share for Largest Multiple System Operators, as of January 1984, 1994, and 2004

	1984		1994		2004	
	Total Basic Subscribers (in millions)[a]	Share of National Total	Total Basic Subscribers (in millions)[b]	Share of National Total	Total Basic Subscribers (in millions)	Share of National Total
Total	31.4		57.2		66.1[c]	
Top Share	2.8	8.9%	10.7	18.7%	21.5	32.5%
Top 2	5.1	16.2%	17.9	31.3%	32.4	49.0%
Top 4	8.6	27.4%	23.5	41.1%	45.0	68.1%
Top 8	13.1	41.7%	30.2	52.8%	57.0	86.2%
Top 10	14.7	46.8%	32.8	57.3%	59.0	89.3%

[a] Basic subscriber totals are from *Cable TV Financial Databook*; MSO basic subscriber estimates are from *Television & Cable Factbook*, 1984.

[b] Basic subscriber totals are from *Cable TV Financial Databook*; MSO basic subscriber estimates are from SEC documents and *Television & Cable Factbook*, 1994.

[c] There are various estimates of the number of cable households nationwide. This estimate is from the FCC annual report on the video marketplace. The estimates contained in the report were 66.05 million cable subscribers in June 2003 and 66.1 million in June 2004. The use of these figures is consistent with earlier sample periods. Multiple system operator subscriber estimates are from SEC documents.

The impact of these mergers and acquisitions on the marketplace is clear. In January 2004, the top four MSOs accounted for 68.1 percent of cable households nationwide, with Comcast and Time Warner accounting for just under half (49.0 percent). That was before the two agreed in 2005 to divide the assets of Adelphia Communications, which would raise their combined total to around 57 percent. Most significant is the fact that just ten multiple system operators accounted for 89.3 percent of cable households nationwide. With the inclusion of direct-to-home satellite providers DirecTV and Dish Network and other noncable recipients of multiple video programming services, the overall share for the top four declines somewhat, from 68.1 percent to 59.3 percent, as does the share for the ten largest. The concentration ratios, however, remain quite high. Given News Corps.' acquisition of DirecTV, moreover, one must question whether this has resulted in an increase in outlet diversity. Table 6.2 documents the market shares for the largest multiple video programming distributors.

There is one indisputable fact that emerges from an examination of cable and direct-to-home satellite distributors: bigness rules the day. The transformation of the marketplace from 1984 when no MSO reached even 10 percent of cable households to 2004 when Comcast reached over 30 percent is profound. To be certain, the infusion of capital required to convert from coaxial to fiber optic cable and to build digital systems is huge and operator expenditures on infrastructure from 1996 through 2004 surpassed $90 billion.[44] What is most critical for this analysis, however, is the degree to which this consolidation placed the control of cable and satellite systems in the hands of vast media conglomerates like Comcast, Time Warner, and News Corp. The

Table 6.2. Multiple Video Programming Distributors with the Most Subscribers in the United States, as of January 2004

	Total Subscribers (in millions)	Share of National Total
Total	91.05[a]	
Comcast Cable	21.5	23.6%
DirecTV	12.2	13.4%
Time Warner Cable	10.9	12.0%
Dish Network	9.4	10.3%
Top Four MVPDs	54.0	59.3%
Charter Communications	6.4	7.0%
Cox Communications	6.3	6.9%
Adelphia Communications[b]	5.3	5.8%
Cablevision Systems Corp.	2.9	3.2%
Bright House Networks	2.2	2.4%
Mediacom Communications Corp.	1.5	1.7%
Top Ten MVPDs	78.6	86.3%

[a] This total is derived from statistics in the FCC report on competition in the video marketplace, issued in 2005. That document estimated total MVPD households at 89.8 million as of June 2003 and 92.3 million as of June 2004. The midpoint in these two estimates is used for January 2004. Totals for individual corporations are based on corporate documents.
[b] The total includes subscribers from systems that Adelphia owned (5.085 million) as well as systems that reached 238,000 that the Rigas family owned and Adelphia operated.

question that must be asked is the degree to which this consolidation impacts on the development of new programming services and limits source and outlet diversity.

PATTERNS OF OWNERSHIP: PROGRAM SERVICES

The roots of cable television might be found in the post-World War II period, but a single day marked its rebirth: September 30, 1975. It was on that day that Home Box Office transmitted the title fight between Muhammad Ali and Joe Frazier via satellite from Manila. "The Thrilla in Manila" was the third in a series of bouts between Ali and Frazier and one of the greatest fights of all-time. The transmission from the Philippines was also a turning point in the evolution of television. It marked the dawn of a new era, with HBO becoming the first in the cable business to use satellites for the regular transmission of programming.

Home Box Office was not the first premium cable service, nor was the Ali-Frazier bout the first cablecast. A division within Paramount Pictures wired 150 homes in Palm Springs in 1953, while a far more ambitious plan emerged a decade later. Pat Weaver, the former president of NBC, developed

Subscription TV as a three-channel service with first-run motion pictures, major sporting events, and other programs not available on broadcast television delivered via cable. The proposed service generated over $23 million in investment capital before it sold a single subscription, and there appeared to be no legal obstacles since it planned to operate within the state of California, with Los Angeles and San Francisco the target markets, which placed it outside the jurisdiction of the FCC.[45] Motion picture theater owners and broadcasters, however, mounted a well-financed campaign entitled "Save Free TV" and a referendum on the November 1964 California ballot outlawed pay television in the state.[46] The Supreme Court of California ruled the referendum unconstitutional in 1966, and while it was too late to save Subscription TV, the ruling and subsequent Supreme Court refusal to overturn did smooth the path for later cable services.[47]

Home Box Office debuted on November 8, 1972, with a National Hockey League game from Madison Square Garden and a motion picture, *Sometimes a Great Notion*, transmitted via microwave link to 365 households in Wilkes-Barre, Pennsylvania. Manhattan Cable, the Time Inc.-owned franchisee for lower Manhattan, built the premium service around sporting events and motion pictures and decided to feed the service to other cable systems in order to amortize costs. The development of satellite transmission allowed HBO to morph into a national service in 1975. Its evolution since then is important to consider as it represents each of the interlinked but distinct processes that contribute to concentration within media industries: vertical and horizontal integration; diversification and internationalization. From the outset, HBO was an example of diversification, as magazines such as *Time, Fortune, Sports Illustrated,* and *People* were the prominent brands within Time. It soon became an example of horizontal integration and internationalization as well, as Time launched Cinemax in 1980 as a companion network that utilized the same management and created HBO International through a joint venture with major motion picture studios in 1983.

Vertical integration is the most critical issue, however. HBO is now a jewel within Time Warner, which also includes a collection of motion picture production and distribution companies, including Warner Bros., New Line Cinema, Warner Independent Pictures, and Picturehouse. HBO debuted long before the Time merger with Warner Communications in 1989, and in the beginning there was no direct connection to a major studio. That does not mean that Time and HBO did not represent vertical integration. When HBO debuted as a satellite service in 1975, Manhattan Cable was a wholly owned subsidiary of Time.[48] Executives made the decision to offer HBO to other cable operators in order to recoup costs and generate additional revenue.[49]

The vertical integration that Home Box Office and Manhattan Cable created is important. It enabled Time to benefit from two revenue streams, since it collected fees paid to both the premium service and cable operator.[50] Moreover, Time's ownership and control of Manhattan Cable guaranteed HBO access to one of the largest and most prominent cable systems in the nation. The significance of such integration cannot be overstated, and remains a critical issue in cable television. Time management understood the importance of distribution, and it acquired the second largest cable MSO in the nation, American Television and Communications (ATC), for $140 million in 1978.[51] The acquisition made Time a force not just in cable programming but also among cable operators, a position that Time Warner Cable maintains to the present.

Home Box Office was not the only premium service to benefit from cable system ownership. Showtime debuted as the first true competitor to HBO in 1976, and it became a satellite delivered premium service in 1978. Viacom International created Showtime, which gave it access to Viacom-owned cable systems. Carriage remained difficult until 1979 when Viacom sold a 50 percent interest in Showtime to TelePrompTer Corp., one of the largest MSOs in the nation. When the deal was completed, TelePrompTer had wired 1.15 million households nationwide, 250,000 of which subscribed to HBO.[52] These subscriptions switched to Showtime on January 1, 1979, when TelePrompTer's contract with HBO expired and the joint venture with Viacom became official.[53]

The genesis of Turner Broadcasting is the antithesis of HBO, which evolved within the womb of one of the most respected, and profitable, media corporations in the United States. In 1963, Ted Turner's father committed suicide after setting in motion the liquidation of his failing billboard business. His son reversed the transactions then in progress, sold his late father's plantation to settle notes, and began to regain parts of the business his father had lost.[54] In time, he transformed his father's business into a multimillion-dollar conglomerate, and he traded $2.5 million worth of stock in his company for the title to WTCG, an independent television station in Atlanta.[55] His foray into television began on a rather inauspicious note, as there was a time in 1970 when not even the Atlanta audience could receive Turner's just-purchased UHF station. When he acquired the station, it was losing $600,000 per year and management had suspended maintenance on the station's equipment. Before Turner could make the needed repairs, a transmission line blew out and it was a week before WTCG could broadcast again.[56]

In 1976, WTCG was renamed WTBS and it became the first broadcast station transmitted via satellite, giving birth to the concept of the "superstation." WTBS placed Turner on the map, but it was with the Cable News Network (CNN) that he made his name. He envisioned an all-news cable service before WTBS transmitted via satellite, but with fewer than five million households wired for cable television at the end of 1975, he determined that it was not feasible to launch such a service.[57] The cable landscape exploded between 1975 and 1980, with the number of homes passed reaching 29.1 million in June 1980.[58] The same month, Turner launched CNN, and eighteen months later, he created a companion service, CNN Headline News. In its formative stage, CNN was news without stars, news without end, and oftentimes news without editing. The use of nonunion production and technical personnel and on-air talent culled from local stations rather than national networks allowed CNN to reduce its costs, but the losses were still substantial, an estimated $2 million a month in the developmental period. The service was close to the breakeven point in 1982 when it launched CNN Headline News, which thrust it back into the red and prompted predictions that Turner would have to take on a partner or CNN would go bankrupt.

Many saw the debut of the Satellite News Channel in June 1982 as a bad omen for Turner. ABC and Westinghouse created the service and when it was launched, the chairman of Westinghouse Broadcasting and Cable, Dan Ritchie, told all who would listen that it would be Turner who would have to sell out, and cheap.[59] After little more than a year in operation and losses of more than $40 million, however, Turner purchased the Satellite News Channel for $25 million and shuttered its doors in October 1983.[60] As part of the sale, ABC and Westinghouse agreed not to launch a cable news service for three years. That Turner was able to meet the challenge that such a service presented is remarkable, given the financial resources those two corporations brought to the table, plus access to a network news operation that ABC could contribute and entry to cable households that Group W Cable could guarantee.[61]

The ultimate demise of the Satellite News Channel is also important to consider. Around the time that the service launched, Turner was calling CNN the "most significant achievement in the annals of journalism." The promise of cable television was that it could enrich the marketplace of ideas, that the pursuit of profit would not be the dominant motive. The Westinghouse annual report, however, suggested that the notion of public service was not prominent in the decision-making at the Satellite News Channel. The service reached 5.4 million subscribers after just six months, and the costs associated with the operation were within the parameters established prior to its launch. The revenues that the service generated, however, were below target and the "time required for an adequate return on its investment was too long to remain in the 24-hour television news market."[62] The Supreme Court opinion that, "the exhibition of motion pictures is a business pure and simple," seemed to fit the case of cable television as well.[63]

There were corporations that built successful cable networks in which cable operators, broadcast networks, and motion picture companies did not hold a financial interest. Turner Broadcasting established CNN, CNN Headline News, and TBS Superstation before Ted Turner turned to cable operators for help in 1986. Other nonaligned programming services emerged in the pre-1984 period, including Country Music Television, The Nashville Network, and The Weather Channel. The evolution of the Entertainment and Sports Programming Network, better known by the ESPN acronym, provides another example. ESPN was the creation of Bill Rasmussen, who envisioned a cable service that could provide statewide coverage of sports events in Connecticut. The capital used to build ESPN came from the Getty Oil Company, which owned 85 percent of the service in mid-1983.[64] Getty Oil was a major industrial corporation, with revenues of over $12 billion in 1983, but it was not a media conglomerate, which indicates that there was some degree of diversification in ownership at this time.

While entrepreneurs were at the roots of many national cable networks, the prominence of cable operators in this period is important, since such ownership could guarantee carriage in a certain number of households and provide a foundation upon which such services could build. Nickelodeon began as a joint venture between Time and Warner Communications, and the cable systems those two corporations controlled reached close to two million subscribers when it launched in 1979. USA Network debuted in 1977 as the MSG Sports Net, a satellite-delivered service projected to program 135 events per year from Madison Square Garden. At the outset, it was a joint venture between Gulf + Western Industries and UA-Columbia Cablevision, the tenth largest cable MSO, although UA-Columbia sold its interest to Time in 1981. The other prominent MSO at the time, Tele-Communications, Inc., made its first inroads into cable programming in 1980 with the launch of Black Entertainment Television.

The Concentration and Conglomeration of National Cable Networks: 1983–2005

The transformation of cable television since this formative period is dramatic, with the industry's exponential growth having a profound impact on the news and entertainment landscape in the United States. When Ted Turner envisioned a worldwide news operation with the word cable in its title and Bill Rasmussen became enamored with four simple letters, no one could imagine CNN and ESPN would one day be as recognizable as NBC or ABC, or that MTV would hold more cachet for some generations than CBS. In almost all measurable standards, the growth has been profound. In terms of subscribers, the number of cable and satellite households in the United States has increased from an estimated twenty-seven million at the start of 1983 to over ninety million in 2004. In terms of revenue, the dollars spent to advertise on cable television at the local and national levels has increased from just under $400 million in 1983 to just under $20 billion in 2004.[65]

These dramatic increases are attributable to the proliferation of cable programming services. A cable television marketplace with hundreds of national networks continues to evolve from a landscape with a mere handful of services. Technological advances in the medium, moreover, made it feasible for more households to receive a higher proportion of these services. In March 1983, around 22 percent of U.S. cable systems had a channel capacity of twelve channels or less, and fewer than one-half had a channel capacity of thirty channels or more.[66] In January 2004, the FCC concluded that the average system had 73 analog video channels plus 150 digital video channels for a total of 223.[67] The penetration of video-on-demand services increases these totals even further.

While there has been significant growth in the size of cable systems, there are still a finite number of channels that a cable system can transmit, so the allocation of a scarce resource becomes critical. This returns one to the questions that Dallas Smythe posed in 1960 when cable television was received in less than a million households and offered little more than retransmitted broadcast signals. In the context of this discussion, the fundamental issues raise a more defined set of questions: Who owns the national cable networks that assume such a significant role in the marketplace of ideas and the dissemination of culture? How concentrated is the ownership of national cable networks, and how does that pattern of ownership relate to the broader configuration discussed in the entertainment and news industries? Who has taken action to permit and promote the allocation of cable and satellite systems and services?

This evaluation of the ownership and control of cable programming services will focus on five benchmark dates between 1983 and 2005. These historical points in the evolution of cable television are important for a number of reasons. First, these dates offer a start point and an end point to the dramatic expansion of cable television that occurred between 1983 and 2005, as well as three additional points along the road. Second, and of equal importance, these dates bridge three pieces of legislation that Congress passed and the FCC enacted: the Cable Communications Policy Act of 1984, the Cable Television Consumer Protection and Competition Act of 1992, and the Telecommunications Act of 1996.

Patterns of Ownership: The 1980s

The Cable Communications Policy Act of 1984 marked a critical point in the evolution of cable television in the United States, and ownership among cable programming services prior to the passage and implementation of that legislation is illustrative. This period is notable for other reasons, as mid-1983 was an intersection in the evolution of cable television, falling after a period of expansion and before a period of consolidation. In the first six months of 1983, three prominent cable networks launched: Disney Channel, The Nashville Network, and Country Music Television. In the final six months of 1983 and the first two months of 1984, Daytime and Cable Health Network merged to form Lifetime; Alpha Repertory Television Service (ARTS) and Entertainment Channel merged to form A&E Television Network; and Showtime and The Movie Channel combined management but remained separate services.

When one examines the ownership and control of cable programming services in mid-1983, one discovers an ownership structure that extended beyond the corporations that controlled the motion picture companies and broadcast networks and the nation's most prominent cable operators. These conglomerates were present, to be certain, but their dominance was not as prevalent as it became later. Bill Rasmussen retained a 15 percent equity interest and remained in operational control of ESPN. ACSN: The Learning Channel, which began as a satellite service to link remote locations in the Appalachian mountains, became a national network in 1980 but it remained a nonprofit organization under the control of the Appalachian Community Service Network. Pat Robertson managed Christian Broadcasting Network, and Ted Turner remained in total control of Turner Broadcasting with beneficial ownership of 86.8 percent of the common stock.

There were forty national cable networks at the end of June 1983, with well over forty different corporations, organizations, and individuals with an equity interest of 5 percent or more in at least one of those networks. The aforementioned Getty Oil Co., Appalachian Community Service Network, Christian Broadcasting Network, and Turner Broadcasting were examples of the range of companies that controlled cable networks. What is significant about these four, moreover, is that the networks in question now rank among the most prominent in the cable landscape, but each has been integrated into a major media conglomerate: ESPN and the remnants of the Christian Broadcasting Network (aka Family Channel) into Disney, The Learning Channel into Liberty Media, and CNN and TBS into Time Warner. The same is true of other cable services that launched in 1983. Country Music Television (CMT) and The Nashville Network (TNN) are now part of the Viacom empire, but in June 1983 the Telstar Corp. owned a majority share of CMT and American General Corp. owned TNN.

The 1984 Cable Act had a profound impact on the regulation of cable television, as it placed substantial limits on the power of local governments to influence cable operators that held franchise rights in their communities and freed the same operators to set prices and increase them at their own discretion. The regulation of cable television rates ceased in 1987, which makes the patterns of ownership and control of cable programming services prior to that date noteworthy. The number of cable networks that distributed their programming on a national basis for over fifteen hours a week increased between 1983 and 1987. There were a total of fifty such networks in operation in January 1987, an increase from 1983, but the number of corporations, organizations, and individuals that held a financial interest of 5 percent or greater in one of those networks had decreased.

The consolidation of various cable networks, in most instances, involved companies that controlled other networks. As discussed earlier, Turner Broadcasting purchased the Satellite News Channel from ABC and Westinghouse and ceased operations in an effort to increase the dominance of CNN. In 1984, Alpha Repertory Television Service and Entertainment Channel merged to form A&E Television Network, and Cable Health Network and Daytime merged to form Lifetime. The dominant companies in those mergers were ABC, Hearst, and Viacom, all of which owned and controlled other services. Viacom, in fact, had become a powerful figure in cable television. In 1985, it launched VH-1: Video Hits One and Viewer's Choice, and in 1986, it acquired MTV: Music Television and Nickelodeon from Warner Amex, in addition to the portion of Showtime and The Movie Channel that it did not own. What is notable about these acquisitions is that two of the most popular basic services, MTV and Nickelodeon, shared a corporate parent with two of the most prominent premium services, Showtime and The Movie Channel. Viacom also collected a pair of music services, MTV and VH-1, and subsequent lawsuits argued that it utilized the power such ownership afforded to limit access to the marketplace.

The patterns of ownership evident in 1987 showed that most of the new services launched after 1983 belonged to cable operators. The Discovery Channel launched in June 1985 with funding from Westinghouse among others, but twelve months later four cable MSOs made financial investments. American Movie Classics, a sister service to Bravo, was also able to take advantage of MSO connections with its link to Cablevision. The power of the cable operators was most evident in the creation of pay-per-view services and home shopping channels. Viacom created Viewer's Choice in November 1985 and added a second channel, Viewer's Choice II, in June 1986. That year saw an explosion of home shopping channels, including Home Shopping Network, QVC Network, and Cable Value Network. While cable operators did not have an equity interest in Home Shopping Network, Comcast was the driving force behind the creation of QVC in November 1986, and TCI and Warner were both among the investors in the Cable Value Network.

The transformation of cable television in the 1980s was profound. In 1980, the largest cable MSO accounted for less than 10 percent of the cable households nationwide, and the market share for the four largest MSOs was around one-third. In 1990, the national market share for Tele-Communications, Inc. alone was around 25 percent through various investments and joint ventures. The merger mania that cut across so many different industries over the previous decade also altered the cable television marketplace, with the combination of Time and Warner the most dramatic. At the end of the decade, Time Warner owned an equity interest in no fewer than twelve national networks and was also prominent in the control of C-Span and C-Span 2, which operated as nonprofit cooperatives of cable operators. Time Warner's investments ranged from complete ownership of services, including HBO and Cinemax, to investments in companies that operated other services, such as Black Entertainment Television, E! Entertainment Television, and QVC Network. Time Warner also held an interest in Turner Broadcasting, whose stable of networks included the Cable News Network, CNN Headline News, TNT, and TBS.

Patterns of Ownership: The 1990s

The number of cable services that qualified as bona fide cable networks under the measurements utilized in this analysis increased 50 percent between 1987 and 1991. What is of interest is the percentage of cable services launched in which a small group of media conglomerates held a financial interest. There were more than ten national cable networks that were launched after the start of 1987 that remained viable services at the end of 1990.[68] The dominant conglomerates assumed a prominent role in this group, with at least one of the parent corporations of the broadcast networks, major motion picture companies, or two dominant cable MSOs holding an equity interest in six of those networks. The list included the most successful launches from this period, including TNT, CNBC, and E! Entertainment Television. It also incorporated Time Warner's The Comedy Channel, which merged with Viacom's Ha! The TV Comedy Network to form Comedy Central.

The level of concentration among national cable programming services as of January 1991 is detailed in table 6.3, which includes the holdings of the four broadcast networks, six major motion picture production and distribution companies, and two cable operators that reached over 10 percent of the cable households nationwide, TCI and Time Warner. The dominance of these corporations is clear, especially among the commercial services that achieved a penetration rate of 50 percent among television households nationwide. The major corporations held a financial interest in nine out of the thirteen such services (69.2 percent).[69] The only networks in which the major corporations did not hold an attributable interest of 5 percent or more were MTV: Music Television and Nickelodeon, which Viacom owned; The Nashville Network, which Oklahoma Publishing Co. owned through Gaylord Broadcasting Co.; and The Weather Channel, which Landmark Communications owned.

The level of concentration was even higher when one combined the four most prominent providers of programming services—TCI, Time Warner,

Table 6.3.   Ownership of Basic, Premium, and Pay-Per-View Cable Networks among the Parent Corporations of Broadcast Networks, Major Motion Picture Studios, and Cable Operators with a 10% Market Share, as of January 1991

Parent Corporation	Services with 50%+ Penetration of U.S. TV Households	Total Domestic Cable Television Services
Tele-Communications, Inc.	5	12
Time Warner Inc.	3	12
Capital Cities/ABC Inc.	3	3
General Electric Co.	1	4
Paramount Communications	1	1
Matsushita Electric	1	1
Walt Disney Co.	0	3
CBS Inc.	0	0
Sony Corp.	0	0
News Corp.	0	0
Total	9 of 13 (69.2%)	24 of 57 (42.1%)

Note: Totals derived from information contained in the *Cable TV Financial Databook*.

Capital Cities/ABC, and Viacom. These four corporations held a financial interest in ten of the thirteen cable networks (76.9 percent) that had achieved a penetration rate of 50 percent or greater. Viacom was a prominent cable operator at the time, but it did not yet own a motion picture studio or broadcast network. Still, the level of concentration is quite high when one considers that the federal government considers an industrial sector to be concentrated when the four dominant providers account for a market share of 40 percent. In this instance, that figure was almost doubled. What is also interesting about the 1990 data is the parent corporations of three of the studios, Disney, News Corp., and Sony, and one of the broadcast networks, CBS, were not major players in cable television, at least not yet.

The dominance of the nine major corporations in the cable television marketplace increased between the end of 1990 and the end of 1997. Table 6.4 documents the end results of a period of consolidation. There were twenty-three cable networks that had penetrated 50 percent of the television households nationwide as of January 1998, and only one of those services, The Weather Channel, was outside the nine dominant corporations in question. Even when one expanded the pool and measured cable services that reached 10 percent of television households nationwide, this same group held a financial interest in over 75 percent. Most evident in these totals is the dominance of the cable operators in this period, with the services that Tele-Communications, Inc., Time Warner, and Viacom owned all benefiting from such vertical integration. The reach of these corporations went even further. C-Span is a nonprofit public

Table 6.4. Ownership of Basic, Premium, and Pay-Per-View Cable Networks among the Parent Corporations of Broadcast Networks, Major Motion Picture Studios, and Cable Operators with a 10% Market Share, as of January 1998

Parent Corporation	Services with 50%+ Penetration of U.S. TV Households	Total Domestic Cable Television Services
Tele-Communications, Inc.	6	53
Time Warner Inc.	4	22
Viacom Inc.	3	18
Walt Disney Co.	4	15
General Electric Co.	3	12
News Corp.	1	7
Seagram Co. Ltd	1	4
CBS Corp.	1	4
Sony Corp.	0	2
Total	22 of 23 (95.7%)	104 of 137 (75.9%)

Note: The core list for this measurement was derived from the Federal Communications Commission's *Annual Assessment of the Status of Competition in Markets for the Delivery of Video Programming*, released on January 13, 1998. The list contained in the FCC report was a valuable point of departure, but the Commission applies no criteria to the classification of cable services. For this table, the FCC's criteria for the classification of broadcast networks were utilized: fifteen hours per week to a minimum of five affiliates.

service organization, and C-Span and C-Span 2 are not included in these totals, but cable operators such as TCI and Time Warner created the service and
continued to exercise some degree of control. For instance, the C-Span board
included numerous cable executives and Leo Hindery, the president and CEO
of TCI, was the chairman of the executive board of C-Span at the beginning
of 1998.

The dominance of these corporations is further illustrated when considering the highest rated cable networks. In the fourth quarter of 1997, the ten
cable networks with the highest prime time ratings had ties to the dominant
corporations: Time Warner (HBO, Cinemax, TNT, and TBS), Seagram (USA
Network), Viacom (Showtime, Nickelodeon, and The Movie Channel), and
Disney (Disney Channel and ESPN). In this context, the issue of ratings and
audience share is an important one. The revenue streams for cable networks
include both carriage fees and advertising, and the lattermost is contingent
on the measurement of a cable network's national audience. Nielsen Media
Research compiles ratings on basic cable services, and thirty-one of the
thirty-five basic networks Nielsen measured (88.6 percent) at the end of 1997
had ownership ties to one of the dominant corporations.[70] The only excep-
tions were Home and Garden Television, The Weather Channel, Television
Food Network, and WGN. The quest for high ratings, while not the end all
and be all as is the case with the broadcast networks since cable networks
also generate revenue through carriage fees, was still quite important.

What is most significant in this period is the dominance of the major corporations in the launch of new networks. There were eight cable networks
that launched after the end of 1990 that had reached ten million subscribers
at the end of 1994: America's Talking, Cartoon Network, Comedy Central,
Court TV, ESPN2, FX, Sci-Fi Channel, and Television Food Network. In every case except one, ownership could be traced to the parent corporation of a
broadcast network or major motion picture studio or one of the two dominant
cable MSOs. Among the broadcast companies, General Electric owned America's Talking and News Corp. created FX, while Capital Cities/ABC held an
80 percent interest in ESPN2. The parent corporations of the motion picture
companies were also quite active. Time Warner held a financial interest in
the Cartoon Network, Comedy Central, and Court TV. Viacom had moved
into this group with the purchase of Paramount Communications and held a
financial interest in two other networks, Comedy Central and Sci-Fi Channel,
while Matsushita also held an interest in the Sci-Fi Channel. TCI held a financial interest in two of the most prominent new cable networks, the Cartoon
Network and Court TV.

The Battle for Carriage

The proliferation of cable programming services through the mid-1990s intensified the battle for carriage on cable systems to an unprecedented level.
While the channel capacity of most systems increased, the promise of a five

hundred-channel universe was just that, a promise, as the bandwidth was filled on most systems. The dominant question toward the end of the decade was what did a new network need to gain the cable carriage required to survive. The allegation was made that TCI had to be involved in a proposed cable network for it to achieve the penetration level that is desired for the sale of national advertisements, approximately thirty million. The evidence did not support the argument that TCI alone could doom a cable network, but the examples of successful services that were not affiliated with the major corporations were few and far between. This raises a broader question: was an investment by one of the major corporations a prerequisite for the successful launch of a cable network.

There are some basic cable networks with such ownership ties for which the accumulation of a base level of subscriptions has proven to be quite difficult, while others have been terminated prior to launch.[71] The Sony-owned Game Show Network, for example, debuted in December 1994, but it did not reach ten million subscribers until December 1997. What is important about this case is that Sony was not a cable MSO, so it could not guarantee carriage on systems that it owned. Moreover, it did not own other cable networks or broadcast stations that could be used as leverage to gain carriage on cable systems. The absence of such assets proved to be a serious weakness for a corporation that launched a cable network. The Game Show Network was still below thirty million subscribers when Sony sold a 50 percent interest to Liberty Media in 2000.

The importance of such assets increased to a dramatic degree, as ownership of other cable networks and broadcast stations became leverage to gain carriage for new networks. Cable services that shared corporate ownership were often bundled in negotiations with cable operators. The Supreme Court ruled that block booking was anticompetitive in the distribution of motion pictures to theaters in the Paramount case and stated that there must be open bidding on motion pictures on a theater-by-theater, picture-by-picture basis. In the case of cable television, however, neither the FCC nor the Federal Trade Commission ruled against such practices. In 1997, Disney and TCI reached agreement on a wide-spread, ten-year carriage deal that covered ESPN and ESPN2, as well as ESPNews, which had struggled to obtain carriage. The agreement also included the Disney Channel and other Disney-owned networks, A&E Television Network, the History Channel, and Lifetime Television.[72] ESPN and Disney claimed that there were separate agreements for each network, but TCI president Leo Hindery described the deal as "one all-encompassing agreement" with the Disney organization.[73]

There was a second component of the carriage agreement between Disney and TCI that was significant. The cable operator received consent to retransmit the ABC affiliates that were owned and operated by the network, as well as the network affiliates of the Hearst Corporation, which owned the other 20 percent of ESPN. The 1992 Cable Act required cable operators to receive retransmission consent from broadcast stations, and that has been used as leverage to gain carriage for cable networks. When one examines the list of cable networks launched in the mid-1990s, five of the most successful, dubbed "retransmission networks," had ties to a large broadcast station group in retransmission consent agreements. In addition to the ESPN2 link to both ABC and Hearst stations, FX Network was tied to the Fox stations that News Corp. owned and operated as well as other Fox affiliates, and MSNBC was connected to the NBC-owned and -operated stations. Retransmission consent for E.W. Scripps network affiliated stations was negotiated with Home and Garden Television, while the Tribune Co. did the same with the Television Food Network.

The case of MSNBC is also quite revealing. In the summer of 1996, MSNBC, a joint venture of General Electric and Microsoft, was launched over the channels that carried another General Electric-owned service, America's Talking. The carriage of that service was tied to retransmission agreements for the NBC-owned and -operated stations. In 1996, however, some cable operators balked when General Electric announced that MSNBC would replace America's Talking in some twenty million households. The operators claimed that the format of the new service did not conform to that described in contracts for the old service and, as such, carriage agreements were null and void. General Electric, however, used its broadcast assets to trump such threats.

Thomas Rogers, the president of NBC Cable, declared that cable operators that did not allow the transfer of America's Talking outlets to MSNBC could not retransmit the NBC Television Network during the 1996 Olympic Games, scheduled for Atlanta that summer.[74] Rogers stated, "As quid pro quo, in the event that an operator dropped the channel, we have every right to drop their NBC television network programming. Why anyone would want to get into that fight, we don't know."[75] Such a tactic is quite remarkable for a corporation that is mandated to operate NBC in the public interest. The threat worked, as MSNBC launched on schedule and was carried in over thirty-six million households at the end of 1997. Whether it was desired or utilized in those households is another question, however. In the third quarter of 1997, MSNBC was watched, on average, in just 99,000 homes, despite the well-publicized use of NBC News personnel and a ratings boost after the death of Princess Diana.[76]

CABLE AND SATELLITE TELEVISION IN THE DIGITAL AGE

The impact of deregulation and consolidation on cable and satellite program services was most evident in coverage of the Olympic Games. When NBC Sports televised the Games of the XXVI Olympiad from Atlanta in 1996, the programming plan was rather simple: 171 hours of coverage and all of them on the NBC network. Flash forward eight years to the Games of Athens and one found an altogether different tale. In 2004, NBC telecast a total of 1,210 hours spread across seven different broadcast and cable outlets: NBC, NBC HD, USA Network, Bravo, MSNBC, CNBC, and Telemundo. The sheer volume represented more hours than the four previous summer Games combined, but the collection of networks was most telling. There was a longstanding link between NBC and the cable news channels, as General Electric launched CNBC in 1989 and MSNBC in 1996. The rest of the networks were new editions to the NBC stable as it completed the acquisitions of Telemundo in 2001 and Bravo in 2002 and took control of USA Network with the creation of NBC Universal in 2004.

The link with USA Network is the most significant of this group, as NBC became the last of the six major broadcast networks to align with one of the prominent general entertainment cable networks. The integration of a major motion picture studio, broadcast network, and basic cable channel under the same ownership, in fact, was one of the major alterations in the landscape between 1994 and 2004. FX Network had such a connection from its launch in 1994 and built its profile upon programming from the Fox network and Twentieth Century Fox studios. TBS and TNT rose to prominence outside of the major media conglomerates, but the merger of Turner Broadcasting and Time Warner in 1996 created vertical integration with the Warner Bros. studio and its fledgling broadcast network, The WB. The importance of such relationships was evident in the first quarter of 1996 when the syndication rights to a pair of marquee prime time programs, *The X-Files* and *ER*, remained in-house, with Twentieth Television selling the rights for the *X-Files* to the FX Network and Warner Bros. doing likewise with the rights for *ER* going to TNT. *The X-Files* was the perfect picture of integration: produced at Twentieth Century Fox Television, broadcast on the Fox network, and syndicated on FX.

The big three broadcast networks took different routes to such integration, but the end result is much the same. CBS acquired The Nashville Network in 1997, which Viacom transformed into TNN: The National Network in 2000 to move it from "Southern regional entertainment to a broad entertainment channel."[77] It renamed the network again in 2003 when it became Spike TV to focus on a male demographic. The merger of Disney and Capital Cities/ABC in 1996 gave the conglomerate two pieces of the puzzle, a major studio and broadcast network, but it lacked the final jewel, a general entertainment cable network that it owned and controlled outright.[78] It filled that hole in the fall of 2001 when it purchased Fox Family from News Corp. for $5.2 billion and renamed it ABC Family.

The connection between the broadcast networks and their cable cousins is quite clear. ABC Family marked its arrival as a member of the Disney family at the start of 2002 with a marathon of *Alias*, a Touchstone Television production broadcast on ABC. Before the first quarter was over, ABC Family was showing episodes of *Alias* and another Touchstone production, *According to Jim*, days after they debuted on ABC.[79] The story was similar at Spike TV, which showed significant rating growth in 2004 thanks to off-network episodes of *CSI: Crime Scene Investigation*, a coproduction of Alliance Atlantis and CBS Productions. What was ironic for a network targeted at men is that much of the ratings increase came from female viewers. That did not stop Viacom and Spike TV from committing a reported $1.9 million per episode for the cable rights to *CSI: NY* after the third member of the CSI franchise had aired for fewer than three months.[80] Sidebar 6.2 explores the prominence of off-network programming on cable networks.

The marriage of NBC and USA Network under the NBC Universal banner in 2004 involved the same concepts. The cornerstones of the NBC prime time lineup at the time were three installments of *Law & Order*: the original, *Special Victims Unit*, and *Criminal Intent*. The USA Network schedule was also built around that franchise, as it owned the off-network syndication rights to *Law & Order: SVU* and repurposed episodes of *Law & Order: Criminal Intent* six nights after their debut on NBC. Vivendi Universal Entertainment owned USA Network and produced *Law & Order* within Universal Television. The formation of NBC Universal brought Universal Television, USA Network, and NBC under common ownership. At the press conference to discuss the completion of the merger, executives of NBC Universal also announced renewals for all three series, a commitment to a fourth, and a long-term extension of creator Dick Wolf's production deal with the newly named NBC Universal Television Studios.[81] Six months later, it announced the sale of syndication rights to *Law & Order: Criminal Intent* for a reported $2 million per episode. The recipient of those rights was not one but two NBC Universal networks, with USA Network holding the Monday–Friday rights and Bravo the weekend rights.[82]

The coordination of such a bid was not as complicated as it might seem. With the creation of NBC Universal, day-to-day control of all of its television assets—the NBC and Telemundo networks and stations, NBC Universal Television Studios, and various cable networks—was handed to NBC Universal Television Group President Jeff Zucker.[83] The management of such properties differed from conglomerate to conglomerate. The month before Zucker took over at NBC Universal, Disney named Anne Sweeney president of Disney-ABC Television, which included the day-to-day management of its entertainment television assets: the ABC network, ABC Family and Disney Channel, and Touchstone Television. There was also coordination in the management of its sports properties, as George Bodenheimer controlled ESPN and ABC Sports. Viacom divided its properties along different lines. Les Moonves handled the broadcast assets, including CBS and UPN, while Tom Freston managed Paramount Pictures as well as the MTV, Showtime, and BET cable groups. And while Viacom chairman Sumner Redstone completed a split of Viacom into two companies in 2006, ultimate control of the parts remained in his hands.

Sidebar 6.2
Cable Television Programming: Promises Unfulfilled

The rise to prominence of cable programming services and the challenge posed to their broadcast brethren prompted debate throughout the 1990s, but the 52nd Annual Emmy Awards in September 2000 eliminated any lingering doubts that cable had arrived. James Gandolfini captured the Emmy for the lead actor in a drama series for his work on HBO's *The Sopranos*, one of eighteen nominations the show received that year. While *The Sopranos* lost the ultimate prize to *The West Wing*, the admiration for the show was still clear. In his acceptance speech for the Emmy for outstanding drama series, *The West Wing* creator Aaron Sorkin conceded, "It's been said before, it's worth saying again, *The Sopranos* is one of the great achievements in the history of television."[1] *The Sopranos* became the first cable series to claim the Emmy for outstanding drama series in 2004, just as *Sex and the City* claimed the first outstanding comedy Emmy for cable in 2001. The shift in the balance of power in television was undeniable.

Michael Chiklis and Tony Shalhoub followed the path Gandolfini forged and collected outstanding actor awards in 2002 and 2003 for their work in *The Shield* on FX and *Monk* on USA Network, respectively.[2] Such programs have garnered innumerable headlines, but the careful analysis of the advertiser-supported, basic cable networks tells a different story. Since the birth of such services, programs originated for cable were quite rare, and off-air network programs were abundant. The Christian Broadcasting Network ranked among the lowest rated cable services after its debut in 1981, but it climbed into fourth behind ESPN, TBS, and CNN in 1984 with a schedule loaded with off-network programs.[3] Pat Robertson argued that, "all-religious programming just doesn't reach people. They want comedy, they want sports, they want news."[4] The name of the service was even changed to diminish the Christian orientation of the network, from the Christian Broadcasting Network to the CBN Family Channel, and then to the Family Channel.

Other reasons support the devotion to off-network programs, with financial ones most prominent. National and regional sports networks such as ESPN and Fox Sports Net are the most expensive on the basic tier, and the acquisition of high-priced programming is the foremost reason. The price tag associated with the development of prime time programs does not approach the $1.1 billion annual fee that ESPN will hand over to the National Football League starting in 2006, but the costs are still considerable and there are no guarantees of success. Far more reliable are off-network hits, and basic cable networks have invested millions in such reruns over the first half of the 2000s. A&E alone committed $800,000 per episode for *Crossing Jordan* in 2002, $1 million per episode for *CSI: Miami* in 2003, and $2.5 million per episode for *The Sopranos* in 2005.[5]

The implication of such an approach was most evident in February 2005, when basic cable outrated the broadcast networks in prime time for the first time in a sweeps month.[6] The four highest rated cable services that month were TNT, USA Network, TBS, and Spike TV, and when one adds two other general entertainment basic networks to the mix, ABC Family and FX, the reliance on recycled content is indisputable. For the February sweeps, the six networks programmed 672 hours between 7:00 p.m. and 11:00 p.m., and reruns of network programming filled 47.2 percent of those hours.[7] *Law & Order* (TNT), *Law & Order: Special Victims Unit* (USA), and *CSI: Crime Scene Investigation* (Spike TV) alone accounted for 19.2 percent. Most striking given the headlines that shows such as *Monk* and *The Shield* have generated is that original scripted series accounted for just twenty hours (3 percent) that month.

In addition to the off-network programs, the six cable services were quite reliant on motion pictures from the Hollywood studios. Three of the six networks, FX, ABC Family, and TBS, allocated between 46.4 percent and 51.3 percent of their program hours to motion pictures. The dominance of the major studios and the mini-majors, moreover, was clear. The six networks aired 155 films in whole or in part between 7:00 p.m. and 11:00 p.m., and 80 percent of those came from one of the six major studios or two prominent mini-majors, Disney's Miramax and Time Warner's New Line. The ownership link was most evident with FX, which aired eighteen different movies at least once in the prime time window, fifteen of which came from Twentieth Century Fox (83.3 percent).

The dearth of original programming is little noticed with most cable services, but that is not the case with BET: Black Entertainment Television. The African-American community was critical of the prominence of music videos and the absence of substantive programming on BET even before it became part of Viacom in 2001, and little has changed since then.[8] The decision to cancel three prominent public affairs programs, *BET Tonight with Ed Gordon, Lead Story,* and *Teen Summit,* in December 2002 drew criticism as did the migration of off-network entertainment programs from UPN, including *The Parkers* and *Girlfriends.* In 2001, BET founder Robert Johnson made it all seem rather simple: "We are not trying to be socially redeeming for black intellectuals. We were running a business. And we had the right to run our business the same way MTV runs its business and Comedy Central runs its business."[9]

While few would question Johnson's right to run his business as he desires, the hopes were much higher in the case of BET, and Johnson contributed to such expectations. Before BET launched in 1980, Johnson said, "It's not that there's too little black programming on TV, it's that commercial television is limited to mass-appeal programming, which means it has to be bland and it can't be specialized. We'll have a special channel that will feature the full creative range of black entertainment."[10] He promised that "three, four or five years down the road" the audience built upon off-network situation comedies and other programs he called "blaxploitation" would enable the network to show "our own, original, made-for-Black Entertainment Television programs. I think that will completely overshadow what we're starting with."[11]

BET long ago surpassed the twenty million subscribers that Johnson once cited as the benchmark for the development of original programming, reaching over sixty million households when it became part of Viacom. There was a time when BET did not have the resources required for original program production, but that is no longer the case. In corporate documents in the mid-1990s, BET argued that the acquisition of syndication rights to "high quality" off-network programming is the most "cost-effective" means to provide its audience with such programs, that the production of original programming is too expensive.[12] Cost-effective programming was evident across the BET schedule. In one week of the 1997–1998 season, programs that featured music videos and stand-up comedians accounted for eighteen of the twenty-two hours cablecast in the prime time period.[13]

(Continued)

The network never approached the vision that Johnson laid forth in 1979. At that time, he cited one program in particular, *Benson*, when he described the limitations of broadcast network programs that featured African-Americans.[14] Johnson wondered why Robert Guillaume's character remained a butler when he was so bright, questioning why he was not an executive.[15] The use of *Benson* as an example proved to be rather poignant, since BET began to cablecast reruns of the show in 1996. The Guillaume character did become the state budget director and attorney general in the show, but one has to question whether the BET decision to purchase the program had as much to do with the transformation of Benson or the minimal cost of acquisition, $36,000 per episode.

NOTES

1. Quoted in Phil Rosenthal, "Commanding Win for 'West Wing,'" *Chicago Sun-Times*, 11 September 2000, 28.

2. Michael Chiklis won the Emmy for outstanding actor in a drama series in 2002 while Tony Shalhoub won for outstanding actor in a comedy series in 2003.

3. The CBN schedule included westerns such as *Wyatt Earp, Rifleman,* and *Wagon Train* and comedies such as *The Best of Groucho, Burns and Allen, I Married Joan,* and *Bachelor Father.* ("Change Brings Success For Christian Network." *New York Times*, 3 September 1984.)

4. Quoted in "Change Brings Success For Christian Network," *New York Times*, 3 September 1984.

5. A&E also acquired off-network rights to *24* in 2004 for between $225,000 and $250,000 per episode. Serials such as *24*, with stories continuing from episode to episode, have not done as well in syndication as series such as *Law & Order* with closure at the end of each episode.

6. R. Thomas Umstead, "Cable Nips a Sweeps Win," *Multichannel News*, 7 March 2005, 31.

7. The sweeps period extended from February 3, 2005, through March 2, 2005. This total includes eight hours of *Sex and the City* on TBS, and while this program originated on HBO rather than one of the broadcast networks, the basic issues are the same.

8. In 1995, a petition circulated on the Internet that presented six demands to the executives of BET, ranging from improved political coverage to more space for black independent films. The petition also called for a reduction of music videos: "decrease the amount of negative imagery that comes into our homes via your station's overabundance of music video shows, particularly those videos which focus on scantily clad women, violence and drugs." In the *Village Voice* article about the petition, the author said that BET was "programming by the lazy, directed at the paralyzed," and that Black History Month programs on other cable channels made "BET's sorry ass hard to ignore." (Colson Whitehead, "Dream On," *Village Voice*, 20 February 1997, 43.)

9. Quoted in Ben Wasserstein, "Back Off, Black Brainiacs, Demand Makes BET Bad," *New York Times*, 31 July 2005, 6.

10. Quoted in Tom Shales, "Beyond Benson: Black-Oriented Channel from a Cable Pioneer," *Washington Post*, 30 November 1979.

11. Quoted in Shales, "Beyond Benson," *Washington Post*, 30 November 1979.

12. BET Holdings, Inc., Form 10-K, 31 October 1997.

13. The week examined extended from October 25, 1997, through October 31, 1997.

14. ABC broadcast "Benson" from September 1979 until August 1986. Robert Guillaume was a butler for a widowed governor.

15. Shales, "Beyond Benson," *Washington Post*, 30 November 1979.

The same ownership patterns were evident in Spanish-language networks. The acquisition of Telemundo made General Electric one of the last major conglomerates with extensive television holdings to venture into that market. The deal also included Telemundo Internacional, a news and entertainment channel that drew upon Telemundo resources, and mun2, targeted at third- and fourth-generation bilingual eighteen- to thirty-four-year-olds. The development of digital cable and proliferation of national program networks included a dramatic increase in the number of Spanish-language networks between 1997 and 2004. Univision and Telemundo had long utilized cable for distribution in markets without affiliated broadcast stations, and networks based in Europe and Latin American were carried on some systems as premium services. Univision-owned Galavision, however, was one of the few U.S.-based, general entertainment, Spanish-language cable networks with widespread distribution prior to 1997.[84] That changed in the years that followed.

Univision dominated in this area and launched a series of digital cable networks in 2003 through a joint venture with Grupo Televisa that included two movie channels, DePelicula and DePelicula Classico, and three different music and lifestyle channels: Bandamax, Ritmoson Latino, and Telehit. Univision was no longer alone in the market, however, as Disney, Liberty Media, News Corp., Time Warner, and Viacom all launched digital Spanish-language services in this same period. Some of these networks were distributed in Latin America, but Hispanic households in the United States were a prime focus. And most of them carried established brand names, including CNN en Espanol, Cartoon Network en Espanol, Discovery en Espanol, ESPN Desportes, Fox Sports en Espanol, HBO Latino, History Channel en Espanol, MTV Espanol, Toon Disney en Espanol, and VH Uno.

The evolution of MTV Espanol is illustrative of the changes that occurred in the cable and satellite market in the United States. Viacom launched MTV Latino in 1993, and while its studios were located in Miami the main target were households in an estimated twenty territories in Latin America.[85] MTV Latino followed the business model that Viacom created with MTV Europe and featured some of the same programming that appeared on MTV: Music Television, including Anglo-artists and English-language video. That was not the case with MTV S when it launched in 1998. It focused on Hispanic artists and Spanish-language videos, and it was distributed to cable and satellite households in the United States. Viacom rebranded the network as MTV Espanol in 2001 to position the service as an essential channel for the twelve to thirty-four-year-old Spanish-speaking demographic.

The development of digital cable and direct-broadcast-satellite increased the number of channels available in most households, but MTV Espanol and the other Spanish-language networks are characteristic of how the major conglomerates attacked these new services. In the summer of 1998, Viacom launched "The Suite from MTV and VH1," which included six different music channels: MTV2, MTV X, MTV S, VH1 Smooth, VH1 Soul, and VH1 Country.[86]

"The Suite" added three children's networks that debuted in the first quarter of 1999: Noggin, Nickelodeon Games & Sports, and Nick Too, a time shifted version of Nickelodeon using an alternate feed.[87] Viacom introduced four more channels to the service in 2002: Nicktoons, MTV Jams, MTV Hits, and VH1 Mega Hits to bring the total to 13.[88]

What is significant about Viacom's approach to "The Suite from MTV and VH1" is that it did not handle carriage deals for the digital services on a channel-by-channel basis and used its market power to leverage carriage for the services. From its launch in 1998, Viacom bundled carriage of "The Suite" and attempted to sell the services en masse. While it was possible for cable operators to negotiate carriage deals for a single channel, there were strong financial disincentives to acquire them on an a la carte basis.[89] There were also discounts for operators who carried MTV, VH1, and Nickelodeon in their basic tier. Viacom acquired the trump card it needed with the acquisition of CBS in 2000. In a speech to investors after the merger was completed, president Mel Karmazin discussed how Viacom could, "use CBS retransmission consent to get additional carriage for its properties."[90]

The power of that link was evident in 2003. In September, Viacom announced a long-term agreement with the National Cable Television Cooperative, which represented independent cable operators that reached more than fifteen million subscribers. The deal covered the core Viacom networks such as MTV: Music Television, Nickelodeon, TV Land, and Spike TV, but it also included carriage for six of the MTV digital networks on the NCTC systems that rolled out digital service, MTV2, MTV Hits, VH1 Classic, Noggin, Nicktoons, and Nickelodeon Games & Sports.[91] In December, Comcast received retransmission consent for the CBS-owned and- operated stations less than two months before the network televised Super Bowl XXXVIII. As part of that agreement, Comcast agreed to launch Nicktoons and MTV Hits as part of its digital service nationwide and increase the distribution of MTV2, Nickelodeon Games & Sports, VH1 Classic, and VH1 Country.[92]

Patterns of Ownership in National Cable Networks: 2004–2005

The detailed examination of ownership in 2004 and 2005 raises serious questions about whether the growth of cable and direct-broadcast-satellite services increased the diversity of voices on television. Graham Murdock argues that one must make a distinction between diversity and multiplicity: "It is possible to greatly increase the number of channels and the number of goods in circulation without significantly extending diversity. More does not necessarily mean different." Frank Hughes of the National Cable Television Cooperative echoed the essence of that argument when MTV Networks announced the addition of four more channels to "The Suite" in 2002: "These guys are trying to stake their claim on digital tiers, and why are we suckers for this repurposed digital programming. It's not new. It's not fresh."[93]

There is little question that the penetration of fiber-based distribution systems and digital platforms increased the number of channels available in the average American household. In the first quarter of 2004, the number of video channels carried by the average cable system was 223, 73 analog channels, and 150 digital channels.[94] This allocation preserved additional bandwidth for high-definition television, video-on-demand, Internet access, and other services.[95] It was also comparable to the distribution of channels on Total Choice Premium on the DirecTV satellite service in the first quarter of 2005.[96] That package carried 173 video channels, plus an average of nineteen local broadcast channels in the five largest television markets, for a total of 192. The DirecTV Spanish-language lineup, Opcion Premier, included 181 video channels, plus the same local broadcast channels.

An examination of the allocation of bandwidth on five of the largest cable systems in the United States at the start of 2005 adds further depth to this discussion. These systems represented five of the most prominent multiple system operators—Comcast, Time Warner Cable, Cox Communications, Cablevision, and Bright House Networks—and included systems that were part of three of the largest system clusters in the nation.[97] These systems are also consistent with the FCC mean, with an average of 76.2 analog channels and 140.6 digital channels. Most striking about these systems are the similarities between them, which extends far beyond the video channels measured above. Each of these systems included forty-six channels of Music Choice, a joint venture that counts among its investors Time Warner, Comcast, Cox Communications, Sony Corp., EMI Group, and Microsoft. Each also designated between twenty-seven and forty channels to sports pay-per-view or subscription services such as NBA League Pass, MLB Extra Innings, and ESPN PPV. In addition to the obvious connection between ESPN PPV and Disney, these services were all distributed through iN DEMAND LLC, a joint venture of Time Warner, Comcast, and Cox Communications. All of them also devoted considerable space to pay-per-view and video-on-demand services.

The allocation of scarce bandwidth to such services and the benefit to the major corporations is important to understand, but it is also crucial to measure the power of these corporations within the analog and digital tiers that reach the most households. In the first quarter of 2004, for example, there were just over sixty-six million basic cable subscribers, about a third of which subscribed to digital cable.[98] As such, access to dozens of pay-per-view channels as well as video-on-demand services is much more limited. The failure to distinguish these differences is one of the fundamental flaws with the Federal Communications Commission's annual assessment of the marketplace for the delivery of video services, which sidebar 6.1 addresses in more detail. In the *Eleventh Annual Report,* issued in February 2005, the FCC identified 388 satellite-delivered national programming networks in 2004, compared to 339 networks in 2003.[99] These totals might suggest that there was a vibrant marketplace, but closer inspection raises serious doubts about such a conclusion.

The FCC total of 388 satellite-delivered national programming networks included ninety-one pay-per-view or video-on-demand channels, including thirty-seven from iN DEMAND and thirty-fve from TVN Entertainment alone. Given relative market power as well as carriage fees and other factors, iN DEMAND outscoring the ESPN networks 37–6 skewed the overall totals and the Commission's conclusions. There were also numerous services included that programmed just a handful of hours per week and some that transmitted a signal without a known destination, free for broadcast stations and public, educational, and government (PEG) access channels to utilize. The FCC also counted defunct services and some networks that had not launched as of December 31, 2004. When one eliminated pay-per-view and video-on-demand services and set reasonable criteria for the rest—services programming a minimum of twelve hours per day, transmitting to designated channel slots on cable and satellite systems, and targeting households in at least one-third of the geographic area of the United States—the number of satellite-delivered national programming networks stood at 263 at the dawn of 2005.[100] Of this total, eight corporations—Disney, NBC Universal, News Corp., Time Warner, Viacom, Liberty Media, Comcast, and E.W. Scripps—held a financial interest in 163 (62.0 percent) and Comcast marketed another seventeen (6.5 percent) foreign language services through International Premium Networks, giving these conglomerates control over 68.4 percent of the national cable and satellite services.

The prominence of this group increased when one examined the national programming services that reached a significant number of television households. Just over ninety million American households received cable or satellite service at the start of 2005, and it is illustrative to look at the national networks that reached two-thirds and one-third of those households, sixty million and thirty million, respectively. The thirty-million household mark is also significant since advertisers have long viewed that as the minimum threshold for national sales.[101] Even this benchmark is not a guarantee for success, however, as Time Warner closed down CNNfn in the fall of 2004, citing the challenge of generating solid ratings with only thirty million households.[102] The ownership of programming services in sixty-million and thirty-million households at the start of 2005 is broken down in table 6.5.

The prominence of the five conglomerates that owned a broadcast network and a major motion picture studio—Disney, NBC Universal, News Corp., Time Warner, and Viacom—was quite evident among the cable and satellite networks that reach sixty million households. There were forty-six advertiser-supported, basic networks that reached this threshold as of January 2005, and the five conglomerates had an ownership interest in thirty-five of the forty-six, 76.1 percent.[103] When one included Liberty Media, the total increased to 89.1 percent for six conglomerates. With Comcast and E.W. Scripps in the mix, eight corporations had an ownership interest in 93.5 percent of the networks with a subscriber base over sixty million.[104] The only networks in this group

Table 6.5. Ownership of Most Prominent Basic and Premium Cable & Satellite Programming Services, as of January 2005

Ownership Group	60+ Million w/o C-Span & C-Span 2	30–60 Million w/o C-Span & C-Span 2	Premium Movie Channels	Totals
NBC Universal	8	4	—	12
News Corp.	6	1	—	7
Sony Corp.	0	1	—	1
Time Warner Inc.	7	1	2	10
Viacom Inc.	8	5	2	15
Walt Disney Co.	8	8	—	16
Subtotal	35 of 46 (76.1%)	18 of 42 (42.9%)	4 of 6 (66.7%)	57 of 94 (60.6%)
Liberty Media	8	8	2	18
Subtotal	41 of 46 (89.1%)	25 of 42 (59.5%)	6 of 6 (100.0%)	72 of 94 (76.6%)
Comcast	1	4	—	5
E.W. Scripps	2	3	—	5
Total	43 of 46 (93.5%)	31 of 42 (73.8%)	6 of 6 (100.0%)	80 of 94 (85.1%)

that one of the conglomerates did not own in whole or part were The Weather Channel, AMC: American Movie Classics, and WGN, owned by Landmark Communications, Cablevision Systems Corp., and Tribune Co., respectively. The percentages were a little lower for networks with between thirty-million and sixty-million households, 59.5 percent for six conglomerates, with Liberty Media once again joining the broadcast/studio group, and 73.8 percent for all eight. When one included the six premium movie channels that A.C. Nielsen included in its rating—HBO, Cinemax, Showtime, The Movie Channel, Encore, and Starz!—the five major conglomerates held an ownership interest in fifty-seven of ninety-four networks, 60.6 percent, while one of the eight dominant corporations had an interest in eighty of ninety-four, 85.1 percent.

The five media behemoths gain much of the attention, with Sony more or less on the sidelines, but the inclusion of Liberty Media, Comcast, and E.W. Scripps in this group is important. One of the basic issues to address is the degree to which corporations with market power in one media sector are able to use that position to extend their reach into other sectors. Such leverage can come in different forms. The FCC has long focused on vertical integration between programming networks and cable system operators, and Comcast and Time Warner are included in such totals. The Liberty Media collection utilized the same leverage for most of its services when it was part of Tele-Communications, Inc. and before AT&T Broadband spun it off into an independent corporation in 2001. And in the case of Scripps, the power wielded was through federal mandated retransmission consent for the prominent local stations in the Scripps Howard group.

The analysis of digital cable networks paints another picture of dominance and adds depth to the discussion. The abundance of diverse voices that digital cable could create is one justification presented for the loosening of ownership regulations, but the concentration of those channels in a limited number of hands would undermine that argument. Measuring digital programming services is problematical, for while some digital channels have reached a critical mass and reliable numbers are available, corporations do not report subscriber figures for many of these channels and there are no reliable estimates. The examination of the twenty-five largest cable systems in the country, however, presents clear trends on how operators are utilizing the digital bandwidth. The top twenty-five systems as of March 2004 covered all four time zones in the contiguous states and included one system in Hawaii. These systems also represented the two largest cable multiple system operators, Comcast and Time Warner, and six of the top nine.[105]

Seventy-six digital services appeared on approximately two-thirds of the largest systems, sixteen or more out of twenty-five, and the dominance of the major conglomerates is undeniable.[106] The results are detailed in table 6.6.

Table 6.6. Ownership and/or Control of Digital Services on the 25 Largest Cable Systems in the United States, as of January 2005

	Digital Services on 16 or more of 25 Largest Systems	Digital Services on 8 to 16 of 25 Largest Systems	Total
NBC Universal	3	4	7
News Corp.	7	2	9
Sony Corp.	0	0	0
Time Warner Inc.	17	1	18
Viacom Inc.	16	8	24
Walt Disney Co.	8	4	12
Sub Total	47 of 76	19 of 38	66 of 114
	(61.8%)	(50.0%)	(57.9%)
Liberty Media	21	2	23
Subtotal	68 of 76	20 of 38	88 of 114
	(89.5%)	(52.6%)	(77.2%)
Comcast	2	1	3
E.W. Scripps	2	2	4
Total	71 of 76	23 of 38	94 of 114
	(93.4%)	(60.5%)	(82.5%)

Note: List of services is based on the twenty-five largest cable systems as of March 2004, according to the National Cable & Telecommunications Association website. This group of systems reflected the dominant MSOs, with seven Comcast and Time Warner systems, six Cox systems, three Cablevision systems, and one each from Bright House Networks and Insight Communications. The cable lineup for each system was accessed in the first quarter of 2005.

Of the networks with carriage on sixteen or more systems, one could trace ownership of 61.8 percent of them to at least one of the five conglomerates with ownership of a broadcast network and major motion picture studio— NBC Universal, News Corp., Time Warner, Viacom, and Walt Disney—and that total increased to 89.5 percent with the inclusion of Liberty Media.[107] With the inclusion of Comcast and E.W. Scripps, one could connect an ownership interest in 93.4 percent to at least one of eight corporations. Two of the five networks without such a connection were owned by Cablevisions Systems Corp., the sixth largest cable MSO at the time, while a third, Cine Latino, was owned by Mexico television giant MVS Communications. The major conglomerates were not quite as dominant with the digital channels found on between eight and sixteen of the twenty-five largest systems, although the group of five still had an interest in 50 percent and the eight combined for ownership in twenty-three of thirty-eight, 60.5 percent.

There is little question that DirecTV and Dish Network created competition in the marketplace for multichannel video programming distributors (MVPD), but it is less certain that these alternatives increased the diversity of program choices. In 1998, the FCC adopted rules related to the Cable Act of 1992 that mandated that direct-broadcast-satellite providers set aside 4 percent of their channel capacity for noncommercial programming of an educational or informational nature.[108] This resulted in some unique program services such as RFD TV, which programmed for rural and agricultural audiences and both DirecTV and Dish Network carried as part of its public interest obligations. When one controls for such services, which are akin to the public, education, and government access channels on cable, there is a remarkable sameness to the offerings on the satellite services. In the case of DirecTV, there were 126 unique national program networks in the Total Choice Premium package once public interest, religious, and shopping channels were eliminated, and 116 (92.1 percent) of those were among the sixty million or thirty million plus subscription groups or the sixteen plus system group discussed earlier.[109] In the case of Dish Network, there were 122 networks in the analogous group for the America's Top 180 package with premium movie channels, and 109 (89.3 percent) of those were in the cable groups detailed above.

Vertical Integration, Retransmission Consent, and other Market Factors

It is impossible to refute the success of the five conglomerates with ownership of broadcast networks and motion picture studios in building cable and satellite carriage for their national programming networks. That group had an ownership interest in 76.1 percent of the national networks with a subscriber base of sixty million or higher and an interest in 61.8 percent of the digital networks found on sixteen or more of the twenty-five largest cable systems. When one includes Liberty Media, Comcast, and E.W. Scripps to the mix, these totals reach 93.5 percent and 93.4 percent, respectively. The critical question is whether market power in one sector, through the ownership of motion picture studios, local broadcast stations, and/or cable or satellite systems, provided the leverage for such gains. The conglomerates would suggest that the excellence of the programming on these networks was the cause for the increases in cable and satellite carriage, but anecdotal evidence points to other factors. This is where the diversification of ownership across traditional media borders becomes critical.

There is little question that vertical integration between multiple system operators or direct-broadcast-satellite (DBS) providers and a national programming network is a significant advantage in the launch and penetration of a service. The connections between Comcast Cable and Time Warner Cable and their respective networks are clear, and the advantages are indisputable. Such connections are perhaps most critical for niche services that appeal to a particular demographic group. TV One launched in January 2004 as a lifestyle and entertainment channel aimed at African-American adults and its subscription base increased from 2.2 million to 18 million within a year. Comcast Corp. held a 38.8 percent equity interest in TV One from its launch, and DirecTV Group made a financial investment when it added the network to its Total Choice package in January 2005.[110] The tale is similar with Sí TV, an English-language service directed at the Latino audience, which debuted a month after TV One. Time Warner Cable and EchoStar Communications, the parent company of Dish Network, invested $60 million in Sí TV and helped drive distribution, which surpassed ten million just after the network's first anniversary.

The Federal Communications Commission measures vertical integration with cable operators and program services in its analysis of the MVPD marketplace, but the FCC does not do the same with DBS operators, so it ignores the connection between DirecTV Group and News Corp.-owned networks. It also ignores the importance such ownership had in the emergence of numerous others. Showtime, Nickelodeon, MTV, and VH1 rose to prominence at a time when Viacom, Inc. was also a large cable operator, with over a million households. Viacom sold its cable systems to Tele-Communications, Inc. in 1995 to lower its debt after the acquisition of Paramount Communications and Blockbuster, but the connection was critical to the success of those services. The influence is much more recent with Liberty Media, the content arm of Tele-Communications, Inc. and AT&T Broadband before it spun off in 2001. The most prominent Liberty Media-owned networks, including Animal Planet, Discovery Channel, The Learning Channel, Travel Channel, and QVC as well as Encore and Starz!, built their subscription base prior to that divorcement.

The balance of power in cable television once favored the prominent multiple system operators like TCI that served as the gatekeepers between programming networks and television households. While Comcast, Time Warner, and other large operators still possess tremendous might, passage of the 1992 Cable Act and advent of retransmission consent shifted significant power from the operators to broadcast stations groups. This was never more evident than in 2000 with the rather public feud Disney waged with Time Warner and then Comcast. At the stroke of midnight on May 1, 2000, Time Warner Cable dropped the feeds of ABC-owned and-operated stations in seven markets, including New York, Los Angeles, Philadelphia, and Houston, after the expiration of an extension of the retransmission consent agreement between the two parties. The ABC stations remained dark for thirty-nine hours amid accusations and finger-pointing from both sides. Disney's chief lobbyist, Preston Padden, claimed that, "Some deranged individual has deprived all of these (viewers) of ABC," while Fred Dressler of Time Warner Cable countered that Disney had threatened to take their stations off the cable systems for months and "started squealing like a pig" when Time Warner did it for them.[111]

Most significant about the feud between Disney and Time Warner is that the quarrel had virtually nothing to do with the ABC Network or its affiliated stations. The battle revolved, instead, around carriage of Disney-owned cable networks on Time Warner systems. At the top of the Disney wish list was the conversion of the Disney Channel from a premium service to the basic cable tier, which increased subscriber revenue for the network. It also sought carriage for two new digital channels, SoapNet and Toon Disney. Less than a month after Time Warner dropped the ABC stations, the two corporations reached a long-term retransmission agreement. Disney received all the concessions that it had sought, as Time Warner agreed to convert all of its premium Disney Channel subscribers to basic service and committed to the rollout of SoapNet and Toon Disney. The deal also included carriage agreements for the ESPN networks, with Time Warner pledging to increase ESPN2 distribution to the same level as ESPN, boost ESPN Classic penetration by an estimated six million households, and carry ESPNews on all its digital systems.[112] Time Warner also made a commitment to support the launch of two undetermined Disney cable networks in the future. Retransmission consent for seven local ABC affiliates in Time Warner Cable markets was the leverage in this battle.

As Disney reached the settlement with Time Warner, it faced a similar battle with Comcast Cable. The retransmission agreement between Disney and Comcast for six markets, including New York suburbs in northern New Jersey, Los Angeles, Chicago, and Philadelphia, expired at the end of 1999, but three extensions later the two corporations headed toward a December 31, 2000, deadline. The issues were identical to the Time Warner case: migration of the Disney Channel from premium to basic service and carriage of SoapNet and Toon Disney. Disney, however, held another card in this game, as Comcast's carriage agreements for the ESPN networks expired at the end of 2000. While Time Warner earned the wrath of Congress and a reprimand from the FCC for dropping ABC stations, Disney believed it could pull ESPN without the same political uproar while viewers directed their displeasure at Comcast.[113] Two days before the consent agreement expired, Disney and Comcast signed a long-term retransmission agreement for the ABC stations that also included the conversion of the Disney Channel, carriage of SoapNet and Toon Disney, and a new deal for the ESPN networks.

The impact of such deals is clear. At the end of 1999, ESPN2 was available in 66.9 million households, while ESPN Classic and ESPNews were carried in twenty and eighteen million, respectively. At the end of 2004, ESPN2 had all but matched ESPN with carriage in 88.1 million cable and satellite households, while the subscriber base for ESPN Classic and ESPNews had more than doubled to 55.3 and 42.8 million, respectively. The increases for SoapNet and Toon Disney were even more dramatic. SoapNet, which re-airs the ABC network soap operas, did not even launch until January of 2000, but it surpassed thirty-nine million households at the end of 2004. Toon Disney debuted in April 1998, but was available in just fourteen million households at the end of 1999. With the help of ABC retransmission deals, Toon Disney was on the verge of fifty million households at the end of 2004.

These tactics were not reserved to The Walt Disney Co. or to cable operators. In March 2004, Dish Network blacked out CBS stations in sixteen markets in which Viacom owned and operated the local affiliate for forty-six hours. Dish Network also pulled ten Viacom-owned cable and satellite services, including MTV and Nickelodeon, nationwide. There were numerous fronts in this battle, including fee increases for the cable services, but the one constant was that Viacom used retransmission consent to maintain current levels or acquire additional carriage for its programming services.[114] EchoStar chairman Charlie Ergen had derided the Viacom-owned children's service Noggin as "obscure" and claimed his children did not watch either Noggin or Nickelodeon Games & Sports.[115] He said that Viacom was "saddling our subscribers with higher prices for programming they really don't want" and forcing Dish Network to "carry unwanted cable channels." In exchange for retransmission consent for the CBS stations, Viacom demanded extended carriage agreements for a package of channels, which included the addition of a new service, Nicktoons. While Viacom is believed to have lowered its carriage fee demands as part of a settlement, Nicktoons did join Noggin and Nickelodeon Games & Sports on the America's Top 180 tier.

SUMMARY

The cable landscape is littered with a remarkable collection of programming services, and one could compose a list that suggests remarkable diversity. Things are not always as they might appear, however, and when one examines the services that have reached a critical mass on cable and satellite systems, ownership of most of them can be traced to a small cadre of conglomerates. In the case of the most prominent programming services, the parent corporations of the five conglomerates that own broadcast networks and major motion picture studios hold a financial interest in over 76 percent of those with over sixty million subscribers in cable and satellite households. When this group is expanded to eight conglomerates, there is an ownership link to forty-three of forty-six services, over 93 percent, among this top tier of networks.

The roots of most of the programming services that eclipsed sixty million households at the start of 2005 are found in the 1980s, so the high penetration of the marketplace is understandable. What is most significant is the prominence of services from these same corporations in the 30 to 60 million household range and within the digital services of the largest cable systems. In the 30 to 60 million household range, thirty-one of forty-two services could be traced to one of eight corporations at the end of 2004, and the same was true of seventy-one of the seventy-six services on the digital tier of sixteen of the twenty-five largest cable systems. The ownership patterns were quite similar on the two prominent direct-to-home satellite services, DirecTV and Dish Network. Proponents of deregulation point to the numerical abundance of digital cable and satellite systems and predict that viewpoint, outlet, and source diversity is guaranteed without government involvement, but the dominance of these same corporations in areas where less mature services are growing suggests otherwise.

What is also evident, and underexamined within the FCC, is the degree to which horizontal and vertical integration and diversification are valuable tools in the acquisition of carriage on cable and satellite systems. In the 1980s, ownership of cable systems was the most expedient route to market penetration of cable services, and some of the biggest brands built a subscriber base while linked to the cable assets of TCI, Time Warner, or Viacom. Passage of the Cable Act of 1992 changed the scene, however, and retransmission consent might now be the most valuable possession. The parent corporations of ABC, CBS, Fox, and NBC have wielded their station groups in countless confrontations with cable and satellite system operators. What makes this remarkable is the fact that the Communications Act of 1934 mandates broadcast licensees to serve the public interest, not corporate expansion.

What is most evident from the analysis of cable and satellite systems and services is the degree to which "bigness" has become dominant. This is evident in the systems of distribution, with the four largest operators—Comcast, DirecTV, Time Warner Cable, and Dish Network—combining for a market share just under 60 percent. The same holds true with programming services, with vast collections under common ownership within Disney, NBC Universal, News Corp., Time Warner, and Viacom. This is where ownership of cable services becomes critical, as these channels are mere cogs within vast media machines. The argument that Douglas Kellner advances in relation to television is worth repeating here. He believes that television has become a dominant force in "integrating individuals into the social order, celebrating dominant values," and in "offering models of thought, behavior, and gender for imitation."[116] When one sees that even the abundance of new technologies does not diminish the dominance of a mere handful of conglomerates, it renews concerns over the current state of ownership and regulation.

NOTES

1. Quoted in Heather Hudson, *Communication Satellites* (New York: The Free Press, 1990), 157–158.

2. Quoted in John Lippman, "How Television Is Reshaping World's Culture," *Toronto Star*, 21 December 1992.

3. Quoted in Michael Gurevitch, "The Globalization of Electronic Journalism," in *Mass Media and Society*, ed. James Curran and Michael Gurevitch, 186 (London: Edward Arnold, 1991).

4. United Nations, *Universal Declaration of Human Rights*, 1949.

5. As of March 2004, Viacom corporate documents identified joint ventures or licensing agreements for MTV networks in ten different countries across Asia and Europe as well as Canada and Australia. These are in addition to the wholly owned MTV services in Asia, Europe, Latin America, and Africa.

6. Majid Tehranian, *Technologies of Power: Information Machines and Democratic Prospects* (Norwood, NJ: Ablex, 1990), 9.

7. There are limitations to the electromagnetic spectrum, but since the 1920s the federal government has made such limitation more dramatic through the allocation of large areas of the spectrum for government use.

8. Ithiel de Sola Pool, *Technologies of Freedom* (Cambridge: Harvard University Press, 1983), 5.

9. Federal Communications Commission, *Frontier Broadcasting v. Collier*, 32 FCC 459 (1962).

10. *U.S. v. Southwestern Cable Co.* 392 U.S. 159 (1968).

11. Federal Communications Commission, *Second Report and Order*, 2 FCC 2nd, 6 RR 2nd (Washington, DC: Government Printing Office, 1966).

12. Stephen C. Godek, *Determinants of Public Interest Cable Communications Policies* (Lanham, MD: University Press of America, Inc., 1996).

13. Federal Communications Commission, *Cable Television Report and Order*, 36 FCC 2nd 143 (Washington, DC: Government Printing Office, 1972).

14. Federal Communications Commission, *Cable Television Report and Order*, 36 FCC 2nd 143.

15. *Home Box Office v. Federal Communications Commission*, 567 F. 2nd 9 (1977).

16. *Federal Communications Commission v. Midwest Video Corp.*, 99 S. Ct. 1435 (1979).

17. Paul Kagan Associates, Inc., *The Cable TV Investor*, 14 April 1998, 3.

18. Direct-broadcast-satellite service does represent an alternative, but this was not the case when Congress passed the 1984 Cable Act.

19. *Cable Communications Policy Act of 1984*, Public Law 98–549, 30 October 1984.

20. *Cable Television Consumer Protection Act of 1992*, 102nd Cong., 1st sess., 5 October 1992.

21. Paul Kagan Associates, Inc., *Marketing New Media*, 16 March 1998.

22. Quoted in "Cable Industry Takes Out Ads Against Retransmission Fees," *The Entertainment Litigation Reporter*, 9 September 1991.

23. "Sec. 6, Retransmission Consent for Cable Systems," *Cable Television Consumer Protection Act of 1992.*

24. Federal Communications Commission, "Must-Carry and Retransmission Consent Provisions," (Washington, DC: GPO, 1993).

25. Quoted in "Committee Chairman Claims Retransmission Consent Jurisdiction," *Entertainment Litigation Reporter,* 23 December 1991.

26. Quoted in Wayne Walley, "Malone: Stations Must Give Extras to Get Fees," *Electronic Media,* 22 February 1993, 2.

27. William Drake, *The New Information Infrastructure: Strategies for U.S. Policy* (New York: Twentieth Century Fund Press, 1995), 314.

28. National Cable & Telecommunications Association, "Infrastructure Expenditures," www.ncta.com (accessed 30 April 2005).

29. Federal Communications Commission, "Inquiry Concerning High-Speed Access to the Internet Over Cable and Other Facilities," FCC 00-185, 15 March 2002.

30. *Brand X Internet Services v. Federal Communications Commission,* 345 F. 3d 1120 (2003).

31. *National Cable & Telecommunications Association v. Brand X Internet Services,* 125 S. Ct. 2688 (2005).

32. *Time Warner Entertainment v. Federal Communications Commission,* 345 U.S. App. DC, 186 (2001).

33. *Time Warner Entertainment v. United States,* 341 U.S. App. DC, 255 (2000).

34. *Time Warner II* (2001).

35. *Time Warner II* (2001).

36. Federal Communications Commission, "The Commission's Cable Horizontal and Vertical Ownership Limits," FCC 05–96, 13 May 2005.

37. Federal Communications Commission, "Notice of Proposed Rule Making in the Matter of 2002 Biennial Regulatory Review," FCC 02–249, 23 September 2002.

38. Dennis Wharton, "Small Cablers Ask FCC to Block Disney ABC Merger," *Variety,* 2 October 1995, 74.

39. Quoted in Wharton, "Small Cablers Ask FCC to Block Disney-ABC Merger," 74.

40. Quoted in Jeannine Aversa, "FCC Approved FCC Takeover of ABC, With Strings," *The Association Press,* 8 February 1996.

41. Godek, *Determinants of Public Interest Cable Communications Policies,* 170.

42. Godek, *Determinants of Public Interest Cable Communications Policies,* 170.

43. Godek, *Determinants of Public Interest Cable Communications Policies,* 170.

44. National Cable & Telecommunications Association, *Cable Developments 2004,* 28, no. 1. (2004), 12.

45. Richard Setlowe, "Many Strands Grew Together to Build Cable," *Variety,* 3–9 November 1997, 66.

46. Setlowe, "Many Strands Grew Together," 66.

47. *S. L. Weaver et al v. Frank M. Jordan, Secretary of State, etc.,* 64 Cal. 2nd 235 (1966); *Jordan, Secretary of State of California v. Weaver et al,* 87 S. Ct. 49 (1966).

48. Manhattan Cable was one of the largest cable systems in the nation, with 80,000 subscribers at the end of 1975 (Time Incorporated, Annual Report, 1975).

49. Setlowe,"Many Strands Grew Together," 66.

50. The revenue generated by Time's publishing activities dwarfed those of Manhattan Cable and Home Box Office. In 1975, publishing generated $531 million of Time's total revenues of $910.7 million, 58.3 percent, compared to just $16.2 million, 1.8 percent, for what were termed "developmental activities" in the Time annual report, which included Manhattan Cable and HBO (Time Incorporated, Annual Report, 1975).

51. At the time, ATC owned ninety-eight cable systems in thirty-one states and had a total of 790,000 subscribers.

52. Jack Egan, "Pay TV Firms Announce Joint Venture," *Washington Post*, 14 September 1978.

53. Egan, "Pay TV Firms Announce Joint Venture."

54. Hank Whittemore, *CNN: The Inside Story* (Boston: Little, Brown and Company, 1990).

55. William M. Henry, "History as it Happens," *Time*, 6 January 1992, 24–27.

56. Whittemore, *CNN: The Inside Story*.

57. Paul Kagan Associates, Inc., *The Cable TV Financial Databook*, 1993.

58. Paul Kagan Associates, Inc., *The Cable TV Financial Databook*, 1993.

59. Howard Rudnitsky, "The Mouth of the South Strikes Again," *Forbes*, 7 November 1983, 82.

60. Sally Bedell Smith, "Turner Buys Sole Rival in Cable News Market," *New York Times*, 13 October 1983, D1.

61. Westinghouse acquired the cable franchises that Teleprompter Corporation owned in August 1981 and had approximately 1.8 million cable subscribers as of December 31, 1982. (Westinghouse Electric Corporation, Annual Report, 1982.)

62. Westinghouse Electric Corporation, Annual Report, 1983.

63. *Mutual Film Corp. v. Industrial Film Corp.*, 35 S. Ct. 387, 1915.

64. Getty Oil Company, Annual Report, 1982.

65. Cable Advertising Revenue: 1982–1987, National Cable Television Association, www.ncta.com/dir_cableadvert.html.

66. "Channel Capacity of Existing Cable Systems," *Television & Cable Factbook*, No. 51 (1983), 1548.

67. Federal Communications Commission, *Annual Assessment of the Status of Competition in the Market for the Delivery of Video Programming*, FCC 04–227, 4 February 2005.

68. There were other services that launched in this period that ceased operations prior to December 31, 1990, including America's Value Network and The Fashion Channel.

69. This total does not include C-Span or C-Span 2. Tele-Communications, Inc. and Time Warner assumed prominent roles in the development and operation of C-Span. Since C-Span and C-Span 2 are nonprofit, public service operations, they are not included in these totals.

70. Linda Moss, "97: Big Year for TNT," *Multichannel News*, 5 January 1998, 1; "Primetime Ratings, 10/27–11/2," *Cablefax*, 7 November 1997.

71. A cable news network that utilized the personnel of ABC News was in the works, but Disney terminated plans for the service due to the costs of development and the inability to guarantee cable carriage for the service.

72. Linda Moss, "TCI Locks Up Disney, ESPN in 10-year Deal," *Multichannel News*, No. 15, Vol. 18 (1997), 1.

73. Moss, "TCI Locks Up Disney, ESPN," 1.

74. Ray Richmond, "NBC Plays Hardball In News Net Carriage Game," *Daily Variety*, 4 June 1996, 27.

75. Quoted in Richmond, "NBC Plays Hardball," 27.

76. Kyle Pope, "As the Focus Shifts, the Picture Brightens at MSNBC," *Wall Street Journal*, 28 October 1997.

77. Tom Freston quoted in Steven J. Stark, "TNN goes National with renamed Net," *Hollywood Reporter*, 20 September 2000.

78. The Walt Disney Co. did own a percentage of A&E Network, Lifetime, and E! Entertainment, as well as the ESPN networks, but the only networks that it owned outright in September 2001 were The Disney Channel, Toon Disney, and SoapNet.

79. Paul Farhi, "A Television Concept that Bears Repeating: 'Repurposing' Gives Rise to Instant Reruns," *Washington Post*, 19 March 2002, C1.

80. Mike Reynolds, "Cable Gets an 'L&O', '24'; USA, Bravo to Show 'Criminal Intent'; A&E Ponies Up for Serial," *Multichannel News*, 6 December 2004, 59.

81. Cynthia Littleton, "First Up for NBC Universal: Lock In Wolf, 'Law' Shows," *Hollywood Reporter*, 13 May 2004.

82. Mike Reynolds, "Cable Gets an 'L&O', '24'," *Multichannel News*, 6 December 2004, 59.

83. The inclusion of Telemundo in NBC's coverage of the Olympic Games represented another important trend. NBC purchased Telemundo Communications for $2.7 billion in 2002 in a bid to reach the high-growth Hispanic market. In short order, it integrated the network and station group into its overall operations, with Jeff Zucker assuming control of its entertainment programming at the start of 2003.

84. Galavision had 8.1 million subscribers at the end of 1996 (Univision Communications, Inc., 10-K, 4-21-1997).

85. Viacom Inc., Form 10-K, 31 March 1994.

86. MTV X featured hard rock, active rock, and heavy metal. VH1 Smooth focused on jazz, new age, and adult contemporary; VH1 Soul spotlighted rhythm and blues.

87. Richard Katz, "MTV Sets Deals for Digital Nets, Noggin," *Daily Variety*, 1 July 1998, 8.

88. Some of the names of the different channels did change between 1998 and 2002. VH1 Smooth became VH1 Classic Rock in 1999 and then VH1 Classic in 2000.

89. Linda Moss, "VH1 Classic Gears for Launch," *Multichannel News*, 1 May 2000, 5.

90. Quoted in Mike Farrell, "Karmazin to Play Retrans Chip for MTVN Cable Nets," *Multichannel News*, 22 May 2000, 1.

91. Linda Moss, "Dealmaking Like Big Guys; NCTC Signs Broad Carriage Deal With MTV Nets," *Multichannel News*, 22 September 2003, 3.

92. "Viacom and Comcast Sign Multi-Year Affiliation Agreement," *PR Newswire*, 19 December 2003.

93. Quoted In Linda Moss, "Animated MTVN Adds Four to Suite," *Multichannel News*, 4 March 2002, 3.

94. Federal Communications Commission, *Annual Assessment of the Status of Competition in the Market for the Delivery of Video Programming*, FCC 05–13, 14 January 2005.

95. According to the NCTA, nearly 95 million homes were passed by cable systems with 750 MHz or higher capacity at the end of 2003. It would take approximately 438

MHz of bandwidth to transmit 73 analog channels and an additional 75 to 150 MHz to transmit 150 digital channels. As such, analog and digital video channels utilized about 65 percent to 70 percent of the bandwidth in the average system.

96. DirecTV.com (accessed 21 March 2005).

97. The systems measured were the third, sixth, seventh, ninth, and tenth largest systems in the nation at that time: Cox Communications, Las Vegas; Time Warner Cable, Manhattan; Bright House Networks, Winter Park, Florida; Comcast, Seattle; Cablevision, Brooklyn, New York. The Cablevision and Time Warner clusters in Metro New York and the Comcast cluster in Seattle all ranked among the ten largest in the nation.

98. There are numerous estimates on the number of cable households. The FCC uses estimates from Kagan World Media, which are lower than the Nielsen figures that the National Cable & Telecommunications Association uses. To remain consistent, the Kagan World Media figures are utilized in all measurements.

99. Federal Communications Commission, *11th Annual Assessment of the Status of Competition in the Market for the Delivery of Video Programming*, FCC 05–13, 14 January 2005, 78.

100. This total included some national program services that were not listed in the FCC annual report but were on the NCTA web page.

101. Louis Chunovic, "Supping at the Subscriber Plate; New Cable Nets May Further Fragment View Base," *Electronic Media*, 20 January 2003, 31.

102. Linda Moss, "CNNfn Cashes in Chips," *Multichannel News*, 1 November 2004, 2.

103. C-Span and C-Span 2 were also in over sixty million households, but these totals do not include these services. Cable operators created C-Span in 1979, and the president of Time Warner Cable, Thomas Baxter, was a member of its Executive Committee in 2005.

104. It is reasonable to drop Sony from these calculations, at it owned just one programming service, GSN, and that was a joint venture with Liberty Media.

105. The twenty-five largest as of March 2004 included seven systems from Comcast and seven from Time Warner Cable, six from Cox Communications, three from Cablevision, and one from Bright House Networks and one from Insight Communications. (NCTA.com, accessed 8 March 2005.)

106. There is some overlap between the services listed within the thirty to sixty million household range in table 6.5 and those listed within the sixteen to twenty-five systems in table 6.6.

107. While Discovery Communications does not "own" BBC America in the traditional sense, it did invest at least $100 million to launch the network and controls marketing rights. The $100 million was part of a $660 million commitment that Discovery made in 1998 for a series of deals with the BBC. Ed Kirchdoerffer, "Upfront: BBC & Discovery Go Public with Alliance Details," *Realscreen*, 1 April 1998, 6.

108. Federal Communications Commission, *Direct Broadcast Satellite Public Interest Obligations* (Washington, DC: 1998), 65.

109. Of the ten remaining networks, six of those were in the eight to sixteen system group. In these totals, multiple feeds of a single service, such as the East Coast feed of HBO and West Coast feed of HBO, were counted only once. The regional sports networks on DirecTV were not counted.

110. R. Thomas Umstead, "DirecTV Buys into TV One," *Multichannel News*, 10 January 2005, 12.

111. Quoted in Lisa de Moraes, "Time Warner, Disney Dispute Leaves Viewers in the Dark," *Washington Post*, 2 May 2000, C1.

112. Linda Moss, "It's A Done Deal: Time Warner, ABC Outline Retrans Details," *Multichannel News*, 29 May 2000, 1.

113. Christopher Stern, "Comcast Upbeat on Talks," *Washington Post*, 1 December 2000, E4.

114. Congress and the FCC extended retransmission to direct-broadcast-satellite services with passage of the Satellite Home Viewer Improvement Act (SHIVA) in 1999.

115. Ted Hearn, "Ergen Says He'd Dump CBS," *Multichannel News*, 8 March 2004, 4.

116. Douglas Kellner, *Media Culture* (London: Routledge, 1995), 235.

7

❖

Why Ownership Matters, Revisited

The proliferation of broadcast networks and local stations, penetration of cable and satellite programming services, and the flood of motion pictures and television programs into homes via DVD sales and rentals and other means prompts claims that the media marketplace is liberated. This explosion of content services and distribution systems inspired an onslaught against the cornerstones of broadcast regulation, with the Federal Communications Commission (FCC) oftentimes leading the charge. This was most evident in the spring and summer of 2003 when the Republican majority in the FCC pushed through a widespread relaxation of ownership rules. In response to the public uproar that followed, Michael Powell agued that, "the United States has the most diverse media marketplace in the world. There are more media outlets, owners, variety and diversity now than at any point in our nation's history."[1] There is no question that there are more media outlets, but it is far from certain that this abundance has resulted in true diversity.

It is worthwhile to revisit the definitions of diversity that the FCC utilized in its 2002 Biennial Regulatory Review. The Commission reaffirmed diversity as one of its core objectives and set forth four factors that promoted its continued existence that are germane to this discussion: viewpoint, outlet, program, and source diversity.[2] Program diversity refers to a "variety of programming formats and content," and the Commission relies on competition to achieve this goal. While one could question the degree to which the broadcast networks feature such diversity given the replication of successful program formats, the increase in the number of cable and satellite program services has contributed to growth in this area. As discussed in sidebar 6.2, the general entertainment cable networks build their schedules around reruns of programs from the broadcast networks and motion pictures from the major studios, but niche services such as Food Network, Home and Garden Television, ESPN, and MTV do increase the range of formats and content on television.

Viewpoint diversity relates to the availability of media content from a variety of perspectives based on the notion that the "widest possible dissemination of information from diverse and antagonistic sources is essential to the welfare of the public."[3] The Commission focus in this area is on sources of news, and it concluded in the biennial review that the growth of the Internet, cable, and satellite services had created a "vast array" of national news outlets. The question is whether this numerical increase resulted in information from "diverse and antagonistic sources." The broadcast networks remain prominent in this discussion, but much is made of cable news services such as CNN, CNN Headline News, CNBC, MSNBC, and Fox News Channel. These same organizations are also important sources of news and information via the Internet. The ownership of all these news operations, however, resides within five of the largest conglomerates in the world, so it is difficult to argue that these sources are diverse and antagonistic. This undermines the conclusion that the marketplace is more diverse.

The concentration of cable outlets in a handful of conglomerates raises related issues. Outlet diversity results from the presence of independently owned firms in a given market, but the explosion in available outlets did not result in an increase in the number of owners in various markets at both the national and local levels. As discussed above, the concentration of cable news outlets in major media conglomerates undermines this conclusion, as do the vast collections of cable services that each controls. The increase in local broadcast television stations, likewise, creates the feeling of abundance, but the elimination of the one-to-a-market ownership rule and increase in the allowable national reach of station groups has promoted "bigness" rather than localism. This is consistent with other areas of the media marketplace, such as cable systems and motion picture theaters, where big has given way to huge.

The issue of source diversity, the availability of media content from a variety of content producers, is the most important to this discussion. The FCC established the Financial Interest and Syndication Rules and Prime Time Access Rule in 1970 to promote source diversity and eliminated them in the 1990s based on perceived changes in the media marketplace. The Commission argued that one transformation was that the broadcast networks were no longer in a position to demand a financial interest in programs in exchange for a slot on their prime time schedules. The record of CBS over the last decades makes clear that this was a flawed conclusion. In rebuffing new calls for regulations requiring broadcast networks to purchase a portion of their prime time schedules from unaffiliated producers, the Commission argued that given the significant increase in the number of channels available in most households, there was no need for government regulations to promote source diversity. The Commission concluded, moreover, that there was no evidence that the quantity of programming sources across the video programming market, both broadcast and nonbroadcast services, was limited.

The substantiation the FCC said was lacking is the focal point of this study, and the level of concentration is extreme. Six conglomerates—Disney, NBC Universal, News Corp., Sony, Time Warner, and Viacom—owned all of the major broadcast networks and motion picture studios at the start of 2005. This consolidation reaches to the local level as well, as four of these corporations also owned vast local station groups, ones that reached close to 45 percent of television households in the case of Viacom and News Corp. Once again, the promise of additional outlets oftentimes did not result in more voices, as either Viacom or News Corp. owned the UPN affiliate in each of the ten largest markets, while the Tribune Co. owned The WB affiliate in eight of those cities in 2005. Two of these corporations also ranked among the most prominent owners in delivery systems, cable in the case of Time Warner and direct-broadcast-satellite in that of News Corp. (DirecTV). Even the breakup of Viacom into two corporations, Viacom Inc. and CBS Corp., in the first quarter of 2006 did not eliminate such links since Sumner Redstone retained an ownership interest of over 70 percent in each of them. Table 7.1 outlines the market shares for each of these corporations in significant areas as well as totals for the group.

The control that these same corporations wield over the production and distribution of content is the most significant conclusion of this study. As discussed earlier, all of these conglomerates own a major motion picture studio, but each of them also controls various specialty distribution companies. This includes the two most prominent mini-majors, New Line Cinema (Time Warner) and Miramax Film Corp. (Disney). Trade publications often herald the success of these "independent" companies, often in line with the Academy Award nominations, but their most prominent films often fail the reasonable measures of independence. The impact of this horizontal integration is evident in the market share of the six conglomerates, which averaged 84.9 percent over 2002, 2003, and 2004, reaching over 90 percent in 2003. This is one piece of the "quantity of programming sources" puzzle, since these same conglomerates feed countless cable and satellite services. These range from premium movie channels to niche services such as Fox Movie Channel and Turner Classic Movies to general entertainment outlets such as TBS, FX, and ABC Family.

The dominance of these same corporations over the production and distribution of prime time programming on the six broadcast networks is a second part of the equation. The Financial Interest and Syndication Rules limited the broadcast networks in this area, but that is no longer the case. That change fueled the vertical integration of broadcast networks and motion picture studios within media conglomerates: ABC and Disney in 1996, CBS and Paramount in 2000, and NBC and Universal in 2004. The impact of this consolidation on prime time programming is clear. At the start of

Table 7.1. Ownership and Control of Prominent Motion Picture and Television Assets for Six Major Media Conglomerates, 2004–2005

	Major Studio & Mini-Major	Major Broadcast Networks	Average Share of Domestic Box Office (2002–2004)[a]	Share of Prime Time Program Hours (2004–2005)	Share of 60+ Million Cable & Sat. Services (2004)
Time Warner	Warner Bros. New Line Cinema	The WB	20.67%	21.72%	15.22%
The Walt Disney Co.	Walt Disney Pictures Miramax Films	ABC	19.52%	19.19%	17.39%
Viacom Inc.	Paramount Pictures Paramount Classics	CBS & UPN	7.21%	26.26%	17.39%
General Electric Co.	Universal Pictures Focus Features	NBC	11.37%	15.66%	17.39%
News Corp.	20th Century Fox Fox Searchlight	Fox	10.97%	15.66%	13.04%
Sony Corp.	Columbia Pictures Sony Picture Classics	— 0%	15.16%	1.52%	0.0%
Group Totals	6 of 6	6 of 6	84.90%	93.94%[b]	76.09%[c]

[a] These totals reflect the average box office shares for 2002, 2003, and 2004. The total for General Electric includes Universal Pictures in each year.
[b] Individual shares equal more than the total because of coproductions that are attributed to each unit but counted once in the totals.
[c] Individual shares equal more than the total because of co-ownership of services that are attributed to each unit but counted once in the totals.

the 2004–2005 season, the five corporations with ownership of a studio and network—Disney, NBC Universal, News Corp., Time Warner, and Viacom—held a financial interest in 93.94 percent of the hours broadcast on the networks with attributable ownership.

The obvious preference for in-house programming is an important consideration. The parent corporation of each of the four established broadcast networks—ABC, CBS, Fox, and NBC—held a financial interest in at least 70 percent of the programs with attributable ownership on their respective schedules, with a high of 95 percent in the case of CBS. When these networks are not scheduling programs produced in-house, moreover, they are most often turning to their alleged rivals for help, raising serious questions as to whether they are true competitors or more akin to collaborators. In 2004–2005, for example, Twentieth Century Fox Television produced programs on ABC and CBS in addition to Fox, while Touchstone Television did the same for CBS and NBC in addition to ABC. When one accounts for all of these links, just two nonreality-based programs remained in which these conglomerates did not hold a financial interest, *That 70's Show* and *Grounded for Life* from Carsey-Werner Productions. In the summer of 2005, its two principal owners, Marcy Carsey and Tom Werner, announced that they were scaling back on program development because of the "odds of getting on the air" as an independent were so long.

The third piece of the "quantity of programming sources" puzzle is the ownership of basic and premium programming services on cable and direct-broadcast-satellite systems. The same six conglomerates held a financial interest in over 75 percent of the cable and satellite programming services that reached sixty million or more television households as well as the most prominent premium services, including HBO and Showtime. When one drops Sony from this group and includes Liberty Media, the old programming wing of Tele-Communications, Inc., six corporations held a financial interest in 89.1 percent of the programming services in over sixty million cable and satellite households.[4] Just as important, this same group of six had a financial interest in 89.5 percent of the digital services with positions on at least sixteen of the twenty-five largest cable systems at the start of 2005.

The dominance of these conglomerates on both the analog and digital tiers of cable programming is significant. The addition of fiber optics to the infrastructure of cable systems resulted in increased channel capacity, but there are still limits on the available bandwidth. To reuse an old term, channel slots are a scarce resource, and the allocation of most of these positions to services from a handful of corporations is important. As discussed in chapter 6, the launch and expansion of programming services is altogether different within these conglomerates. Ownership has been a valuable weapon, whether through the control of delivery systems in cases such as Time Warner and News Corp., other popular services as in a case such as Disney, or the link to retransmission consent for large local broadcast station groups in cases such as Viacom or

NBC Universal. In some instances, all three ownership connections enhanced bargaining power. Comcast, Liberty Media, and E.W. Scripps utilize some of these same advantages.

The measure of the digital services on the largest cable systems supports the contention that it is all but impossible for nonaligned programming services to penetrate the market, even in the digital world. Hundreds of services are available, but most of the ones that are able to reach significant thresholds come from a handful of corporations. The challenge is even greater with prime time programs on the broadcast networks, with five corporations holding a financial interest in close to 94 percent of the program hours on the six networks at the start of the 2004–2005 season. The level of concentration is only a little lower in the distribution of motion pictures, with the parent corporations of the six major studios accounting for an average of 85 percent of domestic box office receipts between 2002 and 2004. And the sale of MGM/UA and Newmarket Films and apparent surrender of Carsey-Werner Productions in 2005 suggests that the plight of independent production will continue.

Framed within the findings of this study, the diversity that Michael Powell celebrated when the FCC released its 2002 Biennial Regulatory Review is nowhere to be found. There is no question that there are more outlets as Powell claimed, but ownership of the most prominent ones reside in fewer and fewer conglomerates. The argument that Graham Murdock advanced in the 1980s holds true: "diversity is not multiplicity . . . More does not necessarily mean different."[5] The multiplicity of outlets has increased in each area of these industries, but at every turn, the federal government allowed greater concentration to occur. This is true at the local level in the ownership of broadcast stations, cable systems, and theaters, but it is most evident at the national level.

Basic math confirms the changes that have occurred. The increase in the number of broadcast networks has not resulted in a corresponding rise in source diversity at the national level. In 1985, there were just three broadcast networks, ABC, CBS, and NBC, to go along with the six major studios, and nine different corporations owned one of them. Two decades later, the number of networks had doubled, but the owners had dwindled to just six. The same is true with program sources. In the 1984–1985 season, 52.7 percent of the prime time programs originated outside the major studios and networks. The number of network program hours increased from 66 to 104 in the years that followed with the addition of Fox, UPN, and The WB, but at the start of the 2000–2001 season, the market share for nonaligned shows stood at just 1.7 percent. At first glance, the distribution of motion pictures would appear to be an exception to the rule, as the major studios claimed just 66.6 percent of domestic box office revenues in 1987 compared to 69.16 percent in 2003. When one accounts for all the subsidiaries that the parent corporations of the major studios owned, however, the market share for six conglomerates reached 90.28 percent.

The same consolidation that has undermined the FCC goal to increase diversity in the marketplace has also diluted the other two core policy objectives of the Commission: competition and localism. The level of concentration has reached a point that an oligopolistic structure exists at the national level in each of these sectors. An important characteristic of an oligopoly, a market in which a few large suppliers dominate, is the interdependence and even collusion between firms. True competition dissipates in such a structure, and the oligarchs become enablers rather than competitors. This is most evident in the coproductions in television programs and motion pictures. As discussed in chapter 4, most of the successful nonanimation films that DreamWorks SKG distributed were coproductions with a major studio, while Twentieth Century Fox and Paramount Pictures shared the up-front costs required to produce *Titanic*.

Localism is among the most serious casualties of this wave of consolidation. The Commission licenses broadcast stations in the communities in which they operate based on the argument that local concerns should take precedent over national ones and individuals and institutions should resolve such issues at the local level. This desire to remain local has run headlong into a broadcast network quest to own more of its local affiliates, and localism emerged from this confrontation battered and bruised. The broadcast networks argue that their survival is contingent upon such expansion, and the federal government raised its national ownership rules three times over the last two decades. This created vast station groups more in tune with corporate objectives than local concerns and altered the power dynamics in the relationship between the networks and their affiliates.

The degree to which the federal government has sanctioned the conglomeration and concentration of television and motion picture properties over the last two decades is also important to consider. Most of the regulations that pertain to ownership of broadcast television networks or stations and cable television services or systems are gone, and those that remain are weakened to the point where such constraints are almost meaningless. What is most remarkable is that some members of the FCC are the head cheerleaders for this wave of conglomeration and consolidation. The Commission assumed an active role in the promotion of the dominant corporations and a series of FCC chairpersons, with Mark Fowler and Michael Powell the most prominent, advocated the marketplace as the ultimate determinant of the public interest. Such a position seems problematical in light of the Communications Act of 1934, which created the FCC to regulate the broadcast television and radio in the public interest.

Ted Turner reached the same conclusions in an article published in the *Washington Monthly* in the summer of 2004 entitled "Break Up This Band!"[6] Turner brings a unique perspective to this discussion since he created TBS and CNN outside of the major conglomerates. He is convinced that such independence is impossible in the current marketplace. The loss of such voices has profound implications—what Turner calls the "triple blight": the loss of quality, loss of localism, and loss of democratic debate. These afflictions evolve in part from the focus on short-term financial results, an emphasis on taking profits rather than taking risks. There is also a dearth of competition, as the oligarchs cooperate to inhibit competition. In Turner's mind, there is little room for the entrepreneurs who innovate and force the big boys to compete and change.

The most compelling aspect of the Turner thesis is that such behavior is predictable within large corporations. This is true in terms of being risk averse and profit-focused, which deprives these industries of individuals who are "less obsessed with earning than they are with ideas," but also in the insatiable quest for horizontal and vertical integration. In the new millennium, the quest is rather basic: "the only way for media companies to survive is to own everything up and down the media chain . . . Big media today wants to own the faucet, pipeline, water, and the reservoir. The rain clouds come next."[7] This road to consolidation, moreover, is a natural one to follow: "As a business proposition, consolidation makes sense. The moguls behind the mergers are acting in their corporate interests and playing by the rules. We just shouldn't have those rules."[8]

Therein lies the rub. It is understandable to focus on the conglomerates that create and disseminate cultural products, but it is the White House and Congress, in addition to the FCC, that allowed the hijacking of these media markets. The Commission and others expressed outrage when the Fox network broadcast an episode of *Married by America* in 2003 featuring salacious scenes from bachelor and bachelorette parties in a Las Vegas hotel, a broadcast the FCC ruled was patently offensive as measured by contemporary community standards. Missing from such recriminations was the acknowledgment that Congress and the Commission allowed networks to own and operate so many local stations, reaching almost 45 percent of television households in the case of Fox, which altered the balance of power in affiliate groups and squelched the voices of nonaligned stations.

Also absent in such debates, and failing to shine a light on the growing concentration of power and influence in a small cadre of conglomerates, is the mainstream media. In democratic societies, the media are supposed to make self-government possible through the creation of a vibrant marketplace of ideas. This requires the dissemination of information from diverse and antagonistic sources. What happens when the issue is with the media themselves? In the first nine months of the 2002 Biennial Regulatory Review, in which the FCC contemplated wholesale changes in its ownership rules, the news divisions at ABC, CBS, and NBC offered no coverage on the deliberations. There was a smattering of stories starting in mid-May when the debate was all but over, but there was silence when commissioners Michael Copps and Jonathan Adelstein called for public hearings and further discussions earlier in the spring. That is not surprising given the fact that the parent corporation of each of the networks was lobbying the FCC for a relaxation of the ownership rules. The major newspaper chains had their own wish list for these deliberations.

With five conglomerates controlling the broadcast networks and prominent cable news outlets, there is no one left to hold the government accountable, and big media becomes even bigger. In a conversation on *Nightline* days before the FCC vote in the spring of 2003, Barry Diller argued that there needed to be appropriate regulation of these industries so that the conglomerates have a little fear "back in their bones."[9] The issue for Diller was the absence of independence and diversity and the need to have rules that "these oligarchs cannot own all of the things that go through their distribution system."[10] The concerns for Turner were much the same, but his solution was more drastic: "We need to write rules that will break these huge companies to pieces."[11] The question is how does media consolidation and concentration get a proper hearing in the marketplace of ideas, and who has the fortitude to confront these behemoths and write new rules.

NOTES

1. Michael Powell, "New Rules, Old Rhetoric," *New York Times*, 28 July 2003, A17.

2. The fifth type of diversity that the Commission discussed was minority and female ownership diversity, which is outside the range of this study.

3. Federal Communications Commission, "2002 Biennial Regulatory Review," 19.

4. Sony Corp. has a financial interest in just one such service, GSN: The Network for Games. That service is a fifty-fifty joint venture between Sony and Liberty Media.

5. Graham Murdock, "Large Corporations and the Control of the Communications Industries," in *Culture, Society and the Media*, ed. Michael Gurevitch, Tony Bennett, James Curran, and Janet Woollacott, 120 (London: Methuen, 1982).

6. Ted Turner, "Break Up This Band," *Washington Monthly* 36, no. 7/8 (2004), 30–36.

7. Turner, "Break Up This Band," 33–34.

8. Turner, "Break Up This Band," 32.

9. Barry Diller, "Media, Inc.," *Nightline*, 28 May 2003.

10. Diller, "Media, Inc."

11. Turner, "Break Up This Band," 32.

Discussion Questions

CHAPTER 1: WHY OWNERSHIP MATTERS

1. Does it matter who owns the media? If so, why? If not, why not? Does it matter more or less with the production and distribution of news and information than it does with motion pictures and prime time television programming?
2. Scholar Graham Murdock makes a distinction between diversity and multiplicity, arguing that it is possible to increase the number of available outlets and products without significantly enhancing diversity. How do we draw a line between an abundance of outlets and true diversity in an analysis of the motion picture and television industries?
3. Laissez-faire economists would argue that the success of Hollywood cultural products in foreign markets results from American producers responding to the demands of sovereign consumers, that the invisible hand of the market dictates what is produced and how it is distributed. What social, economic, and political factors also contribute to Hollywood success outside of the United States?
4. Former Federal Communications Commission chair Mark Fowler once equated a television to a "toaster with pictures" and argued, in turn, that it required no more regulation than other household appliances. Scholar Douglas Kellner argues that television assumes a critical role in the "structuring of contemporary identity and shaping thought and behavior." Does the nature of television make it unique and raise issues that are not prominent with other appliances and industries? If so, what are the most serious concerns?

CHAPTER 2: CONGLOMERATION IN THE MOTION PICTURE INDUSTRY

1. The Supreme Court argued in 1915 that the exhibition of motion pictures is a business, "pure and simple." What are the implications of the commercial origins of the motion picture business in the United States?
2. The Paramount decrees forced the major studios to separate exhibition from production and distribution. What are the structural elements in the motion picture business that have remained constant since the dawn of the studio system in the 1920s?
3. How has the nature of conglomeration changed in the motion picture business since the 1960s and what is the significance of such changes?
4. The media often hails the rise of the independents when Miramax and New Line motion pictures collect Oscars at the Academy Awards. How accurate are such claims and how should independence be measured? Is there a single overriding determinant in this debate and does it matter?

CHAPTER 3: CONGLOMERATION IN THE BROADCAST TELEVISION INDUSTRY

1. What are the connections between the structure of broadcast radio in the United States that emerged in the 1920s and 1930s and the present state of broadcast television? Was such an organization and allocation inevitable in the United States?
2. What are the relationships between the FCC rules that limit local television station ownership at the national level and those that restrict combinations at the local level? Do these restrictions achieve the desired outcomes? Should the thresholds be higher or lower?
3. Scholar Dallas Smythe addresses a critical component of political economic analysis in asking, "Who takes what actions in order to provide what scarce goods and services, when, how and where?" How did changes in laws and policies in Congress and the Federal Communications Commission in the 1990s, including the Financial Interest and Syndication Rules and local and national television station ownership rules, affect the ownership of the major broadcast television networks?
4. How have changes in the ownership rules affected the relationship between the broadcast networks and their local affiliates?
5. To what degree has the creation of additional broadcast television networks to compete with ABC, CBS, and NBC contributed to the diversity of voices, viewpoints, and genres at the local or national level?

CHAPTER 4: PATTERNS OF OWNERSHIP IN MOTION PICTURE DISTRIBUTION

1. What are some of the reasons that film scholars and critics have viewed distribution—the middle point between production and exhibition—as the power position in the motion picture industry for generations?
2. What changes have occurred in the financial dimension of motion picture production and distribution since the 1980s, from first print costs to marketing, and what are some of the implications of these changes on what films reach the theaters?
3. How do the changes in The Walt Disney Co. since the 1970s, including the creation of Touchstone Pictures and acquisition of Miramax Film Corp., represent broader patterns in the motion picture business?
4. What are some of the similarities between mini-majors such as Disney's Miramax Film Corp. and Time Warner's New Line Cinema and corporate cousins such as Walt Disney Pictures and Warner Bros. in how they finance and distribute films?
5. The six major studios averaged a domestic market share of 69.1 percent between 1970 and 1974 compared to 68.6 percent between 2000 and 2004. What are the significant differences between these two periods of time in terms of the overall reach of the majors and their parent corporations?

CHAPTER 5: PATTERNS OF OWNERSHIP IN PRIME TIME NETWORK PROGRAMMING

1. The prominence of independent television production companies in the 1970s is undeniable. How have changes in the patterns of conglomeration since then influenced the production of prime time programming?
2. What structural changes have occurred in the television marketplace over the last three decades that transformed the market for off-network, syndicated programs?
3. What are the incentives for a broadcast network to hold a financial interest in prime time programs on its network? What are the challenges it could face with programs it does not own?
4. Prior to the expiration of the Financial Interest and Syndication Rules, the Federal Communications Commission argued that the broadcast networks no longer had the power to demand ownership in programs. Has this proven to be the case in the decade since Fin/Syn expired?
5. Among the guiding principles of FCC ownership rules were four aspects of diversity, one of which was source diversity: the "availability of content

to consumers from a variety of content producers." How does ownership of prime time programming in the 2000s either advance or undermine such an objective?

CHAPTER 6: CONGLOMERATION IN CABLE AND SATELLITE TELEVISION SYSTEMS AND SERVICES

1. How has the nature of cable television evolved from its roots as a mechanism for retransmission? What are the implications of this transformation on the broadcast networks?
2. The federal regulation of cable television once related to the potential impact of cable on broadcast networks and stations. How has federal regulation changed over time, and how has the federal government limited the power of local governments to influence service in their communities?
3. How has the Congressional mandate that cable operators receive "retransmission consent" from local broadcast stations altered the power dynamics within the television marketplace?
4. Time Warner Cable ranked among the largest multiple system operators in 2005, while Time Warner also owned a collection of prominent programming services. What are the advantages of such vertical integration? What implications are there for nonaligned systems or services?
5. There is no disputing the fact that programming services have increased the number of available outlets on cable and satellite systems. In the news and information arena, the big three broadcast networks now compete with CNN, CNBC, MSNBC, Fox News Channel and others. Has this outlet diversity resulted in a robust range of opinions, values, and ideologies in the marketplace—what the Commission would call viewpoint diversity?

CHAPTER 7: WHY OWNERSHIP MATTERS, REVISITED

1. In 2003, former FCC chair Michael Powell argued that "the United States has the most diverse media marketplace in the world. There are more media outlets, owners, variety and diversity now than at any point in our nation's history." Does the evidence support this conclusion? Does one need to differentiate between outlets, owners, variety, and diversity and assess each on its own terms?
2. Ted Turner created CNN and TBS outside of the major media conglomerates when cable television was in its infancy. He contends that it would be impossible for someone such as himself to do likewise in the current

marketplace. Is this a valid conclusion? And, if so, what are the implications for American society?

3. Many have argued that the rules are broken, that the White House, Congress, and the Federal Communications Commission have allowed too much concentration in motion picture and television markets. The media conglomerates, meanwhile, continue to press for even greater latitude in the acquisition of studios and stations. What is the appropriate level of regulation given the current state of the market and the nature of the cultural products involved?

4. We end where we began. Does it matter who owns the media? If so, why? If not, why not? Does it matter more or less with the production and distribution of news and information than it does with motion pictures and prime time television programming?

Terms and Concepts

allocative versus operational control: an important consideration in discussions of ownership and control. Allocative control involves the power to define the overall goals and scope of a corporation and determines how to deploy resources. Operational control works at a lower level, confined to decisions about the effective use of resources already allocated and the implementation of policies already decided at the allocative level. There are times when allocative and operational control resides in the same hands. The 13-member corporate board of News Corp. at the start of 2006 included Rupert Murdoch and his son Lachlan, as well as four executives or advisers from within News Corp. or one of its subsidiaries. The make-up of the General Electric board was altogether different, as it included just three inside directors on its 15-person board, including NBC Universal chair and chief executive office Bob Wright, so there is far greater separation. *See also* ownership and control.

antitrust laws and regulations: designed to promote competition through the prohibition on anti-competitive behavior and unfair business practices. Such laws prohibit collusion among competitors, including market allocation arrangements, monopolization and attempted monopolization, and anticompetitive mergers and connections. The Sherman Antitrust Act of 1890 remains the foundation of U.S. statutes, although the Clayton Act of 1914 was far more precise, outlawing mergers that "substantially lessen competition or tend to create a monopoly," so that federal action might "arrest . . . monopolies in their incipiency." Antitrust laws were at the foundation of federal litigation against the major motion picture studios in the 1940s that resulted in the Paramount consent decrees. *See also* Paramount decrees.

associative state: concept first advanced in the 1920s by then Secretary of Commerce Herbert Hoover. Central to the "American system" in Hoover's opinion was the development and proper use of cooperative institutions, trade associations and professional societies in particular. These organizations could contribute to the government apparatus "needed for an assured transition to an American utopia." The Motion Picture Producers and Distributors of America (MPPDA) and National Association of Broadcasters (NAB) were created in 1922 and each assumed a prominent role in regulation or self-regulation from the outset. The studios created the MPPDA in a period of scandal in Hollywood and over time it created a form of self-censorship, the Motion Picture Production Code of 1930, better known as the Hays Code. At around the same time, the NAB was instrumental in the reallocation of broadcast radio frequencies in 1928 that occurred with General Order 40, also known as the Davis Amendment, which favored network interests. *See also* corporate liberalism.

block booking: the practice of selling films in packages on an all-or-nothing basis, forcing theaters to feature numerous less desirable films in order to gain access to a single marquee film. The practice evolved in the 1920s with the emergence of the studio system. The studios ensured the sale of mediocre films to theaters with their inclusion in blocks of 20 films or more, with some contracts covering an entire season of production. The films were often sold sight unseen before production even began, a practice called "blind selling." These practices were a financial burden for smaller theater owners since they acquired films for which there was no real audience and made it difficult for independent producers to gain access to first-run theaters. In 1948, the Supreme Court ruled that block booking was anti-competitive, and ordered the studios to sell their products on a theater-by-theater, picture-by-picture basis. *See also* Paramount decrees; runs and clearances.

broadcast television versus cable television: the programming is often the same, but the mechanisms for distribution are quite different. Broadcast television uses radio frequencies to transmit its signal over the air, free of charge. There are limits on the number of local broadcast stations that can operate in a given market because of the scarcity of the electromagnetic spectrum, and it was "chaos" in the 1920s that prompted an expanded government role in the allocation of frequencies. Cable television also uses radio signals, but these are transmitted via fiber optic or coaxial cables rather than through the air. There are still limits on the number of channels a given system can transmit, but the numbers are much higher. Digital television, moreover, allows multiple, compressed signals to be delivered over the space that carries a single analog channel. Because of the pervasiveness of broadcast television, including the fact that stations have no control over who receives their signals, the Federal Communications Commission imposed a higher standard in terms of indecent material in programs.

carriage agreements: contracts between cable operators and programming services that outline the conditions under which cable systems or satellite services can retransmit a given service. This includes the nature of carriage, allocation of advertising inventory and financial compensation. Most programming services receive a portion of cable or satellite bills, ranging from a few cents a month in the case of new digital services to about $2.50 a month per household in the case of ESPN in mid-2005. The major media conglomerates often negotiate carriage agreements for a block of programming services rather than on a channel-by-channel basis, and some are also linked to retransmission consent for local station groups. *See also* must-carry; retransmission consent.

commodification: refers to the transformation of a product whose value is determined by its ability to meet individual and societal needs, its use value, into a product whose value is determined by what it can command in the marketplace, its exchange value. A motion picture, for example, can satisfy certain human wants or needs, such as entertainment or education, but what it can command at the box office determines its exchange value.

competition: the relative degree to which firms in a market compete with other individuals or companies to sell their products to consumers. In its perfect form, there is competition among both buyers and sellers, and none on either side is large enough to impact on the market as a whole. There are four definable levels of competition, from perfect competition at one end to monopoly at the other. *See also* monopolistic competition; monopoly; oligopoly; perfect competition.

concentration: a function of the number of firms selling products or services in a given market and their respective shares within that market. This is often used to describe the extent to which the largest firms in a market sector account for a significant percentage of total market share. The measurement is sometimes based on the market share of the top four firms in a given sector, with markets defined as unconcentrated, moderately concentrated, or highly concentrated. Concentration is the result of various interlinked but analytically distinct processes. *See also* diversification; horizontal integration; internationalization; vertical integration.

conglomerate: a group of diverse companies under common ownership and run as a single corporation. The classic definition is that of a diversified conglomerate, a corporation with business interests in a wide range of industrial sectors. General Electric, for example, includes a vast collection of businesses, from the motion pictures and television programs produced and distributed within NBC Universal to aircraft engines and nuclear power plants. Media and/or entertainment conglomerates that own diverse companies involved in the production and distribution of creative content and the dissemination of news and information are also now common. The Walt Disney Co., for

example, focuses on entertainment industries, but this includes motion pictures, broadcast television, and cable television as well as theme parks and
theatrical productions. *See also* diversification.

corporation: legal distinction for a business or organization formed by a group
of people, with rights and liabilities separate from those of the individuals
involved. For example, while individuals who own shares in a corporation
can lose their investment if it becomes insolvent, creditors cannot access the
personal assets of these investors. Individual and institutional stockholders
invest in a corporation in hopes of obtaining profits through stock apprecia-
tion and dividends.

corporate liberalism: represented not a particular prescription for liberal ends
but "reformist ideologies that accepted the large business corporation as a
permanent and desirable feature of national life." One of the clearest endorsements for this notion came from President Woodrow Wilson in 1914
when he declared that, "The antagonism between business and government
is over." The manifestation of such policies was evident in 1919 with the
federal government orchestrating the creation of the Radio Corporation of
America (RCA) and again following the Radio Act of 1927 when the reallocation of frequencies favored corporate owners over educational, religious,
and other non-profit broadcasters. *See also* associative state.

cross-ownership: the ownership of a television station and newspaper in the
same market. The Federal Communications Commission (FCC) outlawed
such combinations with the Newspaper/Television Cross-Ownership Prohibition in 1975, although groupings that existed prior to passage of that
regulation could continue under common ownership. The prohibition was
designed to increase program and viewpoint diversity in local communities.
The FCC moved to allow such combinations in most markets in 2003, but
federal courts remanded this provision back to the Commission for further
consideration.

diversification: one of the interlinked but analytically distinct processes that
contribute to concentration. In this case, firms acquire holdings in a range
of industries. This enables them to hedge their bets and cushion the effects
of recession in a particular sector. In the media and entertainment industries,
there are examples of corporations diversified across leisure and information-
providing industries, such as Viacom, Inc. and The Walt Disney Co., and
others diversified into non-leisure and non-information related industries,
such as General Electric Co. *See also* concentration; conglomerate.

dual product market: the unique market relationship that exists with some
media products because of the central role of advertising. First, media products are "sold" to consumers. Second, these consumers are "sold" to advertisers. Access to the audience or reader is critical to the second market.

Newspapers and magazines, for example, sell products to consumers through subscriptions and single-copy sales, and then, in turn, sell the readers to advertisers. This differs from book publishing where the sale to the consumer is similar, but the absence of advertisements eliminates the second product market.

duopoly: used in the analysis of media markets to describe the ownership of multiple radio or television outlets of the same kind in the same market. Prior to the 1990s, the Federal Communications Commission (FCC) allowed an individual or corporation to own or operate just one AM and one FM radio station and one television station in a given market. In 1992, the FCC eliminated the rules related to AM and FM radio stations, and in 1999 it relaxed the rules to allow ownership of two television stations in markets where there were at least eight independently owned stations, provided only one was among the four top-rated stations in the market.

economies of scale: the reduction in the average cost of production per unit of output resulting from the production of additional units of a product. This concept has been central to the production and distribution of motion pictures since the 1920s, when the studios realized that they could maximize the profits from a single film with an increase in the number of available outlets. The studios, in turn, acquired chains of theaters and established a network for worldwide distribution. This economic theory addresses technical economies in the actual production of goods, but also relates to managerial economies, financial economies, marketing economies, and others. A motion picture produced within Touchstone Pictures, for example, could take advantage of Disney's line of credit in the financing of the film and corporate-wide advertising agreements, reduced rates predicated on volume, while also utilizing the managerial expertise of Buena Vista in the distribution of the film. *See also* infinitely reproducible, infinitely exportable.

economic structure: media industries in most industrialized nations function within a mixed economy, the combination of a command economy and a market economy. In a command economy, the government makes all decisions regarding production and distribution. The government decides what will be produced and in what quantity; it establishes wages and prices and plans the rate of economic growth. In a market economy, a complex system involving buyers and sellers determines the scope of production and distribution with no government intervention. Mixed economic systems in the media industries feature some government policies and regulations while allowing private ownership of media outlets.

Financial Interest and Syndication Rules: implemented by the Federal Communications Commission in 1970. These rules were designed to increase program diversity and limit the market control of the three broadcast networks. Prior to the introduction of the rules, the networks often demanded distribution and syndication rights to programs from independent produc-ers. The Fin/Syn rules prohibited the networks from participation in domestic syndication of both off-network and first-run programs and from acquiring additional rights to independent productions licensed for broadcast on the networks. These rules expired in 1995.

horizontal integration: one of the interlinked but analytically distinct pro-cesses that contribute to concentration. In this case, firms acquire additional business units at the same level of production, distribution, or exhibition. This enables them to consolidate and extend their control within a particular sector and maximize the economies of scale and shared resources. The cable networks division of Viacom Inc., for example, features the most prominent music channels on cable television—MTV: Music Television, VH1, and CMT: Country Music Television—under common senior management within MTV Networks. *See also* concentration.

infinitely reproducible, infinitely exportable: an important concept in a dis-cussion of motion picture and television content. In most industries, the cre-ation of products for sale, from automobiles to cellular telephones, exhausts the raw materials involved and makes these materials unusable for other consumers. As such, there are significant costs involved in the production of additional units. This is not the case with motion picture and television content. Multiple copies of a motion picture or television program can be made without damage to the original, and each of them can be projected or broadcast repeatedly with little or no damage. Moreover, once all the costs associated with shooting and editing the original are covered, known as the first print cost in films, these products can be reproduced in various formats for little additional cost. For example, when the final installment of the *Lord of the Rings* trilogy opened in December 2003, it did so on over 3,700 screens in the United States and generated over $170 million at the box office in the first nine days. The nature of these products also allows them to be reproduced with subtitles or voice tracks and shipped around the world. The same week *The Return of the King* debuted in the U.S., it also opened in numerous markets around the world, including 1,337 screens in Germany, 550 in Mexico, 513 in Spain, and 494 in Great Britain. The same masters that produced the 6,500 prints needed for those five nations alone also produced the 6 million DVDs and VHS tapes that sold in the U.S. in the first week on the market. *See also* economies of scale.

internationalization: one of the interlinked but analytically distinct processes that contribute to concentration. In this case, firms expand into foreign mar-kets with prominent brands or invest in foreign corporations. As is the case with diversification, this allows firms to cushion the impact of recession in a market. For example, Viacom has utilized the MTV brand to build music chan-nels around the world, and at the start of 2006 there was a Viacom-owned

MTV regional networks on six continents—Asia, Europe, South America, North America, Australia, and Africa—in addition to various joint ventures and licensing agreements for MTV networks in different countries. *See also* concentration.

license agreement: basic contract that exists between television program producers and broadcast networks. The standard license agreement covers four or five seasons, and allows a network to broadcast each episode twice in exchange for a license fee. After those first-run broadcasts, the program rights revert to the producer for off-network syndication. When the initial agreement expires, the program producer can negotiate a higher license fee or shop the show to other networks. It was in such negotiations that *ER* and *Friends* received record fees, $13 million and $10 million per episode, respectively. Since the 1990s, broadcast networks have often attempted to negotiate perpetual or extended license agreements to protect them from such tactics. What complicates the relationship between program producers and networks even further is the fact that the initial per episode license fee does not cover the total cost to produce the show, so program producers must deficit finance the production in the hopes that the show will reap a higher license fee upon renewal or become profitable in syndication. *See also* repurposing; syndication.

local franchise agreements: contracts between cable system operators and local communities. Prior to 1984, these agreements detailed various operational policies, including rate structures. The fact that system operators laid coaxial cable under public roads or along power lines, and most operators functioned as local monopolies, justified the power allocated to local governments. The 1984 Cable Act altered this relationship, eliminating rate regulation at the local level and placing strict limits on the areas in which local governments could exercise control. The Cable Act also placed severe limits on the grounds under which municipalities could deny the renewal of a franchise agreement to cable operators.

local station groups: collection of local television or radio stations under common ownership. Prior to the mid-1980s, a single individual or corporation could control just 12 television stations nationwide, but the size and reach of such groups increased to a dramatic degree in the two decades that followed. The Federal Communications Commission licenses such stations to serve the local communities in which they operate, but much of the decision-making is centralized at the regional or national level within station groups. This is most evident in the owned and operated stations that the broadcast networks own, but it is also true with other large station groups that are affiliated with various networks. The Sinclair Broadcast Group, for example, broadcast a one-hour program, *A P.O.W. Story: Politics, Pressure and the Media,* that incorporated parts of a documentary critical of John Kerry on one of its stations in 39 markets in the fall of 2004.

localism: one of the pillars of broadcast regulation since the 1920s and a reason radio and television stations are licensed in their local communities rather than to national networks. The basic concept is simple: local concerns should take precedent over national ones and individuals and institutions should resolve such issues at the local level. Local stations, moreover, should be responsive to the "unique" interests and needs of the individual communities in which they operate. *See also* public interest, convenience, and necessity.

major studios: a term used to describe the dominant motion picture production and distribution companies. The studios included in this group change over time. In the litigation that ended with the signing of the Paramount decrees, the federal government spoke of the big five—Paramount, Loew's, RKO, Warner Bros., and Twentieth Century Fox—and the little three—Columbia, Universal, and United Artists. In current discussions, the major studios include Columbia Pictures, Paramount Pictures, Twentieth Century Fox, Universal Pictures, Walt Disney Pictures, and Warner Bros., all of which are now part of huge media conglomerates: Sony, Viacom, News Corp., NBC Universal, Disney, and Time Warner, respectively.

market: an economic institution in which buyers and sellers come together to exchange commodities. The functions of the market include price making, allocation of resources, and the rationing of scarce goods. The definition of a market is critical in the analysis of media industries. In discussions of television, for example, one can address the market as a whole, or various segments within that market, such as national or local, broadcast or cable, and more specific segments such as premium movie channels (HBO, Showtime, Cinemax, etc.) or news channels (CNN, Fox News Channel, MSNBC, etc.). *See also* market share.

market model versus public sphere model: two prominent media structures adopted in different locations around the world. The market model suggests that society's needs can best be met through a relatively unregulated process of exchange based on the dynamics of supply and demand. This model treats the media like all other goods and service. It argues that as long as competitive conditions exist, businesses pursuing profits will meet consumer needs. The public sphere model suggests that there are some societal needs that the market's supply and demand dynamic cannot meet and this requires some degree of government regulation. Since the media, moreover, assume a critical role in the marketplace of ideas that makes self-government possible, such content cannot be treated the same as other products.

market share: percentage of the total available market or market segment that is attributable to a given product or service or corporation. The definition of the market segment is critical to this measurement. At the end of the 2004–2005 prime time television season, for example, CBS claimed victory for total viewers, while Fox collected the largest share of the audience in the 18–49-year-old demographic that advertisers covet most. *See also* concentration; market.

marketplace of ideas: one of the cornerstones of democratic theories of the press. This is the belief that the media makes self-government and representative democracy possible through the creation of a marketplace in which citizens can grapple between truth and falsehood in a "free and open encounter."

monopolistic competition: one of four definable levels of competition. This is a market structure in which there are a large number of sellers offering products that are similar, but not perfect substitutes for each other. Some local radio markets and the national magazine market are examples of monopolistic competition. *See also* competition.

monopoly: one of four definable levels of competition. This is a market structure in which there is one dominant seller of a product with no real substitutes, which affords that one seller complete control over pricing. The barriers for entry to the market are high. Prior to the emergence of direct-broadcast-satellite (DBS) service as a viable alternative, cable television systems were monopolies in most local markets. *See also* competition.

multiple system operator (MSO): term used to describe cable operators that control systems in multiple communities. Cable television originated as the ultimate local mechanism, nothing more than a collection of homes connected to a common antenna. The Cable Act of 1984 accelerated the consolidation of cable systems into large groups, and the 10 largest MSOs accounted for close to 90 percent of cable households in 2004. MSOs often organize their systems in regional "clusters" under common management.

multichannel video programming distributor (MVPD): blanket term used within the federal government to describe systems that distribute multiple channels of television programming to multiple households. This measure includes multiple system operators such as Comcast and Time Warner Cable and direct-broadcast-satellite services such as DirecTV and Dish Network.

must-carry: long-standing component of federal regulation of cable television. The current regulations were part of the Cable Television Communications and Competition Act of 1992 and guaranteed local television stations with carriage on cable systems in their communities. This provision of the Cable Act was intended to support marginal broadcast stations that might not otherwise be carried on cable systems. Cable operators fought the regulation up to the Supreme Court, arguing that being forced to carry a given station violated their First Amendment rights. The Supreme Court remanded the law to a lower court in 1994, then upheld must-carry in 1997 upon its return. In 1999, the FCC extended must-carry to direct-broadcast-satellite providers, ruling that such services must retransmit all local television stations that request carriage in markets in which they elect to carry any. *See also* retransmission consent.

network affiliates: connection between the networks and their local stations that is central to the broadcast structure in the United States. The parent corporation of each of the networks owns a number of local stations, concentrated in the major markets, but each of them also contracts with a collection of local stations in other communities. The commercial revenue that fuels the networks is based on the number of viewers nationwide, so having a program broadcast in most markets is critical. In the cases of ABC, CBS, and NBC, the networks provide their affiliates with programming in various dayparts, including prime time, morning talk shows, afternoon soap operas, and late-night talk shows or news magazines, as well as national news programs, sports, and some children's programming. The financial relationship is complex. First, the networks and their affiliates split the advertising inventory in network programs, with each selling a percentage of the time. Second, the long-standing networks have traditionally given their local stations an affiliate fee to carry their programs, although the networks have reduced these fees over the last decade. The Fox network has long followed a different path, receiving reverse compensation from its affiliates.

oligopoly: one of four definable levels of competition. This is a market structure with a few giant sellers, each with a significant share of the market. There is generally some product differentiation, but given the interdependency of members, no firm can make significant changes in price without reactions from others. Entry to the market for new sellers is quite difficult. The production and distribution of motion pictures has featured an oligopolistic market structure since the 1920s. *See also* competition.

ownership and control: some argue that there has been a separation of ownership and control in the modern corporation, with the widespread ownership of stock diluting the share of any individual or group, resulting in a new managerial class that runs corporations. Ownership of just five percent of a corporation is considered to be sufficient for control, with a lower percentage enough in some instances. General Electric is an example of a corporation where the directors and executives do not own enough stock to exercise control, with none holding more than one-tenth of one percent in 2005. That is not the case with Viacom, however, where Sumner Redstone has beneficial ownership of over 70 percent of the common stock. *See also* allocative versus operational control.

Paramount decrees: a series of consent degrees between the United States government and motion picture production and distribution companies. In 1938, the federal government filed suit against the big five studios—Paramount,

Loew's, RKO, Warner Bros., and Twentieth Century Fox—and the little three—Columbia, Universal, and United Artists—under the Sherman Antitrust Act. The government argued that the big five attempted to restrain trade and monopolize the production, distribution, and exhibition of motion pictures, and that the little three combined with the big five in these efforts. After a decade of litigation, the Supreme Court affirmed most of the lower court rulings, that block booking, systems of runs and clearances, and other trade practices were illegal. The Supreme Court set aside a ruling on divestiture between distribution and exhibition and sent the question back to a lower court for further consideration. Rather than continue to litigate the case in court, Paramount and RKO entered into negotiations with the government and signed consent decrees in 1949. The other three majors soon followed. The Paramount decrees mandated that the studios cease all unfair business practices, and forced the studios to break ties between their production and distribution operations and the movie theaters that the studios owned. *See also* block booking; runs and clearances.

perfect competition: one of four definable levels of competition. This is a market structure characterized by a large number of sellers and a large number of buyers. Each seller supplies such a small percentage of the market that no single firm or group of firms dominates the market. The sellers produce products that are homogeneous and new sellers can enter the market with relative ease. *See also* competition.

pilots: final step in the program development process before a network adds a show to its schedule. Each of the networks sifts through hundreds of concepts from in-house production units and other producers during this process, but only a few of these concepts receive the funding to develop a "pilot" production that introduces the major themes and characters. Fewer still receive a slot on a network schedule and a minimum commitment of 13 or so episodes.

Prime Time Access Rule: adopted by the Federal Communications Commission (FCC) in 1970 in conjunction with the Financial Interest and Syndication Rules. The PTAR prohibited network affiliate stations in the top 50 markets from broadcasting more than three hours of network programming or off-network reruns each night in the prime time window, defined as 7:00 p.m. to 11:00 p.m. in the Eastern and Pacific time zones and 6:00 p.m. to 10:00 p.m. in the Central and Mountain time zones. ABC, CBS, and NBC were able to broadcast four hours on Sunday night since the additional hour included feature films or family, news, and public affairs programming, which qualified for an exemption. The FCC promulgated the rule in response to concerns that ABC, CBS, and NBC dominate the program production market and inhibited the development of competing program sources. The adoption of the PTAR opened up the 7:00 p.m. to 8:00 p.m. window for first-run syndication. The FCC abolished the Prime Time Access Rule in 1996, but the "access hour" has remained under the control of local affiliates. *See also* Financial Interest and Syndication Rules.

production, distribution, and exhibition: three interlinked stages in the motion picture process. Production involves the creation of a completed master of a motion picture, what is called the first print. The distributor takes this master, makes additional prints and places them in the hands of exhibitors. In the traditional model, exhibition involves the showing of the motion picture to patrons in theaters, although one could now include home video sales, video-on-demand, etc., at this level of the process.

public interest, convenience, and necessity: part of broadcast regulation in the United States since the 1920s. The roots of the notion can be found in the Radio Act of 1927, which empowered the Radio Commission to regulate the airwaves as the "public convenience, interest and necessity requires," although Congress did not define what the concept meant. The Communications Act of 1934 codified a requirement that broadcast licensees serve the "public interest, convenience and necessity." While Congress or the Commission never provided a concise definition, the roots of the concept are evident in various Federal Communications Commission policies, including the restrictions on children's television, limits on indecent content, and equal time requirements with political figures. *See also* scarcity rationale.

ratings and shares: critical numbers in broadcast and cable television, assuming a central role in the sale of commercial time. The rating is the percentage of *total television households* in the sample area with a television tuned to a given program. For broadcast networks, this is the percentage of total television households nationwide; for a cable channel, this is the percentage of television households that subscribe to the channel. The share is the percentage of *total viewing households* tuned to a given show. This is the percentage of Households Using Television (HUT) at a given time that are tuned to a given program

repurposing: relatively new concept in television production and distribution. The traditional off-network syndication model was for networks to have an exclusive run for four seasons, during which a program accumulates just under 100 episodes (22 to 23 per season). It was at that point that successful programs launched in local and/or cable syndication. In repurposing, however, prime time programs can re-air on cable networks within even a week of their debut on the network. In 2001, for example, episodes of 24 debuted on Fox on Tuesday nights, and then were repurposed on FX in a double run on Sunday and Monday nights. *See also* license agreement; syndication.

retransmission consent: much-debated provision of the Cable Television Communications and Competition Act of 1992 that requires cable operators to receive authorization from local television stations to retransmit their signals. The parent corporations of some large stations groups believed this consent could be worth millions in compensation, but cable operators have all but refused such payments, arguing that cable subscribers should not be charged since broadcast stations are available free of charge over the air. Cable operators have not been against other forms of compensation, however, and media conglomerates have used retransmission consent for their stations groups to leverage carriage of cable programming services they also own. The Satellite Home Viewer Improvement Act (SHIVA) of 1998 extended retransmission consent to satellite services as well. *See also* must-carry.

right to reject: addresses the power of local stations, in theory, to reject or replace programs received from broadcast television networks. The Code of Federal Regulations stipulates that a license will not be granted to a station with a "contract, arrangement, or understanding" that prevents or hinders the station from rejecting network programs it "reasonably believes" to be "unsatisfactory or unsuitable or contrary to the public interest" or from substituting a program that is of greater local or national importance. *See also* localism.

runs and clearances: practice of giving a theater the exclusive first-run engagement of a particular motion picture in a particular area. Competing "runs" of the same film were "cleared" from the theater's protected area. These runs and clearances were the products of long-term arrangements between studios and theaters. The Supreme Court ruled these practices illegal in the Paramount case since it saw them as a geographic division of the market. *See also* block booking; Paramount decrees.

scarcity rationale: one of the cornerstones of broadcast regulation since the 1920s. The basic idea is a simple one: the radio spectrum is limited and so it is not available to all who might wish to use it. It has been argued, therefore, it is reasonable to limit the free speech rights of those who are licensed to use the public airwaves. One of the strongest statements in support of the rationale came in 1943 in *NBC v. United States* when the Supreme Court upheld the power of the FCC to regulate certain aspects of the business practices of networks and their affiliates. The Supreme Court ruled again in the *Red Lion Broadcasting Co., Inc. v. Federal Communications Commission* in 1969, with Justice White arguing that "Where there are substantially more individuals who want to broadcast than there are frequencies to allocate, it is idle to posit an unabridgeable First Amendment right to broadcast comparable to the right of every individual to speak, write, or publish." Former FCC chair Michael Powell was among those who declared, based on the growth of the television marketplace through cable and satellite services, that the scarcity rationale was no longer valid for regulating broadcasting. *See also* public interest, convenience, and necessity.

syndication: process of selling the rights to the exhibition of television programs and other content. This includes agreements between motion picture distributors and broadcast networks and cable channels for national runs of feature films, but the focus is often on the sale of television programs to local stations and cable channels. First-run syndication, original programming such as game shows (i.e., *Jeopardy!*), talk shows (i.e., *Oprah*), and newsmagazines (i.e., *Entertainment Tonight*), and off-network syndication, such as reruns of situation comedies (i.e., *Seinfeld*) and dramas (i.e., *ER*) that debuted on the broadcast networks, are prominent in this market. The syndication of such programs in television markets around the world is an important revenue stream for distributors. *See also* license agreement; repurposing.

vertical integration: one of the interlinked but analytically distinct processes that contribute to market concentration. In this case, firms acquire additional business units at different levels of production, distribution, or exhibition. The extension of operations into other stages of the process enables firms to reduce their vulnerability to fluctuations in the supply and cost of essential materials and services and enables them to regulate and rationalize production and increase their control over the market. The creation of NBC Universal, for example, brought the production and distribution of the *Law and Order* franchise under common ownership, since Universal Network Television produced the shows that were a cornerstone of the NBC schedule. *See also* concentration.

Selected Bibliography

Adams, William C. *Television Coverage of International Affairs*. Norwood, NJ: Ablex, 1992.

Adorno, Theodor W. "Culture Industry Reconsidered." In *The Culture Industry: Selected Essays on Mass Culture*. Edited by J. M. Bernstein. London: Routledge, 1991.

Albarran, Alan B. *Media Economics: Understanding Markets, Industries and Concepts*. 2nd ed. Ames: Iowa State University Press, 2002.

Allen, Robert C., ed. *Channels of Discourse, Reassembled: Television and Contemporary Criticism*. 2nd ed. Chapel Hill: The University of North Carolina Press, 1992.

Altschull, J. Herbert. *Agents of Power*. New York: Longman, 1984.

Anderson, Robin. *Consumer Culture & TV Programming*. Boulder, CO: Westview Press, 1995.

Ang, Ien. *Desperately Seeking the Audience*. London: Routledge, 1991.

———. *Living Room Wars: Rethinking Media Audiences for a Postmodern World*. London: Routledge, 1996.

Aufderheide, Patricia. *Communications Policy and the Public Interest*. New York: The Guilford Press, 1999.

Auletta, Ken. *Three Blind Mice*. New York: Vintage Books, 1992.

Bagdikian, Ben H. *The Media Monopoly*. 6th ed. Boston: Beacon Press, 2000.

———. *The New Media Monopoly*. Boston: Beacon Press, 2004.

Baker, William F., and George Dessart. *Down the Tube: An Inside Account of the Failure of American Television*. New York: BasicBooks, 1998.

Baldwin, Robert, and Martin Cave. *Understanding Regulation: Theory, Strategy, and Practice*. New York: Oxford University Press, 1999.

Balio, Tino, ed. *The American Film Industry*. Revised ed. Madison: The University of Wisconsin Press, 1985.

———. *Hollywood in the Age of Television*. Boston: Unwin Hyman, 1990.

Barnet, Richard J., and John Cavanaugh. *Global Dreams: Imperial Corporations and the New World Order*. New York: Touchstone, 1994.

Barnouw, Erik. *A Tower in Babel: A History of Broadcasting in the United States, Volume I - to 1933*. New York: Oxford University Press, 1966.

———. *The Golden Web: A History of Broadcasting in the United States, Volume II - 1933 to 1953*. New York: Oxford University Press, 1968.

———. *The Image Empire: A History of Broadcasting in the United States, Volume III - from 1953*. New York: Oxford University Press, 1970.

Barnouw, Erik, et al. *Conglomerates and the Media*. New York: The New Press, 1997.

Becker, Samuel L. "Marxist Approaches to Media Studies." In *Critical Studies in Mass Communication* 1 (1984).

Bell, Daniel. *The End of Ideology*. Glencoe, IL: The Free Press, 1960.

———. "The Power Elite—Reconsidered."*American Journal of Sociology*, vol. 64, no. 3 (1958).

Benjamin, Stuart M., Douglas G. Lichtman, and Howard A. Shelanski. *Telecommunications Law and Policy*. Durham, NC: Carolina Academic Press, 2001.

———. *Telecommunications Law and Policy: 2004 Cumulative Supplement*. Durham, NC: Carolina Academic Press, 2004.

Berle, Adolf A., Jr., and Gardiner C. Means. *The Modern Corporation and Private Property*. New York: Macmillan, 1933.

Biskind, Peter. *Down and Dirty Pictures*. New York: Simon & Schuster Paperbacks, 2004.

Blumenthal, Howard J., and Oliver R. Goodenough. *This Business of Television*, 2nd ed. New York, NY: Billboard Books, 1998.

Bogart, Leo. *Commercial Culture*. New York: Oxford University Press, 1995.

Bowditch, John, and Clement Ramsland. *Voices of the Industrial Revolution*, 23rd ed. Ann Arbor: The University of Michigan Press, 1996.

Cantor, Muriel G., and Joel M. Cantor, *Prime-Time Television*, 2nd ed. New York: Sage Publications, 1992.

Chan-Olmstead, Sylvia. "Market Competition for Cable Television: Reexamining Horizontal Mergers and Industry Concentration." *Journal of Media Economics*, vol. 1, no. 2 (1996).

Chan-Olmsted, Sylvia, and B. R. Litman. "Antitrust and Horizontal Mergers in the Cable Industry," *Journal of Media Economics*, vol. 1, no. 1.

Chomsky, Noam. *Media Control: The Spectacular Achievements of Propaganda*. New York: Seven Stories Press, 1997.

Compaine, Benjamin M., Christopher H. Sterling, Thomas Guback, and J. Kendrick Noble, Jr. *Who Owns the Media?* 2nd ed. White Plains, NY: Knowledge Industry Publications, Inc., 1982.

Conant, Michael. *Antitrust in the Motion Picture Industry*. Berkeley: University of California Press, 1960.

Conway, M. Margaret. "PACs in the Political Process." In *Interest Group Politics*, edited by Allan J. Cigler and Burdett A. Loomis. Washington, DC: CQ Press, 1994.

Croteau, David, and William Hoynes. *The Business of Media*. Thousand Oaks, CA: Pine Forge Press, 2001.

Curran, James. *Mass Media and Society*. Edited by James Curran and Michael Gurevitch. London: Edward Arnold, 1991.

Daniellian, N. R. *AT&T: The Story of Industrial Conquest*. New York: The Vanguard Press, 1939.

de Sola Pool, Ithiel. *Technologies of Freedom*. Cambridge: Harvard University Press, 1983.

Dominick, Joseph R., and Millard C. Pearce. "Trends in Network Prime-Time Programming, 1953–74." *Journal of Communication* (1976).

Douglas, Susan J. *Inventing American Broadcasting*. Baltimore: The Johns Hopkins University Press, 1987.

Dow, Bonnie J. *Prime-Time Feminism*. Philadelphia: University of Pennsylvania Press, 1996.

Downing, John, Ali Mohammadi, and Annabelle Sreberny-Mohammadi. *Questioning the Media: A Critical Introduction*. 2nd ed. Thousand Oaks, CA: Sage Publications, 1995.

Dreier, Peter. "The Position of the Press in the U.S. Power Structure." In *Mass Communication Review Yearbook* (1983).

DuBoff, Richard B. *Accumulation & Power: An Economic History of the United States*. Armonk, NY: M. E. Sharpe, Inc., 1989.

Entman, Robert M. *Democracy Without Citizens*. New York: Oxford University Press, 1989.

Ewen, Stuart. *Captains of Consciousness*. New York: McGraw-Hill Book Company, 1976.

Flannery, Gerald V., ed. *Commissioners of the FCC: 1927–1994*. Lanham, MD: University Press of America, Inc., 1995.

Fowler, Mark S., and Daniel L. Brenner, "A Marketplace Approach to Broadcast Regulation." *Texas Law Review* 60, no. 2, p. 207 (1981–1982).

Garnham, Nicholas. *Capitalism and Communication: Global Culture and the Economics of Information*. London: Sage Publications, 1990.

———. "Toward a Theory of Cultural Materialism." *Journal of Communciation*, vol. 33, no. 3 (1983).

Gerbner, George, and Larry Gross. "Living with Television: The Violence Profile." *Journal of Communication* 25 (1976).

Gitlin, Todd. *Inside Prime Time*. New York: Pantheon Books, 1983.

———. *The Whole World Is Watching*. Berkeley: University of California Press, 1980.

Godek, Stephen C. *Determinants of Public Interest Cable Communications Policies*. Lanham, MD: University Press of America, Inc., 1996.

Goldenson, Leonard H. *Beating the Odds*. New York: Charles Scribner's Sons, 1991.

Gomery, Douglas. "Disney's Business History: A Reinterpretation." In *Disney Discourse*. Edited by Eric Smoodin. New York: Routledge, 1994.

Guback, Thomas H. "Are We Looking at the Right Things in Film?" Paper presented at the Society for Cinema Studies conference, 1978.

Guback, Thomas H., and Dennis J. Dombkowski. "Television and Hollywood: Economic Relations in the 1970's." *Journal of Broadcasting* 20:4 (1976).

Gurevitch, Michael, Tony Bennett, James Curran, and Janet Woollacott, ed. *Culture, Society and the Media*. London: Methuen, 1982.

Harris, Richard A., and Sidney M. Milkis. *The Politics of Regulatory Change*, 2nd ed. New York: Oxford University Press, 1996.

Harvey, David. *The Condition of Postmodernity*. Cambridge, MA: Blackwell Publishers Ltd., 1990.

Hawley, Ellis W. "Three Facets of Hooverian Associationalism: Lumber, Aviation and Movies, 1921–1930." *Regulation in Perspective*. Edited by Thomas K. McGraw. Cambridge, MA: Harvard University Press, 1981.

———. "Herbert Hoover, the Commerce Secretariat, and the Vision of an 'Associative State,' 1921–1928." *Journal of American History*, vol. 61, no. 1 (1974).

———. "The Discovery and Study of a 'Corporate Liberalism'." *Business History Review*, vol. 52, no. 3 (1978).

Held, David. *Introduction to Critical Theory: Horkheimer to Habermas*. Berkeley: University of California Press, 1980.

Held, Sydney W. *Broadcasting in America*. Boston: Houghton Mifflin, 1972.

Herman, Edward S. *The Real Terror Network: Terrorism in Fact and Propaganda*. Boston: South End Press, 1982.

Herman, Edward S., and Noam Chomsky. *Manufacturing Consent: The Political Economy of the Mass Media*. New York: Pantheon Books, 1988.

Herman, Edward S., and Robert W. McChesney. *The Global Media: The New Missionaries of Corporate Capitalism*. London: Cassell, 1997.

Hiaasen, Carl. *Team Rodent: How Disney Devours the World*. New York: The Ballantine Publishing Group, 1998.

Horowitz, David, and Laurence Jarvik, ed. *Public Broadcasting & The Public Trust*. Los Angeles: Center for the Study of Popular Culture, 1995.

Howard, Herbert H. "The 1996 Telecommunications Act and TV Station Ownership: 1 Year Later." *Journal of Media Economics*, vol. 11, no. 3 (1998).

Hoynes, William. *Public Television for Sale: Media, Market and the Public Sphere*. Boulder: Westview Press, 1994.

Kasza, Gregory J. "Democracy and the Founding of Japanese Public Radio." *Journal of Asian Studies* 45 (1986).

Kellner, Douglas. "Ideology, Marxism, and Advanced Capitalism." *Socialist Review* 8 (1978).

———. *Media Culture*. London: Routledge, 1995.

———. *Television and the Crisis in Democracy*. Boulder, CO: Westview Press, 1990.

Kubey, Robert, Mark Shifflet, Niranjala Weerakkody, and Stephen Ukeiley. "Demographic Diversity on Cable: Have the New Cable Channels Made a Difference in the Representation of Gender, Race, and Age?" *Journal of Broadcasting & Electronic Media* 39 (1995).

Ledbetter, James. *Made Possible By . . .* London: Verso, 1997.

Lessig, Lawrence. *Free Culture*. New York: The Penguin Press, 2004.

Levy, Leonard W. *Freedom of the Press from Zenger to Jefferson*. Indianapolis, IN: The Bobbs-Merrill Company, Inc., 1966.

Lichter, Robert, Linda S. Lichter, and Stanley Rothman, *Prime Time*. Washington, DC: Regnery Publishing, Inc., 1994.

Lin, Carolyn A. "Diversity in Network Prime-Time Program Formats During the 1980s." *The Journal of Electronic Media* 8 (1995).

Lukes, Steven. *Power: A Radical View*. London: Macmillan, 1974.

MacAvoy, Paul W. *Deregulation of Cable Television*. Washington, DC: American Enterprise Institute for Public Policy Research, 1977.

Mander, Jerry. "In the Absence of the Sacred," *Whole Earth Review* (1991).

Marc, Peter, and Robert J. Thompson. *Prime Time Prime Movers*. Syracuse, NY: Syracuse University Press, 1995.

Mattelart, Armand, and Seth Siegelaub. *Communication and Class Struggle*. vol. 1. New York: International General, 1979.

Mazzocco, Dennis W. *Networks of Power*. Boston: South End Press, 1994.

McChesney, Robert W. *Corporate Media and the Threat to Democracy*. New York: Seven Stories Press, 1997.

———. "Labor and the Marketplace of Ideas." *Journalism Monographs* (1992).

———. *The Problem of the Media*. New York: Monthly Review Press, 2004.

———. *Rich Media, Poor Democracy*. New York: The New Press, 1999.

———. *Telecommunications, Mass Media, & Democracy: The Battle for the Control of U.S. Broadcasting, 1928–1935*. New York: Oxford University Press, 1994.

McCraw, Thomas K., ed. *Regulation in Perspective*. Cambridge, MA: Harvard University Press, 1981.

McDonald, J. Fred. *One Nation Under Television*. Chicago: Nelson-Hall Publishers, 1994.

McQuail, Denis. *Mass Communication Theory*. London: Sage Publications, 1993.

Meehan, Eileen R. "Conceptualizing Culture As Commodity: The Problem of Television." *Cultural Studies in Mass Communication* 3 (1986).

———. "Critical Theorizing on Broadcast History." *Journal of Broadcasting & Electronic Media* 30 (1986).

Meehan, Eileen R., Vincent Mosco, and Janet Wasko, "Rethinking Political Economy: Change and Continuity." *Journal of Communication* 43 (1993).

Meiners, Roger E., and Bruce Yandle, ed. *Regulation and the Reagan Era*. New York: Holmes & Meier, 1989.

Miege, Bernard. "The Cultural Commodity." *Media, Culture and Society*. vol. 1 (1979).

Milton, John. *Areopagitica*. Folcroft, PA: The Folcroft Press, Inc., 1969.

Moran, Albert, ed. *Film Policy*. London: Routledge, 1996.

Mosco, Vincent. *Broadcasting in the United States*. Norwood, NJ: Ablex Publishing Co., 1979.

———. *The Political Economy of Communication*. London: Sage, 1996.

Mosco, Vincent, and Janet Wasko, ed. *The Political Economy of Information*. Madison: The University of Wisconsin Press, 1988.

Mowlana, Hamid. *Global Information and World Communication*. New York: Longman, 1986.

Murdock, Graham. "Large Corporations and the Control of the Communications Industries." In *Culture, Society and the Media*, edited by Michael Gurevitch, Tony Bennett, James Curran, and Janet Woollacott. London: Methuen, 1982.

———. "Programming Needs and Answers." Paper presented at the New Dimensions in Television meeting, March 1981.

Murdock, Graham, and Peter Golding. "For A Political Economy of Mass Communication." In *The Socialist Review 1973*, edited by Ralph Miliband and John Saville. London: The Merlin Press, 1974.

National Cable & Telecommunications Association. *Cable Developments 2004*, vol. 28, no. 1 (2004).

Newcomb, Horace, ed. *Television: The Critical View*. 5th ed. New York: Oxford University Press, 1994.

Nielsen Media Research. *2000 Report on Television*. New York: Nielsen Media Research, 2000.

Nowell-Smith, Geoffrey, and Steven Ricci, ed. *Hollywood and Europe: Economics, Culture, National Identity: 1945–95*. London: British Film Institute, 1998.

O'Sullivan, Tim, John Hartley, Danny Saunders, Martin Montgomery, and John Fiske. *Key Concepts in Communication and Culture Studies*. London: Routledge, 1994.

Palentz, David L., and Robert M. Entman. *Media, Power, Politics*. New York: The Free Press, 1981.

Pendakur, Majunath. "Film Policies in Canada: In Whose Interests?" In *Media, Culture & Society*, 1981.

Porter, Glenn. *The Rise of Big Business*. 2nd ed. Arlington Heights, IL: Harlan Davidson, Inc., 1992.

Rowland, Willard D., Jr., and Michael Tracy, "Worldwide Challenges to Public Service Broadcasting." *Journal of Communications* 40 (1990).

Sabine, George H. *A History of Political Theory*. New York: Holt, Rinehart and Winston, Inc., 1937.

Said, Edward. *Orientalism*. New York: Vintage Books, 1978.

Scholle, David. "Critical Studies: From the Theory of Ideology to Power/ Knowledge." *Critical Studies in Mass Communication* 5 (1988).

Schwarzlose, Richard A. "The Marketplace of Ideas: A Measure of Free Expression." *Journalism Monographs* 118 (1989).

Scott, John. *A Matter of Record*. Cambridge: Polity Press, 1990.

Seltzer, Alan L. "Woodrow Wilson as 'Corporate-Liberal': Toward a Reconsideration of Left Revisionist Historiography." *Western Political Quarterly* vol. 30, no. 2 (1977).

Shawcross, William. *Murdoch*. New York: Simon and Schuster, 1992.

Sklar, Martin J. *Movie-Made America*. Revised ed. New York: Vintage Books, 1994.

——— . "Woodrow Wilson and the Political Economy of Modern United States Liberalism." *Studies on the Left* vol. 1, no. 3 (1960).

Slughart, William F., II. "Antitrust Policy in the Reagan Administration: Pyrrhic Victories?" In *Regulation and the Reagan Era*, edited by Roger E. Meiners and Bruce Yandle. New York: Holmes & Meier, 1989.

Silberman, Jonathan I., and Garey C. Durden. "Determining Legislative Preferences on Minimum Wage: An Economic Approach." *Journal of Political Economy*, 94 (1986).

Smoodin, Eric. *Disney Discourse: Producing The Magic Kingdom*. New York: Routledge, 1994.

Smulyan, Susan. *Selling Radio: The Commercialization of American Broadcasting, 1920–1934*. Washington, DC: The Smithsonian Institution Press, 1994.

Smythe, Dallas. "On the Political Economy of Communications." *Journalism Quarterly* (1960).

Spender, Dale. "Defining Reality." In *Language and Power*, edited by Chris Kramarae, Muriel Schulz, and William O'Barr. Beverly Hills, CA: Sage Publishing, 1984.

Stewart, James B. *Disney War*. New York: Simon & Schuster, 2005.

Streeter, Thomas. *Selling the Air: A Critique of the Policy of Commercial Broadcasting in the United States*. Chicago: The University of Chicago Press, 1996.

Suman, Michael, ed. *Religion and Prime Time Television*. Westport, CT: Praeger, 1997.

Tehranian, Majid. *Technologies of Power: Information Machines and Democratic Prospects*. Norwood, NJ: Ablex Publishing Co., 1990.

Tillinghast, Charles H. *American Broadcast Regulation and the First Amendment*. Ames: Iowa State University Press, 2000.

Turner, Graeme. *British Cultural Studies: An Introduction*. London: Routledge, 1990.

Varis, Tapio. "The International Flow of Television Programs." *Journal of Communication* 34, no. 1 (1984).

Wasko, Janet. *Hollywood in the Information Age*. Austin: University of Texas Press, 1994.

———. *Movies and Money: Financing the American Film Industry*. Norwood, NJ: Ablex Publishing Corporation, 1982.

————. "New Methods of Analyzing Concentration." In *Policy Research in Telecommunications*, edited by Vincent Mosco. Norwood, NJ: Ablex Publishing Corp., 1984.

Watson, Mary Ann. *The Expanding Vista: American Television in the Kennedy Years.* Durham, NC: Duke University Press, 1994.

Wheeler, Mark. "'Trade Follows Film': Hollywood and U.S. Trade Policy." Paper presented at the Political Science Association Conference, April 5–7, 2005.

Whittemore, Hank. *CNN: The Inside Story.* Boston: Little, Brown and Company, 1990.

Williams, Raymond. *Culture.* Cambridge: Fontanta Books, 1981.

————. *Marxism and Literature.* New York: Oxford University Press, 1977.

————. *Towards 2000.* New York: Pantheon, 1983.

Wilson, Woodrow. "Trusts and Monopolies." In *The New Democracy: Presidential Messages, Addresses, and Other Papers*, vol. 1, no. 3. New York: Harper & Brother Publishers, 1926.

Zeitlin, Maurice. "Corporate Ownership and Control: The Large Corporation and the Capitalist Class." *American Journal of Sociology* (1974).

Index

About the Author

William M. Kunz teaches courses on media ownership and regulation, television theory and criticism, and broadcast writing and video production at the University of Washington, Tacoma (UW Tacoma). He earned his PhD in communication and society at the University of Oregon with a focus in the political economy of communication. He and his wife, Miyuki Taguchi, have two children, Maya and Tomo.

Prior to joining the faculty at UW Tacoma, Kunz was a vice president and senior producer at Turner Broadcasting in Atlanta. While at Turner Sports, he was responsible for the day-to-day functions of the production unit before overseeing all aspects of the television operation at the 2001 Goodwill Games in Brisbane, Australia. He also served as the senior producer during the 1998 and 2000 Goodwill Games and 1988 Olympic Winter Games in Nagano, Japan. He spent over a decade working with ABC Sports on a full-time and freelance basis before his tenure at Turner Sports and remains active in the field. He is a four-time National Sports Emmy Award recipient.